POEMS ON AFFAIRS OF STATE

AUGUSTAN SATIRICAL VERSE, 1660–1714

Volume 4: 1685–1688

James II

Poems on Affairs of State

AUGUSTAN SATIRICAL VERSE, 1660–1714

VOLUME 4: 1685–1688

edited by

GALBRAITH M. CRUMP

New Haven & London

YALE UNIVERSITY PRESS

1968

Copyright © 1968 by Yale University.
Designed by John O. C. McCrillis,
set in Baskerville type,
and printed in the United States of America by
Vail-Ballou Press, Inc., Binghamton, N.Y.
Distributed in Canada by McGill University Press.

Library of Congress catalog card number: 63-7938

PREFACE

The poems in this volume not only record the literary, cultural, and political concerns of the reign of James II, but also measure the emotional intensity generating the Glorious Rebellion of 1688. Though only a selection from the great bulk of satire written and circulated during the four years James was on the throne, the poems collected here are witness to the growing power of the satirist. With Juvenal his master he lashed away in crude, anonymous verse, employing the obviously exaggerated and libelous to achieve his desired effects. Yet even while noting his crudeness, one senses the exuberance and self-assurance bred of what every generation believes is its special "reasonableness" in pushing forward to "a better day." Like the Rebellion, much was not glorious about the satire of the period, but more was vital, capturing the essence of an age in which faction gave way to party, and party, grudgingly, to parliamentary trust.

By the nature of his work, an editor invariably accrues debts of assistance too numerous to mention in detail. I am no exception. To all who have helped me over the years in the preparation of this volume I extend my deepest thanks. I am particularly indebted to my co-editors and to George deF. Lord, the project's general editor, who read my manuscript at various stages and was always a source of aid and encouragement. James M. Osborn was my scholarly angel, introducing me to the project and fostering my work with his advice and the material assistance of his invaluable collection of Restoration manuscripts. Earl Miner read the final typescript with extreme care and thoughtfulness, thereby saving me from numerous errors and omissions. F. W. Bateson, Maynard Mack, Louis Martz, and David Vieth offered help and encouragement along the way. Ruth Glick, Marilyn Riley, and Victoria Cudahy aided in the preparation of the text. Susan Holahan took great pains in editing the text for the press and, like so many others, made many invaluable suggestions toward final revision. Also, I wish to express my gratitude to Yale University for helping support my research by granting me a Morse Fellowship for study abroad in 1960-61. Finally, my thanks to my wife Joan for her patience and understanding and to my sons Andrew, Ian, Patrick, and Timothy for their complete imperviousness to things satiric.

G. M. C.

Kenyon College
July 1966

CONTENTS

LIST OF ILLUSTRATIONS

WORKS FREQUENTLY CITED

Broadsides
In the British Museum.

The Luttrell Collection

In the Bodleian Library, Oxford.

Ashmole G. 16
Firth b. 20: This and the following collections are "aggregations"
of single leaves and folds, both printed and in manuscript.*
Firth b. 21
Vetera A3. c. 133
Wood 417

Other Broadside Collections.

Harvard broadsides, Houghton Library, Cambridge, Massachusetts;
formerly in the Marquis of Bute's collection.
New York Public Library broadsides, New York, New York.
Yale quartos, Beinecke Rare Book and Manuscript Library, Yale
University, New Haven, Connecticut.
Yale broadsides, Beinecke Rare Book and Manuscript Library.

Manuscripts
In the British Museum.

Additional Manuscripts.
21094: A folio anthology of political poems, songs, and prose
pieces, formerly in the collection of Basil Fielding, fourth
Earl of Denbigh (1703).

---

* In describing broadside collections and manuscripts, the terms "anthology" and
"aggregation" (i.e. "the bringing together within one binding a number of 'separable
MSS.' ") have been employed following the suggestion of William J. Cameron, "A Late
Seventeenth-century Scriptorium," *Renaissance and Modern Studies, 8* (1963), 25–52. I
have designated manuscripts which Cameron fully describes in his article by his
initials: *WJC.*

27407: An aggregation in folio and quarto of political poems and songs.

27408: *Ditto.*

29497: A folio anthology of political and satirical poems.

Burney 390: A quarto anthology of political poems and songs.

Harleian Manuscripts.

6914: A quarto anthology, with additions, of political poems and songs.

7317: "Satyrs & Lampoons," a quarto anthology.

7319: "A Collection of Choice Poems, 1703," a quarto anthology.

7332: An anthology of poems in various hands.

Sloane 655: An aggregation in folio and quarto of political poems and songs.

2332: An anthology of verse satires.

Stowe 305: An anthology of political poems, songs and prose pieces.

In the Bodleian Library, Oxford.

Doncaster e. 24: "Poems &c. by several hands," a quarto anthology.

Douce 357: A folio anthology with additions, formerly in the collection of Francis Douce.

Eng. Poet. d. 152: An aggregation in folio and quarto of political poems and songs.

Firth c. 15: "A Choice Collection of Poems, Lampoons, Satyrs, &c.," an anthology formerly in the collection of Sir Charles Firth (*WJC*).

Firth c. 16: "Astrea's Book [*sic*] for Songs and Satyrs, 1686 [*corr.*] 1688," an anthology with late additions dating from 1738; formerly in the collection of William Busby, later in that of Sir Charles Firth.

Music School c. 95: A large collection of short English musical pieces, both vocal and instrumental, containing *Lilli burlero;* formerly in the collection of Dr. Richard Rawlinson.

Rawlinson Poet. 19: An aggregation of miscellaneous English and Latin pieces in poetry and prose, formerly in the collection of Dr. Rawlinson.

Rawlinson Poet. 152: An aggregation of seventeenth and early eighteenth century political poems and songs.

Rawlinson Poet. 173: "The Muse's Magazine, or Poeticall Miscelanies [sic], in two parts. . . .1705." For complete description of this anthology as accession 14665, see Falconer Madan, *Summary Catalogue of Western MSS.*, 1895, *3*, 321.

Tanner 306: An aggregation of political poems and songs.

Other Manuscripts.

Advocate 19. 1. 12: "Pasouils [sic] and Satires," an anthology in the National Library of Scotland, Edinburgh.

Dyce 43: An anthology of political poems and songs in the collection of the Victoria and Albert Museum, London (*WJC*).

Folger 473.1: An anthology of political verse, owned by the Folger Shakespeare Library, Washington, D.C. (*WJC*).

Folger m. b. 12: Three "separable MSS." bound together with individual title pages heading each collection: f. 1, "A collection of Poems and Lampoons &c., Not yet printed"; f. 102, "A Collection of Choice Poems, Satyrs, & Lampoons From 1672 to 1688. Never printed"; and on f. 146, "A Collection of Poems. From 1688 to 1699" [later the date "1703/4" was added].

Folger v. b. 94: An anthology of political poems and songs.

Folger x. d. 197: A single sheet or "fold," containing the *Song,* "The widows and maids."

Folger x. d. 198: A single sheet or "fold," containing *The Men of Honor Made Men Worthy.*

Harvard Eng. 585: An anthology of political poems and songs in the collection of the Houghton Library, Cambridge, Massachusetts.

Harvard Eng. 586: A commonplace book in many hands containing a few verse satires.

Longleat xxviii: A volume of over 300 leaves, containing English and Latin works and fragments by Matthew Prior. Among the Prior Papers at Longleat, Warminster, Wiltshire, in the library of the Marquis of Bath.

Ohio State: "A Choice Collection of Poems, &c.," an anthology owned by Ohio State University, formerly in the collection of Thomas Wentworth, Earl of Strafford (*WJC*).

Osborn Box 89 #3: An aggregation of political poems, songs, and prose in folio and quarto in the collection of James M. Osborn, New Haven, Connecticut.

Phillipps 8301: An aggregation, as above, owned by James M. Osborn; formerly in the collection of Sir Thomas Phillipps.

Phillipps 8302: An aggregation as above.

Portland PwV 42: "A collection of Poems and Lampoons, &c. Not
yet printed." An anthology in the collection of the Duke of
Portland at the University of Nottingham. (*WJC*)

Portland PwV 46: An anthology of political poems and songs, formerly owned by William Lord Craven, Baron Craven of Ham-
stead Marshall; vol. 2 [see PwV 47] in a three volume collection
owned by the Duke of Portland on deposit at the University of
Nottingham. (*WJC*)

Portland PwV 47: "A Collection of Poems, Lampoons, Songs, and
Satyrs from the beginning of the Revolution in 1688 to 1695,"
vol. 1 of three; an anthology owned by the Duke of Portland on
deposit at the University of Nottingham. (*WJC*)

Taylor 2: "A Collection of Choyce Poems, Lampoons, and Satyrs
from 1673–1689. Never Extant in Print." An anthology in the
collection of Robert H. Taylor, Princeton, New Jersey. (*WJC*)

Vienna National Library 14090: Österreichische Nationalbiblio-
thek. An anthology, without title-page. (*WJC*)

Primary Printed Sources

In addition to such standard abbreviations as *OED, DNB, EB, N&Q,*
the following short titles are employed in the text and apparatus. Unless otherwise noted, the place of publication is London. The abbreviations *b.c.,* "before correction," and *corr.,* "corrected" are also employed in the apparatus.

180 Loyal Songs: A/Choice Collection/OF/180 Loyal Songs,/ALL
of them written since the/TWO late PLOTS/(*VIZ.*)/The Horrid *Salamanca Plot* in 1678./AND THE/*Fanatical Conspiracy*
in 1683./Intermixt with some New Love SONGS./With a *Table*
to find every Song./To which is added,/*The* Musical Notes *to
each Song.*/————/The Third Edition with many Additions/
————/LONDON, Printed by *N. T.* at the entrance into the/
Old-Spring-Garden near *Charing-Cross,* 1685./Price Bound 2s.

Case 171 (c). 1685

Poetical Recreations, 1688: POETICAL/RECREATIONS:/Con-
sisting of/ORIGINAL POEMS,/SONGS, ODES, *&c.*/With sev-

eral/New *TRANSLATIONS.*/————/In Two PARTS./————
/PART I./Occasionally Written by Mrs. *JANE BARKER.*/
PART II./By several Gentlemen of the UNIVERSITIES,/ and
Others./————. [2 lines of verse, from Virgil]/————/*LON-
DON,*/Printed for *Benjamin Crayle,* at the *Peacock*/and *Bible,*
at the West-end of St. *Pauls.* 1688.

Case 186. 1688

POAS, 1, 1689: A/COLLECTION/OF/POEMS/ON/Affairs of
State;/*Viz.*/[10 titles in 2 columns]/————/BY/*A*————
M————*l* Esq; and other Eminent Wits./————/*Most whereof
never before Printed.*/————/LONDON,/Printed in the Year,
M DC LXXXIX.

Case 188 (1) (a). 1689

POAS, 2, 1689: THE SECOND PART/OF THE/COLLECTION
/OF/POEMS/ON/Affairs of State,/*Viz.*/[21 titles in two col-
umns divided by a single line of rule]/————/By *A*————
M————*l* and other eminent Wits./None whereof ever before
Printed./————/LONDON, Printed in the Year, 1689.

Case 188 (2). 1689

POAS, 3, 1689: THE/THIRD PART/OF THE/COLLECTION
/OF/POEMS/ON/Affairs of State./Containing,/Esquire *Mar-
vel*'s further Instructions to/a Painter./AND/The late Lord
Rochester's *Farewel.*/————/*LONDON:*/Printed in the Year
M DC LXXXIX.

Case 188 (3). 1689

Popery, 1, 1689: A/COLLECTION/OF/The Newest and Most In-
genious/Poems, Songs, Catches, &c./AGAINST/POPERY./Re-
lating to the Times./————/Several of which never before
Printed./————/[ornament]/————/LONDON, Printed in the
Year, MDCLXXXIX.

Case 189 (1) (a). 1689

Popery, 2, 1689: A SECOND/COLLECTION/OF/The Newest
and Most Ingenious/Poems, Satyrs, Songs, &c./AGAINST/Pop-
ery and Tyranny,/Relating to the TIMES./————/Most of
which never before Printed./————/[ornament]/————/LON-
DON, Printed in the Year M DC LXXXIX.

Case 189 (2). 1689

Popery, 3, 1689: A THIRD/COLLECTION/OF/The Newest and Most Ingenious/Poems, Satyrs, Songs, &c./AGAINST/Popery and Tyranny,/Relating to the TIMES./————/Most of which never before Printed./————/[group of ornaments]/————/ LONDON, Printed in the Year M DC LXXXIX.

Case 189 (3). 1689

Muses Farewell, 1689: THE/MUSES FAREWEL/TO/Popery and Slavery,/OR, A/COLLECTION/OF/Miscellany Poems, Satyrs,/Songs, &c./Made by the most Eminent Wits of/the Nation, as the Shams, Intreagues,/and Plots of Priests and Jesuits gave/occasion./————/[1 line of verse, from Horace]/————/ *LONDON,*/Printed for *N. R. H. F.* and *J. K.* and are to/be sold by the Book-Sellers of *London* and/*Westminster,* 1689.

Case 191 (1) (a). 1689

Muses Farewell, 1689, supplement: A/SUPPLEMENT/TO THE/ COLLECTION/OF/*MISCELLANY POEMS*/AGAINST/Popery & Slavery./————/[2 lines of Latin verse]/————/LON-*DON:*/Printed in the Year M DC LXXXIX.

Case 191 (2) (a). 1689

POAS, 1, 1697: POEMS/ON/Affairs of State:/FROM/The Time of *Oliver Cromwell,* to the/Abdication of K. *James* the Second./ *Written by the greatest Wits of the Age.*/VIZ./Duke of *Buckingham,*/Earl of *Rochester.*/Lord *Bu*————*st,*/Sir *John Denham,*/*Andrew Marvell,* Esq;/Mr. *Milton,*/Mr. *Dryden,*/Mr. *Sprat,*/Mr. *Waller.*/Mr. *Ayloffe,* &c./————/With some Miscellany Poems by the same:/Most whereof never before Printed. /————/*Now Carefully examined with the Originals, and*/*Published without any Castration.*/————/Printed in the Year 1697.

Case 211 (1) (a). 1697

POAS, 1, 1697, continuation: POEMS/ON/Affairs of State:/. . . [title as above].

Case 211 (1) (c). 1697

POAS, 2, 1703: POEMS/ON/Affairs of State,/FROM/The Reign of K. *James* the First,/To this Present Year 1703./Written by the Greatest Wits of the Age,/*VIZ.*/The Duke of *Bucking-*/*ham.* /The Earl of *Rochester.*/The Earl of *D*————*t.*/Lord *J*————*s.*

/Mr. *Milton.*/Mr. *Marvel.*/Mr. *St. J*———*n.*/Mr. *John Dryden.*
/Dr. *G*———*th.*/Mr. *Toland.*/Mr. *Hughes.*/Mr. *F*———*e.*/Mr.
Finch./M. *Harcourt.*/Mr. *T*———*n,* &c./———/*Many of*
which never before Publish'd/———/VOL. *II*/———/Printed
in the Year 1703.

Case 211 (2) (a). 1703

POAS, 3, 1703: POEMS/ON/Affairs of State,/From 1640. to this
present/Year 1704./*Written by the greatest Wits of the Age,*/
VIZ./The late Duke of/*Buckingham,*/Duke of *D*———*re,*/Late
E. of *Rochester,*/Earl of *D*———*t,*/Lord *J*———*rys,*/Ld
Hal———*x,*/*Andrew Marvel,* Esq;/Col. *M*———*d*———*t,*/
Mr. *St. J*———*ns,*/Mr. *Hambden,*/Sir *Fleet Shepherd,*/ Mr.
Dryden,/Mr. *St*———*y,*/Mr. *Pr*———*r,*/Dr. *G*———*th,* &c./
———/*Most of which were never before publish'd.*/———/
VOL. *III*/———/Printed in the Year 1704.

Case 211 (3) (a). 1704

POAS, 1698: POEMS/ON/Affairs of STATE:/FROM/OLIVER
CROMWELL,/To this present time. Written by the/greatest
Wits of the Age, *Viz.*/Lord *Rochester,*/Lord *D*———*t,*/Lord
C———*ts,*/Duke of *Buckingham,*/Dr. *K.*/Dr. *Wild,*/Sir *Charles*
S—*dly,*/Sir *Fleetwood S*———*d,*/Mr. *Dryden,*/Mr. *Prior,*
/*Charles Blount, Esq;*/Mr. *Wicherly,*/Mr. *Shadwell,*/Mr. *Tho*
Brown,/*Capt Ayloffe.*/Mr. *H*———*bt,*/———/PART III./
———/With other Miscellany POEMS;/And a new Session of
the present/*POETS.* The whole never before/Printed./———
/Printed in the Year, 1698.

Case 215. 1698

POAS, 1705: A New/COLLECTION/OF/POEMS/Relating to/
State Affairs,/FROM/*OLIVER CROMWEL*/To this present
Time:/By the Greatest/Wits of the Age:/Wherein, not only
those that are Contain'd in/the Three Volumes already Published are/incerted, but also large Additions of chiefest/Note,
never before Published./The whole from their respective Originals,/without Castration./ = /LONDON,/Printed in the Year,
M DCC V.

Case 237. 1705

Poems on Several Occasions: Poems on Several Occasions by the

Earls of Roscommon and Dorset, &c., 1714; also 1720.

Montagu, *Works: The Works and Life of the Rt. Hon. Charles, Late Earl of Halifax*, 1715.

Minor Poets, 1749: *The Works of the most celebrated Minor Poets*, &c., 2 vols., 1749.
A Supplement to the Works of the most celebrated Minor Poets, &c., 1750.

Political Ballads: Political Ballads of the 17th and 18th Centuries, ed. W. Walker Wilkins, 2 vols., 1860.

Bagford Ballads: The Bagford Ballads, Illustrating the Last Years of the Stuarts, ed. J. W. Ebsworth, 4 pts., Ballad Society, Hertford, 1876–78.

Roxburghe Ballads: The Roxburghe Ballads, Illustrating the Last Years of the Stuarts, ed. William Chappell and J. W. Ebsworth, 8 vols., Ballad Society, Hertford, 1871–95.

Pepys Ballads: The Pepys Ballads, ed. Hyder Edward Rollins, 8 vols., Harvard University Press, Cambridge, Mass., 1929–32.

POAS, Yale: *Poems on Affairs of State*, George DeF. Lord, general editor, Yale University Press, New Haven, Conn., 1963— [in progress].

Other Printed Sources

Ailesbury, *Memoirs:* Thomas Bruce, Earl of Ailesbury, *Memoirs*, ed. W. E. Buckley, 2 vols., Roxburghe Club, Westminster, 1890.

Angliae Notitia: Edward Chamberlayne, *Angliae Notitia, or the Present State of England*, from 1669–1704.

Burnet: Gilbert Burnet, *Bishop Burnet's History of His Own Time*, 2 vols., 1724, 1734.

Calamy, *Life:* Edmund Calamy, *An Historical Account of My Own Life, with some reflections on the times I have lived in (1671–1731)*, 2 vols., 1829.

Campana: Marchesa Emilia Campana de Cavelli, *Les derniers Stuarts à Saint-Germain en Laye*, 2 vols., Paris, 1871.

Case: Arthur E. Case, ed., *A Bibliography of English Poetical Miscellanies, 1521–1750*, Bibliographical Society, Oxford, 1935.

Chappell: William Chappell, *Popular Music of the Olden Time*, &c., 2 vols., [1855–59].

Clarendon, *Correspondence* or *Diary:* Henry Hyde, second Earl of Clarendon, *The Correspondence of Henry Hyde . . . and of his brother Laurence Hyde, Earl of Rochester; with the diary of Lord Clarendon from 1687 to 1690,* ed. S. W. Singer, 2 vols., 1828.

Clarke: *The Life of James II,* published from the original MSS. in Carlton House by J. S. Clarke, 2 vols., 1816.

Cokayne, *Baronetage:* G. E. Cokayne, *The Complete Baronetage,* 6 vols., Exeter, William Pollard, 1900–09.

———, *Peerage:* G. E. Cokayne, *The Complete Peerage,* new edn., ed. V. Gibbs, &c., St. Catherine Press, 1910 [in progress]; original edn., 8 vols., 1887–98.

CSPD: Calendar of State Papers, Domestic series (with dates according to contents).

Dalrymple: Sir John Dalrymple, *Memoirs of Great Britain and Ireland,* &c, 3 vols., 1790.

Downes: John Downes, *Roscius Anglicanus,* ed. Montague Summers, Fortune Press, 1928.

Dryden: John Dryden, *Works,* ed. Sir W. Scott; rev. George Saintsbury, 18 vols., Edinburgh, 1882–92.

Poems, ed. John Kinsley, 4 vols., Oxford, Clarendon Press, 1958.

D'Urfey: [Thomas D'Urfey], *Wit and Mirth, or Pills to Purge Melancholy,* 6 vols., 1719.

Dutch Dispatches: Dutch Political Correspondence Relating to England, 1685–88. B.M. Add. MS. 34,508, vol. 2.

Echard: Laurence Echard, *The History of England from the Restoration, &c.,* 3 vols., 1707–18.

EHD: English Historical Documents, 1660–1714 (vol. VIII), ed. Andrew Browning, Eyre & Spottiswoode, 1953.

Ellis Correspondence: George Agar Ellis, *The Ellis Correspondence, 1686–88,* 2 vols., 1829.

Evelyn: *The Diary of John Evelyn,* ed. E. S. de Beer, 6 vols., Oxford, Clarendon Press, 1955.

Fox: Charles James Fox, *A History of the Early Part of the Reign of James II,* 1808.

Gramont: Anthony, Count Hamilton, *Memoirs of Count Gramont,* ed. Allan Fea, Bickers & Son, 1906.

Granger: The Rev. J. Granger, *A Biographical History of England,* 4 vols., 1769.

Hatton Correspondence: Correspondence of the Family of Hatton, being letters chiefly addressed to Christopher, First Viscount Hatton, 1601–1704, ed. E. M. Thompson, 2 vols., Camden Society, 1878.

HMC: Historical Manuscripts Commission [reports cited by collection].

Howell's *State Trials: A Complete Collection of State Trials,* 34 vols., 1809–28 [vols. 1–28 edited by T. B. Howell].

Jesse, *Memoirs:* John Heneage Jesse, *Memoirs of the Court of England during the Reign of the Stuarts,* &c., 4 vols., 2nd edn., 1846.

Kennett: White Kennett, *A Complete History of England,* &c., 3 vols., 1706–19.

Kitchin, *L'Estrange:* George Kitchin, *Sir Roger L'Estrange,* Kegan Paul, Trench, Trübner, 1913.

Lane: Jane Lane, *Titus Oates,* Andrew Dakers, 1949.

Lingard: John Lingard, *The History of England . . . to the Accession of William and Mary in 1688,* 10 vols., Edinburgh, John Grant, 1902.

London Gazette: The London Gazette, 1666 on, twice weekly. [Begun as *The Oxford Gazette,* 1665–66.]

Luttrell: Narcissus Luttrell, *A Brief Historical Relation of State Affairs from September 1678 to April 1714,* 6 vols., Oxford, 1857.

Macaulay: Thomas, Lord Macaulay, *The History of England from the Accession of James II,* ed. Sir Charles H. Firth, 6 vols., Macmillan, 1913–15.

Macdonald: Hugh Macdonald, *John Dryden, A Bibliography of Early Editions and of Drydeniana,* Oxford, Clarendon Press, 1939.

Mazure: F. A. J. Mazure, *Histoire de la révolution de 1688 en Angleterre,* 3 vols., Paris, 1825.

North, *Examen:* Roger North, *Examen, or an Enquiry into the Credit and Veracity of a Pretended Complete History,* &c., 1740.

Observator: Sir Roger L'Estrange, *The Observator, in question and answer.* 13 April 1681–9 March 1687.

Ogg, *Charles II:* David Ogg, *England in the Reign of Charles II,* 2nd edn., Oxford, Clarendon Press, 1956.

Ogg: David Ogg, *England in the Reigns of James II and William III,* Oxford, Clarendon Press, 1955.

Partridge: Eric Partridge, *A Dictionary of Slang and Unconventional English,* 4th edn., Routledge & Kegan Paul, 1956.

Pepys, *Diary:* Samuel Pepys, *Diary,* ed. H. B. Wheatley, 9 vols., 1893–99.

Plomer (1641–67): Henry R. Plomer, *A Dictionary of the Booksellers and Printers who were at work in England, Scotland and Ireland from 1641 to 1667,* Bibliographical Society, 1907.

Plomer (1668–1725): Henry R. Plomer, et al., *Ibid. 1668 to 1725,* Bibliographical Society, Oxford, 1922.

Prior: Matthew Prior, *Literary Works,* ed. H. Bunker Wright and Monroe K. Spears, 2 vols., Oxford, Clarendon Press, 1959.

Public Occurrences: Public Occurrences Truely Stated. No. 1, 21 Feb.–No. 34, 2 Oct. 1688. [By Henry Care, 21 Feb.–7 Aug., and Elkanah Settle, 14 Aug.–2 Oct.]

Reresby: Sir John Reresby, *Memoirs and Selected Letters,* ed. Andrew Browning, Glasgow, Jackson, 1936.

Rump Songs: The Rump: or, a Collection of Songs & Ballads made upon those who would be a Parliament, and were but the Rump of an House of Commons, five times dissolv'd, 2 pts., 1660.

Somers' Tracts: A Collection of Scarce and Valuable Tracts . . . selected from an infinite number . . . in the Royal, Cotton, Sion, and other Public, as well as Private Libraries; particularly that of the late Lord Somers, ed. Sir W. Scott, 13 vols., 1809–15.

Steele: R. R. Steele, *Tudor and Stuart Proclamations, 1485–1714,* 2 vols., Oxford, Clarendon Press, 1910. [Originally part of *Bibliotheca Lindesiana.*]

Tilley: M. P. Tilley, *A Dictionary of the Proverbs in England in the Sixteenth and Seventeenth Century,* Ann Arbor, University of Michigan Press, 1950.

Trevelyan: G. M. Trevelyan, *England Under the Stuarts,* Methuen, 1904.

Turner: F. C. Turner, *James II,* Eyre & Spottiswoode, 1948.

Welwood: James Welwood, *Memoirs of . . . the last Hundred Years preceding the Revolution of 1688,* 1736.

Wheatley: H. B. Wheatley, *London Past and Present,* 3 vols., 1891.

Wing: Donald Wing, *Short-title Catalogue, 1641–1700,* 3 vols., New York, Index Society, 1945.

Introduction

INTRODUCTION

James II came to the throne at fifty-one. For twenty-five years he had stood in the background while his brother reigned. Though he was Charles' chief advisor most of this time, events often made it prudent to conceal the extent of his influence, at the loss of much personal prestige. Three times in the latter years of the reign he had been forced to accept exile to ease tensions largely attributable to the unpopularity of his person and beliefs. For any man these impositions would have been hard to bear. For one of forceful nature and deep convictions, they would, at times, prove almost intolerable. Though self-abnegation is a fact of life for royalty, its impact on a person is no less strong for that. The years of denial and waiting had a profound effect on virtually every aspect of James' personality and character.

I. James' Personal Qualities

On the positive side, James had gained a wealth of military and political experience to draw against as king. His youthful exploits under Turenne had won him a reputation for courage and gallantry. After the Restoration, as Charles' Lord High Admiral, he pursued the naval reforms and improvements recommended by his staff with energy and intelligence, and his reputation for courage was enhanced by his victory over the Dutch at Lowestoft (1665). Politically, James learned much from his father-in-law Edward Hyde, first Earl of Clarendon, particularly in regard to the royal prerogative. When Clarendon fell in 1667 despite James' efforts to save him, James gradually assumed the position of chief advisor. By the beginning of 1669 he was deeply involved with his brother in negotiations for the secret Treaty of Dover (1670), by which the Grand Design to re-convert England was in part to be implemented. James' conversion made it necessary for him to dissemble his faith. For almost seven years he continued to attend the services of the Church of England, often in company with his brother, and for more than half this time he took the sacrament according to its rites at Christmas and Easter.

In 1673 parliament forced Charles to withdraw the Declaration of Indulgence, which he had issued the year before, and began debate on a proposed Test Act bill, requiring holders of public office to take the sacrament according to the English rites and to declare against the doctrine of transubstantiation. James figured prominently in these debates. On enactment, he laid down his offices and withdrew temporarily from public life. He was under constant attack in the years that followed, as the Country party—later known as the Whigs —sought to exclude him from the throne. However misguided their efforts appear, they were in large measure motivated by a sincere apprehension of James and all that he symbolized. In him the opposition saw personified the threat of "Popery and slavery" which haunted the reign. Though Charles never forsook his brother during these years, three times he managed to persuade him that "it was absolutely necessary to yield to this torrent [and] withdraw for some time out of England" (Clarke, *Life, 1,* 541). James' last exile began in October 1680 and continued for almost eighteen months, during which time he conducted the affairs of Scotland with ruthless success. His long apprenticeship to rule was coming to an end, but not before he had experienced for the first time since the 1660s a renewed popularity, largely a reaction to the discredited Whig machinations, though James naturally also felt that it resulted from the achievements of his Scottish administration. Either way, it strengthened his position in the last years of Charles' reign and contributed to the general ease and quiet of his accession in 1685.

A long apprenticeship may be disadvantageous. One may overtrain for a task and go beyond his peak in preparation, or become restricted in purpose and point of view as a result of too limited a share in the responsibilities for and outcome of a specific decision. James' long experience of submission and retirement apparently both narrowed and fixed his ideas. By nature a man of strong convictions like his grandfather James I and his father Charles I, he fervently believed in the divine right of kings, the royal prerogative, and the paternal relationship of king to subject. He was also deeply loyal to Charles, his brother and king, finding it necessary out of that loyalty to accede in almost everything for the good of the reign. In religion alone he would not give way. Devout by nature, by circumstance he became a zealot. As if in direct response to his countrymen's distrust of him and their disdain for his religion, he displayed in things religious the convert's fervor. As early as 1679 the Pope cautioned him against too vehement a pursuit of the Roman Catholic cause in England (Campana, *1, 302*). Charles repeatedly counselled him to cloak his true religious convictions under the trappings of the Anglican faith. Though for a considerable time Charles prevailed, James was determined to make public his faith, just as later, at the outset of his own reign, he resolutely showed himself at mass, having "the doors set wide open" for all those at court to see him at worship (Evelyn, *4, 416*). In the end, the strength of his convictions and the forces pent up by years of restraint had their effect. At his accession, James was not only, as historians have noted, an old man in a hurry, he was also decidedly set in his ways. Whereas certain of his skills had unquestionably been strengthened by use, many of his ideas had suffered a kind of intellectual atrophy.

James came to personify the threat of "Popery and slavery." As a result, he more than Charles was the central figure in the minds of most Englishmen from the Restoration to the Rebellion. From his secret marriage to Anne Hyde on 3 September 1660 to his flight before William's advancing army in December 1688, it is largely his deeds and misdeeds which the State Poems chronicle. They present him in a hundred different guises, from a dull Mark Antony courting his dumpish Cleopatra, Anne Hyde, to a "fumbler royal," at once a political bungler and "an unperforming husband"; from "th'ungrateful Brutus," standing over the bleeding body of his brother "Caesar," to the "pious Samson" who

> would with joy o'erthrow
> The universe and perish by the blow;
> His plots, though known, yet he will ne'er give o'er,
> But still intrigues with his dear Babel whore.

Behind all is the image of him as the leader of a band of Catholic "villains . . . more obedient than a Turkish slave" who, as he is made to boast would

> thrust their bloody knives
> Into their fathers' throats, their children's, wives',
> Or any but their own, they'll freely do't,
> And lay them sprawling at your sacred foot.
> I have Teagues and Tories at my beck

Will wring their heads off like a chicken's neck;
Tri'd rogues, that never will so much as start
To tear from mother's belly infant's heart.
First rape, than rip them up, in one half hour
Two lusts they'll satiate, do but give them pow'r.[1]

Thus the State Poems saw James.

He preferred to see himself, however, as the strict but benevolently wise father of an unruly, wholly dependent progeny—his people. "Be careful that none under you oppress the people," he said to his son in 1692, "or torment them with vexations, suits, or projects. Remember a king ought to be the father of his people and must have a fatherly tenderness for them." And again, "as 'tis the duty of subjects to pay true allegiance to him and to observe his laws, so a king is bound by his office to have a fatherly care of them" (Clarke, 2, 617). The need formally to bequeath "advice" to his son is symptomatic of James' character, however traditional such an act may be. (The idea and form of the "advice" may derive from Charles the I's advice to the Prince of Wales as recorded in John Gauden's *Eikon Basilike*, 1649, sect. xxvii.) Throughout his life, James was deeply influenced, moreover, by the life, ideals, and fate of his father. More than once, he was predisposed, as he said in reference to his treatment of the Seven Bishops, "against the yielding temper which had proven so dangerous to his brother and fatal to the King his father" (James Macpherson, *Original Papers, &c.*, 1775, *1*, 152). In his mind his father had failed not because he had made too few concessions to his people, but because he had made too many. He had not been strong enough. The idea may have been implanted by his disgruntled mother, but James himself nurtured it over the years.

James grew up in the shadow of a gifted and martyred father, was long dominated by his mother, and spent his youth and middle age in face of a brilliant rival brother, who at times seemed to have a positive contempt for him. It is not surprising that an inferiority complex and repressed aggressiveness resulted. On assumption of power, James may have reacted strongly to the years when so much of his own personality had been suppressed. He was now free to act

[1] For the various references to James see *The Second Advice to a Painter* (1666), *POAS*, Yale, *1*, 39–40; *The Statesman's Almanac* (1688), printed below; *The Dream* (1688), printed in *POAS*, *1*, 1697, continuation, p. 146; *Stafford's Ghost* (1682), *POAS*, Yale, *3* (534); and *Popish Politics Unmasked* (1680), *POAS*, Yale, 2, 383–84.

in his own right and in that of the Stuarts. Possibly the image of his father remained with him as he asserted his own integrity, prompting him to it and, perhaps subconsciously, driving him relentlessly on, like his father before him, to a confrontation with the forces of external violence.

Much in James' life lends itself to this interpretation. Paternalism would naturally be associated in the seventeenth century with the divine right of kings and the royal prerogative. But James' general conduct points to a more specific identification with a father image. To his own children it appears that he was devoted and affectionate. He set great store, as well, in his relationship with his "dear son" William of Orange, counselling him, desiring his acceptance and respect, but, above all, fearing him as a rival. His paternal instinct manifested itself, moreover, quite directly in relation to his subjects and with considerable strictness. Evidence appears from the outset of the reign in James' insistence that "the word of a king" was all the assurance and safeguard his subjects could reasonably expect or need, in his efforts to impose a sense of thrift, if not frugality, on his court, and to establish in it a higher moral tone than had been the case under Charles. In addition, he endeavored, on prompting from his Queen and her priests, to set a personal example of continence by repressing his sexual misconduct with Catherine Sedley, while at the same time perhaps seeking to endow that relationship with some degree of dignity by creating her Countess of Dorchester before packing her off to Ireland.

Characteristically, James considered the maintenance of the royal prerogative of prime importance. In his *Advice* to his son he set down a list of necessary advisors for the crown, among whom he suggested "some ingenious young lawyers to have pensions from the Crown to apply themselves to study the prerogative" (Clarke, 2, 641). As head of the realm, the king must be upheld and his rights safeguarded, whatever his subjects might desire. Like spoiled children, the people could be expected to want all manner of things not in their best interest. Ultimately, he felt it fell to the king to see that they did not have their way in such instances. When a difference of opinion arose between him and one of his counsellors, for example, James often sought to settle it by recourse to his own powers of persuasion backed by a sincere belief in the correctness of his position. For extreme cases of disagreement, James developed the practice of closetting which, while it smacked of coercion, apparently operated in his mind, at least, on the principle of the patriarchal interview. Nor was this form of interview reserved for political matters. James did not "think it below his dignity," said one critic, "after the priest had failed to bring in new converts, to try himself how far his own arguments might prevail, and he closetted men for that purpose, too" (Welwood, p. 218). Partially as a result of his own deep involvement in the Catholic cause, James tended to identify intransigence with ingratitude and personal rebuff. Burnet records the following duel of words with the Duke of Norfolk:

> One day the King gave the Duke of Norfolk the sword of state to carry before him to the chapel, and he stood at the door. Upon which the King said to him, "My lord, your father would have gone further." To which the Duke answered, "Your majesty's father was the better man, and he would not have gone so far" (*History of his own Time, 1*, 683–84).

When in November 1688 James was deserted by Churchill and then by Prince George and Princess Anne, he saw their perfidy in a familial context. Churchill's ingratitude reportedly astounded James because he had treated his subject like a son, raising him from nothing to a place of eminence in the court (Reresby, p. 534). Of the indolent Denmark, James mockingly said, "were he not my son-in-law, a single trooper would have been a greater loss." On learning that Anne had followed her husband, however, the King is said to have broken down and wept, "God help me! My very children have forsaken me!" (Lingard, *10*, 352, 354).

The events of James' reign and the measures he took to promote his policies often seem to have been conditioned by an abiding fear of his countrymen. J. P. Kenyon has reminded us that James "lived in daily expectation of rebellion," that "apprehension . . . not aggression, is the key to an understanding of James the II's policy" (*The Stuarts,* p. 162). And James' fears had basis. Within months of his accession, Argyle and Monmouth landed on the shores of Scotland and the west country. The trial and conviction of Titus Oates in May 1685, though a victory for the Crown, was also a bitter reminder of the frenzy of Exclusion and the Popish Plot, to which James had been subjected in the last years of his brother's reign. He feared assassination as well, and the disclosures of the Rye House Plot (1683) to murder the royal brothers confirmed his darkest suspicions. At times he seemed preoccupied with the subject. Once on returning in his coach from a day's hunting, he encountered his brother walking virtually unattended and warned him of the danger to his person. "No kind of danger, James," the King replied, "for I am sure no man in England will take away my life to make you king" (Anthony Hamilton, *Memoirs of the Count of Gramont,* ed. Sir Walter Scott, edn. of 1846, pp. 447–48). The King's cynical estimate of affairs no doubt tallied with James' own realization of the dislike most of his countrymen felt for him. He had had years to grow accustomed to their hostility. The public insults he bore in London, such as those reported in May and June 1686 by the Tuscan envoy Tierriesi, simply reaffirmed his general distrust of his subjects (Campana, 2, 107–08). While the 1685 rebellion of Monmouth had climaxed years of bitter strife with his bastard nephew, James was confronted from 1687 onward with the competition of his son-in-law for the sympathies of his people, culminating in William's campaign against him in 1688.

The example and fate of his father remains as important as any of these things in determining James' reaction to events. James intended to take all steps to avoid a similar fate, but these only led, ironically, to his downfall. When parliament challenged his prerogative, he sought to rule without them. The prerogative must be maintained. He felt his own safety lay in strength, both physical and moral, and in the dismissal of those who opposed him. He sought to build a strong standing army in his defense. He looked for aid to Ireland, Scotland, France. He relied on the support of the high-church leaders within the Anglican clergy. At times it seems almost as if he were impelling himself toward the spectre of his father's tragic end.

During the later years of exile, he saw the loss of his kingdoms as the just punishment of God for his incontinence, and he rehearsed at length the typology of the "unnatural," the "stiff-necked and murmuring" generations who, like himself, had offended God in his bounty (*Papers of Devotion of James II,* ed. Godfrey Davies, 1925, pp. 35 ff.). But in the months of crisis toward the end of his reign, a familial image obsessed him, which "he recounted at length" to the

Papal nuncio. He told d'Adda how he feared the application to the present case of the tragic stories of Richard the Second and Henry the Sixth, plundered of life and realm by the aggression of their closest relatives.[2]

II. THE CLIMATE OF SATIRE

On 24 February 1685 parliament quite predictably renewed for the "space of seven years" the act "preventing the frequent abuses in printing seditious, treasonable, and unlicensed books and pamphlets, and for regulating of printing and printing presses" (*The Statutes at Large,* II Jac. cap. XVII. xiv). Reënactment of the statute was a matter of course. No ordinary overseer, however, had charge of its enforcement. Long known as "the bloodhound of the press," Roger L'Estrange's unstinting efforts at control won for him a knighthood on 30 April 1685, while on 21 May a warrant proclaimed "the King's will that L'Estrange exercise all such powers as he formerly did [under Charles II] in the regulation of the press and see diligently to the execution of these commands and render a report to the King from time to time in case of any disobedience thereunto, the command of the press being a prerogative inseparable from the sovereignty of his imperial crown" (*CSPD,* 1685, p. 159). L'Estrange's activities during the first two years of the reign are amply demonstrated by the various items among the state papers for this period. In addition a general censorship of the mails existed. Giving an account of parliament's activities in relation to James' attempt to suppress the Test Act in November 1685, Owen Wynn, the newswriter, employs code because "the conjecture is [such] that you cannot use too much cipher, for all the packets are opened of late somewhere by the way, and the letters enclosed taken out and sent uncovered" (*HMC, Downshire, 1, i,* 54. *CSPD,* 1686–87, p. 350, provides an instance of the success of this postal inspection). It should be stressed, of course, that these measures were in no way unusual in themselves, especially as Monmouth's Rebellion (June–July 1685)

---

[2] Sir James Mackintosh (*History of the Revolution in England in 1688,* 1835, p. 693), prints the letter:

Disse poi che leggeva nelle istorie d'Inghilterra due successi, ne quali si potevano cavar insegnamenti per il caso presente, e racontò à longo il fine tragico di due Rè si ben mi souviene, Ricardo seconda, ed un Henrico, li quali sotto titolo d'accordo furono spogliati del regno e del vita, da suoi più stretti parenti, ed agressori.

necessitated a tightening up on all restrictions. L'Estrange and his sergeants had a blanket authority, however, which enabled them, for example, on word "that several treasonous and seditious libels [had] lately been dispersed and thrown up and down the streets of the cities of London and Westminster . . . to make a strict and diligent search for the said libels, together with the publishers, dispensers, receivers, or concealers of the same, and to seize the said papers, apprehend the said persons, and particularly to search the houses or lodgings" of anyone under suspicion (*CSPD*, 1686–87, p. 135). The relative paucity of satire during the first two years of James' reign results, in part, from the vigilance of the King's operatives, particularly that of Surveyor L'Estrange.

Though "when James acceded to the throne, the printed newspapers had been suppressed, and many of the newswriters had been laid by the heels" (P. Fraser, *The Intelligence of the Secretaries of State and Their Monopoly of Licensed News, 1660–1688*, 1956, p. 131), in itself suppression may not suffice in muzzling protest. The third Earl of Shaftesbury's remark that the "greater the weight [of constraint] is, the bitterer will be the satire. The higher the slavery, the more exquisite the buffoonery" reminds us that, up to a point, added risks may merely force the satirist to become more efficient and effective in his work (R. C. Elliott, *The Power of Satire*, 1960, p. 264, citing Shaftesbury's *Characteristics*). In this light we may explain the relative satiric quiet from 1685 through the first-half of 1687 as a result less of government surveillance than of English optimism. For most Englishmen recognized that all of James' Romanizing measures must ultimately prove futile so long as the succession remained Protestant. When events began to prove the Englishman wrong in his estimation of James' political as well as his procreational sufficiency, he took up his pen and attacked with all the energy at his command. Throughout the reign, satire kept pace with events, mirroring them and the Englishman's attitude to them quite accurately. Thus with the quickening of affairs of state in the last months of 1687 came a deepening of satiric concern.

Much of the satire of the last eighteen months of the reign keenly perceives cause and effect and artfully achieves its satiric purpose. Still more sinks beneath contempt in matter and manner. Its modern counterpart is the obscene joke and anonymous libel which spring up like weeds whenever the political weather intensifies. Attacks on the Queen during her pregnancy and subsequently on the Prince of Wales at his birth and during the first months of his infancy illustrate the attitude and tenor of the opposition. Richard Lapthorne, a young student, records the stir caused by "a lampoon relating to the late thanksgiving" [in all probability *The Council,* printed below, which circulated in January 1688] and noted that "a strict inquiry is made after the author who, if he be discovered, will according to deserts be severely punished" (*Portledge Papers,* ed. R. J. Kerr and Ida C. Duncan, 1928, p. 24). During the weeks immediately following his son's birth, James lamented that "pamphlets flew about filled with all the ribaldry and calumny that malice and wit were capable of inventing, where under the notion of novels and private relations of what passed at court, the horridest crimes were laid to the Queen's charge" (Clarke, *2, 192).* James' natural bias notwithstanding, it is extremely difficult in face of the mass of invective with which the birth was greeted not to share his abhorrence. Only a small portion of the satire of the reign finds its way into this volume and that which does is generally of a higher tone than most of the discarded specimens. Even on the basis of the poems included here, however, it is hard to avoid the suggestion that the "Whig interpretation of history," strongly elaborated by men like Macaulay, who knew the *State Poems* intimately,[3] to a great extent grew out of the intensity and depravity of the satire everywhere to be found, like debris left in the wake of the emotional flood of the summer and fall of 1688. The newswriter and satirist had set out to destroy James and his Catholic party, just as they had attempted to do in the early 1680s under Shaftesbury's instigation and with Oates' disclosures. Libel and exaggeration became their primary weapons whether to paint an ironic, dark, menacing portrait of the King, as in *Hounslow Heath,* and thus heighten the sense of danger, or to reduce him and his courtiers to absurd and obscene caricature, as in *A Faithful Catalogue of Our Most Eminent Ninnies,* and thus laugh away their potency. In these efforts the satirist recognized, along with Roger North, the difficulty of keeping fact separate from fiction:

---

[3] The first historian to make extensive use of the *State Poems,* Macaulay unquestionably adds color to his account of events by recourse to them, though on occasion at the expense of accuracy. As an instance of his reliance on the poems, his descriptions of the second Earl of Peterborough and fourth Earl of Salisbury (Macaulay, *2, 848*) should be compared with their source, *The Converts,* printed below.

> If libel and history were like oil and vinegar, that, however beaten together, would of themselves divide and go several ways, this trouble might have been spared, but lies to truth are rather as lead to quicksilver, that cling so close that nothing but fire will part them (*Examen,* p. 659).

A measure of the effectiveness of their work may be inferred from a survey of the number of versions that appeared during November and December 1688 of *The Orange* and *Lilli burlero.* At least three versions of the former came out in the six-week period from William's landing to James' flight, the last of these written by Matthew Prior. No less than five sets of lyrics were composed for the more famous *Lilli burlero* in the same period, and the tune had so great an effect that a pro-James version circulated, presumably designed to enhance the Royal cause by capturing for it some of the song's popularity.

On 11 October 1688 James ordered "that no coffee house or public house keep any written or any other news, save the *Gazette,*" the official news organ of the government (*HMC, Le Fleming,* p. 214); on 26 October he issued a proclamation "to restrain the spreading of false rumors." In it the people who "have been of late more bold and licentious" in their discourses than in the past are warned to "presume not henceforth, either by writing, printing, or speaking, to utter or publish any false news or reports whatsoever, or to intermeddle with affairs of state . . . in their common and ordinary discourse" (Steele, n. 3888). The proclamation had little effect, of course, as a newsletter of 28 October attests. Following a vivid description of the state of London in this period of tension, the writer concludes by observing that "concerning the Prince of Wales' birth . . . men are grown very learned. It is shameful to hear what discourse is common amongst them, even to footmen and lackeys. But I forgot the proclamation come out this evening [*sic*] to forbid talking or writing of state affairs upon peril" (*HMC, Portland, 3,* 420; and see the opening lines of *The Progress,* printed below, for further evidence of the crowd's preoccupation with matters of state). The satirist, clearly, was not to be deterred. His songs, lampoons, and libels were everywhere. Not the least of the indignities which the gentle, frightened Queen had to bear were the aspersions on herself and her child. She had never been popular with the rabble, nor had she been able to understand their ways. On their part, however, they had never troubled themselves to think of her as anything more than "a fawning Duchess and a saucy Queen" (*The Dream, POAS*, 1703, *1*, continuation, pp. 146–49). When, on awaking one morning early in December, she found an obscene ballad on the Prince thrust into one of the gloves on her dressing table, her fear and hatred of her husband's countrymen must have been absolute (Campana, 2, 341).

Against the spawn of minor satirists of the period, most of whom remain nameless, Dryden sounds like Leviathan in his greatness. His pindaric on the death of Charles, *Threnodia Augustalis,* gave him his first opportunity to support the new King and offer himself as James' poet royal:

> A warlike Prince ascends the regal state,
> A Prince, long exercis'd by fate:
> Long may he keep, though he obtain it late.
> Heroes in Heaven's peculiar mold are cast,
> They and their poets are not form'd in haste;
> Man was first in God's design, and man was made the last.

Shortly thereafter Dryden celebrated the new reign with the Italianate opera *Albion and Albanius,* which while it was not particularly successful did seek to convey the pageantry and hopes of the moment. By the great work of these years, *The Hind and the Panther,* Dryden hoped to support James and prepare his countrymen for toleration, though the King's precipitant action in proclaiming the toleration in April 1687 largely undercut the poem's political effectiveness. The subject of the last poem Dryden wrote for James, *Britannia Rediviva,* on the birth of the Prince, provided him quite naturally with the image significant to the reign that was ending. In it he saw James as the father of his people, the founder of a line in the "proper character of a king by inheritance, who is born a father of his country" (from Dryden's "Dedication" to his translation of the *Aeneid*). But even Dryden, with all his strength and size, could not "swallow in the fry." Striking at every point, the satirists swarmed until they made the political waters boil. Their effect may be seen in James' indecisiveness, his troops' almost total lack of morale in face of the enemy, the virtually bloodless revolution that resulted, and the very real fear displayed by James and his followers in their flight from the country. The effectiveness of the satirist has lent support to the notion that the Glorious Rebellion was more a national movement than the work of a relatively few disgruntled members of the upper classes in support of William who, no matter what else he may have been, was a not unwilling usurper.

III. THE POEMS

The poems which follow have been selected from the great number surviving with these criteria in mind: 1) the poetic and political interest; 2) the representation of various satiric forms, such as the advice-to-a-painter poem or the court ballad; and 3) the apparent popularity or influence of the poem. Where possible I have also tried to represent both sides of an issue, though not much satire during the reign defends the Crown and its policies.

The text is modernized in spelling, punctuation, and other accidentals. A few basic considerations have prompted the decision to adopt this measure. With some notable exceptions, the anonymous and fugitive nature of this body of political verse fails to produce single, authoritative texts. To anyone who has worked in the field of popular literature, bibliographical chaos is a *donnée*. Certainly some poems, so far as one can tell, exist only in a single manuscript or broadside version; most of the poems, however, have come down to us in many versions and in many forms, both manuscript and printed, all presumably at several removes from the author's holograph. To reproduce the spelling and punctuation of these witnesses would be to perpetrate, by and large, the carelessness, whims, and idiosyncrasies of nameless scribes and harried printers, working under the pressure of popular demand and political injunction. In the printed texts the same problem arises in regard to such typographical devices as italicization, capitalization, and the various other means of "setting-off" at the disposal of the popular press.

For much of the poetry contained in the earlier volumes of the present series no printed text of significance was available, and the basic collections of *Poems on Affairs of State* (1689–1716) were for most purposes too far removed in time from the events to prove particularly useful in establishing individual texts. In this situation the separate manuscript of a single poem, as distinguished from a manuscript collection, was usually found to be preferable to other witnesses as a basis for establishing an accurate text (Cf. *POAS*, Yale, *1*, 441–43). The poems printed in this volume derive, however, more frequently from a printed source. A large number of them exist in one or more broadsides which represent, if not a close approximation of what the satirist wrote, at least the form of the satire read by those most deeply involved in the events of the moment. The first editions of *Poems on Affairs of State* (1689), *Poems . . . Against Popery* (1689), and *The Muses Farewell to Popery* (1689) came out soon enough after the preceding reign and the circumstances contained in their poems were still fresh and controversial enough, moreover, for care to be exercised in preparation, thus enhancing their value to the modern editor and making them for these years of more than usual textual interest. The manuscripts generally represent one of two species; first, those single and separable manuscripts which circulated at the time of the event, and, more often, those manuscripts and manuscript collections produced in the 1690s and later by professional scribes, often working in a commercial enterprise of the kind described by William Cameron in his study of "A Late Seventeenth-Century Scriptorium" (*Ren. & Mod. Studies,* 7 [1963], 25–52). Quite valuable bibliographical evidence of this kind of venture is provided by the file copy or "exemplar" employed in one commercial house, which has served in the present edition as the basis for the text of *A Faithful Catalogue of Our Most Eminent Ninnies.* The "exemplar" is a fair copy of the poem, bearing the marks of a second hand which has "corrected" it and added directions to the scribe for making further copies (see plate #10 and commentary in textual notes).

Ideally, then, the lineage of a particular poem of, say, the summer of 1688 would be (1) a broadside or separable manuscript, (2) a printed collection, and (3) a manuscript collection. Normally, this or some portion of this sequence has determined the choice of copy text, though always with regard to the more important and particular concerns of soundness and accuracy of an individual witness. In preparing these poems I have often found it necessary to emend the copy text when one of its readings is demonstrably inferior to that of another witness or group of witnesses. The textual apparatus records these emendations, as well as those substantive variants which seem to offer plausible alternative readings. The apparatus remains, however, strictly selective and is basically a guide to the historical and satiric vagaries of the time. The basis for the text of each poem is given at the beginning of the apparatus and is followed by a list of all other versions consulted. Because of the numerous texts that have come to the notice of this project since the first volumes were printed, I have felt it convenient to drop the original system of sigla, which did not prove as easily expandible as was anticipated. In each individual section of the textual notes, I have designated the copy text and witnesses by cue titles, plus a letter symbol employed in the apparatus proper to cite variant readings.

Some few final considerations: Proper names, generally indicated by blanks in most printed texts, have been supplied from manuscripts unless otherwise noted. Obscene words have been indicated by initial letters and dashes, following the practice of most of the seventeenth-century texts. Dates are Old Style, except that the year has been regarded as beginning on January 1. Unless otherwise noted, definitions in the notes are taken from the *Oxford English Dictionary*.

1685

The Accession of James the Second
(February 1685)

Among the numerous ballads celebrating the accession, the following "companion" poems rise above eulogy and propaganda to indicate one aspect of the popular feeling of the moment. The *Reward of Loyalty* rehearses James' long military and political apprenticeship to monarchy. Before the Restoration he had won fame in Europe under Turenne and with the Spanish at the battle of the Dunes (1658). As Charles II's Lord High Admiral, he had been generally successful against the Dutch at Lowestoft (1665) and Sole Bay (1672). He was his brother's chief advisor throughout most of the reign, and his renewed popularity during its closing years was, in part, a reaction to the humiliations he had suffered from exclusionist parliaments and anti-Catholic juries and witnesses. His personal qualifications did much, no doubt, to instill confidence, while the public aspirations of a new reign may have diminished the popular fear of Popery. Besides, James had declared in Council his determination "to preserve this government in Church and State as it is now by law established" (Steele, *1*, 457). This assurance, as the Whig Gilbert Burnet pointed out, "was magnified as a security far greater than any that laws could give. The common phrase was, 'we have now the word of a King, and a word never yet broken'" (Burnet, *1*, 620; see also *Observator*, 11 Feb. 1685).

Despite the favorable aspects of the situation, however, fear and resistance remained strong. James and his ministers were anxious about the reception the proclamation of his accession would receive throughout the country. The people's fear of Popery might easily prove stronger than their faith in monarchy. The suddenness, the unexpectedness of Charles' death, with the inevitable rumors as to its cause, could be counted on greatly to increase the danger of reaction. Yet, as Rochester told Ormonde in a letter written four days after the death of Charles, everything remained "calm and quiet to a wonder" (*HMC, Ormonde*, 7, 317). From afar Burnet reported the day was one of "heavy solemnity," with few "shouts of joy for the present King" (*1*, 620), and the Nonconformist Edmund Calamy, who witnessed the demonstrations in Cheapside said he had never seen "so universal a concern as was visible in all men's countenances, at that time," admitting how his heart ached within him "at the acclamations made upon that occasion" (*Life*, p. 116). Despite the optimism of *The Reward of Loyalty*, some nodded ominously at the full implications of both loyalty and reward once the King found himself "at leisure."

On 21 March "his Majesty's free and gracious pardon . . . for 76 prisoners in Newgate" was announced (Luttrell, *1*, 336). The amnesty was calculated to call forth a popular response. The health to "James the Great" raised by the pardoned prisoners in *A Trick for Tyburn* was certainly of the same order as that produced by the free wine distributed in the streets at the accession (Fox, App., xvi). But, though the rogues who promised to reform were as fickle as those the author of *The Reward of Loyalty* charged with "sedition," they were at one with their countrymen in their hatred of England's enemies. Rogues they might be, but they were not traitors. James took over a country tired of internal conflict, a country more united than it had been for years, eager to assert itself in the struggle in Europe. It was, perhaps, not too great an exaggeration to sing of its leader,

> Ne'er was king of more renown
> Than great James that wears the crown.

THE REWARD OF LOYALTY

Being a Song of the Times Advising Every Man to be
Faithful to God, Loyal to His King, and Honest to His
Neighbor, and Not to Meddle with State Affairs

To the tune of "Hark, the Thundering Canons Roar"

1.

> Loyalty's a noble thing;
> Service done unto a king
> Honor and reward doth bring
> And flies up to promotion.
> Treason is a trick of state,

Which the devil makes a bait
To a proud aspiring pate
    To overturn a nation.

2.

I never knew since time began
An open rogue and great trepan   10
Turn a true and faithful man
    To God, or yet be loyal.
He who to a king that's brave
Proves a false deceitful knave
Is sedition's simple slave: 15
    Be true to James the Royal.

3.

Newgate traitor, tell me now
What turns all thy projects to
And exploits thou thought to do
    Against the Lord's anointed?   20
Rebels that the nation hate
Must submit to divine fate,
Which ruleth both the church and state
    And runs as God appointed.

4.

Ne'er was king of more renown   25
Than great James that wears the crown;
Rebels' names he doth write down
    Until he be at leisure;
Loyalists he doth requite;
Gratitude is his delight,   30
But the rascal rout doth slight:
    He's just as was old Caesar.

---

10. *trepan:* One who "entraps or decoys others into actions . . . to his advantage and to their ruin or loss."

32. *old Caesar:* Charles II.

5.

When Hogen Mogen did disdain
To take on Britain's yoke again,
He led the fleet unto the main   35
    And bravely did behave him;
When brains and bullets fled about,
He prov'd himself both wise and stout
And cri'd, "Let's have the other bout;
    We will both fight and slave them."   40

6.

He is the first-rate *Sovereign Blood,*
Laden with the kingdom's good,
Toss'd betwixt the wind and flood
    When Providence ensureth.
Though the church religious vail   45
Were made treason's highest sail,
The hope of hypocrites would fail,
    For truth alone endureth.

33. *Hogen Mogen:* A corruption of *Hoogmogendheiden,* "High Mightinesses," the official designation of the States General of the United Provinces.

33–40. During the Battle of Sole Bay (1672), James' flagship, the *Prince,* was so badly battered that he was forced to abandon her for the *St. Michael,* which in turn he left for the *London* (Clarke, *Life, 1,* 466, 470).

37. *brains . . . fled about:* A reference to the deaths of Charles Berkeley, Earl of Falmouth, Charles MacCarthy, Lord Muskerry, and Richard Boyle, second son of the Earl of Burlington. Cf. Waller's *Instructions to a Painter* (*POAS,* Yale, *1,* 27–28):

> . . . a fatal volley we receiv'd:
> It miss'd the Duke, but his great heart is griev'd;
> Three worthy persons from his side it tore
> And dy'd his garment with their scatter'd gore. (145–48)

See also Marvell's more elaborate treatment of the subject in the *Second Advice,* see *POAS,* Yale, *1,* 44–45.

39. *bout:* Presumably "a round at fighting," but the historical context suggests the possibility of the reading "boat."

41. *first-rate Sovereign Blood:* Refers to both James' legitimate claim to the throne, as the son of Charles I, and to a ship of the first rate, such as the *Sovereign of the Seas,* launched in 1637, twice rebuilt, and finally burned accidentally in 1696. The finest vessel of the fleet, she was also called the *Sovereign, Royal Sovereign,* and *Sovereign Royal.*

45–47. The nautical metaphor is continued here, though syntactically obscure, in reference to the "vailing, or lowering of a sail as an acknowledgement of inferiority."

7.

Heap me a rousing glass with wine;
Let no man at this health repine: 50
To James the Great I'll drink off mine,
   He knows both sword and scepter.
When madness did make Britain dance
The tragedy of base mischance,
His practice did his parts enhance   55
   And was complete still after.

8.

Honest fellow, live content,
Kindly take what God hath sent,
Think what way to pay thy rent
   And strive to fly no higher.   60
He's a fool at any rate
Meddleth with affairs of state;
He'll repent when 'tis too late
   And say that I'm no liar.

9.

Fear the Lord, honor the king,   65
Submit to fate in everything,
Do thy business and sing,
   And never think on sorrow.
In private eat thy honeycomb,
Kiss thy wife when thou'rt at home,   70
Never think on what may come,
   For none hath seen tomorrow.

53–56. A reference to the "madness" of the Popish Plot and attempts to exclude James from the throne.

69–70. Cf. Proverbs 24:12–14. In the context, however, this may be an off-color joke, employing "honeycomb" as a slang expression for "mistress."

A TRICK FOR TYBURN
OR
A PRISON RANT

Being a Song of the Prisoners of Newgate at the
Jail Delivery
To the tune of "Hark, the Thundering Canons Roar"

Trumpets sound and steeples ring,
Every loyal subject sing
With a health to James our King
   For his pardon granted.
Prisoners half dead that lay,   5
Clos'd in stone instead of clay,
Have their liberty today
   Which before they wanted.

Newgate lately did bring forth
Seventy children at a birth,   10
All in wantonness and mirth
   At a jail delivery.
But her keepers they lie in,
Money-sick for want of sin;
They will look both pale and thin   15
   Till a new recovery.

Now the doors are open wide
Jack may take his mare and ride
With a leg on every side,
   And the jade be flinging;   20
Take her halter, Ketch, and try
What's the nearest course to die,
And we'll write thine elegy,
   "He's hang'd for want of hanging."

16. *recovery:* A recovery of the prisoners, the objects of the keepers' extortion, and of the keepers' health.

18. *Jack:* Obs., a knave.
   mare: "Horse" and also "gallows," the two- or three-legged mare.

19. *With a leg on every side:* i.e. without leg irons.

Henceforth we will steal no more 25
Though we should be ne'er so poor.
If by chance we take a whore
    In single fornication,
We get a soldier to the King
Or a seaman who doth bring 30
From the Indies everything:
    It doth not wrong the nation.

We were rebels more than base
To abuse an act of grace;
We'll ne'er do't in any case, 35
    We'll legal be and loyal.
If the French begin to reel
(English hearts are true as steel),
We'll make their breasts our bullets feel
    For James our King, the Royal. 40

Should our case be ne'er so bad,
We will never be so mad
As to go upon the pad
    Whilst our life endureth.
This rogue that was a great trepan 45
Is two parts turn'd a civil man
And honestly drinks off his can
    And nothing deadly feareth.

We wish that those that cannot pay
Their debts may have a jubiley, 50
That poor men for the King may pray
    At his great coronation.
To see the usurers go mourn
And take with Jack a second turn,
When their bills and bonds they burn, 55
    Would overjoy the nation.

37. *reel:* Behave recklessly.
43. *to go upon the pad:* To commit robbery on the highway.
45. *trepan:* A deceiver.
50. *jubiley:* "A time of restitution, remission, or release." The original spelling indicates the pronouncing of this rime-word in normal 17th-century usage.
54. *turn:* Here also "a step off the ladder at the gallows."

Whittington did build an house,
Enough to starve a rat or mouse,
But left allowance for a louse
  To give poor men the fever.   60
But James the Great hath found a way
To turn his scepter to a key
And give his children all the play:
  God bless him then forever.

57–60. Richard Whittington (d. 1423), the famous "Dick," Mayor of London, left legacies to rebuild Newgate prison and to establish, among other institutions, an alms-house.
59–60. Cf. "the louse is a beggar's companion" (Tilley, L471).
63. *the play:* "A holiday."

The Humble Address
(May 1685)

Standing as a warning against the addresses which filled the *London Gazette* in February and March, *The Humble Address* mocks their willingness to welcome, even if only as a matter of form, a Catholic king to the throne of England. Supposedly presented by the leaders of law and religion, the address links Jeffreys with James and ironically prays for their success in subverting English law and religion. The warning was not without reason. Within ten days of his accession James had declared his own religious position by publicly attending mass in the chapel of St. James' Palace (Evelyn, *4, 416*; Fox, App., xxxii–iii), and even moderate Anglicans were ready to admit that Roman Catholics showed themselves "more boldly than ever" at Court (Luttrell, *1, 337*; also Evelyn, *4, 419*). Moreover, though a parliament had been elected, there were strong rumors and some evidence that these elections had not been free of interference from the Crown and its officers (see below, 11–12 and n.).

Only one of the petitioners can be identified. He is William Sancroft (1617–93), Archbishop of Canterbury, who was in James' debt. In 1677 James had been instrumental in obtaining Sancroft's appointment to the archbishopric, opposing the strong candidacy of Henry Compton, Bishop of London. We may safely assume that the representative of the judiciary was equally appropriate to his role— in the satirist's mind at least—although the unintelligible abbreviation in Phillipps 8302 has so far obscured his identity. The poem is endorsed, "Address to King James, 1684," which would indicate that it was written prior to 25 March 1685, but internal evidence suggests a date after the assembly of Parliament on 19 May. The endorsement is presumably a scribal error of the kind so frequently made in the first weeks of a "new year."

The Humble Address

Of the Loyal Professors of Divinity and Law
that Want Preferment and Practice
Introduced by their Graces of Canterbury and B[?].

Great sir, our poor hearts were ready to burst
For the loss of your brother when we heard it at first.
But when we were told that you were to reign
We all fell a roaring out huzzas again.
With hearts full of joy, as our glasses of wine,   5
In this loyal address both professions do join.

May Jeffreys swagger on the bench
And James upon the throne,
Till we become slaves to the French
And Rome's dominion own;   10
May no man sit in Parliament
But by a false return,
Till Lords and Commons by consent

Subtitle: The manuscript bears an abbreviation, beginning with the letter "B,"
which seems to stand for a name or title such as Bedford or Beaufort. A possible
candidate among James' judiciary is Sir Robert Baldock (d. 1691), one of the King's
sergeants, for whom see below, *The Dissenters' Thanksgiving*, note to title.

7. *Jeffreys:* George Jeffreys (1648–89), first Baron Jeffreys of Wem in Shropshire,
1685; educated at St. Paul's School, Westminster, and Trinity College, Cambridge;
called to the bar (1668), named Recorder of London (1678), and Lord Chief Justice
(1683), despite Charles' personal distaste for him. Jeffreys was raised to the peerage
within a few days of the trial of Titus Oates, over which he presided, and on 20
May, four days after passing sentence on Oates, rumor made it "a very hot report"
that he was to supersede Guilford, the Lord Chancellor (Luttrell, *1, 343;* also Evelyn,
4, 445). A vicious portrait of him is in *POAS, 1,* 1697, 171, entitled *The True
Englishman:*

> Let a lewd judge come reeking from a wench
> To vent a wilder lust upon the bench;
> Bawl out the venom of his rotten heart,
> Swell'd up with envy, overact his part;
> Condemn the innocent by laws ne'er fram'd
> And study to be more than doubly damn'd.

11–12. On 22 May Sir Edward Seymour "made a bold speech against many elections
and would have had those members who, he pretended, were obnoxious to withdraw
till they had cleared their being legally returned, but nobody seconded him" (Evelyn, *4,*
444; Fox, App., xciii–iv). Sunderland's care in preparing for the elections is attested to
by his letters to the lords-lieutenant (*CSPD,* 1685, pp. 21–109 *passim*).

Their Magna Charta burn.
Though Smithfield now neglected lie,   15
Oh, may it once more shine
With Whigs in flaming heaps that fry
Of books they call divine;
From whence may such a blaze proceed,
So glorious and so bright,   20
That the next parish priest may read
His mass by Bible light.
Then holy water pots shall cheer
Our hearts like aqua-vitae
Whilst singing monks in triumph bear   25
Their little God Almighty.
More blessings we could yet foretell
In this most happy reign,
But hark, the King's own chapel bell
Calls us to prayers again.   30
May trade and industry decay,
But may the plague increase,
Till it hath swept those Whigs away
That sign not this address.

15. *Smithfield:* Made infamous in the 16th century by the burning of heretics, especially the Marian martyrs.

18. *of books:* i.e. in a fire fed by "books they call divine."

26. *Their little God Almighty:* The Host, or the crucifix.

29. *the King's own chapel:* The oratory connected to James' old lodgings as Duke of York. Charles had closed it, fearing scandal, but James reopened it and made it virtually the Chapel Royal, hearing mass with "the doors set wide open" (Evelyn, *4,* 416).

The Trial and Punishment of Titus Oates
(May 1685)

On 8–9 May at the Court of King's Bar Bench Titus Oates was
tried and convicted on two counts of perjury. A week later he was
sentenced. The day before Parliament assembled, he was pilloried
in Palace Yard. Twice during the following week, as Parliament took
up its tasks, the cries of the perjurer could be heard in the streets
as he was scourged across London. Though the coincidence of the
dates seems to confirm Burnet's conclusion that the whole ghastly
affair was staged "as a preparation" to the sitting of Parliament
(*1*, 637), in fairness to James it should be remembered that Burnet
was biased and that preliminaries to Oates' trial had been going on
for almost a year: Oates had been arrested on 10 May 1684 at the
Amsterdam Coffee-house in an action of Scandalum Magnatum
brought by the Duke of York, fined £100,000, and lodged in King's
Bench Prison in default of payment. When the writs for Parliament
went out late in February 1685, the date of the actual trial was still
uncertain. The Court could easily arrange such an intimidating display, but there was little need to do so. James was pleased with his
Parliament and, indeed, few of the members themselves, as they
listened to the Royal Address on 22 May, would have felt any sympathy for the victim. The nation had been diabolically fooled, and it
would have its revenge.

The poems here printed are selected from the numerous ballads
hawked in the London streets throughout May. They pick up a
thread which had already been spun long and coarse, a thread fretted
with a hundred allusive strands from the angry days of the plot when
Oates' "very breath . . . was pestilential, and, if it brought not
imprisonment or death over such on whom it fell, it surely poisoned
reputation and left good Protestants arrant Papists, and something
worse than that, in danger of being put in the Plot as traitors"
(North, *Examen,* p. 205).

TESTIS OVAT

Behold y⁰ Heroe who has done all this
In a small Triumph stand, such as it is:
A kind of an Ovation onely : true,
But such for Bloudlesse Victories are due
His were not such; he merits more than Egg
Let him in Tryumph swing & ease his Legs

Titus Oates in the Pillory

The Salamanca Doctor's Farewell

Or Titus' Exaltation to the Pillory
Upon his Conviction of Perjury

A ballad, to the tune of "Packington's Pound"

1.

Come listen, ye Whigs, to my pitiful moan,
All you that have ears when the Doctor has none.
In sackcloth and ashes let's sadly be jogging
To behold our dear savior o'th'nation a-flogging.
　　　　The Tories to spite us,   5
　　　　As a goblin to fright us,
With a damn'd wooden ruff will bedeck our friend Titus.
Then mourn all to see this ungrateful behavior
From these lewd Popish Tories to the dear nation-savior.

2.

From three prostrate kingdoms at once to adore me   10
And no less than three parliaments kneeling before me,
From hanging of lords with a word and a frown,
And no more than an oath to the shaking a crown;
　　　　For all these brave pranks
　　　　Now to have no more thanks   15
Than to look through a hole through two damn'd wooden
　　　　planks:

2. A standard joke. Oates did not have his ears "cropped" when he was pilloried.
If the poem were written prior to the passing of sentence, however, the poet would
have expected Oates to undergo this ferocity as punishment for purjury. In *The Last
Will and Testament of Anthony, King of Poland* (*POAS*, Yale, *3*, 397), Shaftesbury
says:

> But first to Titus let my ears be thrown
> For he, 'tis thought, will shortly lose his own. (46–47)

the Doctor: Oates claimed to have been admitted to the degree of Doctor of
Divinity by the University of Salamanca during his brief stay there in 1677.
4. *savior o'th'nation:* At the height of his powers Oates "put on an episcopal garb
(except the lawn sleeves), silk gown and cassock, great hat, satin hatband and rose, long
scarf, and was called or most blasphemously called himself the 'savior of the nation'"
(North, *Examen,* p. 205).
11. *three parliaments:* The three Whig or Exclusion Parliaments, 1679–81.

Oh, mourn ye poor Whigs, with sad lamentation
To see the hard fate of the savior o'th'nation.

3.

Forever farewell, the true, Protestant, famous,
Old days of th'illustrious, great ignoramus!   20
Had the great headsman Bethel, that honest Ketch royal,
But sat at the helm still the rogues I'd defy all.
> The kind Tekelite crew,
> To the Alcoran true,
Spite of law, oaths, or gospel would save poor True-Blue.   25
But the Tories are up and no quarter nor favor
To trusty old Titus, the great nation-savior.

4.

There once was a time, boys, when to the world's wonder
I could kill with a breath more than Jove with his thunder,
But oh, my great *Narrative's* made but a fable,   30
My pilgrims and armies confounded like Babel.
> Oh, they've struck me quite dumb
> And to tickle my bum

20. *great ignoramus:* In July 1681 London grand juries selected by the Whig Sheriffs, Slingsby Bethel and Henry Cornish, threw out the indictments for treason against Stephen College and Shaftesbury as "not true bills." College was later tried and convicted in Oxford. For Shaftesbury's release see the *Medal* poems in *POAS*, Yale, *3*, 38.

21. *great headsman Bethel:* Alludes to a boast Bethel is said to have made that sooner than a headsman should have been lacking to execute Charles I he would have done it himself (Luttrell, *1*, 187).

23. *Tekelite crew:* The Whigs, who sympathized with the Hungarian revolt under Count Imre Tököli in allegiance with Moslem forces, against the tyranny of the Roman Catholic Emperor of Austria, were given this nickname as well as others associated with the rebellion.

25. *True-Blue:* i.e. Whig.

30. *my great Narrative: The True Narrative of the Horrid Plot,* 1679, was concocted by Oates and Israel Tonge, rector of St. Mary Staining and anti-Catholic pamphleteer. It reported the feigned "Popish Plot" to convert England, assassinate Charles II, and establish James, supported by English Catholics under special commission from the Pope and the General of the Jesuit Order.

31. *My pilgrims and armies:* William Bedloe, a witness in the trial of the Catholic lawyer Richard Langhorne, June 1679, deposed that Langhorne was an accomplice in a Jesuit design to land an army of cashiered Irish soldiers disguised as Spanish pilgrims at Milford Haven in Wales (Roger L'Estrange, *The History of the Plot,* 1679, p. 51).

Have my oracles turn'd all to a tale of Tom Thumb.
Oh, weep all to see this ungrateful behavior   35
In thus ridiculing the great nation-savior.

5.

From honor and favor and joys my full swing,
From twelve pound a week and the world in a string,
Ah, poor falling Titus, 'tis a cursed debasement
To be pelted with eggs through a lewd wooden casement.   40
   And oh, muckle Tony,
   To see thy old crony
With a face all benointed with wild locust honey,
'Twould make thy old tap weep with sad lamentation
For trusty old Titus, thy savior o'th'nation.   45

6.

See the rabble all round me in battle array,
Against my wood castle their batteries play;

38. *twelve pound a week:* In Oct. 1678 Oates was assigned a suite of apartments in Whitehall, a bodyguard, and a pension of £600 per annum (Lane, p. 107).

41. *muckle Tony:* Shaftesbury. In 1668 John Locke operated on Shaftesbury for an ulcerous abscess in the liver. To keep it open to drain, first a silver and later a gold pipe was inserted into the wound (see 44).

43. *wild locust honey:* Cf. *The Dunciad,* II.1–5:

> High on a gorgeous seat, that far out-shone
> Henley's gilt tub, or Fleckno's Irish throne,
> Or that where on her Curls the public pours,
> All-bounteous, fragrant grains and golden show'rs,
> Great Cibber sate . . .

46–49. Oates was treated unmercifully when he stood in Palace Yard. But the next day at the Royal Exchange his partisians rioted and overturned the pillory. *A New Song. Perjury Punished, or Villainy Lashed (180 Loyal Songs,* 1685, pp. 260–63) records the scene:

> At City Exchange next day he appears,
> Where whining fanatics saluted his ears;
> Their pillori'd prophet they boldly defend,
> Who can't save them, nor himself, in the end.
> His throne they pull'd down,
> To the city's renown,
> The relics on shoulders they bore up and down.
> But tir'd with procession, 'twas judg'd for the best
> In prison these zealots should take up their rest.

With turnip-grenadoes the storm is begun,
All weapons more mortal than Pickering's screw'd gun.
      Oh, my torture begins   50
      To punish my sins,
For peeping through key-holes to spy dukes and queens,
Which makes me to roar out with sad lamentation
For this tragical blow to the savior o'th'nation.

7.

A curse on the day, when the Papists to run down,   55
I left buggering at Omers to swear plots at London.
And oh, my dear friends, 'tis a damnable hard case
To think how they'll pepper my sanctifi'd carcass.
      Were my skin but as tough
      As my conscience of buff,   60
Let 'em pelt their hearts-blood I'd hold out well enough.
But oh, these sad buffets of mortification,
To maul the poor hide of the savior o'th'nation.

8.

Had the parliament sat till they'd once more but put
Three kingdoms into the Geneva old cut,   65
With what homage and duty to Titus in glory
Had the worshipping saints turn'd their bums up before me:
      But oh, the poor stallion,
      À la mode d' Italian.

---

49. *Pickering's screw'd gun:* Thomas Pickering and John Grove "were ordered to make an attempt upon the King's person . . . to be done with screwed pistols, shorter than some cabines; . . . they had silver bullets, which Grove would have champed [i.e. made jagged by biting] that the wound might prove incurable" (*The King's Evidence Justified; or Doctor Oates' Vindication of Himself,* &c., 1679, p. 9).

52. *peeping through key-holes:* For an example of the oft-prophesied parallel of this activity and the pillory, see *The Complete Swearing Master, POAS,* Yale, *3, 4.*

56. *buggering:* The charge of sodomy was brought against Oates on several occasions, although only once, during his brief career as a naval chaplain, was he actually punished for his vice (Lane, pp. 30–31).

    Omers: Oates obtained admission to the English seminary at St. Omers in Flanders in Dec. 1677 and spent the next six months there, until he was expelled, gathering ideas and "information" for the Plot.

60. *buff:* Thick, tough leather.

65. *cut:* Fashion, style, or make.

To be futter'd at last like an English rapscallion.   70
Oh mourn, all ye brethren of th'Association,
To see this sad fate to the savior o'th'nation.

9.

Could I once but get loose from these troublesome tackles,
A pocky stone doublet and plaguy steel shackles,
I'd leave the damn'd Tories and to do myself justice   75
I'd e'en go a mumping with my honest friend Eustace.
                Little Comins and Oates
                In two pilgrim coats,
We'd truss our black bills up and all our old plots;
We'd leave the base world all for their damn'd rude behav-   80
                iors
To two such heroic true Protestant saviors.

10.

But alack-and-a-day, the worst is behind still,
Which makes me fetch groans that would e'en turn a
                windmill:
Were the pillory all I should never be vext,
But oh, to my sorrow, the gallows comes next;   85

70. *futter'd:* "To coit with," derived from the French, *foutre;* according to Partridge a literary coinage of Sir Richard Burton.

71. *th'Association:* At Shaftesbury's arrest in July 1681, his papers were seized as evidence for the Crown. Among them a document, not in his hand, projected an Association for the defence under Parliament of the Protestant religion and for the exclusion by force, if necessary, of the Duke of York.

74. *stone doublet:* A prison.

76. *mumping:* Begging.

Eustace: Eustace Comins, one of the perjured Irish "evidences" against Dr. Oliver Plunket, the Catholic Archbishop of Dublin. Plunket was tried and executed in the summer of 1681, the last victim of the Plot.

79. *black bills:* A weapon like a halberd. One of the allegations made against Coleman by Oates was that 40,000 of these weapons were to be provided for the projected rebellion in Ireland.

85. *the gallows comes next:* Not part of Oates' sentence. Sir Francis Withins said, nevertheless, after passing sentence, "if it had been in my power to have carried it further, I should not have been unwilling to have given judgment of death upon you. For I am sure you deserve it" (Lane, p. 317). There can be little doubt that the judges intended Oates' punishment to be fatal.

According to MS. notes on the copy text, presumably in Luttrell's hand, this ballad sold for a penny and was purchased (and possibly published) on 20 May 1685, the day

To my doleful, sad fate
I find though too late
To this collar of wood comes a hempen cravat;
Which makes me thus roar out with sad lamentation
To think how they'll truss up the savior o'th'nation.   90

THE TRAGI-COMEDY OF TITUS OATES

Who Sometime Went under the Notion of the Salamanca Doctor;
Who being Convicted of Perjury and Several Other Crimes at
the King's Bench Bar, Westminster, May 16, 1685, Had His
Sentence to Stand in the Pillory, to be Whipped at the Cart's
Arse, and to be Sent Back to Prison

Whet all your wits and antidote your eyes
Before you hazard here to play this prize,
Or gaze like eagles on a show so rare,
No time brought forth an object yet so fair.
Lo, here's the bugbear rampant of the Plot,   5
Which Whig on Tory in a sham begot,

---

of the first whipping, from Aldgate to Newgate. There is a noticeable debt, one way
or the other, of many lines in this ballad and the opening of another called *Epi-
papresbyter,* &c. ("Come hark and hear and draw me nigh") also among the Harvard
broadsides.

Subtitle: Convicted of Perjury and Several Other Crimes: Officially, Oates was tried
and convicted on two counts of perjury: first, that he had falsely sworn to a "consult"
of Jesuits held at White Horse Tavern on 24 Apr. 1678, at which the King's death was
determined; second, that he had falsely sworn to the presence in London between 8–12
Aug. 1687 of William Ireland, whom Oates had claimed had orders to murder the
King. Other crimes only came into the verdict by implication.

3. *gaze like eagles:* Allusion to the old idea that the eagle could look directly at the
sun with open eyes.

5. *bugbear rampant:* Hobgoblin, imaginary terror. Here with a pun on heraldic
forms (cf. 36).

6. *sham:* If we follow Roger North's definition of this word (*Examen,* p. 231), "sham"
is incorrectly used in reference to Oates' plot. "The meaning," says North, "is not
simply a false plot, but the word implies somewhat of trepan joined with it. For
the grand plot of Oates was as false as any other can pretend to be and although it
had a sham-plot, like a jackal on a lion, to attend it, yet itself was no sham-plot,
because all the business was dispatched by pure and direct swearing, under which the
accused were passive, and concerned only in making the best defense they could.
But, when it happens that the accused are drawn in to entangle or to make evidence
against themselves or to accuse others falsely, though there be swearing enough into
the bargain, that is properly a sham-plot."

Here *à la mode* the guardian of the land
In a new-fashion'd pulpit now doth stand.
The tub's o'erwhelm'd and all the hoops are flung,
And depute-Jack he peeps out through the bung.   10
Bar-Cochab's here, the Star of England's sky,
Decipher'd now the Son of Perjury,
Th'Egyptian Cow, the Oaten-Blasted Blade,
Which hath these several years eat up our trade,
The State's Anatomist, the Church Confusion,   15
Who dream'd a Plot and swore it was a vision;
A doctor who degree did ne'er commence,
A rhetorician that spoke never sense:
Like Proteus he still changeth to the time,
His pulse and temper suits with any clime.   20
His birth's equivocal, by generation
Sedition's by-blow, loyalty's privation,
A Linsey Woolsey emp'ric of the state
That hugs the church and knocks it o'er the pate.
He stands in state and well becomes his station,   25
Using a truckling-stool for recreation.
Now should he, in contempt of Peter's chair,
Leap from the pillory to the three-legg'd mare

9. *tub:* Derisively, a pulpit, especially that of a Nonconformist preacher.

10. *depute-Jack:* "The imputed knave," or "the appointed serving-man."

11. *Bar-Cochab:* "Barcochebas" or "Bar Kochba"—"son of a star." In Christian sources the name for Simeon, leader of the Jewish revolt against Rome during Hadrian's reign. He is called "Bar (Ben) Coziba," "son of deceit," in Rabbinic writings after the failure of the rebellion.

13–14. A reference to Gen. 41 and Pharaoh's dreams of the seven lean kine and the seven "blasted" ears which devoured the fat ones. Puns on Oates' name were numerous. As a result of the plot trade suffered considerably; among the many references to the "lean" years, see *The Pepys Ballads, 3*, 86–89, 161–64.

21–22. Cf. Dryden's *Absalom and Achitophel*, 636–37:

> What though his birth were base, yet comets rise
> From earthy vapors, ere they shine in skies.

Here as elsewhere (see 45 below) the general tone of Dryden's famous portrait of Corah informs most of the subsequent attacks on Oates.

23. *Linsey Woolsey emp'ric:* A quack, figuratively a curious medley, neither one thing nor the other.

26. *truckling-stool:* Literally, a stool on truckles, or casters; here perhaps the pillory.

28. *three-legg'd mare:* See *A Trick for Tyburn*, 18.

And, with Empedocles, desire to be
But canoniz'd an oaten-deity,   30
He would spring up, but that he is a sot,
A mandrake to conceive another plot.

His crime no man can balance with a curse,
For still the Hydra doth deserve a worse.
Then let him live a Minotaur of men,   35
Like Hircocervus couchant in his den,
The monument of mischief and of sin,
To spread no farther than the sooterkin
Of old sedition, set before our eye
As buoy and beacon unto loyalty.   40
Yet at the wheels of fortune let him dance
A jig of penance that can make him Prance,
Resenting all his errors though in vain
With fruitless wishes calling time again.
His face is brass, his breech no rod will feel,   45
And who knows but his back is made of steel.
His soul is proof, perhaps his body may

29. *Empedocles:* According to tradition, the philosopher Empedocles, desiring to be a God, jumped to his death into the crater of Mt. Etna (Cf. *Ars Poetica,* 464–66, and *Paradise Lost,* III.471).

31–32. *sot . . . mandrake:* Two noisome growths, with a pun on "sot," meaning "drunkard." The mandrake plant, its flesh-like root growing in the shape of a man's lower limbs, was highly prized as an aphrodisiac and as an aid in facilitating pregnancy.

36. *Hircocervus:* A fabulous creature, half goat, half stag.

38. *sooterkin:* A chimerical kind of afterbirth. Cleveland, *Character of a Diurnal Maker,* 1647: "There goes a report of the Holland women, that together with their children, they are delivered of a sooterkin, not unlike a rat, which some imagine to be the offspring of the stoves."

42. *Prance:* A pun on Miles Prance, the Catholic goldsmith, one of Oates' witnesses. Jailed in 1678 for the murder of Godfrey, he secured his release by inventing a story which charged three innocent men—Robert Green, Henry Berry, and Lawrence Hill—with the deed. They were executed in Feb. 1679. In May 1686, Prance pleaded guilty to perjury in the matter and received sentence similar to that of Oates. (Also mentioned below: *Song,* "What think you of this age now," 44 and n.)

45. *His face is brass:* A humorous development from Dryden's lines, *Absalom and Achitophel,* 632–33, themselves derived from Num. 21:6–9:

> Yet, Corah, thou shalt from oblivion pass;
> Erect thy self thou monumental brass. . . .

Be made of metal harder than the clay.
Then put him to the touch, make Titus roar;
The chase is turn'd now he's son of a whore.   50
Then conjure him with eggs and kennel dirt
And contradictions that his mouth did squirt.
To tell his name we'll Christian him once yet
And mold an agnoun which can with him sit.
He is no doctor, for by horrid lies   55
He cures sedition only tinker-wise.
He is no Papist, for he ne'er had merit;
Nor yet a Quaker, for he hath no spirit;
He is no Protestant, for want of grace
To keep him from a falsifying face.   60
He is no Turk for always, like a swine,
He lov'd to wallow in a tub of wine.
    No name can fit him, therefore, let him be
    The grumbling ghost of old Presbytery.

48. *metal:* A common quibble on "metal" and "mettle." Cf. *Absalom and Achitophel,* 310.

53. *Christian:* i.e. "christen," interchangeable in the 17th century.

54. *agnoun:* Variant spelling of "agname," a sobriquet.

56. *tinker:* An adjective long-popular to describe the kind of "clumsy and inefficient" mending, or botching, of state matters that the Whigs were so caught up in during the last years of Charles' reign (see use below, in connection with Monmouth, particularly in *The Western Rebel*).

JOHN DRYDEN

Prologue and Epilogue
to the Opera Albion and Albanius
(June 1685)

Dryden's opera opened on Saturday evening, 6 June 1685, at the old Queen's Theater in Drury Lane. In his preface to the opera Dryden called it an expansion of what "was originally intended only for a prologue to a play of the nature of *The Tempest* [i.e. *King Arthur*].
. . . But some intervening accidents having hitherto deferred the performance of the main design," he had "proposed to the actors to turn the intended prologue into an entertainment by itself." Parts of the opera had been rehearsed before Charles II, after whose death Dryden put the opera aside for four months. When he took it up again, he found that "the design of it originally was so happy that it needed no alteration, properly so called; for the addition of twenty or thirty lines in the apotheosis of Albion . . . made it entirely of a piece" (author's postscript).

An elaborate allegory on the events of the previous reign, the opera had been set to music by the French composer Lewis Grabu and received a lavish production, the cost of which was never fully recovered (Downes, p. 40). During the sixth performance, word reached London of Monmouth's landing. The audience left in haste to seek further word of events in the west, and the opera was never again performed. What was to have been a suitably light, propitious piece celebrating the new reign, now seemed to many, no doubt, an ill-omen. Not the least because the opera and its music were generally considered uninspired (see contemporary jibes at both cited in Macdonald, pp. 127–28, and the corroborating opinions of historians of music).

PROLOGUE

to the Opera *Albion and Albanius* (1685)

Full twenty years and more our lab'ring stage
Has lost on this incorrigible age;
Our poets, the John Ketches of the nation,
Have seem'd to lash ye, e'en to excoriation;
But still no sign remains, which plainly notes   5
You bore like heroes, or you brib'd like Oates—
What can we do, when mimicking a fop,
Like beating nut-trees, makes a larger crop?
'Faith, we'll e'en spare our pains! and, to content you,
Will fairly leave you what your Maker meant you.   10
Satire was once your physic, wit you food;
One nourish'd not, and t'other drew no blood:
We now prescribe, like doctors in despair,
The diet your weak appetites can bear.
Since hearty beef and mutton will not do,   15
Here's julep-dance, ptisan of song and show:
Give you strong sense, the liquor is too heady;
You're come to farce—that's asses' milk—already.
Some hopeful youths there are, of callow wit,
Who one day may be men, if Heaven think fit;   20
Sound may serve such, ere they to sense are grown,
Like leading-strings, till they can walk alone.
But yet, to keep our friends in count'nance, know,
The wise Italians first invented show;

3. *John Ketches:* Hangmen.

6. *you brib'd like Oates:* There is no evidence for the suspicion that Oates, or friends acting in his behalf, bribed the hangmen to use the lash lightly in carrying out sentence on the perjurer (Lane, pp. 320–21).

8. *beating nut-trees, makes a larger crop:* See Tilley's *Proverbs*, W644.

11–18. Cf. Dryden's prologue to Nahum Tate's *Loyal General*, 1680:

> Weak stomachs with a long disease oppress'd
> Cannot the cordials of strong wit digest;
> Therefore thin nourishment of farce ye choose. . . . (22–25)

16. *ptisan:* "A palatable decoction of nourishing and slightly medicinal quality."

24. In his preface Dryden says, "whosoever undertakes the writing of an opera . . . is obliged to imitate the design of the Italians, who have not only invented, but brought to perfection, this sort of dramatic musical entertainment."

Thence into France the noble pageant pass'd: 25
'Tis England's credit to be cozen'd last.
Freedom and zeal have chous'd you o'er and o'er—
Pray give us leave to bubble you once more;
You never were so cheaply fool'd before.
We bring you change, to humor your disease;   30
Change for the worse has ever us'd to please:
Then, 'tis the mode of France; without whose rules,
None must presume to set up here for fools.
In France, the oldest man is always young,
Sees operas daily, learns the tunes so long,   35
Till foot, hand, head, keep time with ev'ry song:
Each sings his part, echoing from pit and box,
With his hoarse voice, half harmony, half pox.
Le plus grand roi du monde is always ringing,
They show themselves good subjects by their singing.   40
On that condition, set up every throat;
You Whigs may sing, for you have chang'd your note.
Cits and citesses, raise a joyful strain,
'Tis a good omen to begin a reign;
Voices may help your charter to restoring,   45
And get by singing what you lost by roaring.

EPILOGUE

After our Aesop's fable shown today,
I come to give the moral of the play.
Feign'd Zeal, you saw, set out the speedier pace;
But the last heat, Plain Dealing won the race:
Plain Dealing for a jewel has been known,   5
But ne'er till now the jewel of a crown.
When Heaven made man, to show the work divine,
Truth was his image, stamped upon the coin;

27. *chous'd:* "Swindled" or "cheated."
28. *bubble:* "To delude with 'bubbles' . . . to befool, cheat, humbug."
45. *help your charter to restoring:* In Oct. 1683, Charles finally succeeded in subduing the city of London, forcing a new charter on them which remodelled the corporation (See *POAS*, Yale, *3, Prologue to the King and Queen, at the opening of their theater,* 24 and n. and Ogg, *Charles II, 2,* 634–39).

And when a king is to a god refin'd,
On all he says and does he stamps his mind: 10
This proves a soul without alloy, and pure;
Kings, like their gold, should every touch endure.
To dare in fields is valor, but how few
Dare be so throughly valiant—to be true!
The name of great, let other kings affect: 15
He's great indeed, the prince that is direct.
His subjects know him now, and trust him more
Than all their kings, and all their laws before.
What safety could their public acts afford?
Those he can break, but cannot break his word.   20
So great a trust to him alone was due;
Well have they trusted whom so well they knew.
The saint who walk'd on waves, securely trod,
While he believ'd the beck'ning of his God;
But when his faith no longer bore him out,   25
Began to sink, as he began to doubt.
Let us our native character maintain;
'Tis of our growth, to be sincerely plain.
T'excel in truth we loyally may strive,
Set privilege against prerogative: 30
He plights his faith, and we believe him just;
His honor is to promise, ours to trust.
Thus Britain's basis on a word is laid,
As by a word the world itself was made.

12. *touch:* "The action or process of testing the quality of gold or silver by rubbing it upon a touch stone."

23–26. Matt. 14:29–31.

32–33. Cf. headnote, above, *The Accession of James the Second.* "From this Epilogue we learn, what is confirmed by many proofs elsewhere, that the attribute for which James desired to be distinguished and praised, was that of openness of purpose, and stern, undeviating inflexibility of conduct" (Scott-Saintsbury, *Dryden*).

Monmouth's Rebellion
(June–July 1685)

The political exiles who had sought asylum in Holland during the early 1680s were a widely diverse group, ranging from cowards and malcontents to brave and principled men driven from England by Charles II's legal vengeance. They shared the exile's tendency, however, to see the situation at home in terms of their own frustrations rather than as it really was. For a time James Scott, Duke of Monmouth, remained indifferent to their schemes, content to live quietly with his mistress, Henrietta Wentworth, at Gouda. But the death of the King added point to their importunities. While Charles lived, Monmouth could convince himself that his father might have a change of heart and find a legal means of bringing him to the throne. He had been reminded on more than one occasion of "how easy 'tis for parents to forgive," most recently in November 1684, when he had returned in secret for what was to be his final interview with the King. In less than three months Charles was dead, and the unchallegend accession of James dashed whatever hopes the "son of David" had peacefully to succeed his father.

In the spring of 1685 Monmouth joined in a plan urged chiefly by Robert Ferguson, "The Plotter," and Forde, Lord Grey of Wark. There were to be two landings. In the first Archibald Campbell, Earl of Argyle, would lead an attack on the west coast of Scotland. There this prominent Presbyterian, who had fled in 1681 to escape a sentence of death and forfeiture on trumped up charges of treason, perjury, and assumption of the legislative power, could expect strong support from the members of his powerful clan. The second attack was to be led by Monmouth. It would begin in the southwest of England, where his own popularity was assured. Faulty intelligence magnified the unrest in England, claiming that the lower classes, who had suffered long under the penalties imposed on dissent, would come in, as would the Whig nobility in the south and northwest counties. London itself was thought sympathetic and might lend support. On every count the plotters had grossly miscalculated.

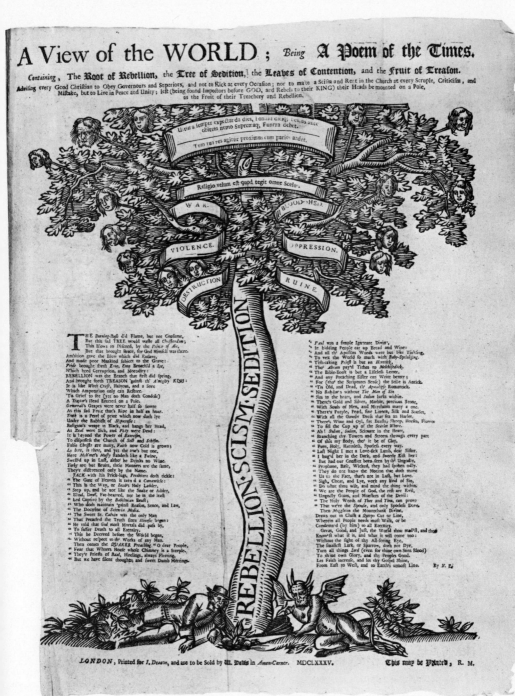

The Tree of Sedition

Argyle put to sea on 2 May, touched at the Orkneys on the 6th, and sailed on, reaching Dunstaffnage Castle on the 11th. From the outset his small force was torn by strife. He himself did not have complete command, having been placed under a committee before leaving Holland. The expedition was, as Trevelyan writes, "little more than the hunt, capture and execution of a chief who knew how to die" (p. 429). Argyle was captured on 18 June and beheaded twelve days later in Edinburgh.

Monmouth was to sail within a week of Argyle, but there were delays. He procrastinated, ostensibly hoping for a redisposition of James' troops to meet the threat in Scotland. Channel winds were unfavorable. Finally, on 30 May, the three vessels which comprised Monmouth's fleet put out from the Texel and began the long journey to the Dorset coast. The crossing was "prosperous" and when on 11 June the ships reached Lyme, Monmouth "with his small company came ashore with some order, but with too much daylight, which discovered how few they were" (Burnet, *1, 641*). As soon as it was evident who the invaders were, most of the townsmen came forward enthusiastically. In the initial tumult, however, the mayor and two others rode out toward Honiton to give the alarm. Within a few hours of their landing, the rebels' blue flag had been raised at the market cross, the declaration read which proclaimed the causes and aims of the mission while averring Monmouth's right to the throne, and the first recruits enlisted and armed. The beginning was auspicious: by the evening of the 12th more than a thousand men were under arms. On the morning of Monday, 15 June, Monmouth rode out of Lyme leading a ragged but resolute army of 3,000. Yet already Monmouth had cause to despair. He had lost Thomas Dare and Andrew Fletcher of Salton, one of his most able officers, in an absurd altercation over a horse. His second-in-command, Lord Grey of Wark, once a prominent exclusionist whose suspected complicity in the Rye House Plot had brought on his arrest and flight in 1683, had skirmished with the militia at Bridport only to turn and bolt with his raw cavalry. Perhaps most distressing was that among the recruits who had come into Lyme there was not one man of substance. The gentry held back, waiting.

By the afternoon of the 15th, Monmouth's forces were drawn up outside Axminster ready to encounter Christopher Monk, the Duke of Albemarle, who led the Devonshire militia. Though his forces outnumbered the rebels, Albemarle could not rely on their loyalty, such was the popularity of Monmouth. Albemarle ordered retreat. At this point, had Monmouth acted with decision, the entire western campaign might have turned in his favor. He had not yet to fear the regular army. The trainbands which threatened him were unreliable, were ready, indeed, to side with him. A clear victory would have won their support, and even the gentry might have been stirred to action. To the west the wealth of Exeter lay exposed. But Monmouth had always been irresolute, perhaps diffident, and he was content to ignore that hoard for the dross of armaments scattered by the fleeing Devonshiremen and for the more certain welcome of the "factious town of Taunton."

From this point, though there were other missed chances—notably outside Bristol—Monmouth's campaign degenerated into a harassed march through Somerset, leading irrevocably to the debacle at Sedgemoor before Feversham's regular army. There was never a chance that the desperate night attack across the moors could achieve a victory of any proportion. When, at about two o'clock on the moonlit morning of 6 July, Monmouth's troops were unable to locate the bridges across the Bussex Rhine and were prevented from falling on the enemy, their leader's despair must have been complete. Grey and his cart-horse cavalry had once again broken and fled. In the darkness Monmouth also withdrew from the battle and safely on a nearby hill watched his gallant followers stand firm for almost an hour before the regulars crushed them.

The carnage following defeat need not be described at any length. The slaughter of the Duke's followers immediately after the battle could not compare with the rapaciousness of "Kirke's Lambs" or that of Jeffreys' own western "campaign," as James called it (Dalrymple, *1*, ii, 206). The haughty judge rode through the west with "four troops of the county horse attending him," which he commanded "as generalissimo" (*HMC, Portland, 3*, 388). As a result, the country was left a shambles; for months the air was heavy with the odor of death and decay (*Hatton Correspondence, 2*, 60). Horrible as the retribution was, however, it seems to have called forth little comment from the nation. Not only were people accustomed to brutal reprisal, but they were unsure of its extent and feared for themselves. Moreover, Monmouth and his fellows had committed high treason; punishment could not but be severe.

Grey and Monmouth were captured near Ringwood in the New Forest. The former made himself infamous in the eyes of his contemporaries by compounding for his life (see *Song,* "The widows and maids," 49–54), forfeiting to the crown his large estates. Monmouth, after desperate pleas and groveling submission to James, resolved to die courageously and was executed on 15 July at Tower Hill.

The ballads of the summer and autumn firmly support James. There are a few mild expections, like *Lymonides, or the Western Expedition,* contained in several MSS. including Harvard Eng. 585 and B.M. Harleian 7319, but the great mass of song proclaims the victory. Nor is there, as has been said, horror at reprisal. It is not until 1688, in the moment of Whig triumph when the government was crumbling, that *Dangerfield's Ghost to Jeffreys* (*POAS,* 2, 1689), invokes the "ghastly train behind":

> Far, far from the utmost west they crowd away
> And, hov'ring o'er, fright back the sickly day.

One cannot but feel, as well, that the attack turns less on cause than opportunity. In general, Monmouth and his followers are ridiculed. *The County's Advice* presents, however, a comparatively moderate review of the rebellion and is strikingly devoid of party raillery. The solemn tone of the poem is enhanced by the use of the *ottava rima* stanza and by the introduction of imagery of civil war, calculated still to have a profound effect on his readers, though the seriousness of the poem is somewhat diminished by the author's near bathetic description of Charles' extravagant fondness for his handsome prodigal. Except for this poem, little else even suggests sympathy. True, George Stepney expresses light sarcasm against the Cambridge dons who burned the portrait of their former Chancellor; and Matthew Prior expresses compassion for a human tragedy. But the sarcasm and compassion are justified by the subjects. Nowhere do we find a hint of sorrow at the failure of rebellion or at the success of the government.

THE WESTERN REBEL

Or the True Protestant Standard Set Up

To the tune of "Packington's Pound"

1.

See, the visor's pull'd off and the zealots are arming,
For our old Egypt-plagues the Whig locusts all swarming.
The true Protestant Perkin in lightning has spoke
And begins in a flash to vanish in smoke.
    Little Jemmy's launch'd o'er   5
    From the old Holland shore,
Where Shaftesbury march'd to the devil before.
The old game's a-beginning, for high shoes and clowns
Are turning state tinkers for mending of crowns.

2.

Let his desperate frenzy to ruin spur on   10
The rebel too late and the madman too soon;
But politic noddles without wit or reason,
When empty of brains, have the more room for treason.
    Ambition bewitches
    Through bogs and through ditches   15
Like a will-with-a-wisp, for the bastard blood itches;
And the bully sets up with his high shoes and clowns,
A true Protestant tinker for mending of crowns.

3. *Perkin:* Monmouth. The allusion to the handsome, young, bastard claimant Perkin Warbeck (1474–99), first made by Nell Gwynne in 1679, proved prophetically apt during Monmouth's own abortive attempt to fight a western campaign and thereby win a crown.

5. *Little Jemmy:* Another of Monmouth's nicknames. James was known as "Old Jemmy."

7. *Where Shaftesbury march'd:* Shaftesbury fled to Holland in Nov. 1682 and died there two months later.

8. *high shoes and clowns:* Rustics, or plain men, who wore high shoes in the 17th century.

9. *state tinkers:* See *The Tragi-Comedy of Titus Oates,* 56 and n.

16. *will-with-a-wisp:* An early form of will-o'-the-wisp.

    the bastard blood: Monmouth was the natural son of Charles II by Lucy Walter.

17. *bully:* Chiefly in the sense of a "blustering gallant."

3.

Let him banter religion, that old stale pretense
For traitors to mount on the neck of their prince,   20
But clamor and nonsense no longer shall fright us,
Our wits are restor'd by the flogging of Titus.
    Their canting delusion
    And Bills of Exclusion
No longer shall sham the mad world to confusion.   25
The old cheat's too gross, and no more boors and clowns,
For perching on thrones and profaning of crowns.

4.

So the great murder'd Charles, our church, freedom, and laws
Were all martyrs of old to the sanctifi'd cause.
Whilst Gospel and Heaven were the popular name,   30
The firebrands of Hell were all light from that flame.
    Reformation once tun'd,
    Let religion but sound,
When that kirk bagpipe plays, all the devils dance round.
But the whining tub cheat shall no longer go down,   35
No more kings on scaffolds and slaves on a throne.

5.

Let his hot-brain'd ambition with his renegade loons
Mount the son of the people for lord of three crowns.
The impostor on one hand and traitor on t'other
    Set up his false title, as crack'd as his mother.   40
    But whilst peacock-proud

19. *that old stale pretense:* The "Good Old Cause" of Republicanism and Puritanism, constantly referred to by the Tories who implied that the basic motive of the Whigs was the same as that of the rebels in the Civil War.

25. *boors:* Peasants, rustics; particularly Dutch peasants.

27. *perching:* "To raise or exalt oneself, to push or set oneself up aspiringly."

34. *kirk bagpipe:* The tune is Presbyterianism, the Scottish religion. There was a widespread Tory belief that the Whigs were working for the restoration of the Commonwealth.

35. *tub:* A pulpit. (See *The Tragi-Comedy of Titus Oates,* 9 and n.)

37–8. *loons:* "Rogues or scamps;" rhymes with "crowns."

40. *false title:* Though Monmouth did not allow himself to be proclaimed "King" until 20 June in Taunton, his pretensions had been clear for more than five years.

    crack'd: Blemished, of ill-repute.

He struts and talks loud,
The head of the rabble and idol o'th' crowd,
From his false, borrow'd plumes and his hopes of a crown
To his black feet below, let th' aspirer look down.   45

6.

Then let him march on with his Politic Pol
To perch up his head by old Bradshaw and Nol;
Whilst the desperate Jehu is driving headlong
To visit the relics of Tommy Armstrong.
    But there's vengeance a-working   50
    To give him a jerking
And humble the pride of the poor little Perkin.
Great James his dread thunder shall th'idol pull down,
Whilst our hands, hearts, and swords are all true to the crown.

46. *Politic Pol:* Perhaps Argyle, but probably Grey. The meaning of *poll*, "to cut off or cut short horns," would have an ironic bearing on the report that Monmouth had had an illicit affair with Grey's wife. Cf. *POAS*, Yale, *3, The Last Will and Testament of Anthony, King of Poland,*

> To thee, young Grey, I'll some small toy present,
> For you with any thing can be content;
> Then take the knife with which I cut my corns,
> 'Twill serve to pare and sharp your lordship's horns,
> That you may rampant Monmouth push and gore
> 'Till he shall leave your house and change his whore. (37–42)

47. *Bradshaw and Nol:* The regicides John Bradshaw and Oliver Cromwell. Their bodies were exhumed in 1661 and hung on the gallows at Tyburn on Jan. 30, the anniversary of Charles I's execution. Subsequently, their heads were displayed on poles atop Westminster Hall.

48. *Jehu:* "A fast and furious driver" in humorous allusion to 2 Kings 9:20. Originally one of Shaftesbury's numerous epithets (cf. Dryden, *The Medal*, 119 ff.), the term here applies perhaps to Ferguson, "The Plotter," or John Wildman.

49. *Tommy Armstrong:* Sir Thomas Armstrong (1624?–84), implicated in the Rye House Plot; he fled to Holland in 1683, where he was apprehended a year later. He was executed without trial on the order of Jeffreys in June 1684 (see Evelyn, *4,* 323, 382).

Monmouth Degraded

Or, James Scott, the Little King in Lyme

A song to the tune of "Hark, Hark, the Thundering Canons Roar"

1.

Come beat alarm, sound a charge
As well without as in the verge,
Let every sword and soul be large
    To make our monarch shine, boys.
Let's leave off whores and drunken souls   5
And windy words o'er brimming bowls,
Let English hearts exceed the Poles'
    'Gainst Perkin, King in Lyme, boys.

2.

Such a fop-king was ne'er before
Is landed on our western shore,   10
Which our black saints do all adore,
    Inspir'd by Tub-Divine, boys.
Let us assume the souls of Mars
And march in order, foot and horse,
Pull down the standard at the cross   15
    Of Perkin, King in Lyme, boys.

2. *in the verge:* i.e. within the palace; the "verge" was the area of jurisdiction of the Marshalsea, embracing the royal palace.

7. *Poles':* Polish forces under John Sobieski (John III of Poland) helped stop the Turks by raising the Siege of Vienna in the late summer of 1683.

12. *Tub-Divine:* Derisively, one who preaches from the Nonconformist's pulpit, or "tub"; here specifically Robert Ferguson (d. 1714), "The Plotter," originally a Presbyterian minister. A strong supporter of Shaftesbury and one of the contrivers of the desperate Rye House Plot to assassinate the royal brothers, he was outlawed in 1683, but escaped to the Netherlands. The Judas in Dryden's *Absalom*, he helped goad Monmouth to rebellion, served as his expedition's chaplain, and wrote the infamous *Declaration of James, Duke of Monmouth, &c.*, issued 11 June 1685, which charged James II with numerous crimes, including the burning of London in 1666 and the poisoning of Charles II. Ferguson escaped after Sedgemoor and, at the Revolution in 1688, turned Jacobite because he felt he had received insufficient recognition from William of Orange.

3.

Pretended son unto a King,
Subject of delights in sin,
The most ungrateful wretch of men;
    Dishonor to the shrine, boys,   20
Of Charles, and James the undoubted right
Of England's crown and honors bright:
While he can find us work, let's fight
    'Gainst Perkin, King in Lyme, boys.

4.

The Sainted Sisters now look blue,   25
Their cant's all false if God be true;
Their teaching stallions dare not do
    No more but squeeze and whine, boys;
Exhorting all the clowns to fight
Against their God, King, Church, and Right,   30
Takes care, for all their wives at night,
    For Perkin, King in Lyme, boys.

5.

"Poor Perkin" now he is no more,
But James Scott as he was before;
No honor left but soul to soar   35
    Till quite expir'd with time, boys.
But first he'll call his parliament
By Ferguson and Grey's consent,

25. *The Sainted Sisters now look blue:* At Taunton 26 girls from Miss Musgrave's
school presented Monmouth with a Bible and a beautifully embroidered banner. The
multiple pun on "blue" involves the color of the rebel's standard, the mood of the
maidens, and the reminiscence of the Good Old Cause of True-Blue Protestantism. An
obscene ballad (Bodleian MS. Wood 417 #144) entitled *The Glory of the West,* "In
Lyme began a rebellion," elaborates on the scurrilous imputation suggested in 25–32.

34. *James Scott as he was before:* Parliament brought a Bill of Attainder against
Monmouth for high treason, stripping him of his titles and putting a price of £5000
on his head (*Journals of the Lords and Commons,* 13–16 June 1685; *CSPD,* 1685, p.
201).

37. *call his parliament:* Cf. *The Declaration of James, Duke of Monmouth, &c.,*
printed and distributed in London by William Disney. (See above, 12; also *Roxburghe
Ballads,* 5, 731–37, where the declaration is reproduced.)

Satirical Playing Cards Illustrating Monmouth's Rebellion

Trenchard and all the boors in's tent,
Fit for the King in Lyme, boys.   40

6.

'Gainst these mock kings, each draw his sword;
In blood we'll print them on record,
"Traitors against their sovereign lord;"
Let's always fight and join, boys.
Now they're block'd up by sea and land,   45
By treason they must fall or stand,
We only wait the King's command
To burn the rogues in Lyme, boys.

7.

But now we hear they're salli'd forth,
Front and flank 'em, south and north,   50
Nobles of brave England's worth,
Let your bright honors shine, boys.
Let guns and cannons roar and ring
The music of a warlike King,
And all the gods just conquest bring   55
Against the rogues in Lyme, boys.

THE COUNTRY'S ADVICE

to the Late Duke of Monmouth and those in Rebellion with Him.

1.

You who the gazing world did once admire,
And you who were extoll'd and prais'd by all,

39. *Trenchard:* John Trenchard (1640–95), prominent Whig politician from Taunton imprisoned for complicity in the Rye House Plot. It was expected that Trenchard would raise the West, but as early as 19 May warrants were out for his arrest, which forced him into hiding (*CSPD*, 1685, pp. 157, 166). On word of Monmouth's landing he fled to Weymouth, where he secured passage to the continent.

boors: Peasants; particularly Dutch peasants.

49. *they're salli'd forth:* Monmouth drew his troops out of Lyme on Monday morning, 15 June (*London Gazette*, 15–18 June 1685).

Title: The Late Duke: Monmouth was officially stripped of his titles on 16 June, see *Monmouth Degraded*, 34 and n.

You who each sighing virgin did desire
And you who once we might great Monmouth call;
Wherefore do you against our peace conspire   5
And in a bloody war our land enthrall?
    Thus Lucifer aspiring to be great
    Was thrown from Heav'n to his infernal seat.

2.

When to great Charles's arms you did return
(Not of your fore-committed crimes to tell),   10
How did that sacred Prince's bosom burn
In hopes you from your former ills had fell.
But oh! too much indulgence makes us mourn,
And sighs instead of joy our bosoms swell.
    Thus mercy freely given is abus'd,   15
    And pardon'd rebels for sham princes us'd.

3.

Weigh with yourself the fall of Absalom;
Let his example teach you to be wise.
He justly had a rebel's martyrdom
And climb'd a tree 'cause he'd a mind to rise.   20
Just Heav'n in thunder will with vengeance come
And on your head avenge your treacheries.

7–8. In *Absalom and Achitophel*, 273–74, Dryden has Shaftesbury apply the parallel to
Charles II.

13–16. These lines recall David's lament at the end of *Absalom and Achitophel:*

> But oh! that yet he would repent and live!
> How easy 'tis for parents to forgive!
> With how few tears a pardon might be won
> From nature, pleading for a darling son!
> Poor piti'd youth, by my paternal care,
> Rais'd up to all the height his frame could bear,
> Had God ordain'd his fate for empire born,
> He would have given his soul another turn;
> Gull'd with a patriot's name, whose modern sense
> Is one that would by law supplant his prince:
> The people's brave, the politician's tool;
> Never was patriot yet, but was a fool. (957–68)

20. Cf. 2 Sam. 18:9–14, the account of Absalom's being caught in an oak tree, where
Joab found and killed him. Here "tree" means "gallows" as well.
21–22. Cf. *Absalom and Achitophel*, 1026–27.

Think on the guiltless blood you hourly spill,
Where brother brother, father son does kill.

4.

In vain, alas! rebellious arms you use,   25
In vain you mighty preparations make,
And but in vain our Monarch you abuse,
And skulking round about poor women take.
In vain you your rebellion would excuse
By saying 'tis for pure religion's sake;   30
   What your religion is I cannot tell,
   But Protestants, I'm sure, can ne'er rebel.

5.

Though with your weak pretenses you delude
And bring in some who're traitors in despair,
A wretched, hopeless, gaping multitude   35
Whose desp'rate souls know neither sense nor care,
Yet all in vain your treasons are pursu'd;
Your stratagems but weak and feeble are,
   For the Almighty has his angels spread
   To guard our sacred, lawful Monarch's head.   40

6.

What show of right, what law can you pretend
To justify this bold, this bloody deed?
What is't you'd have? Wherefore do you contend,
That thus you make the shaking country bleed?
Is this our "liberties"; are you our friend?   45
Dear liberties and a fast friend, indeed!
   Our souls at liberty you set—our wives,
   Our goods, and children perish with our lives.

7.

When on ambition's wings you first were toss'd,
And the curs'd faction did your mind invite,   50
They spar'd no time, no labor, nor no cost
To puff you up with a supposed right;

32. *Protestants . . . can ne'er rebel:* A reference to the doctrine of Passive Obedience and Non-Resistance, an essential part of the Church of England policy towards the hereditary monarchy.

But 'cause you should not in your pride be lost
Your Royal Father clear'd your misted sight,
   Who, wise as just and powerful as great,   55
   Declar'd you to be illegitimate.

8.

And you deluded souls that are engag'd
In arms against your just and lawful Prince
Consult the grounds on which this war is wag'd,
Call back your reason and alarm your sense   60
That this sad, bloody conflict be assuag'd
In which you ne'er can hope for recompense;
   Ask God forgiveness, your wrong'd Sov'reign greet,
   And lay your arms at his imperial feet.

9.

Good God! that ever people thus should be   65
Into such base, unnat'ral wars betray'd
Under the old sham tale of liberty,
Which at that very time they do invade
When we before had all things just and free,
Nor any fear or cause to be afraid.   70
   Now treason, murder, rape, and massacre
   Must the bless'd title of religion bear.

10.

But if you will not now be wise in time
And choose repentance ere it be too late,
May you with speed be punish'd for your crime   75
And meet the scourge of your deserved fate;
And for your head, who would to empire climb
Upon the ashes of a ruin'd state,
   Since neither pardon nor a Prince's love
   Can the sweet bait of mighty crowns remove,   80
   Let him unpiti'd in a dungeon lie
   Till with despair and envy he shall die.

56. *Declar'd you to be illegitimate:* In face of Whig promotion of Monmouth's claim to the throne, Charles twice officially denied his favorite son. See *His Majesty's Declaration to all his Loving Subjects,* 1680, for the statements of 6 Jan. and 3 March 1679 that he was never contracted to or married to any one but Catherine.

GEORGE STEPNEY

ON THE UNIVERSITY OF CAMBRIDGE'S BURNING
THE DUKE OF MONMOUTH'S PICTURE, 1685,
WHO WAS FORMERLY THEIR CHANCELLOR

In answer to this question:

In turba semper sequitur fortunam et odit damnatos.

Yes, fickle Cambridge, Perkin's found this true,
Both from your rabble and your doctors too,
With what applause you once receiv'd His Grace
And begg'd a copy of his godlike face.
But when the sage Vice-Chancellor was sure   5

Title: Shortly after his appointment as Chancellor to the University on 14 July 1674, Monmouth sent the Vice Chancellor a portrait "drawn by Mr. Lely in full proportion, to be placed in the Regent House" (C. H. Cooper, *Annals of Cambridge*, 1845, *3, 563*). Monmouth was removed from the office by order of Charles II on 4 April 1684, and the portrait was taken down. On 3 July 1685 it was ordered "by a grace of the senate" to be burned by "the yeoman beadle." Eight days later Monmouth's name was struck from all catalogues of university officials. The 26th of July was proclaimed a day of thanksgiving for the suppression of the abortive western rising (Cooper, *3*, 611–13).

Epigraph: Juvenal, x. 73:   Sed quid

> turba Remi? sequitur fortunam ut semper et odit
> damnatos.

> How goes the mob . . .
> They follow Fortune, and the common cry
> Is still against the rogue condemn'd to die.
>   (Dryden's translation)

Author: George Stepney (1663–1707) was elected a scholar of Trinity College, Cambridge, in 1682, where he gained a considerable reputation for his Latin verse. He was graduated B.A. in 1685, M.A., 1689. In 1687 he was elected a major fellow of his college. Stepney praised James in an elegy on the death of Charles. In the present poem, as its epigraph indicates, he is more concerned with the foolish rout at Cambridge than with the new monarch. In time, he found himself turning to William. In 1688 he supported William and, with the assistance of his friend Charles Montagu, gained a diplomatic appointment from the new government. There seems to be no reason to doubt the ascription of this poem to Stepney. No text offers an alternative, and most do ascribe it to him.

5. *the sage Vice-Chancellor:* MSS. gloss, "Dr. [Samuel] Blyth, Master of Clare Hall"; see below, 19.

The original in limbo lay secure,
As greasy as himself he sends a lictor
To vent his loyal malice on the picture.
The beadle's wife endeavors all she can
To save the image of the tall young man,   10
Which she so oft when pregnant did embrace,
That with strong thoughts she might improve her race;
But all in vain since the wise House conspire
To damn the canvas traitor to the fire,
Lest it like bones of Scanderbeg incite   15
Scythemen next harvest to renew the fight.
Then in comes Mayor Eagle and does gravely allege
He'll subscribe if he can for a bundle of sedge.
But the man of Clare Hall that proffer refuses,
'Snigs, he'll be beholden to none but the muses,   20
And orders ten porters to bring the dull reams
On the death of good Charles and crowning of James,
And swears he will borrow of the Provost more stuff
On the marriage of Anne, if that ben't enough.
The heads, lest he get all the praise to himself—   25
Too greedy of honor, too lavish of pelf,
This motion deny and vote that Tite Tillet

6. *in limbo:* See above, note to title. The grace for burning the portrait passed three days before the battle of Sedgemoor and five days before Monmouth was captured.

10. *tall:* Lusty, valiant.

13. *House:* i.e. the University senate.

15. *Scanderbeg:* The Turkish name for George Castriota (1403–67), who championed Albanian independence and long resisted the Ottoman forces. His body was exhumed by the Turks, and pieces of it worn to induce "fortune, felicity, and privilege" (*The History of George Castriot*, 1596, p. 496). Cf. Dryden's *Medal* (*POAS*, Yale, 3, 38), "Epistle to the Whigs:" "I believe, when he [Shaftesbury] is dead, you will wear him in thumb-rings, as the Turks did Scanderbeg; as if there were virtue in his bones to preserve you against monarchy." Also note *Scanderbeg Redivivus, An Historical Account of the Life and Actions of John III, King of Poland*, 1684 (Wing G26).

17. *Mayor Eagle:* Nicholas Eagle, Mayor of Cambridge. According to the MSS. he "could neither read nor write."

19. *the man of Clare Hall:* Dr. Blyth; see note to 5.

20. *'Snigs:* A minced oath.

21. *dull reams:* Stepney is poking fun at the ballads, elegies, and panegyrics (his own included) written by every devotee of the muses on any important state occasion. James' daughter Anne (see 24) married George, Prince of Denmark, in July 1683; Stepney's Latin ode on the marriage was included in *Hymenæus Cantabrigiensis*, 1683.

27. *Tite Tillet:* Titus Tillet, the yeoman beadle.

Should gather from each noble doctor a billet.
The kindness was common and so they'd return it;
The gift was to all, all therefore would burn it. 30
Thus joining their stocks for a bonfire together,
As they club for a cheese in the parish of Cheddar,
Confusedly crowd on the sophs and the doctors,
The hangman, the townsmen, their wives, and the proctors,
While the troops from each part of the country in mail 35
Come to quaff his confusion in bumpers of stale.
But Rosaline, never unkind to a Duke,
Does by her absence their folly rebuke.
The tender creature could not see his fate
With whom she had danc'd a minuet so late. 40
The heads, who never could hope for such frames,
Out of envy condemn'd six score pounds to the flames;
Then his air was too proud, and his features amiss,
As if being a traitor had altered his phiz!
So the rabble of Rome, whose favor ne'er settles, 45
Melt down their Sejanus to pots and brass kettles.

32. *club for a cheese:* To combine or join together in the making of cheese. The industry dates from the seventeenth century. Cf. Marvell's *Clarendon's Housewarming*, *POAS, Yale, 1,* 92: As all Cheddar dairies club to th'incorporate cheese. (68)

37. *Rosaline:* According to notes in most MSS., she was "Walker's wife," but Walker's identity remains a mystery.

45–6. Cf. Juvenal, x.61–4:

> iam strident ignes, iam follibus atque caminis
> ardent adoratum populo caput et crepat ingens
> Seianus, deinde ex facie toto orbe secunda
> fiunt urceoli pelves sartago matellae.
> . . . the lung'd bellows hissing fire provoke;
> Sejanus, almost first of Roman names,
> The great Sejanus crackles in the flames.
> Form'd in the forge, the pliant brass is laid
> On anvils, and the head and limbs are made
> Pans, cans, and pisspots, a whole kitchen trade.
> (Dryden's translation)

See also Jonson's *Sejanus,* V.759 ff.

MATTHEW PRIOR

ADVICE TO THE PAINTER

On the Happy Defeat of the Rebels in the West
and the Execution of the Late Duke of Monmouth

*—Pictoribus atque Poetis
Quidlibet—*

Since by just flames the guilty piece is lost—
The noblest work thy fruitless art could boast—
Employ thy faithful pains a second time;
From the Duke's ashes raise the King of Lyme,
And make thy fame eternal as his crime.   5
    The land, if such it may be counted, draw,

Author: Like George Stepney, Matthew Prior (1664–1721) was at Cambridge (St. John's College) in 1685 and was a close personal friend of Charles Montagu, with whom he later collaborated in the writing of *The Hind and Panther Transversed.* Since Prior and Stepney were men of similar political sympathies, it seems probable that their poems on Monmouth are directly related in inception as well as in subject matter. Though Prior's poem represents that genre which instructs a painter in order to build up a detailed and ironic "visual" representation of a series of events (see Mary T. Osborne, *Advice-to-a-Painter Poems, 1635–1856: An Annotated Finding List,* 1949), the events in this case gain in ironic complexity, as Stepney and Prior would have recognized, by the actual destruction of one image (or painting) of Monmouth and the resultant need to create another.

Epigraph: Horace, *Ars Poetica,* 9–10:

> "pictoribus atque poetis
> quidlibet audendi semper fuit aequa potestas"
> "Painters and poets," you say,
> "always have had an equal right in venturing anything."

1. "The Duke of Monmouth's picture burnt at Cambridge" (MS. gloss in Rawl. Poet. 19. With slight variations this and the following glosses occur in most witnesses to the text.).

2. Sir Thomas Lely (d. 1680) painted the portrait Monmouth presented to the university. Here, of course, Prior intends a fictional painter.

4. *King of Lyme:* Monmouth, cf. *Monmouth Degraded,* 8 ff.

6. *The land:* "Holland" (Rawl.). It was thought, and is still possible that Monmouth sailed from Holland with the connivance of the Dutch authorities. The animosity the English bore the Dutch throughout the reign of Charles II is very much alive in this and in the following lines.

Den Hartog van Montmouts binnen Londen
met de byl opentlyk onthalft den 25. Iuly. 1685.

Le Duc de Mommouth est decapité a Londres
en public le 25. Iuillet 1685.

Adr. schoonebeck ex.

The Execution of the Duke of Monmouth

Where int'rest is religion, treason law;
Th'ungrateful land whose treach'rous sons are foes
To the kind monarchy by which they rose,
And by instinctive hatred dread the power 10
Join'd in our King and in their conqueror.
Amidst the counsels of that close divan,
Draw the misled, aspiring, wretched man,
His sword maintaining what his fraud began;
Draw treason, sacrilege, and Julian nigh, 15
The curst Achitophel's kind legacy.
And lest their horrid force too weak should prove,
Add tempting woman's more destructive love;
Give the ambitious fair————
All nature's gifts refin'd by subtlest art 20
Too able to betray his easy heart
And, with worse charms than Helen's, to destroy
That other hope of our mistaken Troy.
     The scene from dullness and Dutch plots bring o'er
And set the hopeful parricide ashore, 25
Fraught with the blessings of each boorish friend
And the kind helps their prayers and brandy lend,
With those few crowns————

11. *their conqueror:* Prior is probably thinking of James' naval successes against the
Dutch at Lowestoft and Sole Bay in the Second and Third Dutch Wars (see headnote
to *The Accession of James II*).
12. *divan:* "An oriental council of state;" here specifically alludes to the Turk
and the association of Whig sympathies with his aid of the Hungarian revolution (see
The Salamanca Doctor's Farewell, 23 and n.).
15. *Julian:* The Rev. Samuel Johnson (1649–1703), a Whig divine and controversialist,
published in 1682 an attack on the Duke of York entitled *Julian the Apostate* for which
he was imprisoned on a conviction of seditious libel.
16. *curst Achitophel:* Cf. Dryden's *Absalom and Achitophel*, 150–51:

> Of these the false Achitophel was first:
> A name to all succeeding ages curst.

Wright-Spears point out that Prior employs Dryden's names throughout this poem
and apparently imitates the style of *Absalom and Achitophel* (Prior, 2, 817).
18. *tempting woman's love:* "The Lady Henrietta Wentworth" (Rawl.) had been
Monmouth's mistress since 1680 and, perhaps guided by her own ambitions, assisted
him by pawning her jewels to raise enough capital to undertake the rebellion.
25. *parricide:* The charge assumes that Monmouth was an accomplice in the Rye
House Plot to assassinate Charles and James (1683).
26. *boorish:* Cf. *Monmouth Degraded*, 39.

Some English Jews and some French Christians send.
Next in the blackest colors paint the town   30
For old hereditary treasons known,
Whose infant sons in early mischief bred
Swear to the Cov'nant they can hardly read,
Brought up with too much charity to hate
Aught but their prayer book and their magistrate;   35
Here let his gaudy banner be display'd,
Whilst the kind fools invoke their neighbor's aid
T'adore the idol which themselves have made,
And peasants from neglected plows resort
To fill his army and adorn his court.   40
   Near these exalted on a drum unbrac'd
Let Heav'n's and James's enemy be plac'd,
The wretch that hates like his Argyle the crown,
The wretch that like our Oates defames the gown,
And through the speaking-trumpet of his nose   45
Blasphemously Heav'n's sacred word expose,
Bidding the long-ear'd rout, "With one accord
Stand up and fight the battles of the Lord."
   Then near the Pageant Prince, alas! too nigh,
Draw Grey with a romantic constancy,   50
"Resolv'd to conquer, or resolv'd to—fly."
And let there in his guilty face appear
The rebel's malice and the coward's fear,
That future ages in thy piece may see
Not his wife falser to his bed than to his party he.   55

---

29. *English Jews:* Cf. *Absalom and Achitophel*, 45 ff.

30. *the town:* "Taunton" (Rawl.). Taunton had long been the stronghold of Presbyterianism. During the Civil War it was twice besieged by Royalist forces under Goring, but the spirit of the townspeople and their leaders remained indomitable. Almost two centuries earlier the town had figured in the abortive invasion of the pretender Perkin Warbeck (for whom, see above, *The Western Rebel*, 2n.).

38. Cf. Exod. 32:1–6.

42. *enemy:* "Ferguson" (Rawl.). See *Monmouth Degraded*, 12n.

47. *long-ear'd:* Cf. *Hudibras*, I.1.9–10:

> When gospel-trumpeter, surrounded
> With long-ear'd rout, to battle sounded.

50. *romantic:* "Fantastic" or "extravagant."

51. *Resolv'd to conquer or resolv'd to—fly:* Cf. Waller's *Instructions to a Painter*, 18 "Resolv'd to conquer or resolv'd to die" (*POAS*, Yale, *1*, 22).

Now let the curst triumvirate prepare
For all the glorious ills of horrid war;
Let zealous lust the dreadful work begin,
Back'd with a sad variety of sin;
Let vice in all its num'rous shapes be shown—   60
Crimes which to milder Brennus were unknown,
And innocent Cromwell would have blush'd to own;
Their arms from pillag'd temples let 'em bring
And rob the Deity to wound the King.

Excited thus by their camp priest's long prayer,   65
Their country's curses, and their own despair,
Whilst Hell combines with its black offspring Night
To hide their treach'ry or secure their flight,
The watchful troops with cruel haste come on,
Then shout, look terrible, discharge, and run.   70

Fall'n from his short-liv'd power and flatter'd hopes,
His friends destroy'd by hunger, swords, or ropes,
To some near grove the Western Monarch flies
In vain. The grove her innocent shade denies.
The juster trees————   75
Which when for refuge Charles and virtue fled
By grateful instinct their glad branches spread
And round the sacred charge cast their enlarged head—
Soon as the outcast Absalom comes nigh
Drop off their trembling leaves and blasted die.   80

57. *horrid war:* Cf. Virgil's "horrida bella," *Aeneid* VI.86, VII.41.
59. Cf. Dryden, *The State of Innocence,* I.1.5–6:

> In liquid burnings, or on dry to dwell,
> Is all the sad variety of Hell.

61. *Brennus:* The leader of the Gauls, who defeated the Romans at the Allia in 390 B.C. He besieged Rome for six months then quitted the city after receiving a ransom of 1000 pounds of gold. It was said he threw his sword onto the scales in which the ransom was being weighed and cried, "Vae victis."

63. *pillag'd temples:* "The rebels unleaded the Cathedral of Bath to make bullets" (Rawl.). At Wells on 30 June Monmouth's forces took lead from the roof of the cathedral and desecrated the building, stealing some of its plate.

65. On the eve of the battle of Sedgemoor, Ferguson and other Puritan ministers held a lengthy service at Bridgewater. Ferguson selected as his text Josh. 22:22: "The Lord God of gods, the Lord God of gods, He knoweth, and Israel He shall know; if it be in rebellion or if in transgression against the Lord (save us not this day)."

74. *The grove:* New Forest, where Charles II had found refuge after the battle of Worcester (1651). The image also fits the account of the death of Absalom in 2 Sam. 18:9–14 (see above, *The Country's Advice,* 20 and n.).

Not earth itself would hide her guilty son
Though he for refuge to her bowels run.
Seditious Corah to her arms she took
When angry Heav'n his Good Old Cause forsook,
But now provok'd with a more just disdain   85
She shrinks her frightened head and gives our rebel back again.
　　Now, artist, let thy juster pencil draw
The sad effects of necessary law.
In painted words and speaking colors tell
How the great, piti'd, stubborn traitor fell.   90
On the sad scene the glorious rebel place,
His pride and sorrow struggling in his face;
Describe the labors of his tortur'd breast
(If by thy imag'ry thought can be express'd),
Show with what diff'rence two vast passions move   95
And how the hero with the Christian strove.
　　Then draw the sacred prelate by his side
To raise his sorrow and confound his pride
With the dear, dreadful thought of a God crucifi'd.
Paint if thou canst the powerful words which hung   100
Upon the holy man's persuasive tongue,
Words sweet as Moses writ or Asaph sung,
Words whose prevailing influ'nce might have won
All but the haughty, harden'd Absalon.
　　At distance round the weeping mother place   105

81. "Duke of Monmouth taken in a ditch" (Rawl.). For an account of his capture see
the *London Gazette*, 6–9 July 1685.

83. *Seditious Corah:* Though this was Dryden's name for Oates, the reference here
points directly to the biblical text (Num. 16:32).

88. Cf. *Absalom and Achitophel*, 1003: "Oh curst effects of necessary law!"

97. *the sacred prelate:* "The Bishop of Ely" (Rawl.). Francis Turner who, with Ken,
Bishop of Bath and Wells, Tenison, then Vicar of St. Martin's, and Dr. George Hopper,
Rector of Lambeth, ineffectually tried to persuade Monmouth to confess the sinfulness
of his affair with Lady Henrietta Wentworth and to acknowledge the doctrine of Non-
Resistance.

102. *Asaph:* One of David's chief musicians; also a compliment to Dryden. Cf. Asaph
in *Absalom and Achitophel* II, *POAS*, Yale, 3, 278.

105–08. While the "Grecian artist" may be Anacreon, the probable originator of the
poetic genre of "advice-to-a-painter," more likely Prior was thinking of Waller's lines
from *Of His Majesty's Receiving the News of the Duke of Buckingham's Death:*

　　　　The famous painter could allow no place
　　　　For private sorrow in a prince's face:
　　　　Yet, that his piece might not exceed belief,

The too unmindful father's beauteous race,
But like the Grecian artist spread a veil
O'er the sad beauties of fair Annabel;
No art, no muse those sorrows can express
Which would be render'd by description less.   110
Now close the dismal scene, conceal the rest—
That the sad orphans' eyes will teach us best—
Thy guilty art might raise our ill-plac'd grief too high
And make us, whilst we pity him, forget our loyalty.

He cast a veil upon supposed grief.
'Twas want of such a precedent as this
Made the old heathen frame their gods amiss. (17–22)

Thorn-Drury says of these lines, "The allusion is to the picture by Timanthes of the sacrifice of Iphigenia, wherein the painter having expressed various degrees of grief in the faces of Calchas, Odysseus, Ajax, and Menelaus, represented Agamemnon, the father of the victim, with his face buried in the folds of his drapery" (Waller's *Works,* 1893, 2, 157).

108. *Annabel:* "Duchess of Monmouth" (Rawl.). See *Absalom and Achitophel,* 34.

110. Macaulay, 2, 616–20, assembles the various accounts of Monmouth's execution in a graphic description. Despite Prior's admonition, I give Burnet's admittedly partial report of the event:

And he went to the place of execution on Tower Hill with an air of undisturbed courage that was grave and composed. He said little there, only that he was sorry for the blood that was shed; but he had ever meant well to the nation. When he saw the axe, he touched it, and said it was not sharp enough. He gave the hangman [Ketch] but half the reward he intended; and said, if he cut off his head cleverly, and not so butcherly as he did the Lord Russell's, his man would give him the rest. The executioner was in great disorder, trembling all over; so he gave him two or three strokes without being able to finish the matter, and then flung the axe out of his hand. But the sheriff forced him to take it up; and at three or four more strokes he severed his head from his body; and both were presently buried in the chapel of the Tower (*1,* 646).

1686

Quick, easy victory over Monmouth brought James to the height of his power—he had money, military strength, influence abroad, and no serious opposition at home. A politically cautious and intelligent man would have nourished these advantages with unhurried care, content to await an abundant harvest. But James was not inclined to be overly cautious, and his political shrewdness was open to question. He was gradually coming more directly under the influence of the radical and opportunistic elements led by the Jesuit Edward Petre, Jefferys, and Sunderland, men whose husbandry knew only reaping. In allowing the advice of these men to dominate his thinking, James turned from the counsel of the moderate Catholic party led by William Herbert, Marquis of Powis, and John, Lord Belasyse, and failed to act in accordance with the will of the majority even of his own faith. James' chief aims had been, from the beginning, to secure toleration for Roman Catholics under the law. The early successes of the reign and the constant prodding of the radical faction worked insidiously to reshape this policy, however, into a program which aimed at no less than the reconversion of England. To the moderates, this was a dangerous plan. Although they considered James the rightful king, they could see that the succession must soon revert to the Protestant line, if there were no male heir. At that time, they could expect to pay dearly for gains too forcibly won.

Their fears at James' growing ambitions were undoubtedly increased by James' opening speech at the reassembly of Parliament (9 November 1685). He was blunt and uncompromising on his need for a strong standing army and on his right to retain the Catholic officers he had appointed during the summer emergency. Parliament had grown more certain of itself since its adjournment in July, but it was ready to grant a sizeable supply and, perhaps, to concur with the King's desire for a strengthened army. It could not tolerate the employment of Roman Catholic officers in that army. Compliance on this point would subvert the laws of the realm which guaranteed the Established Church. Exasperated and fearing a possible court pronouncement on the legality of his position, James prorogued Parliament until 10 February 1686. In the interval a chastened opposition might reconsider its arguments. A flurry of civil and military dismissals followed, but as the time approached for Parliament to reconvene, James grew apprehensive. Throughout December the dismissals, particularly that from the Council of Henry Compton, Bishop of London, occupied town and court (*HMC, Rutland, 2,* 97–9; *Downshire, 1,* i, 77; and see below, *Song,* "The widows and maids," 31–42 n.). There were also fresh rumors about a toleration (Luttrell, *1,* 367; *HMC, Downshire, 1,* i, 79). In January the printing of letters from Charles' strongbox, which seemed to prove he died a Catholic, caused general consternation, though some had known of their existence since October. The old fears were growing. Gossip said *quo warranto* proceedings could be expected against the universities and some of the bishops (*HMC, Downshire, 1,* i, 100; Luttrell, *1,* 368). The factions at court were strong in their concern over James' renewed attentions to his mistress Catherine Sedley (*Downshire, 1,* i, 114). The result of all this was, for Parliament, a further prorogation until August. To most it seemed an act of arbitrary power. Yet one might also argue that it was the act of a strong king faced with an ungrateful and recalcitrant people. James was not alone in seeing the situation as analogous to his father's dilemma. The author of the panegyric on *England's Happiness* emphasized the analogy in his exhortation to loyalty, developing in sombre tones the theme of the martyred King. For many the poem undoubtedly represented a reasonable appraisal of affairs, and in attacking the "self-will'd man" and upholding divine providence, it followed the orthodox Anglican position on the relationship between Church and State. But against this position, like an insistent recitative, sounded fear of Popery. This theme overrode all others as the year progressed and turned the *Song,* "What think you of this age now," a commemorative poem on Monmouth's rebellion, into a searing attack on every manifestation of treachery and bad faith that could be claimed against James and the Roman Church. By mid-summer James' intentions seemed only too clear. Ruefully Englishmen acknowledged the aptness of the following description of the reign:

Unhappier age who e'er saw!
  When truth doth go for treason,
Every blockhead's will for law,
  And coxcomb's sense for reason.
Religion's made a bawd of state
  To serve the pimps and panders;
Our liberty a prison gate,
  And Irishmen commanders.
Oh, wretched is our fate—
  What dangers do we run!
We must be wicked to be great,
  And to be just, undone!
'Tis thus our sov'reign keeps his word
  And makes the nation great,
To Irishmen he trusts the sword,
  To Jesuits the state.[1]

A Poem on England's Happiness

In vain did Heav'n its miracles produce
When man would put them to no pious use;
In vain the Deity our good design'd
When self-will'd man was otherwise inclin'd.
Bliss from above but to no purpose flows   5
When men will stubbornly the bliss oppose.
In vain the Heav'ns do man with good caress
When man resisteth his own happiness.
Unconstant man that for uncertain noise
Would hazard all the good he now enjoys,   10
And but to satisfy unbridled will
Would change a present good for future ill;

1.This lampoon, *Over Lord Dover's Door*, was not published until 1688, when it appeared with four other poems in a broadside of *Lampoons*. It was probably written about the middle of July, when the Catholic Henry Jermyn, Lord Dover, was made a member of James' Privy Council, with Catholic Lords Powis, Arundell, and Belasyse (Luttrell, *1*, 383), a result of the decision in the trial of Hales *v.* Godden discussed below. Earlier, James had "trusted the sword" to Irish Catholic Richard Talbot by giving him the Duke of Ormonde's regiment (Luttrell, *1*, 337), in his "first breach of the Test Act" (Turner, p. 384).

Who when a godlike Monarch does command
In the hard rule of this unworthy land—
A godlike Monarch who, beyond what we   15
Have merited from such great dignity,
His virtue in abundant measure show'd
By winking at our black ingratitude,
Whilst with a bounty scarce heard of before
He offers to increase our blessings' store—   20
The brutish land so strangely does reject
The good we might from such a King expect.
In meager stubbornness they'd rather live
Than on the Canaan of his bounty thrive.
We, like the Jews when the Supreme Power   25
Did down from Heav'n his pleasant manna shower,
With envy murmur and shall murmur on
Till Heav'n its pestilential wrath send down
And by affliction teach us how to prize
The manna of our first felicities;   30
And if its goodness should at last restore
The bliss we might have well enjoy'd before,
Rememb'ring th'ill we did ourselves create,
Should prudently avoid our former fate:
So an old mariner by tempest split   35
Upon a rock again remembers it
And with a dear-bought skill will turn aside
From the vast danger he before had tri'd.
But senseless England to itself unkind
Will thwart the happiness the Heav'ns design'd,   40
Would dally with the fire and tempt the flame
That once had like to have consum'd its frame;
With matchless boldness would that sea repass
In which the beauteous island shipwreck'd was;
Would once more handle these injurious arms   45
By which she had receiv'd so many harms.
Self-vexing nation, when all things agree
To make thy sum up of felicity!
Thou, only thou, with a malicious hand   50
Against thy own advantages wilt stand!

26. *manna:* The image from Exod. 16, became a commonplace in the poetry, tracts, and sermons, illustrating God's providence.

Ill-natur'd people who, when they may taste
Of every fruit within that compass plac'd,
Contemn the proffer and with lustful eyes
To th'top of the forbidden tree will rise,
Or possess all or none of Paradise.   55
Remember, England, how thy giddy zeal
For the supporting of the Commonweal
Did willfully your own enthraldom seal.
And is't so long you wore the chains you would
Again go under such a servitude?   60
Oh, rather change your purpose and consent
To the completion of thy own content;
Sincerely weigh your int'rest, and you'll find
Each honest subject of another mind
Will alter thoughts and not with stubborn pride   65
But humble loyalty be beautifi'd.
Ah, happy island! if thou couldst it know
Or wouldst be satisfi'd in being so;
Oh, happy isle! in thy luxuriant land
And in great James, who does o'er that command—   70
Like the meridian sun he does dispense
O'er all the soil his fruitful influence—
Unclouded let him shine with glorious rays,
Dispel those fogs that would eclipse his face,
While strengthen'd with the vigor of his heat   75
We learn of him to be sincerely great
And better humors from his influence get.
So shall the land be truly bless'd: he reign
For our protection; we his rights maintain.

SONG

To the tune of "A Begging We Will Go"

1.

What think you of this age now
When Popery's in request,

76. *sincerely*: "Completely, thoroughly, wholly." Cf. Dryden's *Absalom and Achitophel*, 43, "But life can never be sincerely blest."

And he's the loyal'st subject
  Slights not the laws the least?
When a-Torying they do go, do go, do go,   5
  When a-Torying they all go.

2.

What think you of a Whiggish plot
  And of their evidence,
When all the laws cannot protect
  The people's innocence?   10
When a-swearing they do go, do go, do go,
  When a-swearing they do go.

3.

What think you of a General
  That did betray his Lord,
For which he does deserve to swing   15
  In Ketch's hempen cord?
Such a rogue you ne'er did know, did know, did know,
  Such a rogue you ne'er did know.

4.

What think you to be tri'd, sir,
  By proclamation laws,   20
And zealously destroy a Prince
  T'advance the Popish cause?
And to mass to make us go, us go, us go,
  And to mass to make us go.

5.

What think you of the Chancellor,   25
  Be sure he'll do the work,

13. *a General:* "Gray" (gloss in *POAS, 3,* 1704).
14. *a Lord:* "Monmouth" (textual gloss).
16. *Ketch:* Jack Ketch, the hangman.
20. *proclamation laws:* Monmouth was executed on 15 July 1685 without benefit of trial. His death was followed by numerous proclamations for the apprehension of suspected rebels. See Luttrell, *1,* 356–57.
21. *a Prince:* "Monmouth" (textual gloss).
25. *Chancellor:* Jeffreys was appointed Lord Chancellor on 28 Sept. 1685. See *The Humble Address,* 7 and n.

Establish a religion
  Although it were the Turk?
And for int'rest he'll do so, do so, do so,
  And for int'rest he'll do so.   30

6.

In Lime Street now we do say mass
  T'advance the Popish cause
And set the mayor to guard it
  Against his oath and laws.
To the court you must bow low, bow low, bow low,   35
  To the court you must bow low.

7.

And what think you of proving
  A Popish army awful
And bant'ring the Church with
  Arguments unlawful?   40
But a-fiddling let him go, him go, him go,
  But a-fiddling let him go.

8.

What would you give to be, sir,
  In contrite Prance's place
And sentenc'd to a pillory   45
  For one small mite of grace?
When recanting he did go, did go, did go,
  When recanting he did go.

31. *Lime Street:* In 1686 a Roman Catholic chapel was set up on this East London street by the resident of the Elector Palatine. Protests from members of the corporation met with a stern rebuke from James (Luttrell, *1*, 373). On Sunday, 18 April, shortly after the chapel was opened, riots broke out "so that the lord mayor and aldermen were there with the trained bands to quell the same; some of the chief ringleaders were taken and his majesty, having had an account of it, sent for the lord mayor and told him to take care of the peace of the city, or otherwise he should be forced to send some assistance to them" (ibid. *1*, 375).

41. *a-fiddling let him go:* Roger L'Estrange (see below, *A Heroic Scene*) was a capable bass-violinist. In early 1686 his *Observator* was full of discussions of toleration, church law, and the like.

44. *Prance:* Miles Prance, one of the perjured witnesses of the Popish Plot, was sentenced on 15 June 1686 (Luttrell, *1*, 380). See *The Tragic-Comedy of Titus Oates*, 42 and n.

9.

What think you of our penal laws
    That made the Pope to bow?   50
If damn'd rogues had not betray'd us
    They'd been as penal now.
But their opinions were not so, not so, not so,
    Their opinions were not so.

10.

Yet fear we not that bugg'ring dog   55
    That sits in the porph'ry chair,
That swears he is infallible
    'Cause he's St. Peter's heir.
'Tis a lie we all do know, do know, do know,
    'Tis a lie we all do know.   60

49. *penal laws:* Known to those afflicted by them as the "bloody" or "sanguinary" laws, the penal laws were severe, though not always scrupulously enforced. Dating from the reign of Elizabeth, the chief elements of the laws against the Catholics have been concisely summarized by Turner:

> The penal laws against the Catholics then in force, in addition to the prohibition of Catholic rites, can be summed up under four heads: to attribute jurisdiction to the Pope was praemunire in the first offense, high treason in the second; to harbor any Jesuit or priest was felony without benefit of clergy; to withdraw any subject to the Romish religion was high treason both to the withdrawer and the withdrawn, and a concealment of such withdrawal by a third party was misprison of treason; and to send a child abroad for education by the papists, or to send money for this purpose, disabled the sender from any suit at law and from holding property (p. 116).

51. *damn'd rogues:* The judges who, on 16 June 1686, handed down the verdict in the test case of Godden *v.* Hales (see below, *To the Respective Judges*). This poem thus dates from after this verdict and perhaps as late as 15 July 1686, the anniversary of Monmouth's execution.

Town and Court
(January–April 1686)

Soon after his accession James promised the Queen that he would give up his mistress Catherine Sedley, "spoke openly against lewdness and expressed a detestation of drunkenness" (Burnet, *1, 624*). For a time, indeed, "the face of the whole court [was] exceedingly changed into a more solemn and moral behavior, the new King affecting neither profaneness nor buffoonery" (Evelyn, *4, 415*). Despite his own overt sexuality (see *A Faithful Catalogue of Our Most Eminent Ninnies*), James undoubtedly sought and expected from his court something more than a show of morality after the dissoluteness of his brother's reign. But even a king's wish could not long prevail against his own or his court's inclinations. Before the spring of 1686 several scandals of major proportion provided the wits full scope for their scurrility. Dozens of lampoons were circulated, attacking the innocent as well as the guilty. Interest was strong, as always, in such matters, particularly as court intrigue usually meant political intrigue as well. Newsletters and ballads conveyed the gossip from London to the provinces. People like Katherine Manners, Countess of Rutland, read the news avidly, and undoubtedly some, like her, wrote out poetic squibs to be, in their turn, circulated among friends.[1]

Two examples have been selected from the numerous poems of this kind which have come down to us. The *Song,* "The widows and maids," rehearses most of the scandal of the first year of the reign with a particularity of detail and analysis that is surprising, especially in its treatment of the disgrace of the newly-created Countess of Dor-

---

1. See *HMC, Rutland*, ii. The countess received numerous letters from her friends and relations in London. These she used as raw material for her lampoons, which she returned to her informants for their amusement. Hers was an interest not without danger as she was reminded in a postscript to a letter from her sister Bridget Noel: "I hope you are as just in burning all my letters as I am in showing your verses" (p. 99). The countess did not heed the advice.

chester. *The Town Life* is a much more general—and traditional—
diatribe on the perversions of the city. Despite this, however, it
achieves a freshness of wit that is genuinely pleasing. It is difficult to
avoid the conclusion that Pope, who knew the *State Poems* well, had
read this one with more than usual interest.

THE TOWN LIFE

Once how I doted on this jilting town,
Thinking no heav'n was out of London known,
Till I her beauties artificial found,
Her pleasures but a short and giddy round.
Like one who has his Phyllis long enjoy'd,   5
Grown with the fulsome repetition cloy'd,
Love's mists then vanish from before his eyes
And all the lady's frailties he descries—
Quite surfeited with joy I now retreat
To the fresh air, a homely country seat,   10
Good hours, books, harmless sports, and wholesome meat.
And now at last I've chose my proper sphere,
Where men are plain and rustic, but sincere.
I never was for lies nor fawning made,
But call a wafer bread, and spade a spade.   15
I tell what merits got Lord ——— his place
And laugh at marri'd Mulgrave to his face.
I cannot veer with ev'ry change of state,
Nor flatter villains though at court they're great,
Nor will I prostitute my pen for hire,   20
Praise Cromwell, damn him, write the *Spanish Friar*—
A Papist now, if next the Turk should reign,
Then piously transverse the Alcoran.
Methinks I hear one of the nation cry,

16. *Lord———:* There is some authority for filling the blank with "Wem," in reference to George Jeffreys, created Baron Jeffreys of Wem in May 1685. Most MSS. do not
attempt to supply a candidate, however, and there is little reason to question their
reading the line as one of general satiric intent.

17. *Mulgrave:* See the following *Song*, 31–42 and n.

20–23. The references are to Dryden, of course. For details of his career see below,
Dryden's Conversion.

Queen Mary of Modena

Catherine Sedley, Countess of Dorchester

"Bee Chreest, this is a Whiggish calumny,   25
All virtues are compris'd in loyalty."
Might I dispute with him I'd change his note,
I'd silence him—that is, he'd cut my throat!
This powerful way of reasoning never miss'd,
None are so positive but then desist,   30
As I will ere it come to that extreme,
Our folly not our misery is my theme.
Well may we wonder what strange charm, what spell,
What mighty pleasures in this London dwell
That men renounce their ease, estates, and fame   35
And drudge it here to get a fopling's name;
That one of seeming sense, advanc'd in years,
Like a Sir Courtly Nice in town appears;
Others exchange their land for tawdry clothes
And will in spite of nature pass for beaux.   40
Indulgent Heav'n, who ne'er made aught in vain,
Each man for something proper did ordain,
Yet most against their genius blindly run,
The wrong they choose and what they're made for shun.
Thus Arran thinks for state affairs he's fit,   45

25. *Bee Chreest:* The author probably intended this and the following line to be
read with something resembling an Irish inflection. The MS. spelling makes this
clearer than does the printed version.

38. *Sir Courtly Nice:* The pompous fool in John Crowne's comedy of the same name,
produced in 1685.

45-6. *Arran . . . Hewitt . . . Chomly:* James Douglas (1658–1712), styled Earl of
Arran (Scotland) until 1698, when he became fourth Duke of Hamilton in succession
to his mother. Sir George Hewitt (1652–89). George, second Earl of Cholmondeley
(d. 1733), poet and general. The three men were constantly satirized by their contemporaries. Etherege may have based his character of Sir Fopling Flutter on Hewitt
(A. Sherbo, "Sir Fopling Flutter and Beau Hewitt", *N & Q,* 9 July 1949). In *To Julian,*
"Dear friend I fain would try once more," appear these lines on Arran (Harleian 7317,
p. 115):

> Arran, by some ill planet curs'd,
> Still aims at what becomes him worst;
> Hath broke himself and many a shop
> To be esteem'd a first-rate fop:
> Affecting to appear sublime
> Talks, as he dances, out of time;
> And is at length become the sport
> Of both the French and English court. . . .

Hewitt for ogling, Chomly for a wit;
But 'tis in vain so wise these men to teach,
Besides the King's learn'd priests should only preach.
We'll see how sparks the tedious day employ
And trace them in their warm pursuit of joy.   50
If they get dress'd—with much ado—by noon,
In quest of beauty to the Mall they run,
Where like young boys with hat in hand they try
To catch some flutt'ring, gaudy butterfly.
Thus Grey pursues the lady with a face   55
Like forty more and with the same success,
Whose jilting conduct in her beauty's spite
Loses her fame and gets no pleasure by 't;
The secret joys of an intrigue she slights
And in an equipage of fools delights: 60
So some vain heroes for a vain command
Forfeit their conscience, liberty, and land.
But see High Mass is done, in crowds they go;
What, all these Irish and Moll Howard too!

The poem *Madam le Croy, POAS, 2,* 1703, 152–56, includes a brief "portrait" of Cholmondeley, provoking a suitable rebuke from the well-known fortune-teller (for whom see *HMC, Rutland, 2,* 104):

> With love and indignation warm,
> Chomly begins to huff and storm.
> "I dress and keep an equipage
> With any coxcomb of the age.
> Pray tell me then a reason why
> Each tinker has his trull but I?"
> "Your hand (you need not be so stout),
> My Lord, your line of love is out.
> Learn then, if you would have success,
> More wit and less affectedness."

55. *Grey pursues the lady with a face:* Probably refers to Forde, Lord Grey of Wark's infatuation with Lady Cartwright. Cf. *Madam le Croy:*

> Fine Lady Cartwright in her chair
> To know her doom does next repair;
> Pursu'd by Fenwick, Frank, and Grey,
> Who sigh all night and dodge all day—
> As beggars dream of golden heaps,
> Each longs, but none the treasure reaps.

64. *Moll Howard:* A notorious bawd and procuress, frequently mentioned by the wits of her time, including Rochester and Sackville (cf., e.g. *Dorset's Lamentation for*

" 'Tis very late, to Locket's let's away;   65
The Lady Frances comes, I will not stay."
Expecting dinner, to discourse they fall,
Without respect of morals censuring all:
The nymph they lov'd, the friend they hugg'd before—
He's a vain coxcomb, she's a common whore.   70
No obligation can their jests prevent,
Wit like unruly wind in bowels pent
Torments the bearer till he gives it vent,
Though this offends the ear as that the nose,
No matter, 'tis for ease and out it goes;   75
But what they talk, too nauseous to rehearse,
I leave for the late ballad-writer's verse.
      After a dear-bought meal, they haste away
To a dessert of ogling at the play.
What's here, which in the box's front I see,   80
Deform'd old age, diseases, infamy—
Warwick, North, Paget, Hinton, Martin, Willis,
And that epitome of lewdness, Ellis—
I'll not turn that way but observe the play;
Pox! 'tis a tragic farce of Banks today,   85
Besides some Irish wits the pit invade
With a worse din than cat-call serenade.
I must be gone, let's to Hyde Park repair;

Moll Howard's Absence). In 1685 she apparently became a Roman Catholic and may be
the woman Evelyn mistakenly names in speaking of Dryden's conversion (4, 497).
      65. Locket's: A famous restaurant at Charing Cross, named for its landlord Adam
Locket (d. 1688). Its reputation was proclaimed by most of the Restoration wits
(Wheatley, pp. 413–14).
      66. Lady Frances: The context here precludes positive identification. Possibly the
satirist intends Frances Hamilton, for whom see the following Song, 66 and n., or her
mother, Frances, wife of Tyrconnel.
      77. the late ballad-writer: Presumably Robert Julian; cf. A Familiar Epistle to Mr.
Julian, Secretary of the Muses, POAS, Yale, 1, 387–91; he was temporarily succeeded by
one Captain Warcup, towards the end of 1684 (ibid. p. xxxviii), when he was imprisoned (CSPD, 1685, p. 233).
      82–83. Warwick, North, Paget, Hinton, Martin, Willis . . . Ellis: Well-known
strumpets and women of the town during Charles' reign mentioned throughout the
court poems of the period.
      85. a tragic farce of Banks: John Banks (fl. 1696) wrote seven tragedies. Dryden com-
posed a prologue and epilogue for the best of these, The Unhappy Favorite, 1682.
"A dreary and illiterate writer" (DNB).

If not good company, we'll find good air.
Here with affected bow and side-glass look   90
The self-conceited fool is easily took.
There comes a spark with six in tassels dress'd,
Charming the ladies' hearts with dint of breast—
Like scullers on the Thames with frequent bow
They labor, tug, and in their coaches row   95
To meet some fair one, still they wheel about
Till she retires, and then they hurry out.
    But next we'll visit where the beaux in order come—
'Tis yet too early for the drawing-room—
Here Novel's and Olivia's abound,   100
But one plain Manly is not to be found.
Flatt'ring the present, the absent they abuse
And vent their spleen and lies, pretending news;
Why such a lady's pale and would not dance,
This to the country gone, and that to France,   105
Who's marri'd, shipp'd away, or miss'd at court;
Others' misfortunes thus afford them sport.
A new song is produc'd, the author guess'd,
The verses and the poet made a jest:
"Live laureat Exeter, in whom we see   110
The English can excel antiquity—
Dryden writes epic, Wolseley odes in vain,
Virgil and Horace still the chief maintain—
He with his matchless poems has alone

90. *side-glass look:* "To ogle through the side-glass of a coach."
93. *dint:* A blow or stroke.
100–1. *Novel's . . . Olivia's . . . Manly:* Characters in Wycherley's *Plain Dealer.*
106. *shipp'd away:* I adopt the MS. reading because of its topicality, see the following
Song, 6 and n.
110. *laureate Exeter:* Presumably John, fifth Earl of Exeter (d. 1700), see *HMC,
Rutland,* 2, *passim,* and cf. *Letter to Captain Warcup, POAS,* 2, 1703, 143–46:

> And that we may to all due justice render,
> Exeter's songs most move the maidens tender;
> Yet Lady Bridget does so cruel prove,
> Six songs a day can't her compassion move. (24–27)

112. *Wolseley:* Robert Wolseley (1649–97) wrote a preface to Rochester's *Valentinian,* 1685 edition, in which he defended the author against the attacks made on him by Mulgrave in his *Essay on Poetry.* Wolseley once fought a duel with a brother of Thomas Wharton over a "poetical quarrel" (*DNB*).

Bavius and Mævius in their way outdone."   115
   But now for cards and play they all propose,
While I who never in good breeding lose,
Who cannot civilly sit still and see
The ladies pick my purse and laugh at me,
Pretending earnest business drive to court,   120
Where those who can do nothing else resort.
The English must not seek preferment there,
For Mac's and O's all places destin'd are.
No more we'll send our youth to Paris now—
French principles and breeding once would do—   125
They for improvement must to Ireland sail,
The Irish wit and language now prevail.
But soft my pen, with care this subject touch,
Stop where you are, you soon may write too much!
Quite weary with the hurry of the day   130
I to my peaceful home direct my way;
While some in hack and habit of fatigue
May have, but oft pretend, a close intrigue,
Others more open to the tavern scour,
Calling for wine, and every man his whore,   135
As safe as those with quality perhaps,
For Newburgh says great ladies can give claps.
Some where they're kept, and many where they keep,
Must see an easy mistress ere they sleep.
Thus sparks may dress, dance, play, write, fight, get drunk,   140
But all the mighty pother ends in punk.

SONG

To the old tune of "Taking of Snuff is the Mode of
the Court"

1.

The widows and maids
May now hold up their heads

115. *Bavius and Mævius:* The spiteful poetasters who attacked the poetry of Virgil
and Horace.
137. *Newburgh:* See the following *Song,* 25-30.

There are men to be had for all uses,
   But who could presage
   That ever one age   5
Should be furnish'd with two Tom Lucys?

2.

[No wonder we see
Why old Goodman should be
So very much angry with her son,
   If his lady's estate   10
   Be encumber'd with debt,
Since she always was free of her person.]

3.

Since his grace could prefer
   The poulterer's heir
To the great match his uncle had made him,   15
   'Twere just if the King
   Took away his Blue String
And sew'd him on two to lead him.

---

6. *two Tom Lucys:* Early in March, 1686, George Fitzroy, Duke of Northumberland, natural son of Charles II by Castlemaine, married Catherine, daughter of Robert Wheatley of Bracknell, Berkshire, said to have been a poulterer near Fleet Bridge, and widow of Thomas Lucy of Charlecote (d. 1684). The marriage achieved singular notoriety (see *HMC, Rutland, 2,* 107–10; *Downshire, 1,* i, 135–69; also Evelyn, *4,* 505; Luttrell, *1,* 373–74). It greatly displeased James, who had attempted to arrange a match between Northumberland and a daughter of the second Duke of Newcastle. Shortly after the marriage Northumberland and his brother, the Duke of Grafton, spirited the unfortunate woman, "rich only in beauty," out of the country to put her in a nunnery on the continent. Though their reasons for such action remain obscure, it was said Northumberland had married her without knowing she was Catholic (*Downshire, 1,* i, 151). In April James ordered her sent for, and by mid-June she was at court.

8. *old Goodman:* Castlemaine. To add to the general mirth over the "Lucy Affair," it was reported in the beginning of April 1686 that Northumberland's "gracious mother," as a result of her liaison with the actor Cardonnell Goodman, had been delivered of "a son which the town has christened Goodman Cleveland" *HMC, Rutland, 2,* 107).

17. *Blue String:* The blue sash or ribbon of the Garter. Northumberland had been installed Knight of the Garter on 8 April 1684.

4.

That the lady was sent
To a convent at Ghent   20
Was the counsel of kidnapping Grafton,
    And we may now foretell
    That all will go well
Since the rough blockhead governs the soft one.

5.

Moll Hinton best knows   25
Why Newburgh kept close,
But it need never trouble her conscience;
    'Twas duty to clap
    That impertinent fop,
For it sav'd us abundance of nonsense.   30

6.

[King John, who once past
For a coward, as last

20. *Ghent:* Famous for its numerous religious houses, particularly for the great
Béguinage, established in 1234.

24. *blockhead:* Charles' numerous illegitimate children were constantly ridiculed for
their stupidity; e.g. *An Answer to the Poem to Captain Warcup* (Harleian 7319, pp.
398–405):

> 'Tis wonderfully strange to me
> The children should such blockheads be,
> And yet the sire so witty.

25–30. The details of the encounter of Newburgh—Charles Livingstone (c. 1662/6–94),
second Earl of Newburgh (Scotland)—with this well-worn bawd (see *The Town Life,*
82 n.) are not certain, but the affair is often alluded to in the satires of the time.
Cf. *The Town Life,* 137, and *Madam le Croy, POAS,* 2, 1703, 152–56:

> With shoulder belt and gaudy feather,
> Ten yards of cravat ti'd together,
> Comes Newburgh, by these lines express'd;
> As you'd a narrow 'scape i'th'west,
> This demi-circle here declares
> You'll meet worse wounds in Venus' wars.

31–42. Another scandal involving a widow. This woman was Ursula, daughter and
coheiress of George Stowel of Cotherstone, Somerset, and widow of Edward, first Earl
of Conway. Her hand was sought both by George Compton, fourth Earl of Northampton, and by "King John" Sheffield, third Earl of Mulgrave (see *HMC, Rutland,* 2,
98–107; *Downshire, 1,* i, 79–138; *Portland, 3,* 392–95). Though rumor had it that she

Gives evident signs of his courage,
    There's many a man
    Scorns pistol and gun   35
Would scarce venture on such a marriage.]

7.

For one that loves peace
And would live at his ease
Northampton the best way has chosen,
    Leaves courting the fair   40
    To his uncle's care
And the combatting part to his cousin.

8.

In Shrewsbury we find
A generous mind
So kindly to live with his mother,   45

---

preferred Northampton and that on the day she should have married Mulgrave she
took horse and "rode twenty miles off," she finally married Mulgrave on 18 March 1686.
In Northampton's behalf his uncle, Henry Compton, Bishop of London, had pursued
the match. It was jocularly given out that the Bishop's dismissal from the Council
was the result of his travelling to Conway's "on the Lord's day" (*HMC, Portland, 3,*
392, 29 Dec. 1685). A Mr. Hatton Compton, presumably cousin to Northampton, fought
a duel in Feb. 1686 in connection with the Conway romance (*HMC, Rutland, 2,* 105).

32. *coward:* In 1668 Mulgrave challenged Rochester to a duel, having been informed
that Rochester "had said something . . . very malicious" against him. When the
antagonists met, however, they decided to call off the duel. The notoriety of their
quarrel and its outcome damaged the reputations of both men (*The Works of John
Sheffield,* &c., 1723, "Memoirs," pp. 8–10).

43–48. Charles Talbot (1660–1718), twelfth Earl of Shrewsbury, was known for an
"unaccountable faint-heartedness" (Dartmouth's note to Burnet, 1823 edn., 5, 453),
popularly considered the result of the tragic deaths of his father and brother. Pepys
recounts the infamous duel fought on 16 March 1668 between the eleventh Earl
and the Duke of Buckingham over Anna Maria Brudenell, Countess of Shrewsbury
and mistress to Buckingham. An apocryphal story says she witnessed the fight, dressed
as a page and holding the Duke's horse, and spent that night with her lover, whose
shirt still bore the bloodstains of the encounter. Shrewsbury died of his wounds two
months after the duel. On 2 Feb. 1686 John Talbot, brother to Charles, was killed in a
duel with the Duke of Grafton. The match is satirized in *The Duel,* "Well did the
fates guide this unlucky arm" (Harleian 7319, pp. 414–15). Gossip said that Talbot
had "danced in a shroud at the Earl of Devonshire's late ball, and that he was foretold that he should be killed by a tall black man before he was twenty-one years old"
(*HMC, Portland, 3,* 394).

And never try yet
To revenge the sad fate
Of his father and only brother.

9.

Thus fighting we see
With some folks won't agree,   50
A witness a much safer post is,
And though my Lord Grey
In the field ran away
He could charge in a court of justice.

10.

'Tis pleasant to hear   55
An eminent peer
Make whoring a case of conscience,
When 'tis so well known
His favor begun
By pimping to Portsmouth not long since.   60

11.

'Tis a very plain case
That the Countess' disgrace
The Catholic cause advances,
'Tis also as plain

52. *Lord Grey:* After the defeat of Monmouth's forces, Grey compounded for his life, forfeiting large sums of money and agreeing to testify against others implicated in the Plot, though he was assured "that nobody should die upon his evidence" (Burnet, *1,* 646; see also Luttrell, *1,* 364–65, 379; Howell's *State Trials, 11,* 538–40).

56. *An eminent peer:* According to a textual gloss, Robert Spencer, second Earl of Sunderland (1640–1702); his success in the last years of Charles' reign had been attributed to his cultivation of Portsmouth and her personal maid, Mrs. Wall, and to his allowing himself to lose large sums to the former at basset.

62. *the Countess' disgrace:* On 19 Jan. 1686 Evelyn records the amazement and annoyance of the court when it learned that James had created his mistress Catherine Sedley Countess of Dorchester. He had presumably dismissed her on his accession. Sunderland and Richard Talbot, Earl of Tyrconnel, played on the anxieties of the Queen and her Catholic advisors, falsely implicating Laurence Hyde, Earl of Rochester and James' Lord Treasurer, as the instigator of a plot to influence James through his Protestant mistress. Sunderland obtained Dorchester's banishment to Ireland early in Feb. and discredited Rochester in James' eyes. (The text is glossed "Dorchester.")

That Tyrconnel's chief aim   65
Was to bring in his daughter Frances.

12.

That church will dispense
With no heretic wench,
And yet we have this for our comfort:
Though the priest at the court   70
Forbid us that sport,
The Chancery allows us a Mountfort.

13.

Thrice fortunate boy
Who canst give double joy
And at every turn be ready   75
With pleasures in store
Behind and before
To delight both my lord and my lady.

66. *his daughter Frances:* Frances Hamilton, daughter of Lady Tyrconnel by her first husband, George, brother of Anthony Hamilton. One of the famous "three viscountesses" of the Irish "court," she married Henry, eighth Viscount Dillon, in 1687 (G. E. Cokayne, *Baronetage*). See *The Town Life*, 66.

72. *The Chancery allows us a Mountfort:* Another obscure but oft-met allusion—to William Mountfort (1664?-92), the actor. A friend of Jeffreys, he lived with him for a time in 1686, apparently withdrawing from the stage. Reresby describes a dinner with Jeffreys on 18 Jan. 1686: "After dinner the Chancellor, having drunk smartly at dinner (which was his custom), called for one Mountfort, a gentleman of his that had been a comedian, an excellent mimic, and to divert the company, as he called it, made him give us a cause, that is, plead before him in a feigned action, where he acted all the principal lawyers of the age, in their tone of voice, and action or gesture of body, and thus ridiculed not only the lawyers but the law itself" (p. 408). Mountfort must have carried his impudence too far, however, if this poem and the ironic *Vindication, Part I,* "Since scandal flies thick," can be believed (see Harleian 7319, pp. 453-60):

> There's a story of late
> That the Chancellor's mate
> Has been f———d and been f———d by player Mountfort;
> Which though false, yet's as true,
> My Lord gave him his due,
> For he had a small tilt at his bum for it.

Dryden's Conversion
(January–April 1686)

No two literary figures received more abuse during James' reign from their fellow writers than did Sir Roger L'Estrange and John Dryden. By many of their contemporaries they were regarded as political opportunists who would "with all revolutions still comply" to insure their well-being. In the case of the politico-journalist L'Estrange the charges of changeability and self-interest were recognized by attacker and attacked alike as more or less occupational. But for Dryden, the foremost poet of the age, the attacks were much more damaging. Though the charges were groundless, turning back to the poet's youth for what seemed to be evidence of his willingness to embrace with equal fervor first Cromwell and then Charles, contemporary opinion was largely set against Dryden. When he became a convert, attacks renewed and multiplied (see Macdonald, pp. 3–4). His name was linked with L'Estrange's, both because L'Estrange's staunch support of Tory policy "under pretense to serve the Church of England . . . gave suspicion of gratifying another party" (Evelyn, *4*, 439), and because Dryden apparently had lowered himself once again to the hack estate. There was money to be got—or so it seemed to many observers. Evelyn writes of the man and his conversion, "such purchases were no great loss to the Church" (*4*, 497). Not all felt the loss to be so inconsiderable; the King and his religion had gained a valuable adherent.

Dryden's sincerity in becoming a convert to the Roman Catholic faith is no longer an issue. He had little to gain in material reward and much to lose as a Catholic even in James' England. Dryden described his own situation in *The Hind and the Panther*, III:

Panther: Methinks in those who firm with me remain,
It shows a nobler principle than gain.
   Your inf'rence would be strong, the Hind repli'd,
If yours were in effect the suff'ring side;

Your clergy sons their own in peace possess,
Nor are their prospects in reversion less.
My proselytes are struck with awful dread,
Your bloody comet-laws hang blazing o'er their head.
The respite they enjoy but only lent,
The best they have to hope, protracted punishment.

(374–83)

One of the three poems printed below receives tentative though contemporary ascription. Most MSS. of *To Mr. Bays* agree in assigning it to Charles Sackville, sixth Earl of Dorset (1638–1706). Dorset's biographer, Brice Harris, says, however, "though the line sounds uncomfortably like some of Dorset's, the attribution is open to question, for he was at this very time assisting Dryden financially" (*Charles Sackville,* Illinois Studies in Language and Literature, *26,* nos. 3–4 [1940], p. 123). The ascription to Dorset may have been intended, of course, to make the poem's satiric impact stronger, to enhance it. But Dorset had cut himself off from James' court and was by no means inclined to the Romanizing spirit of the first years of the reign. Perhaps the most that can be said for retaining the ascription is that the contemporary reader met the poem in this guise.

Of further interest is the evidence one MS. copy of the poem affords concerning the date of Dryden's conversion. Bodleian MS. Tanner 306 contains the poem in a letter from John Newton of the Inner Temple to Arthur Charlett, fellow of Trinity College, Oxford, "commonly called," according to Hearne, "the Gazetteer or Oxford Intelligencer" (*Remarks and Collections,* 1885, *1,* 214). The letter is dated 20 April 1686 and thus supports the assertions of Tom Brown (*The Reasons of Mr. Bays Changing his Religion,* 1688) and Evelyn that Dryden turned to the Roman church toward the end of 1685 or at the latest in the beginning of 1686.

The other poems included here repeat most of the charges which had accumulated against Dryden. The effectiveness of *An Heroic Scene* results from the gusto with which it pilfers from the bombast of the early rhymed tragedies and from the strength of its ending. Pope knew the poem and in his copy of the 1705 edition of the *State Poems* marked many of the lines as "Dryden's, or like 'em."

To Mr. Dryden

Upon his Declaring himself a Roman Catholic

Great truckling soul, whose stubborn honesty
Does with all revolutions still comply!
Thy youthful muse gilt an usurper's bays
And for king-killing smoothly sang his praise,
Nay, valiantly and wisely fawn'd on's hearse   5
And strove t'embalm his name in loyal verse;
And then reformers were not call'd prick-ear'd,
But plain religion primitive appear'd
Because like its first master all its charms
Were truth and peace, not juggling shows nor arms.   10
When Heav'n was pleas'd our Princes to restore,
Thou with the first didst servilely adore
Those earthly gods thou hadst blasphem'd before;
In high, weak verse them fulsomely didst load
With titles due only to th'Heavenly God—   15
By thee as much unknown as are his ways untrod.
The miter, which mere priestcraft and priest-pride
With Gordian Knots have to the crown fast ti'd,
As if one empire could not stand by law
But by another within to keep't in awe,   20
Receiv'd thy homage too, and then our creed
Seem'd only some weak Christian's feeble reed,

3–10. See *Heroic Stanzas* on the death of Oliver Cromwell. Cf. *The Address of John Dryden, Laureate, to his Highness the Prince of Orange, POAS,* 1698, pp. 295–300:

> Nor doubt thy convert, I who well could raise
> Immortal trophies even to Cromwell's praise,
> I who my muse's infant quill could fledge
> With high sung murder, treason, sacrilege. . . . (18–21)

This mock-address is attributed to Shadwell in the table of contents.

7. *prick-ear'd:* Puritan.

12. See *Astraea Redux,* 1660, and Dryden's *Panegyric* on the coronation, 1661. "The reproach of inconstancy was, on this occasion, shared with such numbers that it produced neither hatred nor disgrace; if he changed, he changed with the nation. It was, however, not totally forgotten when his reputation raised him enemies" (Samuel Johnson, *Lives of the English Poets,* ed. G. B. Hill, Oxford, 1905, *1,* 334).

And true religion, which must save mankind,
T'indifferent, necessary rites confin'd.
So like, thou thought'st, thine and the Church's scene   25
That Poet Squab would fain have been a dean,
But thy lewd life and public blasphemies
Made a loose clergy gross vice despise.
    Being thus deni'd the loaves, thou didst decry
The miracles as a mere forgery,   30
No sect nor clergy could secure their fame,
"All priests and all religions were the same;"
E'en holy church was lugg'd into thy farce,
And ghostly fri'r made pimp to bully's tarse;
A mere Almanzor grew'st in e'ery sin,   35

26. *Poet Squab:* Rochester gave Dryden this nickname in his satire *An Allusion to Horace, POAS,* Yale, *I,* 361–2:

> Dryden in vain tri'd this nice way of wit,
> For he to be a tearing blade thought fit,
> But when he would be sharp he still was blunt,
> To frisk his frolic fancy he'd cry "c———!"
> Would give the ladies a dry, bawdy bob,
> And thus he got the name of Poet Squab. (71–76)

In referring to Dryden's attempts to affect the manner of the Court Wits, Rochester neatly brings together in the name "Squab" Dryden's short, fat stature, his poetic "bluntness," and his ineffectual "titillation" of the ladies, which Rochester likens to a "dry bob," or incomplete coition.

    would fain have been a dean: Many contemporary references to Dryden's alleged desire to obtain an academic post connect him with various positions, including the Presidency of Magdalen. (See MacDonald, pp. 138, 231, 265; also cf. *Dryden's Ghost,* 89–90, below.)

    32. Cf. *Absalom and Achitophel,* 99: "For priests of all religions are the same." Prior adapted the line in his *Satire on the Poets,* 1687 (Prior, *1,* 28), and Brown cited it in *The Reasons of Mr. Bays Changing his Religion,* 1688, p. 12.

    34. Cf. *The Spanish Friar,* 1681, directed against the papists. In the play Elvira is aided by Dominic, the friar, in conducting an intrigue with Lorenzo, who turns out to be her brother.

    ghostly: An adjective applied to a father confessor.
    tarse: Penis.

    35–6. *Almanzor . . . Maximin:* See *Almanzor and Almahide, or the Conquest of Granada,* 1670, and *Tyrannic Love, or the Royal Martyr,* 1669. The plays were ridiculed in *The Rehearsal,* 1672, for their bombastic rant and absurd plots. Dr. Johnson cites the following remarks made by Martin Clifford, Master of the Charterhouse, and perhaps a collaborator with Buckingham in *The Rehearsal:* "I am . . . strangely mistaken if I have not seen this very Almanzor of yours in some disguise about this town and passing under another name. Prithee tell me true, was not this Huffcap once the Indian Emperor, and at another time did he not call himself Maximin? . . .

In atheism didst outvie thy Maximin;
Lampoon'st our God, thy patrons, e'en the great
And sacred David's self who gave thee meat.
No vice which thy lewd thought and poverty
Could reach but was us'd and disgrac'd by thee.   40
Thus by bad men despis'd, abhorr'd by good,
Thou bungled'st out a life like a loath'd toad,
Impatiently then waiting a new wind
Of doctrine fit for thy licentious mind,
Till a curst western blast of Popery came—   45
Pop'ry, of Christendom the plague and shame,
The yoke of princes, the true politic cheat
To cramp the honest and to make knaves great—
Thou suck'd'st th'infection in the very nick,
And pliant conscience veer'd to Catholic.   50
Thy zeal e'en nimble Harry Hills outran
And turncoat Nich. Butler the publican.
Should Mohammed this antichrist o'erthrow,

You are therefore a strange unconscionable thief; thou art not content to steal from others, but dost rob thy poor wretched self too" (*Lives, 1,* 350).

37. *Lampoon'st . . . thy patrons:* Another oft-met charge against Dryden, and one well-suited to the general censure of "inconstancy." It arose out of his quarrel with Rochester and culminated—or so most people thought—in Dryden's cudgelling in Rose Alley (1679). The libel may have been kept alive by false ascription of satires to Dryden's pen (see below, headnote to *The Dismissal of Rochester*).

38. *sacred David:* The charge relates to the various Whig attacks on *Absalom and Achitophel* which accused Dryden of making Charles "a broad figure of scandalous inclination" (see Macdonald, pp. 223–26, and *POAS,* Yale, *3,* 274).

51. *Harry Hills:* Henry Hills (1641–89) the printer, who became a papist shortly after James' accession. At the Revolution he fled to St. Omer. See *A View of Part of the Many Traitorous, Disloyal, and Turn-about Actions of H. H., Senior,* &c, 1684, and *The Life of H. Hills,* &c., 1688.

52. *Nich. Butler the publican:* Early in April 1687 Luttrell noted that "Sir Nicholas Butler, one of the commissioners of the customs, hath declared himself a papist" (*1,* 400). In October he was sworn a member of the Privy Council and appointed to Jeffreys' committee, set up to regulate corporations. The reference here presumably is to his political intriguing prior to his conversion.

53–4. Cf. *The Town Life,* 22–23; also *The Address of John Dryden, Laureate,* &c.:

When the bold Crescent lately attack'd the Cross,
Resolv'd the empire of the world t'engross,
Had tottering Vienna's walls but fail'd,
And the Turks over Christendom prevail'd,
I long ere this had cross'd the Dardanello

Thy crucifix would to the crescent bow.
At thy conversion, Jack, thus Whigs rejoice,   55
Who see not through the prudence of thy choice.
What so fit refuge for thee as new Rome,
Which like the old receives all nations' scum?
Or what so fit retirement could'st thou choose
For an old bawdy, profane, thieving muse,   60
When all her stock of purloin'd wit was gone,
As making the dry, fumbling jade a nun?
Now she may translate legends for our land
"According to his majesty's command"
And drivel out her dregs of poetry   65
In hymns on all the sacred trumpery
Of reverend relics, pretty miracles
Which the monk forges, then devoutly sells:
How Mary's image weeps for sinning souls,
Though with dry eyes she bore the carver's tools,   70
When through her trunk he drill'd the squirting holes;
How the milk which from her paps did distill
Is grown a flood enough to drive a mill;
How the curs'd cross, at first but one man's weight,
Is now increased to a navy's freight—   75
And 'tis but fit they multiply the wood,
Who so oft make and crucify the God—
Such lofty themes I leave thee to pursue,
So, Jack of all faiths, and of none, adieu.

> And sat the mighty Mohammed's hail fellow,
> Quitted my duller hopes, the poor renown
> Of Eton College or a Dublin gown,
> And, commenc'd graduate in the great divan,
> Had reign'd a more immortal Mussulman. . . . (93–102)

62. *making the . . . jade a nun:* Dryden reputedly had an affair with Anne Reeves, a comedienne in the King's Company. She became a nun early in 1675 (Macdonald, p. 96).

69–79. In recounting the religious themes which, he feels, Dryden will now pursue, the satirist attacks Mariolatry and transubstantiation (77), two aspects of the Roman Catholic religion which particularly enraged Protestants.

[CHARLES SACKVILLE, SIXTH EARL OF DORSET]

To Mr. Bays

Thou mercenary renegade, thou slave,
Thou ever changeling, still to be a knave;
What sect, what error wilt thou next disgrace?
Thou art so lewd, so scandalously base,
That anti-Christian Popery may be   5
Asham'd of such a proselyte as thee.
Not all the rancor and felonious spite
Which animates thy lumpish soul to write
Could have contriv'd a satire more severe,
Or more disgrace the cause thou would'st prefer.   10
Yet in thy favor this must be express'd:
It suits with thy poetic genius best.
There thou ———
Thy mind disus'd to truth may'st entertain
With tales more monstrous, fanciful, and vain   15
Than e'en thy poetry could ever feign.
Or sing the lives of thy old fellow saints—
'Tis a large field and thy assistance wants.
There copy out new operas for the stage
And with their miracles divert the age: 20
Such is thy faith (if thou hast faith indeed,
For well we may distrust the poet's creed.)
Rebel to God, blasphemer to thy king,
Oh, tell whence could this strange compliance spring:
So may'st thou prove to thy new gods as true   25

2. *changeling:* A waverer, turncoat, or renegade.
17. Dryden translated Bouhours' *Life of St. Francis Xavier* in 1686.
19. *new operas:* See above, Prologue and Epilogue to *Albion and Albanius.*
23. Cf. Tom Brown's epigram *To Mr. Dryden, and His Conversion (Works,* 1707,
1, ii, 17), which often occurs in MS. following the present poem:

> Traitor to God and rebel to thy pen,
> Priest-ridden poet, perjur'd son of Ben,
> If ever thou prove honest, then the nation
> May modestly believe transubstantiation.

As your old friend, th' Devil, has been to you.
Still conscience and religion's the pretense,
But food and drink the metalogic sense;
'Twas int'rest reconcil'd thee to the cheat,
And vain ambition tempted thee to eat.   30
Oh, how persuasive is the want of bread!
Not reasons from strongbox more strongly plead.
A convert thou! Why, 'tis past all believing;
'Tis a damn'd scandal of thy foes' contriving,
A jest of that malicious monster, Fame: 35
The honest Layman's Faith is still the same.

A Heroic Scene

Enter Oliver's Porter, Fiddler, and Poet
In Bedlam

The scene adorned with several of the poet's own flowers

PORTER: Oh glory, glory, who are these appear?
My fellow servants, poet, fiddler here:

28. James continued Dryden's office and the pension of £100 granted by his brother, but he omitted the Laureate's butt of sack.

  metalogic: i.e. "after logic."

32. *strongbox:* See headnote to *Survey of Events, 1686.* In 1686 Dryden assisted in the preparation of *A Defence of the Papers* reputed to have been written by Charles and by Anne Hyde. The latter, whose statement gave her reasons for becoming a convert, was defended by Dryden against attack from Edward Stillingfleet.

36. *Layman's Faith:* The subtitle of Dryden's *Religio Laici.* Sloane 2332 has a marginal note to this effect.

  Subtitle: Several references to Oliver's Porter occur in Restoration literature. See *Rump Songs,* 1662, p. 343; the prologue to D'Urfey's *Sir Barnaby Whig,* 1681: *A Satire in Answer to the Satire against Man,* in *Poetical Recreations,* 1688, II, 82. The origin of the character is obscure, but he more than likely signifies the fanatical Puritan. "Oliver's fiddler" was L'Estrange, a capable bass-violinist, who received this nickname as a result of a chance visit Cromwell made to the home of one Mr. Henckson, where he found L'Estrange and five or six other musicians privately playing (Kitchin, pp. 39–40).

1. Cf. *The Indian Emperor,* I.2: "O mercy, mercy, at they feet we fall," and IV.4: "Ah pity, pity, is no succor nigh!" For the use of "glory" as an ejaculation peculiar to the religious fanatic in Bedlam, see Etherege's *Man of Mode,* I.1.325–7:

  Medley: . . . were I so near marriage, I should cry out by fits as I ride in my coach, "cuckold, cuckold," with no less fury than the mad fanatic does "glory" in Bedlam.

Old Hodge the constant, Johnny the sincere.
Who sent you hither, and pray tell me why
An horrid silence does invade mine eye   5
While not one sound of voice from you I spy?
JOHNNY: I come to let thee know the time is now
To turn and fawn and flatter as we do,
And follow that which does too fast pursue.
Be wise, neglect your int'rest now no more—   10
Int'rest the prince we serve, god we adore!
I for the royal martyr first declar'd,
But ere his head was off I was prepar'd
To own the Rump and for that cause did rhyme,
But those kick'd out, next moment turn'd to him   15
Who routed them, call'd him my sovereign
And prais'd his opening of the kingly vein.
HODGE: I by my low'ring planets was accurst
To be for barren loyalty at first,
But when to Nol's our Charles's fate gave place,   20
I could abjure th'unhappy royal race.
To Nol I all my fingers' skill did show
And charm'd his highness with my nimble bow;
Besides, I serv'd him as a faithful spy
And did decoy the Cavalierish fry.   25
Gold from his bount'ous highness charm'd my eyes;

5–6. Cf. *Astræa Redux* 7–8 for which, as Johnson pointed out in his defense of the
lines, Dryden "was persecuted with perpetual ridicule" (*Lives*, ed. Hill, *1*, 334):

> An horrid stillness first invades the ear,
> And in that silence we the tempest fear.

9. Cf. *The Indian Emperor*, IV.3: "And follow fate, that does too fast pursue."
Dryden defended himself from an early attack on this line in his preface to the
second edition of *Tyrannic Love*, 1672 (see Macdonald, pp. 93 and 104).

17. Cf. *Heroic Stanzas*, 48: "To stanch the blood by breathing of the vein," and
the editors' defense of the line in Scott-Saintsbury, *9*, 14–15.

21, 24. "A damn'd lie": marginal note in MS. Firth c. 16. Although there is no
evidence that L'Estrange was ever in Cromwell's employ as a spy, gossip to this effect
was strong enough in 1660 for him to write in *L'Estrange, His Apology*:

> When I first heard myself suspected for an instrument of Cromwell, his pensioner,
> and a betrayer of his sacred Majesty's party and designs, I could not choose but
> smile. . . . But when I came to find that divers of my nearest friends were cau-
> tioned, and with monstrous secrecy designs were carried for fear of me . . . I
> began to look about me. . . . Upon further inquiry I found that this intelligence
> was as current about the King as here, and that many eminent persons were
> possessed with the same opinion.

My old whore Baltinglass could ne'er suffice
For the expense and equipage of spies.
JOHNNY: Come join with us to make our party strong
    And you can never be in Bedlam long.   30
HODGE: Were you yet madder you might serve the state
    And be concern'd in things of greatest weight.
JOHNNY: For, as the Turks their Santons, we adore
    The fools and madmen and their aid implore;
    They're such who share my panegyric verse.   35
HODGE: To such I write, not to philosophers.
PORTER: Such frequent turns should you to Bedlam bring,
    From Rump to Cromwell, Cromwell to the King,
    Then to your idol church, next to the Pope—
    Which may one day prefer you to the rope!   40
    I amongst madmen am confin'd, 'tis true,
    But I have more solidity than you.
JOHNNY: A windmill is not fickle, for we find
    That it is always constant to the wind;
    I never change, I'm still to int'rest true,   45
    The conqu'ror ever does my muse subdue;
    And with whatever tossing she shall meet,
    She, like a cat, shall light upon her feet.
HODGE: How long did I write for the English church,
    Yet now think fit to leave her in the lurch?   50
    Like will-o'-th'-wisp th'inferior clergy I
    Led into quagmires, where I let them lie;
    Some into bogs and ditches I have cast,
    Where, let them flounder what they will, they're fast;
    So far crape-gown is plung'd into the mire   55
    It is not possible it should retire.

27–8. On 17 Oct. 1665 L'Estrange wrote Arlington, the Lord Chamberlain, that his receipts from his newspaper were only £400 a year, while he was spending £500 "entertaining spies" (CSPD, 1665–66, p. 17: quoted by Kitchin, pp. 152–53).

    Baltinglass: Kitchin suggests, pp. 39 and 260, that this woman may have been the "Lady Baltinglass, a heap of flesh and brandy," whom Titus Oates was said to have married while in King's Bench prison (Ailesbury, Memoirs, 1, 144).

33. Santons: European designation for a kind of monk or hermit among Mohammedans.

55. crape-gown: Cant term for clerics derived from the fine worsted of which their gowns were often made.

PORTER, *aside:* My spirit boils within my troubled breast;
   These rogues are come to interrupt my rest.
JOHNNY: When the exalted Whigs were in their pride
   I spent my oil and labor on their side,   60
   Wrote a Whig play and Shaftesbury outran,
   For all my maxims were Republican;
   For the Excluding Bill I did declare,
   Libell'd and rail'd and did not Monarch spare.
   When they began to droop I fac'd about   65
   And with my pen I damn'd the Whiggish rout.
   Nay, every turn beforehand I can find,
   As your sagacious hog foresees the wind.
HODGE: You nimbly turn to that which does prevail;
   No seaman e'er could sooner shift his sail.   70
JOHNNY: Like a true renegado still I maul
   The party I forsook with utmost gall.
HODGE: So I ere long shall damn the heretic souls
   Of my old comrade coffee-priests near Paul's.
   Spies upon all their pulpits I maintain,   75
   And if of Rome or slavery they complain,
   Or for their own against our church they preach,
   I roar as if they did sedition teach.
   I brand the parson with most ven'mous lies,

57. Pope indicated this was a Dryden line; cf. *The Indian Queen*, I.1.73: "*Montezuma:* Bid children sleep, my spirits boil to high."

59–64. The allegation is made on the basis of that "Whig play" (60), *The Spanish Friar*, first performed in March 1680 and published the next year as a "Protestant play" dedicated to a "Protestant patron," John Holles, Lord Haughton (1662–1711). For Dryden's supposed attack on Charles, see above, *To Mr. Dryden*, 38 and n.

63. "That's true": marginal note in Firth.

66. *I damn'd the Whiggish rout:* In *Absalom and Achitophel* and *The Medal*.

68. *sagacious:* Acutely perceptive, especially by the sense of smell. "Betray'd again": marginal note in Firth.

74. *coffee-priests near Paul's:* The coffee house was Sam's in Ludgate Street, near St. Paul's (and not its more famous counterpart in Exchange Alley). Run by Sam Parson, it was described as "a coffee house where the inferior crape-gown men meet with their guide Roger, to invent lies for the further carrying on the Popish Plot" (note to 1st edn. of *The Medal of John Bays*, 1682: see *POAS*, Yale, *3*, 76; cf. *The Observator* ("Stand forth, thou grand Imposter of our time") in *Popery*, *1*, 1689, 15:

     While you at Sam's like a grave doctor sate,
     Teaching the minor clergy how to prate,
     Who lick'd your spittle up and then came down
     And shed the nasty drivel o'er the town. (94–97)

If I want truth, invention still supplies.   80
JOHNNY: But a reserve I kept for Monmouth still
    Should he prevail, I with such equal skill
    With satire mingled praise he could not take it ill.
    And had that prince victorious been at Lyme,
    I the Black-box had justifi'd in rhyme.   85
    I was prepar'd to praise or to abhor him,
    Satire I had and panegyric for him.
PORTER, *aside:* Oh, seed of locusts! the infernal lake!
    You'll cause my anger and I'll make you quake.
HODGE: Long my sly pen serv'd Rome and I achiev'd   90
    Ample rewards, whole shoals of priests deceiv'd;
    I wrought with such imperceptible tools
    That I of heaps of guineas gull'd those fools:
    The only bubbles in the world they be
    Who to their cost must feel before they see.   95
    In public yet the English church I own
    Though I am subtly writing of it down,
    For yet it is not time I should declare
    Lest fools to whom I write should be aware.
JOHNNY: Men best themselves 'gainst open foes defend   100
    But perish surely by a seeming friend.
    One son turn'd me, I turn'd the other two
    But had not an indulgence, sir, like you.
    I felt my purse insensibly consume
    Till I had openly declar'd for Rome.   105

81. *a reserve I kept for Mommouth still:* By his treatment of him in *Absalom and Achitophel.*

85. *Black-box:* The much advertised, though entirely fictional, box containing the secret marriage papers of Charles II and Lucy Walter, mother of Monmouth.

88. These oaths may be derived from the symbolism of the Book of Revelation, see esp. 9:3; 15:2. The Jesuits were commonly represented by locusts in contemporary satire.

94. *bubbles:* Dupes or gulls.

98. "a sly knave, the poet, and a plaguy guess": marginal note in Firth with last two words cancelled.

102. Dryden's three sons, Charles (1666–1704), John (1667–68–1701), and Erasmus Henry (1669–1710), became converts and later travelled to Rome seeking employment and perferment under the sponsorship of their uncle Cardinal Philip Howard (Charles Ward, *The Life of John Dryden*, 1961, p. 248 and n.). There is no evidence that one of the sons was responsible for his father's conversion.

HODGE: Now fellow servant, pray at length be wise
    And follow our example and advice.
PORTER: What! turn to Rome who did our city burn
    And would our ancient government o'erturn?
HODGE: Hold! is not the inscription blotted out?   110
PORTER: Therefore who burn'd the city none need doubt.
JOHNNY: It was almighty fire from Heav'n came down
    To punish the rebellious, stiff-neck'd town,
    All which had perish'd in devouring flames
    Though on the fire y'had emptied all the Thames.   115
    Had all its waves been on the houses toss'd,
    It had but basted them as they did roast.
    But Heav'n a crystal pyramid did take,
    Of that a broad extinguisher did make,
    In firmamental waters dipp'd above,   120
    Too hood the flames which to their quarry strove.
PORTER: A pryamid extinguisher to hood?
    'Tis nonsense never to be understood!
HODGE: What, you believe the Plot of varlet Oates?
PORTER: Ten proclamations and four senate's votes.   125

---

106. "very wittily spoke": marginal note in Firth.

108–9. "spoke like himself": marginal note in Firth.

110. *is not the inscription blotted out:* On 17 June 1681 Wren's monument commemorating the Great Fire of 1666 received an addition to its inscription by which the Roman Catholics were blamed for the disaster. Four years later the inscription was "erased and cut out" (Evelyn, 17 June 1685). It was restored in 1689 and finally obliterated in 1830. See Charles Welch, *History of the Monument,* 1893; and W. G. Bell, *The Great Fire of London in 1666,* 1920 (rev. 1923), pp. 208–09. B.M. MS. Add. 29497 reads: "Hold, did Coston th'inscription blunder out." I have not been able to identify Coston.

112–15. Cf. *Annus Mirabilis,* 857–60, 889–92, for the suggestion "that the fire served as a penalty for treason and rebellion" (*The Works of John Dryden,* ed. E. N. Hooker and H. T. Swedenberg, Jr. [Berkeley, 1956], *1,* 92, 311). A gloss in Firth claims that "none but Shadwell and the madman could have given such a reason."

118–21. Cf. *Annus Mirabilis,* stanza 281:

> An hollow crystal pyramid he takes,
>   In firmamental waters dipped above;
> Of it a broad extinguisher he makes,
>   And hoods the flames that to their quarry strove.

125. *ten proclamations:* Toward the end of 1678 and at the beginning of 1679 at least ten royal proclamations were issued to urge "the further discovery of the late horrid design" of the Popish Plot. The "strict execution" of the proclamations was

JOHNNY: That Godfrey's life was by the Papists sped?

PORTER: Oh, no! He kill'd himself when he was dead.

HODGE: To Jesuits dying you will credit give?

PORTER: Yes, full as much as all the while they live,

But dying Protestants I'll not believe,   130

For they allow of neat equivocation

And of flat lies with mental reservation.

JOHNNY: Hark, Hodge, to gain him we in vain contend,

Our fellow servant is a wag, dear friend.

HODGE: I'll try him farther, for his parts are such   135

To bring him o'er must needs avail us much,

Who are for Rome and France 'gainst th'English and the Dutch.

Come, fellow servant, you believe our Plot

Of Russell, Hampden, Sidney, and what not,

Of Bedford, Walcot, Bowsteeple, and the Rye?   140

PORTER: For Russell would, but Hampden would not lie,

Rumbold and Walcot, too, did both deny,

Ayloffe to boot, but cowards are not brave,

------

ordered several times by the council (*CSPD*, 1678, pp. 472–581 passim; 1679, pp. 33, 135–297 passim). "The more shame for 'em": marginal note in Firth.

126–27. Sir Edmund Berry Godfrey received Oates' deposition concerning the Popish Plot in Sept. 1678. On Oct. 12 Godfrey left home at 9 AM, attended to some business during the day, but failed to return home that evening. On Oct. 17 his body was discovered in a ditch on Primrose Hill, near Hampstead. He had been strangled to death, and his sword run through his chest in an attempt to make the death look like suicide. The Papists were blamed for Godfrey's murder and eventually three men were executed for the crime (see above, *The Tragi-Comedy of Titus Oates*, 42 n., and J. D. Carr, *The Murder of Sir Edmund Godfrey*, 1936). MS. Firth has the following query next to 127: "Why so?"

130. "A jest": marginal note in Firth. Against 135 it reads: "There again."

139. *Russell, Hampden, Sidney:* Lord Russell, John Hampden, and Algernon Sidney, alleged conspirators in the Rye House Plot.

140. *Bedford, Walcot, Bowsteeple, and the Rye:* Various assassination plots were outlined. Charles might be murdered on his way to Whitehall "under Bedford Wall in Convent Garden, where assassins might walk unsuspected in the piazza"; again it could be accomplished "out of Bowsteeple, as his Majesty was passing to Guildhall." The most famous location was, however, Rye House at Hoddesdon in Hertfordshire, the farm of Capt. Richard Rumbold. Here Charles was to be attacked on his way to or from the Newmarket races. (See Sprat's *True Account of the Horrid Conspiracy*, 1686, pp. 32, 68.)

Walcot: Lt. Col. Thomas Walcot, an old Cromwellian soldier, executed for his complicity in the plot.

143. *Ayloffe to boot:* Capt. John Ayloffe was executed on 30 Oct. 1685 for his complicity in the Rye House Plot. His scathing satire against the Stuarts, *Marvell's Ghost*

For fear's a passion which all cowards have.
Yet to the Plot I firm belief afford,   145
Of th'evidence I credit not one word.
JOHNNY: Can you distrust what Grey and Escrick say?
PORTER: What, two such excellent, moral men as they!
HODGE: Others there are swore home as men could do.
PORTER: Who for their lives must swear, swear home 'tis true.   150
Against the Popish crew none ever swore,
But a full pardon he obtain'd before.
These swearers are like cormorants, for they
On Whigs with ropes about their gullets prey.
JOHNNY: What then? Will you not be to int'rest true?   155
We both are of the same belief with you,
But we know better what we have to do.
PORTER, *aside:* Did ever hell send such a brace of knaves,
Such abject cowards, mecenary slaves? [*Exit, frowning.*]
JOHNNY: His looks are wild, his fiery eyeballs roll,   160
A raging tempest's lab'ring in his soul;
Let's prudently retire.
[*Porter reenters with a great Bible given him by Nell Gwynne.*]
PORTER: You sneaking rogues, would you   [*He knocks them down
be gone?   with the Bible and
Here's that shall knock both you and   stamps upon them;
Popery down!   they get up.*]
HODGE: Rash man! for this I full revenge   165
will take

(1678) is printed in *POAS,* Yale, *1,* 284–86. A member of an underground organization
run by Peter du Moulin and directed against French and Catholic influence, he placed
beside the Speaker's chair sometime during the Parliamentary session of 1673 a wooden
shoe, bearing the arms of England and France and the motto "Utrum horum mavis
accipe" ("Choose whichever of these you prefer").
   147. *Grey and Escrick:* Informers. For Grey see above, headnote to *Monmouth's Rebellion.* William Howard (1626?–1694), third Baron Howard of Escrick, was apprehended in June 1683 for his part in the Rye House Plot. He turned informer and
was the principal witness against Russell, Sidney, and Hampden.
   149–50. "plaguy arguments": marginal note in Firth.
   160–1. Cf. *The Indian Emperor:*

   Montezuma: I feel my hair grow stiff, my eyeballs roll,
            This is the only form could shake my soul. (II.1)
   Cortez: A raging fit of virtue in the soul. (II.2)
   Cortez: Her looks grow black as a tempestuous wind;
            Some raging thoughts are rolling in her mind. (IV.4)

And set our evidence upon your back.

JOHNNY: Audacious fool! how dare you tempt your fate,
　　　Provoking me, a pillar of the state,
　　　Who with my pen alone have turn'd the scale
　　　And made the Tories o'er the Whigs prevail?　　　　　　170

HODGE: Your pen alone! —
　　　Can I this arrogance endure to hear,
　　　Would you usurp the garland I should wear?

JOHNNY: You with your forty-eight and forty-one,
　　　With screws and antependiums plagu'd the town;　　　175
　　　While even the Whigs admir'd my lofty verses,
　　　Your witless prose did fodder forty arses.

HODGE: I'll through your arse touch honor to the quick
　　　And find if you have any by this kick.　　　　[Kicks the poet.]

JOHNNY: Kick on, old fool, till you your toes shall maul,　　　180
　　　I have had several and can bear them all—
　　　Besides, I'm us'd to't.

PORTER:　　　　　　　　　Hence you wretched slaves,
　　　There is contagion in such fools and knaves,
　　　I'll wring your necks off if you ever more　　　　　　185
　　　Presume to set your feet within this door;
　　　I'm chief and have dominion in this place.

JOHNNY: I'll spend my gushing blood upon thy face,
　　　And if thou dar'st effect thy dire design,
　　　With my two hands I'll fling my head at thine.　　　190

PORTER: Holloa, St. Denis, have at you!
　　　　　　　[He kicks and beats them; they run roaring out.]

167. According to Pope a Dryden line, or like one.

168. *a pillar of the state:* i.e. poet laureate.

169–70. In *Absalom and Achilophel, The Medal,* and *The History of the League.*

174. *forty-eight and forty-one:* 1648 and 1641, crucial years in the Civil War.

175. *antependiums.* A covering or a veil for the front of an altar. See Evelyn's comment on L'Estrange's support of Tory policy, quoted in headnote.

184. Cf. *Conquest of Granada,* I.1: "Besides, there is contagion in my fate." Pope identified the line as like Dryden's.

188–90. Cf. *Tyrannic Love,* IV.1:

　　　Porphyrius: Where'er thou stand'st, I'll level at that place
　　　　　　　My gushing blood and spout it at thy face.
　　　　　　　Thus, not by marriage, we our blood will join;
　　　　　　　Nay more, my arms shall throw my head at thine.

191. *St. Denis:* Patron saint of France. The first bishop of Paris, he was decapitated in 280 on Montmartre. By legend he and two friends similarly executed carried their heads to the spot where the town of Saint Denis was afterwards built.

JOHNNY: Murder, murder!
HODGE: Help, help!
PORTER: I on these knaves shall never more complain,
    They have call'd back my wand'ring sense again.   195
             [*He pauses and seems to come to himself.*]
    Of all mankind happy alone are we,
    From all ambition, from all tumults free.
    No plots nor vile informers need we fear,
    No plagues, nor tortures for religion here.
    Our thoughts, nay, e'en our very words are free,   200
    Not damn'd by fines or loss of liberty.
    None here's impeach'd by a vile table spy,
    Who with an innuendo backs his lie.
    Words and lampoons we laugh at and ne'er care
    What's said by men, if actions they forbear.   205
    Anger at words is weakness understood,
    Since none can ridicule aught that is good;
    'Tis womanish and springs from impotence,
    For no great man at words e'er took offense.
    At Rome in all her glory words were free,   210
    Just governments can never jealous be;
    But when to tyranny Rome did decline,
    Weak emperors with delators did join
    To plague the people and themselves undo,
    For when they're fear'd, they must be hated too: 215
    And whom men hate with ruin they'll pursue.
    One witness and a circumstance for facts
    Is not enough, we must prove overt acts.
    Our happy government makes no offense
    But open and rebellious violence,   220
    Which we to quell no standing army need,
    Nor can dragoons upon free quarter feed.
    Booted apostles we have none that come
    To knock and beat men to the church of Rome;
    When its butt-end prevails not, torments will,   225
    For Louis's not yet so merciful to kill.

213. *delatores:* i.e. delators, or professional informers.
216. "Excellent principles": marginal note in Firth.
226. In Nov. 1685 Louis XIV revoked the Edict of Nantes and stepped up his persecution of the Huguenots—Luttrell records news of the latter in September (*1*, 358).

Here we divided from the troubled world
Rest and are into no confusions hurl'd,
For all our wants does our wise state provide,
Here ev'ry vacant place is still suppli'd   230
With persons that are duly qualifi'd,
No favor raises a desertless knave,
Nor infamy, nor yet the gold he gave;
How would all subjects envy us, should we
Publish the secrets of our hierarchy.   235

Large numbers of refugees had been coming to England since late in 1681, but Louis'
actions in 1685 considerably increased their number.
    235. "A speech very proper for a madman": marginal note in Firth.

The Trial of Godden v. Hales
(June 1686)

Lacking parliamentary acquiescence in his policy of appointing Catholics to military posts, James sought support from the bench for his use of the royal prerogative to dispense with the Test Act, which required public servants to receive the sacrament according to the rites of the established church and take the oaths of allegiance and supremacy, within three months of their appointment to office. If he could secure a ruling in favor of the prerogative, James reasoned that he would then be free to install Catholics in whatever post he saw fit. He had contemplated recourse to the judiciary from the time of his return from Scottish exile in 1682, when the possibility was first put into his mind by Edward Herbert, then Chief Justice of Chester, and approved in principle by Chief Justice Jeffreys (Clarke, 2, 80–81).

With the elevation of Herbert to the office of Chief Justice of the King's Bench (23 October 1685), the advice to seek a judicial ruling on the dispensing power was, no doubt, renewed with vigor by its chief proponent. The first step was to prepare a case which could be tested. It was arranged that Arthur Godden, coachman to Colonel Edward Hales, should bring an action against his master, a convert in November 1685, to secure the £500 due to an informer under the Act of 25 Car. 2 for preventing "dangers from popish recusants" (Howell's *State Trials*, *11*, 1165 ff.). Tried and convicted at the assizes held at Rochester on 29 March 1686, Hales appealed on grounds that he had received "letters patent under the Great Seal" which dispensed with the oaths in his case (Howell's *State Trials*, *11*, 1180–82).

During April James took it upon himself to sound judicial opinion through a system of personal interview, which came to be known as "closetting," in hope that he could convince or coerce the opposition to support his point of view. The upshot was that Sir Thomas Jones,

Chief Justice of the Common Pleas, and three other refractory judges were dismissed. In reply to James' determination to have twelve judges of his own opinion, Jones had said that possibly his majesty "might find twelve judges of his opinion, but he could scarce find twelve lawyers of that mind" (Echard, *3*, 797; Reresby, p. 422). And indeed when James sought counsel to defend the dispensing power, he met with another set-back. Heneage Finch, Solicitor General, refused the brief and, as a result, was turned out of office. Some thought that the refusal to comply with the King's wishes was less a result of conscientiousness than of "apprehension of being called to account for compliance by Parliament at some future time" (Leopold von Ranke, *History of England,* 1875, *4*, 290).

James was undaunted by the resistance to his plans, however, and by mid-June he felt he could proceed in his attempts to secure judicial sanction for the dispensing power. Accordingly, he had Herbert assemble the judges beforehand to obtain their opinion on the case. Herbert said of the meeting:

> Truly, upon the argument before us, it appeared as clear a case as ever came before this court. But because men fancy I know not what difficulty, when really there is none, we were willing to give so much countenance to the question in the case, as to take the advice of all the judges in England. They were all assembled at Sergeant's Inn, and this case was put them . . . whether the dispensation . . . were legal, because upon that depended the execution of all the law of the nation. And I must tell you that there were then ten upon the place that clearly delivered their opinions that the case . . . was good law. (Howell's *State Trials, 11,* 1302)

Justice John Powell required additional time to consider his opinion, but later concurred. Only Baron Street dissented. On 21 June Herbert delivered judgment in favor of Hales, thus upholding the dispensing power as part of the royal prerogative.

James had won a major victory, though there can be little doubt that the decision was unpopular (Clarke, *2*, 82 ff.). It aggravated the danger of a Catholic and thus hostile standing army. It supplied what seemed to be a clear instance of the corruptibility of the judiciary, as well, with the resultant destruction of the legal safeguards to the church and state. Despite these aspects of the decision, however, there was apparently little actual demonstration against it during the remainder of the summer. The following two poems, for example, are the only ones so far uncovered which concern themselves with the decision, and one of these, *To the Respective Judges,* may not have been written until 1688 (see 29 and n.). The paucity of satiric attack probably reflects either the populace's tendency to wait and see, secure in the knowledge that the succession was Protestant, or its fear of the power James had secured to himself during the first year of his reign.

A Stanza Put on Westminster Hall Gate

When nature's God for our offenses di'd
Amongst the twelve one Judas did reside.
Here's twelve assembled for the nation's peace
Amongst which twelve, eleven are Judases.
One's true to's trust, but all the rest accord   5
With Jews and pagans to betray their Lord.
What madness, slaves! What is't could ye provoke
To stoop again unto the Romish yoke?
May ye be curs'd and all your hopes demolish'd—
And perish by those laws ye have abolish'd!   10

To the Respective Judges

Dignifi'd things, may I your leaves implore
To kiss your hands and your high heads adore?
Judges you are—but you are something more.

5. *One's true to's trust:* The dissenting judge was Baron Street. Macaulay thought he was acting collusively to lend the bench an appearance of independence (2, 738). Turner feels that this suggestion "does not carry any conviction" (p. 320) and cites evidence from Bramston which shows that Street was "closetted" with James for a considerable time after the trial, but that he was not dismissed. Whatever the truth of the matter, this poem indicates that the popular attitude to Street's dissension was unequivocally behind him.

Title: In the *Muses Farewell to Popery,* 1689, this poem is called *To the Ten Dispensing Judges.* This title suggests that the poem may have been circulated in MS. prior to 21 June, when Herbert announced the court's decision and explained Powell's initial hesitancy in coming to an opinion in line with the majority.

May I draw near and with a rough-hew'd pen
Give a small draft of you, the worst of men,   5
Tell of your merits and your mighty skill
And how your charms all courts of justice fill?
Your laws, far stronger than the Commons' votes,
So finely flow from your dispensing throats,
What Rome will ask, you must not her deny,   10
If Hell command you, too, you must comply!
There's none but you would in this cause combine—
Things made like men but act like brutes and swine.
Law books are trash, a student—he's a drudge;
Learn to say "yes"—he's an accomplished judge: 15
He wins the scarlet robe and wears it too,
Aye, and deserves it well, for more's his due—
All that completes a traitor dwells in you.
Thus you like villains to the benches get
And in defiance to the laws you sit,   20
And all base actions that will please commit.
There must you toil for Rome and also try
Your Irish sense and cobweb policy:
Complete your crimes—and then you're fit to die!
True loyal babes, pimps to the Church of Rome!   25
Tresilian's heirs, heirs to his crimes and doom!
Was e'er the hall fill'd up with such a brood
All dipp'd in treason, villainies, or blood!
Worse than fanatic priests, for they being press'd
By a wise prince preach'd to repeal the Test.   30
Then here's the difference 'twixt you Popish tools:
You're downright rogues, they only knaves and fools.

23. *Irish:* Suggests papistical loyalty to James and his policies.
    cobweb: i.e. unsubstantial.

26. *Tresilian's heirs:* Sir Robert Tresilian, Lord Chief Justice during the reign of Richard II, was hanged in 1388 for the extraordinary cruelty with which he tried the rebels of the Wat Tyler rising.

29. *fanatic priests:* Presumably a general reference to those members of the Anglican church who, by pursuing the doctrine of Passive Obedience or Non-Resistance, were willing to assent to the repeal of the Test Act. The phrase may, however, allude quite specifically to those Anglican priests in 1688 willing to read the second Declaration of Toleration from their pulpits. If so, the date of the 'poem's publication (1688) would, of course, also be the date of its composition.

30. *wise prince:* James. The reference is ironic, but the satirist may intend further to condemn the priests' stupidity by showing James to be wise in comparison.

1687

The Dismissal of Rochester
(January 1687)

The year began with the dismissal of Laurence Hyde, Earl of Rochester, who as Lord Treasurer had been James' chief advisor. Officially, James argued reasonably enough that the Treasury had become too complex for one man to handle, but in appointing a five-man commission to run the government's financial affairs, he overlooked his former chief minister. In his place he named the moderate Catholic, John, Baron Belasyse, to head the body, and another moderate Henry Jermyn, Lord Dover, as a commissioner. These appointments gave rise to Anglican suspicions that James' motives were really religious rather than financial. But whereas James certainly attempted to introduce Catholic officers into his government wherever he could, he was prudent enough to turn to the moderate element, and he supported them with three experienced and capable financial administrators: Sidney, first Baron Godolphin, Sir John Ernle, and Sir Stephen Fox (*CSPD*, 1686–87, p. 330). In retiring Rochester, James arranged for him to receive an income large enough to meet all his needs (*Cal. Treasury Books*, 1685–89, p. 1103).

Clearly, James had the efficiency of the treasury uppermost in his mind, but Rochester's dismissal provided the King's opponents with a cause to exploit. Other appointments were prejudicial to the position of the established church, notably those during the summer of 1686 which brought five Catholics into the Council (see *Survey of Events, 1686,* note to headnote), but Rochester's removal, the first important administrative change in the government, considerably diminished the Anglican voice in James' counsels. Though Rochester had been out of favor for more than a year (see *Song* "The widows and maids," 62 and n.), he could be championed as a "pillar of the church."

An event of December 1686 seemed to support the notion that Rochester's dismissal was primarily a religious matter. Hoping to convert Rochester to his own mind and therefore to his own church,

James had arranged a conference between Roman and Anglican di-
vines in the presence and for the enlightenment of the Lord Treasurer. Writing on 17 December, Luttrell says of the conference and
its outcome:

> There hath been lately a dispute between Dr. Jane and Dr.
> Patrick of the Church of England and Dr. Godden and Mr. Gif-
> ford of the Romish Church. 'Tis said 'twas held in his Majesty's
> presence and for the satisfaction of the Earl of Rochester, who,
> 'tis reported, is thereby more confirmed a Protestant. (*1*, 391)

In estimating the effect this conference had on James' later step in
removing the Treasury from Rochester's hands, it should be remarked that Fox had also been approached by James earlier in the
reign and had been offered a peerage in return for his conversion to
the Roman Catholic church. Like Rochester, Fox had refused to comply with James' desires, but unlike him Fox had not been removed
from the King's service (*Memoirs of the Life of Sir Stephen Fox,*
1717, p. 114).

The following poems were circulated after Rochester's fall, both
independently and together. The *Epitaph,* certainly not written by
Dryden as several MSS. claimed, apparently dates from August 1684
when Rochester was, in Halifax's words, "kicked upstairs" to the
Presidency of the Council and thus frustrated in his original hopes
for the office of Lord Treasurer. Of the ascription Macdonald says,
"I suppose this attack on Laurence Hyde was ascribed to Dryden to
bring discredit on him for attacking a patron" (p. 319). Evidence
not available to Macdonald, however, points to another conclusion.
Two MSS. show that the poem was written and circulated in 1684
with *A Gentle Ballad Called Lamentable Lory.* Upon Rochester's
dismissal in 1687, the poem was apparently revived by Tory sympathizers and furnished with an answer eulogizing Rochester. The satire of the original poem was then undercut by ascribing it to an
author whose name, synonymous with "turncoat," was an antonym
for "constancy."

AN EPITATH ON LAMENTABLE LORY

Here lies a creature of indulgent fate,
From Lory Hyde rais'd to a chit of state;

In chariot now, Elijah-like, he's hurl'd
To th'upper empty regions of the world;
The airy thing cuts through the yielding sky,   5
And as it goes does into atoms fly,
While we on earth see with no small delight
The bird of prey turn'd to a paper kite.
With drunken pride and rage he did so swell,
The hated thing without compassion fell;   10
By powerful force of universal prayer
The ill-blown bubble is now turn'd to air;
To his first less-than-nothing he is gone
By this preposterous translation.

AN ELOGY

Here lives a peer rais'd by indulgent fate,
A shining sun from a fall'n star of state;
In chariot now, Elijah-like, he's bore
A pitch beyond the Roman eagle's soar;
Through th'yielding air he makes his glorious flight   5
And scatters as he goes new beams of light,
While Papists see with envy from the porch
The statesman turn'd a pillar of the church.
With faith and holy resolution crown'd,
Unmov'd the noble patriot stands his ground;   10
By powerful force of weighty argument
The baffl'd fathers back again are sent,
While to his first best principles he's just:
True to his God and faithful to his trust.

3. *Elijah:* The Hebrew prophet in the reign of Ahab (1–2 Kings), who was carried to Heaven in a fiery chariot. The MS. reading "Elias," a variant form of Elijah, gave rise to a mistaken identification with Elisha in one or two texts.

8. *kite:* A pun on "kite," both the bird of prey of the falconiform family and the child's toy, with the additional implication, of course, that Hyde was a "rapacious person."

Title: An obs. Anglicized form of "elogium," that is, "an explanatory inscription, especially on a monument or a portrait."

12. *baffl'd fathers:* The priests whose efforts to convert Hyde were "frustrated or foiled" by his standing firm in his own arguments.

The Declaration of Indulgence
(March–April 1687)

The success James had achieved in clearing the way for Roman Catholic leadership brought with it a new problem of staffing. There were not enough qualified Catholics willing to commit themselves wholeheartedly to James' schemes. Originally, James sought a coalition with the Church of England, depending on that church's submissiveness in accordance with its doctrine of Non-Resistance. But throughout the summer and fall of 1686, the supporters of Anglicanism had stiffened in their opposition to what they saw as a calculated policy, rigorously pursued.

As an alternative James considered an alignment of all the forces of nonconformity against the established church. For more than a year rumors of toleration had been current. Then on 12 February 1687 James issued a partial toleration in Scotland. By this declaration he presumably intended either to test Anglican reaction or to shake its obstinacy. There followed about five weeks of intensive interview between the King and his Anglican opponents, both lay and clerical, in the King's last attempt to gain support for his position (see Reresby, pp. 447–49). When all else failed, on 18 March James went before the Privy Council and told them of his resolve "to issue out a declaration for the general Liberty of Conscience to all persons of what persuasion soever" (*London Gazette,* 17–21 March 1687). Two weeks later the official proclamation was carried by the *Gazette* (4–7 April 1687):

> We cannot but heartily wish, as it will easily be believed, that all the people of our dominions were members of the Catholic Church. Yet we humbly thank almighty God it is, and hath of long time been, our constant sense and opinion . . . that conscience ought not to be constrained, nor people forced in matters of mere religion. . . . We therefore out of our princely care and affection unto all our loving subjects, that they may live at

ease and quiet, and for the increase of trade and encouragement of strangers, have thought fit by virtue of our royal prerogative to issue forth this our Declaration of Indulgence, making no doubt of the concurrence of our two houses of parliament, when we shall think it convenient for them to meet.

In the first place we do declare that we will protect and maintain our archbishops, bishops, and clergy, and all other our subjects of the Church of England in the free exercise of their religion as by law established. . . .

We do likewise declare that it is our royal will and pleasure that from henceforth the execution of all and all manner of penal laws in matters ecclesiastical, for not coming to church, or not receiving the sacrament, or for any other nonconformity to the religion established, or for or by reason of the exercise of religion in any manner whatsoever, be immediately suspended. And the further execution of the said penal laws and every of them is hereby suspended.

However we estimate James' sincerity in this act, historically we must recognize both the dangers apparent to those whose favor he sought and the very real relief that was given them by the lifting of the "sanguinary" penal laws. Addresses of thanks filled the pages of the *London Gazette* from this point forward in the reign, and their sincerity need not be doubted. But there were warnings, as well. Halifax put them most forcefully in his *Letter to a Dissenter,* cautioning that "the Church of Rome doth not only dislike the allowing liberty, but by its principles it cannot do it." Indeed, it was difficult for members of the dissent to avoid his conclusion that they were "to be hugged now" only to be "better squeezed at another time." Halifax's advice was to enjoy quietly the benefits of the act without actively supporting it, cautioning against throwing away the advantages to be gained in "the next probable revolution." Though the Declaration of Indulgence has been called "no more than an incident in the campaign . . . to win over the Dissenters" (Ogg, p. 181), it established, as the remainder of this volume shows, firmly and finally the lines of battle for the rest of the reign.

A POEM OCCASIONED BY HIS MAJESTY'S MOST
GRACIOUS RESOLUTION DECLARED IN HIS MOST
HONORABLE PRIVY COUNCIL, MARCH 18 1686/7, FOR
LIBERTY OF CONSCIENCE.

What heav'nly beam thus antedates the spring
And summer's warmth with autumn's fruits doth bring,
That spreads new life throughout Great Britain's isle
And, making the most sullen tempers smile,
Does all the jarring factions reconcile?   5
'Tis an indulgence from the royal breast,
More fragrant than the spices of the east,
More welcome than to greedy misers wealth,
To rebels pardon, or to sick men health.
Sudden, yet calm as the bless'd angels fly,   10
His resolution comes for liberty:
Liberty in things sacred, that each tread
That path which safest him to bliss may lead,
That elephants may swim, that lambs may wade,
And none each other worry or invade.   15
In heav'n are many mansions, and why then
Not several tracts, though but one road, for men?
Keep the foundations sure, join holy life,
And what need circumstantials cause such strife?
So a kind father does with equal care   20
Cherish his children, though perhaps they wear
Each diverse features, each a different hair.
    Religion is God's work upon the soul,
Which penal laws may startle, not control.
E'en truth's profession, when enjoin'd by force,   25
Does rarely make men better, often worse;
For once compell'd unto hypocrisies,
The sense of virtue and religion dies,
And then, on next fair opportunity,

16. "In my Father's house are many mansions": John 14:2.

17. *tracts:* Here a "course" or "route"; not yet employed to mean a short pamphlet
of a political or religious nature.

24. *penal laws:* For a summary of these laws, see above, *Song,* "What think you of
this age now," 49 and n.

With greater heats they to wild furies fly: 30
For true religion never faction breeds,
Nor the support of impious weapons needs.
Let Mohammed prescribe his Alcoran
To be advanc'd by arms, fast as it can;
Christ's gospel is a law of peace and love 35
And by conviction on the heart doth move.
When Solomon of old God's temple rear'd,
No noise of axes was, nor hammers heard.
Hard upon hard no lasting work will make,
Nor can one flint another kindly break. 40
But moderation is a cement sure,
'Tis that which makes the universe endure,
'Tis that which makes these realms a temp'rate zone
Betwixt the torrid and the frozen one.
   More than one hundred years the state had tri'd 45
To uniform those sects that would divide,
But still the teeming Hydra multipli'd;
Whilst one resolve of mighty James allays
The tempests of the past and following days,
Unites his subjects, makes 'em friends, and so 50
All seeds of faction wholly does o'erthrow.
Holland no longer shall our people drain,
No more our wealthy manufactures gain:
Henceforth rebellion can have no pretense

38. 1 Kings 6:7.

39. *Hard upon hard:* Presumably, a form of the proverb *durum et durum non faciunt murum* ("hard with hard will not make a wall"). Cf. Tilly, *Proverbs,* H145, which cites Fuller, *Church History, 2,* ii, I, 121: "Hard with hard, saith the proverb, makes no wall; and no wonder, if the spiritual building went on no better, wherein the austerity and harshness of the pastor met with the ignorance and sturdiness of the people."

40. *kindly:* By nature, naturally, as well as gently.

43. A commonplace justifying English moderation in political matters.

46. *To uniform those sects:* From early in Elizabeth's reign various attempts were made to enforce compliance with the doctrine of the Anglican Church. Under Charles II, the Act of Uniformity (1662) was the latest such attempt.

52–53. *Holland:* Throughout the century Holland received emigrants and exiles from England fleeing religious and political persecution. It had also opposed the pursuit under Charles and James of vigorous, nationalistic economic policies.

54–55. An obvious allusion both to the Civil War and, more recently, to Monmouth's Rebellion.

To arm the rabble for their faith's defense.   55
Since each mode of religion now is free,
They'll all, I hope, conspire in loyalty.
　　Let no bold, peevish man, prone to excess,
Abuse this favor to licentiousness,
Refine too much on sovereign decrees   60
Of God or's king, but with true humbled knees
Thank both for all the freedom they enjoy,
And cheerfully each follow his employ.
No rivalship be found in any sect,
But who most souls to heaven shall direct.   65

DR. WILD'S GHOST

On his Majesty's Gracious Declaration
for Liberty of Conscience, April 4, 1687

How! Liberty of Conscience! that's a change
Bilks the crape-gowns and mortifies L'Estrange;
Two lines of brisk *Gazette* in pieces tears
The *Observator*'s pains of many years;
The clergy-guide himself is left i'th'lurch,   5
To which he quail-pip'd easy daughter Church;
So the foul fiend at Halberstadt, they say,
In fiddler's guise so charmingly did play
That all the buxom youth of the mad town

Title: Robert Wild (1609–79) was a Puritan minister with Royalist views and a popular, though controversial poet. Called by Dryden "the very Wither of the city," Wild sought poetically to defend the loyalty to the Crown of his Nonconformist brethren and praised Charles' Declaration of Liberty of Conscience in 1672. For several of his best poems see *POAS*, Yale, *1*.

2. *crape-gowns:* Clerics.

　　L'Estrange: Sir Roger L'Estrange, author of the Tory newssheet *The Observator* See above, *A Heroic Scene.*

3. *Gazette:* The *London Gazette* published the Declaration of Indulgence on 7 April 1687.

6. *quail-pip'd:* To lure, as with a quail-call. L'Estrange employed the term in his attacks on Presbyterians (*State Divinity*, 1661, p. 14), "to give over . . . their quail-piping in a pulpit to catch silly women."

7. *Halberstadt:* A town in Saxony. I have not been able to determine whether it has its own version of the Pied Piper legend.

Follow'd his tweedling music up and down, 10
Till the whole troop an unseen gulf did drown.

What's now become of our informing crew,
The Browns, the Hiltons? O loyal men and true!
Once pillars of our church—true church by law—
For more were bugbear'd to her out of awe 15
Then all our sermon-readers e'er could draw;
Those useful sparks, implements orthodox,
Soon as they found their church was i'th'wrong box,
Fled from her faster than from whore with pox—
So rats by instinct quit a falling house, 20
So dying beggar's left by every louse.

Pinfold, that spiritual dragoon, who made
By soul-money a pretty thriving trade,
Gave to old Nick each refractory ninny
But whisk'd him back for a repentant guinea, 25
Is now grown bankrupt, weary of his life,
And almost wild and frantic as his wife.

Those that erewhile no mortal sin could spy
So bad, so gross as Nonconformity
Are now become the only malcontents, 30
And each in sullen sighs his passion vents;
Passive Obedience once was all their clutter,
But soon as their own nails were par'd they mutter:

13. *Browns . . . Hiltons:* "One Brown and [John] Hilton, and one Shafto, a woman, the chief informers against conventicles, having been discovered to be guilty of perjury in those matters, are prosecuted by the justices of Middlesex for the same" (Luttrell, *1, 387*, and *1, 241*).

18. *i'th'wrong box:* In the wrong position; perhaps derived from the boxes of an apothecary.

20-1. For the belief that rats leave a falling house, see Tilly's *Proverbs*, M1243, and cf. *Hudibras*, I.ii.939. I find no such belief recorded about lice.

22. *Pinfold:* Dr. Thomas Pinfold, an official of Doctors' Commons for Nonconformity under Charles and James. In Nov. 1692, he was arraigned before the Council "about money levied on the Protestant dissenters and not returned into the exchequer" (Luttrell, *2, 606, 612; CSPD, 1691-2*, p. 499).

23. *soul-money:* Money subscribed to pay for masses for the soul of a dead person.

32. *Passive Obedience:* The doctrine of Passive Obedience or Non-Resistance demanded respect for and compliance with the office of the lawful king. Resistance was thought both wicked and sacrilegious. The lawful demands—even the doubtful ones—of the king were to be obeyed.

clutter: Arch. or dial., "noisy turmoil or disturbance, hubbub."

"Dear Whigs! dissenting brethren! pray forbear
To meet. Indulgence is a royal snare,   35
This Declaration is a Trojan Horse;
The form's illegal and the matter worse;
There is a snake i'th'grass!"—That, that's their cry,
Which is in short to give their Prince the lie
And charge the best of Kings with treachery.   40
Is this your Church of England Loyalty?

Hark! the hunt's up, backwards they chime their bells,
And every one a frightful story tells;
The doctors stand aghast, and country vicar
Fancies there's holy water in his liquor;   45
Each pulpit echoes, Bellarmine, thou li'st,
And Pelling swears the Pope is Antichrist.
Does not the inundation make you quake:
The Roman Sea join'd with the Leman Lake?
How soon will Father Peters make a hand on's,   50
When Baxter's self has seiz'd on petty canons?

41. *Church of England Loyalty:* In a sermon of this title preached to the Commons
on 29 May 1685, Dr. William Sherlock concluded " 'tis a Church of England loyalty
I persuade you to. This our King approves, commends, relies on as a tried and experienced loyalty, which has suffered with its Prince but never yet rebelled against
him—a loyalty upon firm and steady principles and without reserve. And therefore
to keep us true to our Prince we must be true to our Church and to our Religion,
and its legal securities, for if we change our Religion, we must change the principles
of our loyalty and, I am sure, the King and the Crown will gain nothing by that,
for there is no lasting and immovable loyalty as that of the Church of England"
(publ. 1685; Wing S3345).

42. *backwards they chime their bells:* "To give the alarm . . . [derived from] the
practice of beginning with the bass when the bells were rung" (Partridge, p. 25).

46. *Bellarmine:* Roberto Bellarmino (1542–1621), the great cardinal and theologian.
His *Disputationes de Controversiis Fidei adversus hujus temporis Haereticos* (1581–
93) provided the finest contemporary statement of Roman Catholic doctrine. So forceful and uncompromising was it that for more than a century most Protestant attempts
to vindicate their position found it necessary to begin by answering the *Disputationes.*

47. *Pelling:* Edward Pelling (d. 1718), vicar of St. Martin's, Ludgate, and prebendary
of Westminster. An Anglican controversialist, he attacked Roman Catholics and dissenters both from the pulpit and through the press. His *True Mark of the Beast* was
first published in 1682 and reprinted in 1685.

50. *Father Peters:* Jesuit Edward Petre (1631–99), clerk of the Royal Closet, and
one of the most influential figures at Court. The Tuscan ambassador said he acted
without reflection, attempting the impossible (Campana, 2, 113).

51. *Baxter:* Richard Baxter (1615–91), Presbyterian divine. In May 1685, he was
brought to trial before Jeffreys on a charge of libelling the church in his *Paraphrase*

Turn out, my masters! aloft! aloft, all hands—
Religion that's our tithe-pigs and glebe lands—
The Protestant religion now will fall;
Bel and the Dragon will devour us all!   55

   O tender, zealous hearts! O sad condition!
Idolatry will eat up superstition;
The calf at Bethel fears the calf at Dan:
The English cannot Latin mass withstand;
And now the jacks have lost their wonted prey,   60
They dread the sharks will carry all away;
So conjurers grow towards their end in fear
That their familiar devil will them tear.

   But why this sudden zeal when t'other day
With Popery you could so freely play?   65
Their church you then acknowledged was true—
A rev'rence to the western patriarch due—
And from that coast no danger you could view;
On each occasion Papists favor found,
And all your cry was knock Dissenters down!   70
Yet now you bawl Tiber the Thames will drown,
But why, pray, must our faith be quite undone
Because your persecuting pow'r is gone?
The wise suspect religion's not your fear,
But you are vext, you cannot domineer,   75
And rail at Jesuits for cruel elves,
Because you'd have none spoil us but yourselves.

---

of the New Testament, 1685, grossly insulted, fined, and imprisoned until the fine was
paid. He was released on 24 Nov. 1686, when "James had need of the Nonconformists
as a make-weight (if possible) against a recalcitrant clergy." If the Crown hoped to
turn him to its cause, it was deceived. Even in prison he apparently worked on a
"Defense of his Paraphrase" (Frederick J. Powicke, *The Reverend Richard Baxter*,
1927, pp. 152, 160 ff).

   55. *Bel and the Dragon:* A book of the Apocrypha. The Babylonian idols, the one
brazen and the other live, were exposed by Daniel.

   58. *Bethel . . . Dan:* The sites where Jeroboam set up the golden calves for his
people to worship (I Kings 12:28–33).

   60. *jacks:* Pike; see below, *Dryden's Ghost*, 106 and n.

   61. *sharks:* Those who enrich themselves "by taking advantage of the necessities of
others."

   67. *western patriach:* The pope.

Well, rev'rend sirs, if Popery must be,
You'll find the nuns are pretty company,
And if the fiery trial should return,   80
Most of you wet yourselves too much to burn.
But though you will not hazard your dear lives,
You may be glad to part with your old wives.
At worst—
'Tis but conforming t'other step and then,   85
Jure divino, whip and spur again.

86. *Jure divino:* **By divine right.**

Diplomatic Relations with the Vatican
(*January–July 1687*)

As early as September 1679, the moderate Pope Innocent XI had counselled James against too zealously pressing the Roman Catholic cause in England (Campana, *1, 302*). Himself deeply embroiled with the Jesuits and Louis XIV, Innocent fully understood the dangers from the extremist position, which he opposed, and recognized that long-term suffering and imposition would be the cost to English Catholics of short-lived gains won by James and his Jesuit supporters. But James, always impatient with counsels of moderation, was eager to display both publicly and officially his true allegiances. For a short time after his accession he had been content, as Burnet said (*1, 703*), to manage "his correspondence with Rome secretly." But by the fall of 1685 he had decided to send Roger Palmer, Earl of Castlemaine "on a solemn embassy to Rome . . . [the King being] persuaded it was suitable to his dignity to be represented in that Court by a *titolato*, as they termed it, and [Castlemaine] having been a sufferer and tried for his life in Oates' . . . Plot, was supposed a proper person for that employment" (Clarke, *Life, 2, 75*). All Palmer's genuine qualifications for such an embassy were compromised by his position as the long-suffering, time-serving, husband of Barbara Villiers. The letter of French Ambassador Barillon to Louis XIV explains: "qu'il y ait quelque ridicule à envoyer un homme, si peu connu par lui-même, et si connu par Madame de Cléveland" (Mazure, *2, 77*).

Palmer's departure from Court, though not from the country, roughly corresponded with the arrival in England of the Papal nuncio, Ferdinand, Count d'Adda, in November 1685, in the guise of a foreign visitor (Campana, *2, 80–81*). D'Adda remained in England for three years as the Pope's representative; Palmer in Rome for just over a year as James'. Both men proved largely ineffectual in their offices—d'Adda because of his grace and meekness, Palmer because of his pride and violence. Each was unwittingly responsible for a major blow to James' Papist policy.

Palmer's party embarked at Greenwich for Dieppe on the yacht *Henrietta Maria,* arriving in France two-and-a-half days later. From thence the party journeyed overland, reaching Rome on the eve of Easter, 3 April 1686. For the next year Palmer did his best to achieve James' desires for cardinal's caps for Queen Mary's uncle, Prince Rinaldo d'Este, and for the Jesuit Edward Petre, but seems only to have alienated the Pope more and more by his overbearing manner. "Whenever [Palmer] began to talk business, the Pope was seasonably attacked with a fit of coughing, which broke off the ambassador's discourse for that time and obliged him to retire" (Welwood, p. 185; Ailesbury, *1,* 152–53, describes the Pope's dismissing Palmer by ringing his silver bell when the ambassador "had scarce begun his discourse"). Palmer's formal reception was put off on several occasions. The last time was in November 1686, when all had been got ready. The Pope was suddenly indisposed by an attack of the gout, and the official presentation was postponed until January 1687. The banquet Palmer finally staged was sumptuous to a fault. More than 1,000 attended and were treated to a three-hour feast. Among the table decorations were huge *trionfi* made of sugar paste afterwards sent as gifts to the greatest ladies of Rome (John Wright, *Account . . . of Castlemaine's Embassy,* &c., 1687, p. 69). But all was to no avail. The Pope was disinclined to listen to Palmer, who was at length "advised to come to threats and to give out that he would be gone. . . . Innocent was so little concerned for the ambassador's resentment that when they told him of it he answered with his ordinary coldness . . . 'Well, let him go! And tell him it were fit he rise early in the morning that he may rest himself at noon, for in this country it's dangerous to travel in the heat of the day' " (Welwood, p. 185–6). On 23 June, Castlemaine left the Vatican, accompanied by the English Cardinal Philip Howard; by August he was back in England, where on the 12th he kissed the King's hand at Windsor (Wright, *Account,* p. 111).

In the meantime, Windsor itself had been the scene of another official presentation, which for James had gone equally badly. From the first James had sought to persuade Count d'Adda to proclaim himself publicly as representative of the Vatican. D'Adda had constantly refused on the basis of his own unfitness for the office and of his lack of a Papal directive to this end (Campana, *2,* 93–5). It was not until the summer of 1687 that he allowed himself to be received officially as nuncio. According to Clarke, it was James' "misfortune to think [the entry] would render the people less averse to suffer the exercise of the Catholic religion amongst them, by familiarizing the nation not only with the ceremonies of the Church of Rome, but of the Court of Rome, too" (2, 116). James was circumspect enough, however, to move the ceremonies from Whitehall to Windsor, where there would be less chance of disturbance from the spectators. On 23 July the entry was undertaken with considerable pomp (for a good contemporary account see *Somers' Tracts, 9, 267–8*). The ceremonies were marred, however, by the absence of several important courtiers, chief among them Charles Seymour, Duke of Somerset. When James asked him to introduce the nuncio, he

> humbly desired of the King to be excused. The King asked him his reason. The Duke told him he conceived it to be against law; to which the King said he would pardon him. The Duke replied he was no very good lawyer, but he thought he had heard it said that a pardon granted to a person offending under assurance of obtaining it was void. (John, Viscount Lonsdale, *Memoir of the Reign of James II*, 1808, pp. 23–24.)

Somerset was immediately dismissed from all his offices, but in the moment he had handed James a severe rebuff he had become an Angelican hero.

Of the following poems, the first is by Nahum Tate (1652–1715), poet and dramatist, who became laureate in 1692 on the death of Shadwell. Tate seldom missed an opportunity to produce a panegyric. This particular piece was appended to John Wright's *Account* of Palmer's embassy, published with elaborate illustrations early in 1688. It is mainly interesting in the present context as an example of the kind of "propaganda" James could count on to support his cause. *The Entry* is, however, a very different matter; moreover, it may bear a direct, palinodic relation to Tate's poem.

NAHUM TATE

ON THE EARL OF CASTLEMAINE'S EMBASSY TO ROME IN KING JAMES II'S REIGN, 1687

Let mighty Caesar not disdain to view
These emblems of his power and goodness, too:
A short essay, but fraught with Caesar's fame,
And shows how distant courts esteem his name.
Here may'st thou see thy wond'rous fortunes trac'd,   5
With suff'rings first, and then with empire grac'd;
Long toss'd with storms on Faction's swelling tide,
Thy conduct and thy constancy was tri'd,
As Heaven design'd, thy virtue to proclaim,
And show the crown deserv'd before it came.   10
Troy's hero thus, when Troy could stand no more,
Urg'd by the Fates to leave his native shore,
With restless toil on land and seas was toss'd,
Ere he arriv'd the fair Lavinian coast;
Thus Maro did his mighty hero feign.   15
Augustus claim'd the character in vain,
Which Britain's Caesar only can sustain.
Permit, dread sir, my Muse, though mean, to own
A truth to Albion and to Europe known.

1. *Caesar:* Applied to both Charles and James, suitable by connection with Rome for either praise or blame. Here, however, the name has additional significance since the motif of "the old Roman" was carried out by Castlemaine in his public entry (see Wright's *Account,* p. 22).

5–29. This paean to James, which recounts his sufferings in exile before the Restoration and his later difficulties during his brother's reign, also was inspired by Wright's *Account* of the various entertainments of the embassy. At a banquet given by Cardinal Pamphilio tablets commemorating James' career adorned the walls. One displayed "a ship, her sails furled and lying close against the weather" inscribed "While dangers are abroad." Another depicted a leopard looking on his spots with the motto, "They beautify, not blemish," intimating that James was "unstained by the obloquies against him" and was rather "enhanced by them." Throughout the entertainments the motif of Hercules, a common type of the King but here, in particular, representing James' valor, was much in evidence.

12–14. Cf. *Aeneid,* I.1–7.

The Earl of Castlemaine Making Obeisance to the Pope

You are what Virgil feign'd his prince to be,   20
Your valor such, and such your piety:
Now Theseus' deeds we can receive for true,
And Hercules was but a type of you—
He made the fierce Lernaean monster bleed;
From Hydra-faction you have Albion freed.   25
The paths of glory trod and danger past,
Just Heav'n allows a peaceful throne at last:
At home to show th'indulgence of a god
And send your peaceful ministers abroad.
   While Palmer hastens to the Roman court   30
(And fraught with worth that honor to support),
His glorious train and passing pomp to view
(A pomp that e'en to Rome itself was new),
Each age, each sex the Latian turrets fill'd,
Each age and sex in tears of joy distill'd,   35
While wonder them to statues did convert;
Those seem'd to live that were the works of art
Emblems and figures of such life and force,
As, wanting speech, did to the eye discourse
And show, what was despair'd in ages past,   40
An universal language found at last.
   Hail Palmer, hail illustrious minister!
To Caesar, Britain, Fame, and Virtue dear;
Caesar to represent, great Caesar's voice,
Nam'd Castlemaine; the British shores rejoice,   45
And Tyber's banks applaud great Caesar's choice.
   How therefore could the Muses silent be,
And none can want a Muse that writes of thee!
From thine, no Phoebus' tree, my song I'll raise,
And crown'd with palm, I will contemn the bays.   50

25. *From Hydra-faction you have Albion freed:* By suppressing Monmouth. Palmer carried out the hydra motif in the various tablets and decorations for the entertainments during his embassy.

32–35. "The weather was somewhat rainy, but that hindered not even the streets as well as the balconies and windows from being crowded with people, all shouting and crying out, *'viva il grand Re d'Inghilterra!'* " (Wright's *Account*, p. 51).

49–50. *Phoebus' tree:* The laurel, of course, from which comes the bay. Tate puns on Castlemaine's name, on the religious "palmer," and on the tree with its honorific symbolism.

The Entry of the Pope's Nuncio

Old Westminster, the seat of kings, whose law
So many years has kept the beast in awe,
Henceforth to Windsor must resign thy power—
The loyal Windsor, which in one short hour
Has cancell'd all that thou hast done before!   5
The Gordian Knot, so many ages ti'd,
One Alexander can with ease divide.
And what is more pernicious than the fact,
He has his tools to carry on the act.

Can any nation know a greater curse   10
Than have a Judas to betray the purse?
Sworn to maintain those articles and own
The very laws he labors to run down.
What value all the statutes of our nation
To guard us against popish innovation,   15
If by so vile an upstart trampled on
To sway at court and domineer in town?

But what are servile judges, when e'en they
Of Levi's tribe, the priests, are gone astray?
Apostate Durham! what could be thy hope,   20
What work of merit to bring in the Pope?
If thou must trim to please the King and Queen,
Keep to thy music, 'tis the safer mean.

Chester did not so much betray his trust;
He to his principles was only just.   25

11. *a Judas to betray the purse:* Presumably Sir Thomas Jenner (1637–1707), appointed a Baron of the Exchequer on 5 Feb. 1686. With the majority of the judges Jenner had voted in favor of the King's dispensing power in the trial Godden *v.* Hales.

20. *Apostate Durham:* Nathaniel Crew, third Baron Crew of Stene (1633–1721), and Bishop of Durham. A most obsequious adherent to James' policies, he apparently attended the entry and walked in d'Adda's retinue. Later when d'Adda was Archbishop of Milan he continued to inquire "after his brother the Bishop of Durham, and drinks his health . . ." (Kennett, 3, 494n.)

24. *Chester:* Thomas Cartwright (1634–89), Bishop of Chester, nominated to that see in Dec. 1686. His appointment was ill-received, and opponents attempted to

Who has so long a vassal been to Rome
Must joy to see her brought in triumph home.

Nor is the rough tarpaulin in the wrong
To crowd a member in the sacred throng.
He'd be a fool recorded if his grace 30
For conscience should refuse so great a place,
Whose vile compliance to a monarch's will
Has made the noted blockhead greater still.

But Somerset, to thee what pen can frame
A monument as lasting as thy fame, 35
Who scorns to stoop beneath the vulture's wing
And quits the torrent to embrace the spring;
Firm to his honor, to his country just,
He slights his int'rest to perform his trust;
Scorns all the glories of a flatt'ring court 40
And what they think his ruin counts his sport:
Here thorny satire would transform to bays,
But I must cease, 'cause none can reach thy praise.

---

prevent his consecration. Burnet voiced the general opprobrium in which he was held: "He was a man of good capacity and had made some progress in learning. He was ambitious and servile, cruel and boisterous, and, by the great liberties he allowed himself, he fell under much scandal of the worst sort. He had set himself long to raise the King's authority above law, which, he said, was only a method of government to which kings might submit as they pleased. . . . So he was looked upon as a man that would more effectually advance the design of popery, than if he should turn over to it" (*1*, 695).

28. *the rough tarpaulin:* The "sailor," Henry Fitzroy (1663–90), first Duke of Grafton, and second son of Charles II by Barbara Castlemaine, who, on his father's resolve, had been brought up for the sea as a volunteer under Admiral Sir John Berry. At the entry he conducted the Nuncio.

33. *blockhead:* An epithet commonly applied to Charles and his illegitimate children.

37. A common image in the controversialist writing of the time; see, particularly, Dryden's *The Hind and the Panther,* II.277–78.

"The Rule of Transversion": Attacks
on The Hind and the Panther
(May–July 1687)

Within two months of the first Declaration of Indulgence, the greatest poem of the reign, Dryden's *The Hind and the Panther*, appeared in support of the Roman Catholic cause (entered in the *Stationers' Register* on 27 May 1687; see Macdonald, p. 44). Primarily Dryden's final statement in his long debate between reason and faith—he had first poetically considered the problem in *Religio Laici* (1682)—*The Hind and the Panther* was undoubtedly read by many with considerably more malice than even Dryden had come to expect, because they preferred to see the poem as propaganda, commissioned in support of the toleration, rather than as a sincere statement of faith and argument for understanding. Dryden's preface to the poem made his position as advocate of toleration abundantly clear:

> As for the poem in general, I will only thus far satisfy the reader—that it was neither imposed on me, nor so much as the subject given me by any man. It was written during the last winter and the beginning of this spring, though with long interruptions of ill health and other hindrances. About a fortnight before I had finished it, his Majesty's Declaration for Liberty of Conscience came abroad, which, if I had so soon expected, I might have spared myself the labor of writing many things which are contained in the third part of it. But I was always in some hope that the Church of England might have been persuaded to have taken off the penal laws and the Test, which was one design of the poem when I proposed to myself the writing of it.

Of the many poems attacking Dryden and his poem, the best-sustained and most humorous came from the pens of Matthew Prior and Charles Montagu, who by 19 July 1687 had completed *The Hind and the Panther Transversed* (Macdonald, p. 254 n.). Sir James Montagu, Charles' brother and an intimate friend of Prior, gave the following account of the composition of the poem:

> *The Hind and Panther* being at that time in everybody's hands, Mr. Prior accidentally came one morning to make Mr. Montagu a visit at his brother's chambers in the Middle Temple, London, where the said Mr. Montagu lodged when he was in London. And the poem lying upon the table, Mr. Montagu took it up and read the four first lines in the poem of *The Hind and Panther* . . . where stopping, he took notice how foolish it was to commend a four-footed beast for not being guilty of sin and said the best way of answering that poem would be to ridicule it by telling Horace's fable of the city mouse and country mouse in the same manner. Which being agreed to, Mr. Prior took the book out of Mr. Montagu's hands and in a short time after repeated the four first lines, which were after printed in *The City Mouse and Country Mouse*. . . . The repeating these lines set the company in laughter, and Mr. Montagu took up the pen by him and wrote on a loose piece of paper, and both of them making several essays to transverse, in like manner, other parts of the poem, gave beginning to that work which was afterwards published to the great satisfaction of many people. And, though no name was set to the book, yet it was quickly known who were the authors of it. . . . ("Memorandums Concerning the Late Celebrated Poet and Statesman, Mr. Matthew Prior, etc.," a MS. in the Longleat collection, reprinted in part by Wright-Spears, 2, 831–32)

The success of the Montagu-Prior production was probably no greater than it deserved. Tom Brown's statement "that *The City Mouse and Country Mouse* ruined the reputation of the divine, as *The Rehearsal* ruined the reputation of the poet" is what we would expect from the hostile and facetious lampoonist (see the preface to his *Reasons for Mr. Bays Changing his Religion*, 1688). The parody remains, however, the most important single attack on Dryden's poem, though throughout the summer and into the autumn a host of others appeared. Most of these are catalogued by Macdonald and are as available to the modern reader as their intrinsic merit warrants. Given here, in addition to the Montagu-Prior burlesque, are three

short poems that apparently have not previously been printed. They
occur, with other Drydeniana, in Folger MS. 473.1, a seventeenth-
century commonplace book which may have been prepared by a
scriptorium. Of the three poems, *Dryden's Ghost* maintains a spar-
kle of wit that raises it above the average riposte and thus warrants
its inclusion here on its own merits as satire.

In the text of *The Hind and the Panther Transversed* the italicization of the original has been maintained to indicate passages which
directly parody Dryden. Line references to *The Hind and the Panther* are to James Kinsley's edition.

CHARLES MONTAGU AND MATTHEW PRIOR

THE HIND AND THE PANTHER TRANSVERSED

to the Story of the Country Mouse
and the City Mouse

Much malice mingled with a little wit: *Hind and Panther,* III.1
Nec vult Panthera domari: Quae Genus

Preface

The favorers of *The Hind and Panther* will be apt to say in its
defense that the best things are capable of being turned to ridicule,
that Homer has been burlesqued and Virgil travestied without suffer-

---

Title. Transversed: In *The Rehearsal,* I.1, Bays says: "Why, sir, my first rule is the
rule of transversion, or *regula duplex:* changing verse into prose, or prose into verse,
alternative as you please. . . . I take a book in my hand, either at home or elsewhere,
for that's all one, if there be any wit in't, as there is no book but has some, I transverse it; that is, if it be prose, put it into verse (but that takes up some time), and
if it be verse, put it into prose."

Epigraph: Nec vult Panthera domari. "A tag from Lily's *Grammar,* the section
'De Nominibus Heteroclitis,' beginning, 'Quae genus aut flexum variant'" (Wright-
Spears).

Authors: For Prior, see above, *Advice to a Painter;* Charles Montagu (1661–1715),
later Earl of Halifax, had first attracted attention as a poet by his verses on the death
of Charles II. He pursued his poetic attack on Dryden in his own "Reply" to *The
Hind and Panther* (see Helene Maxwell Hooker's transcription and discussion of the
poem in *ELH, 8* [1941], 51–62).

ing anything in their reputation from that buffoonery, and that, in like manner, *The Hind and the Panther* may be an exact poem, though 'tis the subject of our raillery. But there is this difference, that those authors are wrested from their true sense, and this naturally falls into ridicule; there is nothing represented here as monstrous and unnatural, which is not equally so in the original. First as to the general design, is it not as easy to imagine two Mice bilking coachmen and supping at the Devil, as to suppose a Hind entertaining the Panther at a hermit's cell, discussing the greatest mysteries of religion, and telling you her son Rodriguez [a] writ very good Spanish? What can be more improbable and contradictory to the rules and examples of all fables, and to the very design and use of them? They were first begun and raised to the highest perfection in the eastern countries, where they wrote in signs and spoke in parables and delivered the most useful precepts in delightful stories, which for their aptness were entertaining to the most judicious and led the vulgar into understanding by surprising them with their novelty and fixing their attention. All their fables carry a double meaning. The story is one and entire; the characters the same throughout, not broken or changed, and always conformable to the nature of the creatures they introduce. They never tell you that the dog which snapped at a shadow lost his troop of horse. That would

[a.] *Rodriguez:* Refers to a complicated aspect of the controversy between Dryden and Edward Stillingfleet, later Bishop of Worcester, over the "royal papers," i.e. *Copies of Two Papers Written by the Late King Charles, together with a Copy of a Paper Written by the late Duchess of York,* purporting to prove Charles and the Duchess died Roman Catholics. Stillingfleet had composed *An Answer* to these documents which elicited *A Defense,* of which Dryden wrote the third part, dealing with the Duchess' paper. Dryden's conclusion called upon Stillingfleet to display a "spirit of meekness and humble charity," adding that "he is such a stranger to the spirit, because among all the volumes of divinity written by the Protestants there is not one original treatise . . . which has handled . . . that Christian virtue of humility." In his *Reply* Stillingfleet answered that "within a few years (besides what hath been printed formerly), such a book hath been published in London." Thinking he had found Stillingfleet in error, Dryden said in his preface to *The Hind and the Panther* that Stillingfleet should continue to "look out for some original *Treatise of Humility* . . . for the magnified piece of Duncomb on that subject, which either he must mean, or none . . . was translated from the Spanish of Rodriguez, though with the omission of the 17th, the 24th, the 25th, and the last chapter." Recently Prof. Earl Miner has unravelled what had come to seem a hopeless tangle of allusion ("Dryden and 'The Magnified Piece of Duncomb'," *HLQ* xxviii [1964], 93–98), and proves that Dryden had in mind a Protestant translation of Rodriguez entitled *A Treatise of Humility,* published in 1654 by Eleazar Duncon, "a royalist divine of marked Laudian convictions."

be unintelligible. A piece of flesh is proper for him to drop, and the reader will apply it to mankind. They would not say that the daw, who was so proud of her borrowed plumes, looked very ridiculous when Rodriguez [a] came and took away all the book but the 17th, 24th, and 25th chapters, which she stole from him. But this is his new way of telling a story and confounding the moral and the fable together.

> "Before the Word was written," said the Hind,
> "Our Savior preach'd the faith to all mankind." [II.305–06]

What relation has the Hind to our Savior, or what notion have we of a Panther's Bible? If you say he means the Church, how does the Church feed on lawns or range in the forest? Let it be always a church, or always the cloven-footed beast, for we cannot bear his shifting the scene every line. If it is absurd in comedies to make a peasant talk in the strain of a hero, or a country wench use the language of the court, how monstrous is it to make a priest of a Hind, and a parson of a Panther—to bring 'em in disputing with all the formalities and terms of the school? Though as to the arguments themselves, those, we confess, are suited to the capacity of the beasts, and if we would suppose a Hind expressing herself about these matters, she would talk at that rate.

As to the absurdity of his expressions, there is nothing wrested to make 'em ridiculous. The terms are sometimes altered to make the blunder more visible; *knowledge misunderstood* [I.276] is not at all better sense than *understanding misunderstood,* though 'tis confessed the author can play with words so well that this and twenty such will pass off at a slight reading.

There are other mistakes which could not be brought in, for they were too gross for Bays himself to commit. 'Tis hard to conceive how any man could censure the Turks for gluttony [I.376–79], a people that debauch in coffee, are voluptuous in a mess of rice, and keep the strictest Lent, without the pleasures of a carnival to encourage them. But 'tis almost impossible to think that any man, who had not renounced his senses, should read Duncomb for Allen: He had been told that Mr. Allen had written a *Discourse of Humility,* to which he wisely answers that *that magnified piece of Duncomb's was translated from the Spanish of Rodriguez,*[b] and to set it beyond

<hr>

[b.] A gloss refers to Thomas Tenison's *Difference Betwixt the Protestant and Socinian Methods: in Answer to a Book Written by a Romanist and Entitled, The Protestant's*

dispute makes the infallible guide affirm the same thing [III.332–40]. There are few mistakes, but one may imagine how a man fell into them, and at least what he aimed at; but what likeness is there between Duncomb and Allen? Do they so much as rhyme?

We may have this comfort under the severity of his satire, to see his abilities equally lessened with his opinion of us; and that he could not be a fit champion against the Panther till he had laid aside all his judgment. But we must applaud his obedience to his new mother Hind. She disciplined him severely. She commanded him, it seems, to sacrifice his darling fame [III.282–90], and to do it effectually he published this learned piece. This is the favorable construction we would put on his faults, though he takes care to inform us that it was done from no imposition [Preface, 56–57] but out of a natural propensity he has to malice and a particular inclination of doing mischief. What else could provoke him to libel the Court, blaspheme Kings, abuse the whole Scotch nation, rail at the greatest part of his own, and lay all the indignities imaginable on the only established religion? And we must now congratulate him this felicity that there is no sect or denomination of Christians whom he has not abused.

> Thus far his arms have with success been crown'd.
> [*Tyr. Love*, I.1.1]

Let Turks, Jews, and Infidels look to themselves. He has already begun the war upon them. When once a conqueror grows thus dreadful, 'tis the interest of all his neighbors to oppose him, for there is no alliance to be made with one that will face about and destroy his friends, and like a second Almanzor ᵉ change sides merely to keep his hand *in ure*. This heroic temper of his has created him some enemies that did by no means affect hostility, and he may observe this candor in the management, that none of his works are concerned in these papers but his last piece; and I believe he is sensible this is a favor. I was not ambitious of laughing at any persuasion, or making religion the subject of such a trifle, so that no man

---

Plea for a Socinian, 1687, p. 62, in which Tenison refutes Dryden's claim that among "Protestants there is no one original treatise" on humility. Though Stillingfleet clearly had in mind *A Practical Discourse of Humility*, 1681, by William Allen, he does not mention Allen's name, as Montagu and Prior suggest. They invented this to make Dryden look absurd (see Prof. Miner's article, cited above).

ᵉ *Almanzor:* The hero in Dryden's *Almanzor and Almahide, or The Conquest of Granada.*

is here concerned but the author himself, and nothing ridiculed but his way of arguing.

But, gentlemen, if you won't take it so, you must grant my excuse is more reasonable than our author's to the Dissenters.[d]

The Hind and the Panther, Transversed to the Story of the Country and the City Mouse.

BAYS, JOHNSON, SMITH

Johnson: Hah! my old friend Mr. Bays, what lucky chance has thrown me upon you? Dear rogue, let me embrace thee!

Bays: Hold, at your peril, sir, stand off and come not within my sword's point, for if you are not *come over to the Royal Party, I expect neither fair war nor fair quarter from you* [Pref., 1–2].

Johnson: How, draw upon your friend and assault your old acquaintance? O' my *conscience* my intentions were honorable.

Bays: Conscience! Aye, aye, I know the deceit of that word well enough. Let me have the *marks* of your *conscience* before I trust it, for if it be not of the same stamp with mine, gad, I may be *knocked down,* for all your fair promises.

Smith: Nay, prithee Bays, what damned villainy hast thou been about that thou'rt under these apprehensions? Upon my honor I'm thy friend, yet thou lookest as sneaking and frighted as a dog that has been worrying sheep.

Bays: Aye, sir. *The nation is in too high a ferment for me to expect any mercy,* or, egad, to trust anybody [Pref., 1].

Smith: But why this to us, my old friend, who you know never trouble our heads with national concerns till the third bottle has taught us as much of politics as the next does of religion? [e]

d. Cf. Dryden's preface to *HP:*

> On the other side, there are many of our sects, and more indeed than I could reasonably have hoped, who have withdrawn themselves from the communion of the Panther, and embraced this gracious indulgence of his Majesty in point of toleration. But neither to the one nor the other of these is this satire any way intended; 'tis aimed only at the refractory and disobedient on either side.

e. The following lines from *The Rose Tavern Club,* an obscene ballad circulating in manuscript early in 1687, provide an amusing gloss:

> Much wine had pass'd with much discourse
> Of who's a rogue and who's a worse,
> Such as most usually does close

Bays: Ah, gentlemen, leave this profaneness. I am altered since you saw me and cannot bear this loose talk now. Mr. Johnson, you are a man of parts, let me desire you to read *The Guide of Controversy,* and, Mr. Smith, I would recommend to you *The Considerations on the Council of Trent,*[t] and so, gentlemen, your humble servant. —*Good life be now my task* [I.78].

Johnson: Nay, faith, we won't part so. Believe us, we are both your friends. Let us step to the Rose for one quarter of an hour and talk over old stories.

Bays: I ever took you to be men of honor, and for your sakes I will transgress as far as one pint.

Johnson: Well, Mr. Bays, many a merry bout have we had in this house, and shall have again, I hope. Come, what wine are you for?

Bays: Gentlemen, do you as you please. For my part he shall bring me a single pint of anything.

Smith: How so, Mr. Bays, have you lost your palate? You have been more curious.

Bays: True, I have so, but *senses* must be *starved* that the *soul* may be *gratified* [I.366]. Men of your kidney make the senses the *supreme judge* and therefore bribe 'em high, but we have laid both the use and pleasure of 'em aside.

Smith: What, is not there good eating and drinking on both sides? You make the separation greater than I thought it.

Bays: No, no, whenever you see a fat *rosy-colored* fellow, take it from me, he is either a Protestant or a Turk [I.370].

> The night with bottle at the Rose;
> When I, who silently had sat
> To hear Will Richards' clapper-chat—
> He did a grinning knave abhor,
> As we wrote c——t, nam'd Rochester—
> "Prithee," quoth I to trusty Will
> And double glass myself I fill,
> "Leave off your speaking underhand—
> Here's t'ye and damn Lord Sunderland,
> And all such dogs as he's by nature;
> Betray'd the Church, the Whigs' own creature,
> To mass now goes in form and feature,
> I'th'chamber chapel of Father Peter."
> "Odzoons!" quoth Will. "What, art thou mad,
> To talk so loud of Chit and Dad?" (Taylor 2, p. 188)

[t.] Two books by Abraham Woodhead (1609–78) published in 1666–67 and 1671. Woodhead was the "Romanist" answered by Tenison in *Difference Betwixt the . . . Methods.*

Johnson: At that rate, Mr. Bays, one might suspect your conversion. Methinks thou hast as much the face of an *heretic* as ever I saw.

Bays: Such was I, such by nature still I am [I.76]. But I hope ere long I shall have drawn this *pampered paunch* fitter for the *straight gate* [I.373–74].

Smith: Sure, sir, you are in ill hands. Your confessor gives you more severe rules than he practices; for not long ago a *Fat Friar* ᵍ was thought a *true character.*

Bays: Things were misrepresented to me. I confess I have been unfortunate in some of my writings, but since you have put me upon that subject, I'll show you a thing I have in my pocket shall wipe off all that, or I am mistaken.

Smith: Come, now thou art like thyself again. Here's the King's health to thee—communicate.

Bays: Well, gentlemen, here it is, and I'll be bold to say, the exactest piece the world ever saw, a *nonpareillo,*ʰ i'faith. But I must bespeak your pardons if it reflects anything upon your persuasion.

Johnson: Use your liberty, sir, you know we are no bigots.

Bays: Why then you shall see me lay the Reformation on its back, egad, and justify our religion by way of fable.

Johnson: An apt contrivance, indeed! What, do you make a fable of your religion?

Bays: Aye, egad, and without morals, too; for I tread in no man's steps; and to show you how far I can outdo anything that ever was writ in this kind, I have taken Horace's design,ⁱ but, egad, have so outdone him, you shall be ashamed for your old friend. You remember in him the story of the Country Mouse and the City Mouse? What a plain, simple thing it is! It has no more life and spirit in it, egad, than a hobbyhorse; and his mice talk so meanly, such common stuff, so like mere mice, that I wonder it has pleased the world so long. But now will I undeceive mankind, and teach 'em to heighten and elevate a fable. I'll bring you in the very same mice disputing the depth of philosophy, searching into the fundamentals of religion, quoting texts, fathers, councils, and all that, egad, as you shall see

ᵍ· *Fat Friar:* Dryden's *Spanish Friar,* 1680.

ʰ· *nonpareillo:* A quasi-Italianate form. Cf. *The Rehearsal,* I.1: "*Bays.* I think you'll say this is a *nonpareillo.* I'm sure nobody has hit upon it yet."

ⁱ· *Horace's design:* See *Satires,* II.4.79 ff.

either of 'em could easily make an ass of a country vicar. Now, whereas Horace keeps to the dry naked story, I have more copiousness than
to do that, egad. Here I draw you general characters and describe all
the beasts of the creation; there I launch out into long digressions
and leave my Mice for twenty pages together; then I fall into raptures
and make the finest soliloquies, as would ravish you. Won't this do,
think you?

Johnson: Faith, sir, I don't well conceive you. All this about
two mice?

Bays: Aye, why not? Is it not great and heroical? But come, you'll
understand it better when you hear it; and pray be as severe as you
can. Egad, I defy all critics. Thus it begins:

> A milk-white Mouse, immortal and unchang'd,
> Fed on soft cheese, and o'er the dairy rang'd;
> Without unspotted, innocent within,
> She fear'd no danger, for she knew no gin. [I.1–4]

Johnson: Methinks, Mr. Bays, soft cheese is a little too coarse
diet for an immortal Mouse. Were there any necessity for her eating,
you should have consulted Homer for some celestial provision.

Bays: Faith, gentlemen, I did so, but indeed I have not the Latin
one, which I have marked, by me and could not readily find it in
the original.

> Yet had she oft been scar'd by bloody claws
> Of winged owls and stern grimalkins' paws
> Aim'd at her destin'd head, which made her fly,
> Though she was doom'd to death, and fated not to die. [I.5–8]

Smith: How came she that *fear'd no danger* in the line before, to
be *scar'd* in this, Mr. Bays?

Bays: Why then you may have it *chas'd* if you will, for I hope a
man may run away without being afraid, mayn't he?

Johnson: But pray give me leave, how was she *doom'd to death,* if
she was *fated not to die?* Are not *doom* and *fate* much the same
thing?

Bays: Nay, gentlemen, if you question my skill in the language,
I'm your humble servant. The rogues, the critics, that will allow me
nothing else, give me that. Sure I that made the word know best

what I meant by it. I assure you, *doomed* and *fated* are quite different things.

Smith: Faith, Mr. Bays, if you were *doomed* to be hanged, whatever you were *fated* to, 'twould give you but small comfort.

Bays: Never trouble your head with that, Mr. Smith, mind the
business in hand.

> Not so her young, their Linsey Woolsey line
> Was hero's make, half human, half divine. [I.9–10]

Smith: Certainly these *heroes half human, half divine* have very
little of the Mouse, their mother.

Bays: Gadsokers! Mr. Johnson, does your friend think I mean
nothing but a Mouse by all this? I tell thee, man, I mean a Church,
and these young gentlemen, her sons, signify priests, martyrs, and
confessors that were hanged in Oates' Plot. There's an excellent
Latin sentence which I had a mind to bring in, *sanguis martyrum
semen ecclesiae,*[j] and I think I have not wronged it in the
translation:

> Of these a slaughter'd army lay in blood,
> Whose sanguine seed increas'd the sacred brood;
> She multipli'd by these, now rang'd alone,
> And wander'd in the kingdoms, once her own.
> [I.13, 17–18, 25–26]

Smith: Was she *alone* when *the sacred brood* was *increas'd?*

Bays: Why, thy head's running on the Mouse again, but I hope a
Church may be *alone,* though the members be *increas'd,* mayn't it?

Johnson: Certainly, Mr. Bays, a Church which is a diffusive body
of men can much less be said to be *alone.*

Bays: But are you really of that opinion? Take it from me, Mr.
Johnson, you are wrong; however, to oblige you, I'll clap in some
simile or other about the children of Israel, and it shall do.

Smith: Will you pardon me one word more, Mr. Bays? What
could the Mouse (for I suppose you mean her now) do more than
range in the *kingdoms,* when they were her own?

Bays: Do? Why she *reigned,* had a diadem, scepter and ball, till
they deposed her.

[j.] *sanguis . . . ecclesiae:* Cf. Tertullian, *Apologeticus,* 50; Tilley, B457.

Smith: Now her sons are so *increas'd,* she may try t'other pull [k] for't.

Bays: Egad, and so she may before I have done with her. It has cost me some pains to clear her title. Well, but mum for that, Mr. Smith.

> The common hunt, she tim'rously pass'd by,
> For they, made tame, disdain'd her company;
> They grinn'd, she in a fright tripp'd o'er the green,
> For she was lov'd, wherever she was seen. [I.27–34]

Johnson: Well said, little Bays, i'faith the critic must have a great deal of leisure that attacks those verses.

Bays: Egad, I'll warrant him, whoe'er he is, *offendet solido.* But I go on:

> The independent beast—[I.35]

Smith: Who is that, Mr. Bays?

Bays: Why, a Bear. Pox, is not that obvious enough?

> —In groans her hate express'd. [I.36]

Which, egad, is very natural to that animal. Well! there's for the *Independent.* Now the *Quaker.* What do you think I call him?

Smith: Why, a Bull, for ought I know.

Bays: A bull! O Lord! A bull! No, no, a *Hare, a quaking Hare—armarillis,*[l] because she wears armor—'tis the same figure, and I am proud to say it, Mr. Johnson, no man knows how to pun in heroics but myself. Well, you shall hear:

> She thought, and reason good, the quaking Hare
> Her cruel foe, because she would not swear
> And had profess'd neutrality. [I.37–38]

Johnson: A shrewd reason that, Mr. Bays, but what wars were there?

Bays: Wars! why there had been bloody wars, though they were pretty well reconciled now. Yet to bring in two or three such fine things as these, I don't tell you the Lion's peace was proclaimed till

---

[k.] *pull:* "A trial of strength . . . a bout, a set-to."

[l.] *armarillis:* Cf. *The Rehearsal,* I.1: "*Bays.* Why, I make 'em call her *armarillis,* because of her armor—ha, ha, ha!"

fifty pages after, though 'twas really done before I had finished
my poem.

> Next her, the buffoon Ape, his body bent,
> And paid at church a courtier's compliment. [I.39–42]

That galls somewhere. Egad, I can't leave it off, though I were cudg-
elled every day for it.

> The bristl'd baptist Boar, impure as he—[I.43]

Smith: As who?
Bays: As the *courtier,* let 'em e'en take it as they will, egad, I
seldom come amongst 'em.

> Was whiten'd with the foam of sanctity.
> The Wolf with belly gaunt his rough crest rears
> And pricks up—[I.161, 164]

Now in one word will I abuse the whole party most damnably—*and
pricks up*—egad, I am sure you'll laugh—*his predestinating ears!*
Prithee, Mr. Johnson, remember little Bays, when next you see a
Presbyterian, and take notice if he has not predestination in the
shape of his ear. I have studied men so long, I'll undertake to know
an Arminian by the setting of his wig.

His predestinating ears—egad, there's ne'er a Presbyterian shall
dare to show his head without a border!ᵐ I'll put 'em to that
expense.

Smith: Pray, Mr. Bays, if any of 'em should come over to the
Royal Party, would their ears alter?
Bays: Would they? Aye, egad, they would shed their fanatical
lugs and have just such well-turned ears as I have. Mind this ear—
this is a true Roman ear. Mine are much changed for the better
within this two years.
Smith: Then if ever the Party should chance to fail, you might
lose 'em—*for what may change, may fall.*
Bays: Mind, mind—

> These firey Zwinglius, meager Calvin bred. [I.180–81]

Smith: Those I suppose are some outlandish beasts, Mr. Bays.
Bays: Beasts! A good mistake! Why they were the chief Reformers,

---

ᵐ· *border:* "A plait or braid of hair . . . worn round the forehead or temples."

but here I put 'em in so bad company because they were enemies to my Mouse, and anon when I am warm'd, egad, you shall hear me call 'em *doctors, captains, horses,* and *horsemen* in the very same breath [II.114–20]. You shall hear how I go on now,

> Or else reforming Corah spawn'd this class,
> When opening earth made way for all to pass. [I.184–89]

Johnson: For *all,* Mr. Bays?
Bays: Yes. They were all lost there, but some of 'em were thrown up again at the Leman Lake, as a Catholic Queen [n] sunk at Charing Cross and rose again at Queenhythe.

> The Fox and he came shuffled in the dark,
> If ever they were stow'd in Noah's Ark. [I.190–91]

Here I put a *quaere,* whether there were any Socinians before the Flood, which I'm not very well satisfied in. I have been lately apt to believe that the world was drowned for that heresy, which, among friends, made me leave it.

> Quicken'd with fire below, these monsters breed
> In fenny Holland and in fruitful Tweed. [I.208–09]

Now to write something new and out of the way, to elevate and surprise and all that, I fetch, you see, this *quickening fire* from the bottom of bogs and rivers.
Johnson: Why, faith, that's as ingenious a contrivance as the virtuoso's making a burning glass of ice.
Bays: Why, was there ever any such thing? Let me perish if ever I heard of it. The fancy was sheer new to me, and I thought no man had reconciled those elements but myself. Well, gentlemen, thus far I have followed Antiquity, and as Homer has numbered his ships so I have ranged my beasts. Here is my Boar and my Bear, and my Fox and my Wolf, and the rest of 'em all against my poor Mouse. Now what do you think I do with all these?

[n.] Catholic Queen: In *Animadversions,* Milton refers to "that old wives' tale of a certain Queen of England that sunk at Charing Cross and rose up at Queenhythe." A popular ballad confused Queen Eleanor, the wife of Edward I, whose memorial stood at Charing Cross, with Queen Eleanor, Edward's mother and wife of Henry III, associated with Queenhythe: *A Warning Piece to England Against Pride and Wickedness. Being the Fall of Queen Eleanor, Wife of Edward the First, King of England, who by her Pride, by God's Judgment, sunk into the ground at Charing Cross and rose at Queenhythe* (Wright-Spears).

Smith: Faith, I don't know. I suppose you make 'em fight.

Bays: Fight! Egad, I'd as soon make 'em dance. No, I do no earthly thing with 'em, nothing at all, egad. I think they have played their parts sufficiently already. I have walked 'em out, showed 'em to the company, and raised your expectation. And now whilst you hope to see 'em baited and are dreaming of blood and battles, they skulk off, and you hear no more of 'em.

Smith: Why, faith, Mr. Bays, now you have been at such expense in setting forth their characters, it had been too much to have gone through with 'em.

Bays: Egad, so it had. And then I'll tell you another thing, 'tis not everyone that reads a poem through. And therefore I fill the first part with flowers, figures, fine language, and all that, and then, egad, sink by degrees, till at last I write but little better than other people [Preface, 113–123]. And whereas most authors creep servilely after the Old Fellows ° and strive to grow upon their readers, I take another course. I bring in all my characters together, and let 'em see I could go on with 'em, but, egad, I won't.

Johnson: Could go on with 'em, Mr. Bays! There's nobody doubts that. You have a most peculiar genius that way.

Bays: Oh! dear sir, you are mighty obliging, but I must needs say at a fable or an emblem, I think, no man comes near me, indeed, I have studied it more than any man. Did you ever take notice, Mr. Johnson, of a little thing that has taken mightily about town, a *Cat with a Top-knot?* ᵖ

Johnson: Faith, sir, 'tis mightily pretty. I saw it at the coffeehouse.

Bays: 'Tis a trifle hardly worth owning. I was t'other day at Will's throwing out something of that nature, and, egad, the hint was taken and out came that picture. Indeed, the poor fellow was so civil to present me with a dozen of 'em for my friends. I think I have one here in my pocket. Would you please to accept it, Mr. Johnson?

Johnson: Really, 'tis very ingenious.

Bays: Oh Lord! Nothing at all. I could design twenty of 'em in an hour, if I had but witty fellows about me to draw 'em. I was proffer'd a pension to go into Holland and contrive their emblems. But, hang 'em, they are dull rogues and would spoil my invention.

°· *the Old Fellows:* i.e. the Ancients.

ᵖ· *Cat with a Top-knot:* Scott notes that "there is a copy of this old caricature in Luttrell's Collection" (*10,* 257). I have been unable to locate the print.

But come, gentlemen, let us return to our business, and here I'll give you a delicate description of a man.

Smith: But how does that come in?

Bays: Come in? Very naturally. I was talking of a Wolf and that supposes a wood, and then I clap an epithet to 't and call it a Celtic Wood. Now when I was there, I could not help thinking of the French persecution, and, egad, from all these thoughts I took occasion to rail at the French King and show that he was not of the same make with other men, which thus I prove:

> The Divine Blacksmith in th'abyss of light,
> Yawning and lolling with a careless beat,
> Struck out the mute creation at a heat.
> But he work'd hard to hammer out our souls;
> He blew the bellows and stirr'd up the coals;
> Long time he thought and could not on a sudden
> Knead up with unskimm'd milk this reas'ning pudding.
> Tender and mild within its bag it lay
> Confessing still the softness of its clay,
> And kind as milkmaids on their wedding day.
> Till pride of empire, lust, and hot desire
> Did overboil him, like too great a fire,
> And understanding grown, misunderstood,
> Burn'd him to th'pot and sour'd his curdled blood.
>
> [I.253–60; 270–77]

Johnson: But sure this is a little profane, Mr. Bays.

Bays: Not at all. Does not Virgil bring in his god Vulcan working at the anvil?

Johnson: Aye, sir, but never thought his hands the fittest to make a pudding.

Bays: Why do you imagine him an earthly, dirty blacksmith? 'Gad, you make it profane, indeed. I'll tell you there's as much difference betwixt 'em, egad, as betwixt my Man and Milton's. But now, gentlemen, the plot thickens, here comes my t'other Mouse, the City Mouse.

> A spotted Mouse, the prettiest next the white,
> Ah! were her spots wash'd out, as pretty quite,
> With phylacteries on her forehead spread,

> Crosier in hand and miter on her head,
> Three steeples argent on her sable shield—
> Liv'd in the city and disdain'd the field.
>
> [I.327–29, 399, 395; III.194]

Johnson: This is a glorious Mouse, indeed! But, as you have dressed her, we don't know whether she be Jew, Papist, or Protestant.

Bays: Let me embrace you, Mr. Johnson, for that. You take it right. She is a mere Babel of religions, and therefore she's a spotted Mouse here and will be a Mule, presently. But to go on:

> This Princess—

Smith: What Princess, Mr. Bays?

Bays: Why this Mouse, for I forgot to tell you an old Lion made a left-hand marriage with her mother [I.351–56], and begot on her body Elizabeth Schism, who was married to Timothy Sacrilege, and had issue Graceless Heresy. Who all give the same coat with their mother, *three steeples argent,* as I told you before.

> This Princess though estrang'd from what was best,
> Was least deform'd, because reform'd the least. [I.408–09]

There's *de* and *re* as good, egad, as ever was.

> She in a masquerade of mirth and love
> Mistook the bliss of Heav'n for bacchanals above,
> And grubb'd the thorns beneath our tender feet,
> To make the paths of Paradise more sweet. [I.382–87]

There's a jolly Mouse for you. Let me see anybody else that can show you such another. Here now have I one damnable severe reflecting line, but I want a rhyme to it. Can you help me, Mr. Johnson?

> She—
> Humbly content to be despis'd at home,

Johnson: Which is too narrow infamy for some.

Bays: Sir, I thank you, now I can go on with it.

> Whose merits are diffus'd from pole to pole,
> Where winds can carry, and where waves can roll. [II.552–53]

Johnson: But does not this reflect upon some of your friends, Mr. Bays?

Bays: 'Tis no matter for that. Let me alone to bring myself off. I'll tell you, lately I writ a damn'd libel on a whole party, sheer point and satire all through, egad. Called 'em rogues, dogs, and all the names I could think of, but with an exceeding deal of wit—that I must needs say. Now it happened, before I could finish this piece, the scheme of affairs was altered, and those people were no longer beasts. Here was a plunge now. Should I lose my labor or libel my friend? 'Tis not everybody's talent to find a salvo for this. But what do me? I but write a smooth, delicate preface, wherein I tell them that *the satire was not intended to them* [Preface, 21–22], and this did the business.

Smith: But if it was not intended to them against whom it was writ, certainly it had no meaning at all.

Bays: Poh! There's the trick on't. Poor fools, they took it, and were satisfied, and yet it mauled 'em damnably, egad!

Smith: Why faith, Mr. Bays, there's this very contrivance in the Preface to *Dear Joy's Jests.*[q]

Bays: What a devil, do you think that I'd steal from such an author? Or ever read it?

Smith: I can't tell, but you sometimes read as bad. I have heard you quote *Reynard the Fox.*

Bays: Why, there's it now. Take it from me, Mr. Smith, there is as good morality and as sound precepts in the delectable *History of Reynard the Fox,* as in any book I know, except Seneca. Pray tell me, where in any other author could I have found so pretty a name for a wolf as Isgrim? But prithee, Mr. Smith, give me no more trouble and let me go on with my Mouse.

> One evening, when she went away from Court,
> Levees and couchees pass'd without resort. [I.511, 516]

There's Court language for you. Nothing gives a verse so fine a turn as an air of good breeding.

Smith: But, methinks, the *levees* and *couchees* of a Mouse are too great, especially when she is walking from Court to the cooler shades.

Bays: Egad, now have you forgot what I told you—that she was a Princess! But pray mind, here the two Mice meet:

q. *Dear Joy's Jests:* "Dear joy" was a "familiar appellation for an Irishman." If such a book really existed, it has thus far not been identified. The reference may be more broadly to a "Dear joy's witticism—a distinction without a difference": *Vox cleri pro rege,* 1688, p. 47.

> She met the Country Mouse, whose fearful face
> Beheld from far the common watering place,
> Nor durst approach—[I.528–30]

Smith: Methinks, Mr. Bays, this Mouse is strangely altered since she *feared no danger.*

Bays: Gadsokers! Why no more she does not yet fear either man or beast. But, poor creature, she's afraid of the water, for she could not swim, as you see by this:

> Nor durst approach, till with an awful roar
> The sov'reign Lion bade her fear no more. [I.530–31]

But besides, 'tis above thirty pages off that I told you she *feared no danger,* and, egad, if you will have no variation of the character, you must have the same thing over and over again. 'Tis the beauty of writing to strike you still with something new. Well, but to proceed:

> But when she had this sweetest Mouse in view,
> Good Lord, how she admir'd her heav'nly hue! [I.542–43]

Here now to show you I am Master of all styles I let myself down from the majesty of Virgil to the sweetness of Ovid.

> Good Lord, how she admir'd her heav'nly hue!

What more easy and familiar! I writ this line for the ladies. The little rogues will be so fond of me to find I can yet be so tender. I hate such a rough, unhewn fellow as Milton, that a man must sweat to read him. Egad, you may run over this and be almost asleep.

> Th' immortal Mouse who saw the viceroy come [I.549]
> So far to see her, did invite her home.

There's a pretty name now for the spotted Mouse, the *viceroy!*

Smith: But pray, why d'ye call her so?

Bays: Why! Because it sounds prettily. I'll call her the *crown-general* presently, [II.410] if I've a mind to it. Well—

> did invite her home
> To smoke a pipe and o'er a sober pot
> Discourse of Oates and Bedloe, and the Plot.
> She made a curtsy, like a civil dame,
> And, being much a gentlewoman, came. [I.570]

Well, gentlemen, here's my first part finished, and I think I have kept my word with you, and given it the *majestic turn of heroic poesy.* The rest *being matter of dispute, I had not such frequent occasion for the magnificence of verse* [Preface, 113–23] though, egad, they speak very well. And I have heard men, and considerable men, too, talk the very same things a great deal worse.

Johnson: Nay, without doubt, Mr. Bays, they have received no small advantage from the smoothness of your numbers.

Bays: Aye, aye, I can do't, if I list, though you must not think I have been so dull as to mind these things myself, but 'tis the advantage of our coffeehouse, that from their talk one may write a very good polemical discourse without ever troubling one's head with the Books of Controversy. For I can take the slightest of their arguments and clap 'em pertly into four verses, which shall stare any London divine in the face. Indeed, your knotty reasonings with a long train of majors and minors, and the Devil and all, are too barbarous for my style, but, egad, I can flourish better with one of these twinkling arguments, than the best of 'em can fight with t'other. But we return to our Mouse, and now I've brought 'em together let 'em e'en speak for themselves, which they will do extremely well, or I'm mistaken; and pray observe, gentlemen, if in one you don't find all the delicacy of a luxurious City Mouse and in the other all the plain simplicity of a sober, serious Matron.

> "Dame," said the lady of the spotted muff, [I.572]
> "Methinks your tiff is sour, your cates mere stuff."

There, did not I tell you she'd be nice?

> "Your pipe's so foul that I disdain to smoke,
> And the weed worse than e'er Tom Jenner took." ʳ

Smith: I did not hear she had a *spotted muff* before.

Bays: Why no more she has not now. But she has a skin that might make a *spotted muff.* There's a pretty figure now, unknown to the Ancients.

ʳ· *Tom Jenner:* Thomas Jenner (fl. 1631–56), author, engraver, and publisher. In 1631 he published a group of engravings entitled *Soul's Solice,* the last of which "represents a person in gay attire, . . . sitting and smoking at a table, and is accompanied by a poem" the burden of which is, "thus think, then drink tobacco" (*DNB*).

"Leave, leave" (* she's earnest, you see) "this hoary shed
    and lonely hills,
And eat with me at Groleau's, smoke at Will's.
What wretch would nibble on a hanging-shelf,
When at Pontack's he may regale himself?
Or to the house of cleanly Rhenish go,
Or that at Charing Cross, or that in Channel Row?" [s]

Do you mark me now? I would by this represent the vanity of a
town fop, who pretends to be acquainted at all those good houses,
though perhaps he ne'er was in 'em. But hark! she goes on:

"Come, at a crown a head ourselves we'll treat,
Champagne our liquor and ragouts our meat.
Then hand in hand we'll go to Court, dear cuz,
To visit Bishop Martin and King Buz.[t]
With evening wheels we'll drive about the park,
Finish at Locket's [u] and reel home i'th'dark.
Break clattering windows and demolish doors
Of English manufactures—pimps and whores." [II.563–64]

Johnson: Methinks a pimp or a whore is an odd sort of a *manu-
facture*, Mr. Bays.

Bays: I call 'em so, to give the Parliament a hint not to suffer so
many of 'em to be exported, to the decay of the trade at home.[v]

With these allurements Spotted did invite
From hermit's cell the female proselyte.
Oh! with what ease we follow such a guide,
Where souls are starv'd and senses gratifi'd. [I.365–66]

Now would not you think she's going? But, egad, you're mistaken.
You shall hear a long argument about infallibility, before she stirs
yet.

[s.] "The Rhenish Wine Tavern in Channel Row was kept by Prior's uncle, Arthur
Prior; the Rummer Tavern at Charing Cross was kept by another relative, Samuel
Prior" (Wright-Spears).
  Pontack's: A famous French ordinary located in Abchurch Lane.
  Groleau's: Unidentified.
[t.] *Bishop Martin and King Buz:* Father Edward Petre, James' chief advisor, and
Gilbert Burnet, represented by the Buzzard in *HP*, III.
[u.] *Locket's:* The well-known ordinary at Charing Cross.
[v.] *the decay of the trade:* A common complaint, of course, but particularly apt since
the days of the Plot and during the first months of James' reign; see, for example,
The Tragi-Comedy of Titus Oates, 13–14 and n. and *Pepys Ballads, 3,* 298.

But here the White, by observation wise,
Who long on Heav'n had fix'd her prying eyes, [II.665–66]
With thoughtful countenance and grave remark,
Said, "Or my judgment fails me, or 'tis dark.
Lest therefore we should stray and not go right,
Through the brown horror of the starless night,
Hast thou infallibility, that wight?"
Sternly the savage grinn'd and thus repli'd:
"That mice may err was never yet deni'd." [II.60–65]
"That I deny," said the immortal Dame,
"There is a guide—Gad, I've forgot his name—
Who lives in Heav'n or Rome, the Lord knows where. [II.66–68]
Had we but him, sweetheart, we could not err.

Spotted
Mouse
loquitur.

But hark you, sister, this is but a whim,
For still we want a guide to find out him."

Here you see I don't trouble myself to keep on the narration, but
write *White speaks* or *Dapple speaks* by the side. But when I get
any noble thought which I envy a mouse should say, I clap it down
in my own person with a *poeta loquitur*, which, take notice, is a surer
sign of a fine thing in my writings than a hand in the margin any-
where else. Well, now says White:

> "What need we find him? We have certain proof
> That he is somewhere, dame, and that's enough;
> For if there is a guide that knows the way,
> Although we know not him, we cannot stray."

That's true, egad! Well said, White! You see her adversary has
nothing to say for herself, and therefore to confirm the victory, she
shall make a simile.

Smith: Why then I find similes are as good after victory, as after
a surprise.

Bays: Every jot, egad! or rather better. Well, she can do it two
ways, either about *emission or reception of light* [II.75–76], or
else about Epsom waters, but I think the last is most familiar. Therefore speak, my pretty one!

> "As though 'tis controverted in the school,
> If waters pass by urine or by stool.
> Shall we who are philosophers thence gather
> From this dissension that they work by neither?"

And, egad, she's in the right on't. But mind now, she comes upon her swap!

> "All this I did, your arguments to try."

And, egad, if they had been never so good, this next line confutes 'em.

> "Hear and be dumb, thou wretch; that guide am I." [II.398]

There's a surprise for you now! How sneakingly t'other looks! Was not that pretty now, to make her ask for a *guide* first and then tell her she was one? Who could have thought that this little Mouse had the *Pope* and a whole *General Council* in her belly? Now Dapple had nothing to say to this, and therefore you'll see she grows peevish:

> "Come, leave your cracking tricks and, as they say,
> Use not that barber that trims time, delay—" [III.499–501]

Which, egad, is new and my own—

> "I've eyes as well as you to find the way."
> Then on they jogg'd. "And since an hour of talk
> Might cut a banter on the tedious walk,
> As I remember," said the sober Mouse,
> "I've heard much talk of the Wits' coffeehouse."
> "Thither," says Brindle, "thou shalt go and see
> Priests sipping coffee, sparks and poets tea;
> Here rugged Frieze, there Quality well dress'd,
> These baffling the Grand Seigneur, those the Test.
> And hear shrewd guesses made and reasons given,
> That human laws were never made in Heav'n. [III.679]
> But above all, what shall oblige thy sight
> And fill thy eyeballs with a vast delight
> Is the Poetic Judge of sacred wit,
> Who does i'th'darkness of his glory sit.
> And, as the moon who first receives the light
> With which she makes these nether regions bright,
> So does he shine, reflecting from afar
> The rays he borrow'd from a better star. [I.501–04]
> For rules, which from Corneille and Rapin flow,
> Admir'd by all the scribbling herd below;

From French Tradition while he does dispense
Unerring truths, 'tis schism—a damn'd offense—
To question his, or trust your private sense."

Hah! Is not that right, Mr. Johnson? Gad forgive me, he is fast
asleep! Oh, the damn'd stupidity of this age! Asleep! Well, sir, since
you're so drowsy, your humble servant!
Johnson: Nay, pray, Mr. Bays. Faith, I heard you all the while.
"The white Mouse. . . ."
Bays: "The white Mouse!" Aye, aye, I thought how you heard me.
Your servant, sir, your servant.
Johnson: Nay, dear Bays. Faith, I beg thy pardon. I was up late
last night. Prithee, lend me a little snuff—and go on.
Bays: Go on! Pox, I don't know where I was. Well, I'll begin here,
mind, now they are both come to town.

But now at Piccadilly they arrive
And taking coach t'wards Temple Bar they drive;
But at St. Clement's Church eat out the back
And slipping through the palsgrave bilk'd poor hack.

There's the *utile* which ought to be in all poetry. Many a young
Templar will save his shilling by this strategem of my Mice.
Smith: Why, will any young Templar eat out the back of a coach?
Bays: No, egad, but you'll grant it is mighty natural for a Mouse.

Thence to the Devil and ask'd if Chanticleer
Of clergy kind or Councellor Chough was there,
Or Mr. Dove, a Pigeon of renown,
By his high crop and corny gizzard known,
Or sister Partlet, with the hooded head.
"No, sir. She's hooted hence," said Will, "and fled."
"Why so?" "Because she would not pray abed."
[III.1072, 959, 1024–25]

Johnson (aside): 'Sdeath! Who can keep awake at such stuff? Pray,
Mr. Bays, lend me your box again.
Bays: Mr. Johnson, how d'ye like that box? Pray, take notice of it.
'Twas given me by *a person of honor* [w] for looking over a paper of

w. *a person of honor:* "Dryden assisted Sir William Soames with his translation of
Boileau's *Art of Poetry*, 1683, and Mulgrave . . . and possibly Roscommon with
several pieces" (Wright-Spears).

verses, and indeed I put in all the lines that were worth anything in
the whole poem. Well, but where were we? Oh! Here they are, just
going up stairs into the Apollo, from whence my White takes occasion to talk very well of *Tradition*.

> "Thus to the place where Jonson sat we climb,
> Leaning on the same rail that guided him;
> And whilst we thus on equal helps rely,
> Our wit must be as true, our thoughts as high.
> For as an author happily compares
> Tradition to a well-fix'd pair of stairs, [II.218–21]
> So this the *scala sancta* we believe,
> By which his Traditive Genius we receive.
> Thus every step I take my spirits soar,
> And I grow more a wit, and more, and more."

There's humor! Is not that the liveliest image in the world of a
Mouse's going up a pair of stairs? *More a wit, and more, and more!*

Smith: Mr. Bays, I beg your pardon heartily. I must be rude. I
have a particular engagement at this time, and I see you are not near
an end yet.

Bays: Gadsokers! Sure you won't serve me so. All my finest descriptions and best discourse is yet to come.

Smith: Troth, sir, if 'twere not an extraordinary concern I could
not leave you.

Bays: Well—but you shall take a little more, and here I'll pass
pass over two dainty *episodes of Swallows, Swifts, Chickens, and
Buzzards.*

Johnson: I know not why they should come in, except to make
yours the longest fable that ever was told.

Bays: Why, the excellence of a fable is in the length of it. Æsop,
indeed, like a slave as he was made little, short, simple stories, with
a dry moral at the end of 'em, and could not form any noble design.
But here I give you fable upon fable, and after you are satisfied
with beasts in the first course, serve you up a delicate dish of fowl
for the second. Now, I was at all this pains to abuse one particular
person, for, egad, I'll tell you what a trick he served me. I was once
Varillas   translating a very good *French author,*[x] but, being something long

---

[x.] *French author:* "Dryden translated, or intended to translate Varillas' *History of
Heresies* . . . ; but the translation was never published. Gilbert Burnet assumed that

about it—as you know a man is not always in the humor—what does this Jack do, but puts out an Answer to my friend, before I had half finished the translation. So there was three whole months lost upon his account. But I think I have my revenge on him sufficiently, for I let all the world know that he is a *tall, broadbacked, lusty fellow,* of a *brown complexion, fair behavior,* a *fluent tongue,* and *taking* amongst the *women;* and, to top it all, that he's much a *scholar,* more a *wit,* and owns but *two sacraments* [III.1141–58, *passim*]. Don't you think this fellow will hang himself? But besides, I have so nicked his character in a name as will make you split. I call him— egad, I won't tell you unless you remember what I said of him.

Smith: Why, that he was much a scholar and more a wit—

Bays: Right. And his name is *Buzzard!* Ha, ha, ha!

Johnson: Very proper indeed, sir.

Bays: Nay, I have a farther fetch in it yet than perhaps you imagine, for his true name begins with a *B,* which makes me slily contrive him this to begin with the same letter. There's a pretty device, Mr. Johnson. I learned it, I must needs confess, from that ingenious sport, "I love my love with an *A,* because she's *A*miable," [y] and if you could but get a knot of merry fellows together, you should see how little Bays would top 'em all at it, egad!

Smith: Well, but good faith, Mr. Bays, I must leave you. I am half an hour past my time.

Bays: Well, I've done, I've done. Here are eight hundred verses upon a rainy night and a bird's nest, and there's three hundred more, translated from two *Paris Gazettes,* in which the Spotted Mouse gives an account of the Treaty of Peace between the *Czars of Muscovy* and the *Emperor* [III.1277], which is a piece of news White does not believe, and this is her answer. I am resolved you shall hear it, for in it I have taken occasion to prove *Oral Tradition* better than *Scripture.* Now you must know 'tis sincerely my opinion that it had been better for the world if we ne'er had any *Bibles* at all—

"E'er that *Gazette* was printed," said the White,
"Our Robin told another story quite.

---

his attack upon Varillas (*Reflections on Mr. Varillas' History* . . . Amsterdam, 1686) caused Dryden to abandon the project, and that the incident explained Dryden's animus against him in *HP*" (Wright-Spears).

[y]. Cf. Marvell's *Rehearsal Transpros'd, Complete Works,* ed. Rev. Alexander Grosart, 1873, *3,* 62.

This Oral Truth more safely I believ'd:
My ears cannot, your eyes may be deceiv'd.
By word of mouth unerring maxims flow,
And preaching's best, if understood, or no.
Words, I confess, bound by and trip so light,
We have not time to take a steady sight; [I.31–32]
Yet fleeting thus are plainer than when writ,
To long examination they submit.
Hard things—"

Mr. Smith, if these two lines don't recompense your stay, ne'er trust John Bays again—

"Hard things at the first blush are clear and full;
God mends on second thoughts, but man grows dull." [I.252–56]

Egad, I judge of all men by myself. 'Tis so with me. I never strove to be very exact in anything but I spoiled it.

Smith: But allowing your character to be true, is it not a little too severe?

Bays: 'Tis no matter for that. These general reflections are daring and savor most of a *noble genius* that spares neither *friend nor foe.*

Johnson: Are you never afraid of a drubbing for that daring of your *noble genius?*

Bays: Afraid! Why Lord, you make so much of a beating,[z] egad, 'tis no more to me than a flea biting. No, no, if I can but be witty upon 'em, let 'em e'en lay on. I'faith, I'll ne'er balk my fancy to save my carcass. Well, but we must dispatch, Mr. Smith.

Thus did they merrily carouse all day,
And like the gaudy fly their wings display;
And sip the sweets, and bask in great Apollo's ray.

Well, there's an end of the entertainment. And, Mr. Smith, if your affairs would have permitted, you would have heard the best bill of fare that ever was serv'd up in heroics. But here follows a dispute shall recommend itself, I'll say nothing for it. For Dapple, who you must know was a Protestant all this while, trusts her own judgment and foolishly dislikes the wine, upon which our Innocent does so run her down that she has not one word to say for herself, but what I

[z.] *beating:* A reference to the infamous assault on Dryden in Rose Alley on 18 Dec. 1679.

put in her mouth; and, egad, you may imagine they won't be very good ones, for she has disobliged me like an ingrate.

> "Sirrah," says Brindle, "thou hast brought us wine,
> Sour to my taste, and to my eyes unfine."
> Says Will, "All gentlemen like it." "Ah!" says White,
> "What is approv'd by them must needs be right.
> 'Tis true, I thought it bad, but if the House
> Commend it, I submit—a private Mouse."

Mind that, mind the decorum and deference which our Mouse pays to the company.

> "Nor to their Catholic consent oppose
> My erring judgment and reforming nose."

Ah! ah! there she has nicked her. That's up to the hilts, egad, and you shall see Dapple resents it.

> "Why, what a devil, shan't I trust my eyes?
> Must I drink stum because the rascal lies
> And palms upon us Catholic consent
> To give sophisticated brewings vent?"
> Says White, "What ancient evidence can sway,
> If you must argue thus and not obey? [I.62–63]
> Drawers must be trusted through whose hands convey'd
> You take the liquor, or you spoil the trade.
> For sure those honest fellows have no knack
> Of putting off stumm'd claret for Pontac.[a]
> How long, alas, would the poor vintner last,
> If all that drink must judge, and every guest
> Be allow'd to have an understanding taste?"
> Thus she. Nor could the Panther well enlarge
> With weak defense against so strong a charge. [II.267–68]

There I call her a *Panther* because she's spotted, which is such a blot to the *Reformation* as, I warrant 'em, they will never claw off, egad!

> But with a weary yawn that show'd her pride,
> Said, "Spotless was a villain, and she lied."

[a.] *stumm'd claret:* Wine with grape-juice added to revive fermentation.
  Pontac: A sweet red wine of the Basses Pyrénées in the south of France.

White saw her canker'd malice at that word,
And said her prayers and drew her Delphic sword.
T'other cri'd "Murder," and her rage restrain'd;
And thus her passive character maintain'd.
But now alas—

Mr. Johnson, pray mind me this. Mr. Smith, I'll ask you to stay no
longer, for this that follows is so engaging; hear me but two lines,
egad, and go away afterwards if you can.

But now, alas, I grieve, I grieve to tell
What sad mischance these pretty things befell,
These birds of beasts—

There's a tender expression, *birds of beasts*. 'Tis the greatest
affront that you can put upon any *bird* to call it *beast of a bird;* and
a *beast* is so fond of being called a *bird,* as you can't imagine
[III.1013].

These birds of beasts, these learned reas'ning Mice,
Were separated, banish'd in a trice.
Who would be learned for their sakes, who wise?

Aye, who indeed? There's a *pathos,* egad, gentlemen, if that won't
move you, nothing will, I can assure you. But here's the sad thing
I was afraid of—

The Constable, alarmed by this noise,
Enter'd the room, directed by the voice,
And speaking to the Watch, with head aside,
Said, "Desperate cures must be to desperate ills appli'd.
These gentlemen, for so their Fate decrees,
Can ne'er enjoy at once the butt and peace.
When each have sep'rate int'rests of their own,
Two Mice are one too many for a town. [III.759, 1277–78]
By schism they are torn, and therefore, brother,
Look you to one, and I'll secure the other."
Now whether Dapple did to Bridewell ᵇ go,
Or in the stocks all night her fingers blow,
Or in the counter ᶜ lay, concerns not us to know.

ᵇ· *Bridewell:* A house of correction, principally for vagabonds and loose women.
ᶜ· *counter:* The name of certain city prisons for debtors (formerly spelled "compter").

But the immortal Matron, spotless White,
Forgetting Dapple's rudeness, malice, spite,
Look'd kindly back and wept, and said, "Good night."
Ten thousand watchmen waited on this Mouse,
With bills and halberds, to her country house. [III.1297]

This last contrivance I had from a judicious author that makes *ten thousand angels* wait upon his *Hind,* and she asleep too, egad!

Johnson: Come, let's see what we have to pay.

Bays: What a pox, are you in such haste? You han't told me how you like it.

Johnson: Oh, extremely well. Here, drawer!

On the Author of The Hind and Panther

Predestination how can he deny,
Whose nimble Hind is "fated not to die"?
Yet how can she who this receives from fate
Of her own strength receive immortal state?
But in that faith it is not strange to see   5
Choice transubstantiat'd into decree;
Our poet's choice is mere necessity.
His vocal wants admonish him to "range,"
And 'twere great pity he should starve and change.
His praise of Nol obtain'd no lasting boon,   10
Because his hated mem'ry stank so soon.
Now sure he cannot fail of a supply
From a rich mother "fated ne'er to die"?
But how can he receive it from the cowls,
Who likens their beloved nuns to owls?   15
Nor can the sov'reign hand reward his tongue,
Who counts it his prerogative to wrong.
The lawyers' maxims he's allow'd to blame,
"Whose old possession stands till th'elder quits his claim;"

1–9. These lines reemploy various of the strains from *HP,* I.1–8.

10. *His praise of Nol:* Dryden's *Heroic Stanzas* on Cromwell.

15. This statement probably arises from a misreading, deliberate or otherwise, of *HP,* III.1024–25.

19. Cf. *HP,* II.237.

Which since the elder is not pleas'd to quit,　　　20
That this should yield unto its fate, 'tis fit,
Like th' craz'd ruins of's monumental wit,
Whose darkness in th' abyss of light is set;
Though glory blazes round, 'tis darkness yet.

ON THE SAME

To put religion into dogg'rel rhyme
May well befit the Trentists of our time;
For being naked found in holy writ,
They fly for refuge to her fig-leaf'd wit.

DRYDEN'S GHOST

When martial Caesar came to th'crown,
The northern heresy tumbling down,
Prerogative sitting aloft,
And charters in subjection brought,
Then I, the mighty King of Me,　　　5
Became the friend of liberty:
Not liberty of subject, no!
There is no need of that, we know,
When law's well kept, and armies stout
Fence the three nations round about;　　　10

23–24. Cf. *HP*, I.66–67.

4. *fig-leaf'd:* Here, presumably, meaning "flimsy."

1. *Caesar:* James II.

2. *northern heresy:* The Good Old Cause of Presbyterianism (see above, *The West-ern Rebel,* 19 n.).

3. *charters in subjection:* After the failure of the Whigs, Charles endeavored to destroy the remains of the opposition, prevailing upon many of the principal cities of the realm in 1683–84 to forfeit their charters under the threat of *quo warranto* proceedings.

5. Cf. the first part of *Conquest of Granada,* I.i:

> *Almanzor:* No man has more contempt than I of breath,
> But whence hast thou the right to give me death?
> Obeyed as sovereign by thy subjects be,
> But know that I alone am King of Me.

But Liberty of Conscience dear—
That's the beloved character,
When th'Inquisition shall come here.
And now w'are sure we can't but please you:
Mahomet, Nol, Maria, Jesu,   15
Nayler, or Muggleton to ease you.
'Tis known where my vast empires be,
Conscience the Kingdom is of Me.
That Kingdom solely is my own;
To it I being gave alone.   20
The New Atlantis is a banter,
And The Wives' Island of the painter;
All o' Brazil and fairyland
In doting fancy only stand,
While this great kingdom calls me master—   25
The Renegado Poetaster;
And when I die, the Holy Father
Shall my executor be the rather,
Since this and Purgatory stand
Under the same meridian.   30
Here screech owls and night ravens join
Notes to make harmony divine;
Here priest with cloven foot and brother
With cloven tongue claw one another;
And cant does spiritual prayer commence,   35
And memory supplies lost sense;
Loud noise, deep sighs, distorted eyes
Ingredients are of sacrifice;
As if Dissenting son knew way

15–16. *Nol . . . Nayler . . . Muggleton:* Leaders of "heretical" sects: Cromwell; James Nayler (1617?–60), called by Richard Baxter the Quakers' "chief leader" before William Penn; Lodowicke Muggleton (1609–98), founder with John Reeve in about 1651 of the sect that was named after him. He and Reeve claimed to be the "two witnesses" of Revelation (11:3–6). For a similar treatment of the "catholic" nature of the church, see *A Character of the Church of Chichester, POAS,* Yale, *1,* 312.

17–18. Cf. *HP,* Preface, 41–49.

21. *The New Atlantis:* Francis Bacon's philosophic romance, which recounts a visit to the imaginary Pacific island of Bensalem.

22. *the Wives' Island:* Unidentified.

26. *The Renegado Poetaster:* Cf. the attack on Dryden entitled *The Renegado Poet, POAS,* 2, 1703, 168–69.

To Holy Father what to say 40
Without a solemn embassy.
Call the Cornuto home, send d'Adda back,
Envoys and Nuncios we don't lack—
Conclaves and Conventicles in one pack.
The Kings of Brentford ride on steed, 45
And love and honor are agreed.
We Cromwell call the best of Kings,
And of dead Charles say the same things;
And when his successor shall die,
Like strains shall eternize his memory. 50
To this blest kingdom all may come
From Poland, Amsterdam, or Rome:
Here you are welcome, all and some;
Haste, w'are agreed in the same cause,
Recusants t'a few paltry laws; 55
Laws that speak big but cannot bite,
While their interpreters are Wright,
Herbert, and Holloway, and the Baron,
Who over-rules by sturdy warrant.
A Nunnery's here all one with Conventicle; 60
In this they differ: there a mickle
Priest plays his pranks; here the whole brood
Ride, whip, and spur the sisterhood.
A married clergy smells so rank,
No puddle ever so ill stank; 65
But we're agreed that holy Monk
Or Priest come reeking from his punk,
With the same tongue the slaver'd doxy
Can make bread God without a proxy;
As gifted brother first can plead 70

42–3. *Cornuto:* Roger Palmer, Earl of Castlemaine, the oft-cuckolded husband of the Countess.

45. *Kings of Brentford:* Cf. *The Rehearsal,* II.ii, by George Villiers, second Duke of Buckingham; and below, *Hounslow Heath,* 146 and n.

52. *Poland:* Blamed for the Socinian heresy.

57–58. *Wright, Herbert . . . Holloway . . . the Baron:* Robert Wright, Edward Herbert, Richard Holloway, and George Jeffreys, Baron of Wem—all more or less notorious members of James' judiciary. Jeffreys was, of course, Lord Chancellor.

69. *make bread God:* From the Restoration transubstantiation came increasingly to seem the real distinction between Anglican and Catholic.

Two hours with God in prayer, then read
Twelve chapters ere he go to bed,
And in the dark, by conscience led—
Well-guided conscience—find the place
Where dear Tabitha, babe of grace,   75
With longing expectation lies,
Turns up and down the whites of eyes,
Impatient at the strange delays:
And casuists have found out at last
That drunkenness does not break fast.   80
Thus in our morals we agree,
Nor differ we in policy;
Give us but opportunity, and then
Rebels for Conscience once again,
Conclaves' and Conventicles' true men.   85

Le Envoy
To the Poet

Fate often beats the wise and brave,
Degrades the just, advanceth th'knave,
And gives the prince none, or a common, grave.
   Could Bays have been but made a dean
With license to have held his quean,   90
You ne'er had heard of holy church,
Nor atheist Hobbes left in the lurch.
Could holy father done the feat
By argument or pious cheat,
By dint of sword or church's curse,   95
Indulgence still had been at nurse.
   But tender love to Good Old Cause
Suspends the useless penal laws,
Pardons old traitors that they may
Be true to them another day—   100
For loyalty's quite out of play—
Owns all religious pretensions

75. *Tabitha:* The woman of good works raised from the dead by Peter (Acts 9:36–43).
   89. For a discussion of Dryden's candidacy for an academic post, see above *To Mr. Dryden, upon his Declaring himself a Roman Catholic,* 26 n.
   90. *quean:* Dryden's supposed mistress, was Anne Reeves, an actress in the King's Company who became a nun in 1675 (Macdonald, p. 96).

And joins all sects by Comprehensions.
So fiends at wizard's stern command
Are forc'd to make a rope of sand;
And when the jacks have made a pother,
Draining this pool of fish, and t'other,
At last they eat up one another.

103. *Comprehensions:* "Ecclesiastical inclusion; especially the inclusion of Noncon-formists within the Established Church by enlarging the terms of ecclesiastical com-munion."

106. *jacks:* The pike. A curious reference in a pamphlet entitled *A Dialogue between Father Peters and William Penn* [1687] (Wing D1310) may explain:

> *F.P.:* How do you find the Quakers stand affected? I hope you have at least pro-cured me some friends among them.
> *Will.:* I must confess my small endeavors hain't been wanting, but that damned simile of my brother Mead's fish-pond does so stick in their stomachs, that if they should but see one of your character, they'd presently believe they should be devoured as fast as the Devil in the picture swallows down Jesuits, when he s——s whole armies of soldiers. Besides, instead of a pike, they take you for a more devouring otter.

I have not been able to locate the source of the "simile," but it would appear to have come from the pen of William Mead (1628–1713), the Quaker divine, or from the pen of one masquerading as Mead. Penn and Mead had stood trial together in their famous defence of the right to free worship (1670). On 6 Nov. 1687, a Mr. Mead preached before the lord mayor at a conventicle held in Grocers' Hall (*HMC, Downshire*, p. 276; Luttrell, *1*, 419). According to A. G. Matthews, *Calamy Revised*, 1934, pp. 347–48, how-ever, this was Matthew Mead, curate of Shadwell, Stepney, Middlesex. For a similar use of the word "jacks," see above, *Dr. Wild's Ghost*, 60.

The Progress of Popery—I
(Summer–Fall 1687)

"The great design cannot be carried on without numbers; numbers cannot be had without converts, the old stock not being sufficient; converts will not venture till they have such a law to secure them as hath no exception to it"—thus Halifax writing to William of Orange on 31 May 1687 of the dilemma which confronted James in his attempts to consolidate his position and capitalize on the gains he had made for his faith in the first eighteen months of the reign (Dalrymple, Pt. I, Bk. V, App., p. 70). Halifax's appraisal of affairs was accurate and astute. Despite all James' efforts, conciliatory or coercive, he found Anglican opposition stiffening, while few adherents had come to him. Even after the Toleration, nonconformists realized they could expect no long-term gains. As long as the succession was secure in the Protestant line, Catholic and Dissenter alike could only win a short surcease from the harsh penalties laid on them by the law. For that brief moment of relief they would probably suffer severely. Just as this understanding of the situation undoubtedly prevented many from coming forward to take public office in support of James, so too it inhibited many who might have thought deeply about becoming converts. Few allurements awaited those who might have been willing to support James in his program. The converts generally acted either out of devoutness, as did Dryden, or out of venality. To the Anglican, however, all converts were time-servers. This attitude led to the contradictory point of view that proselytism in high places threatened to subvert the government, but that nevertheless there had been few, if any, conversions of importance. The following hudibrastic satire, *The Converts*, adopts this point of view in its attempt to show all who adhered to James to be beneath contempt.

In addition to the problem of gaining supporters, James found that opposition among the Anglicans was solidifying. Early in March Evelyn, discussing the results of the King's attempts to secure parliamentary backing for the repeal of the Test and penal laws, summed up the general state of affairs:

> . . . to this end most of the parliament men [were] spoken to in his Majesty's closet, and such as refused, if in any place or office of trust, civil or military, put out of their employments. This was a time of great trial. Hardly one of them assenting, which put the Popish interest much backward. The English clergy everywhere very boldly preaching against their superstition and errors, and wonderfully followed by the people. (*4*, 540–41)

Throughout the summer opposition mounted. On 2 July 1687 James finally gave up on his original parliament and dissolved it. By September, when the King began his progress toward Bath, Halifax could report to Orange:

> . . . we do not hear that his observations, or his journey, can give him any great encouragement to build any hopes upon, as to the carrying on some things, which appear every day to be more against the grain. Besides the considerations of conscience and the public interest, it is grown into a point of honor, universally received by the nation, not to change their opinion. (Dalrymple, Pt. I, Bk. V, App., p. 84)

The Englishman's determination was, no doubt, strengthened by verse such as Charles Montagu's *Man of Honor,* purporting to answer William Penn's *Advice to Freeholders and Other Electors of Members who serve in Parliament in Relation to the Penal Laws and the Tests,* &c., 1687, the postscript of which begged "the Church of England to yield to Christ his own throne in the Kingdom of God, and to magistrates their thrones in the kingdom of the world." *The Man of Honor,* one of Montagu's earliest poems, was first ascribed to him in *POAS, 1,* 1697. It later appeared among his *Works* in 1715 and then in *Minor Poets,* 1749. Though none of these witnesses can be called unimpeachable, the ascription seems reasonable enough in light of Montagu's other satire. Whatever we conclude about authorship, however, we may infer something of the poem's success and significance from its position at the head of the collections in *Popery, 1,* 1689, and *The Muses Farewell,* 1689, from the numerous manuscript copies surviving, and from the two pro-James "answers" to

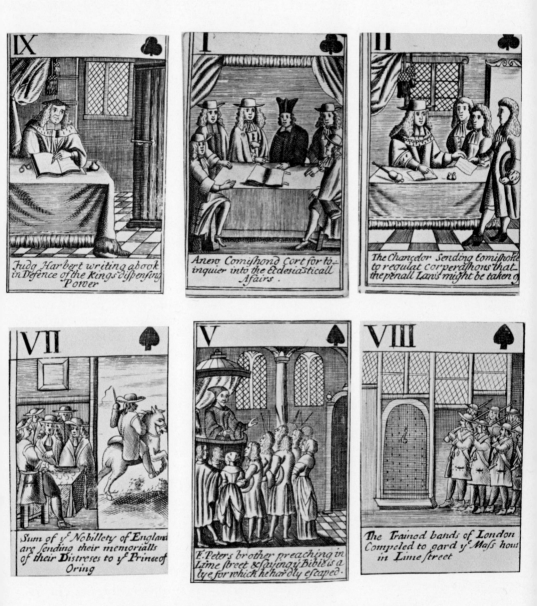

Satirical Playing Cards Illustrating the Progress of Popery, 1686–88

it entitled, *The Man of No Honor* and *The Men of Honor Made Men Worthy*. This last, printed below, displays the vigorous scurrility more normal in verse of the opposition than in that of the party in power.

THE CONVERTS

I did intend in rhymes heroic
To write of converts apostolic,
Describe their persons and their shames,
And leave the world to guess their names;
But soon I thought the scoundrel theme   5
Was for heroic song too mean;
Their characters we'll then rehearse
In burlesque or in dogg'rel verse;
Of earls, of lords, of knights I'll sing
That chang'd their faith to please their King.   10

The first, an antiquated lord,
A walking mummy, in a word;
Moves cloth'd in plasters aromatic,
And flannel, by the help of a stick,
And like a grave and noble peer   15
Outlives his sense by sixty year;
And—what an honest man would anger—
Outlives the fort he built at Tangier;
By pox and whores long since undone,
Yet loves it still and fumbles on.   20
Why he's a favorite few can guess:
Some say it's for his ugliness,
For often monsters, being rare,
Are valu'd equal to the fair

11. *an antiquated lord:* MS. note in Firth b. 21 (broadside) refers to Henry Mordaunt (1624?–97), second Earl of Peterborough. He had been appointed first Governor of Tangier (see 18) in 1661 at the time of its acquisition from Portugal as part of Catherine of Braganza's dowry. Insufficient funds and manpower kept him from developing the fort, and in 1662 he resigned his post. Tangier was evacuated and its fortifications demolished in 1683–84.

(For in his mistresses kind James   25
Loves ugliness in its extremes);
But others say 'tis plainly seen,
'Tis for the choice he made o'th'Queen,
When he the King and nation blest
With off-spring of the House of Este,   30
A dame whose affability
Equals her generosity:
Oh, well-match'd pair, who frugally are bent
To live without the aids of parliament!
All this and more the peer perform'd,   35
Then to complete his virtues, turn'd;
But 'twas not conscience or devotion,
The hopes of riches or promotion,
That made his lordship first to vary,

25–26. James' mistresses were nortoriously unattractive. His brother once quipped that James "had his mistresses given him by his priests for penance" (Burnet, *1*, 169).

28. *the choice he made o'th'Queen:* Peterborough in 1673 travelled about the continent as James' ambassador extraordinary interviewing possible candidates for the royal hand. Peterborough's activities and the occasional reports he returned to England caused considerable amusement. Late in the summer he was sent to Italy to offer a proposal of marriage to Princess Mary, daughter of Alfonso IV d'Este, Duke of Modena. The Princess, who had long desired to devote her life to religious works by entering a nunnery, hesitated at first. Finally, she was persuaded to the marriage by a brief from Pope Innocent X, which stressed the service she would do her faith by pursuing the marriage. (The strength of her faith, which at times reached the point of superstition or fanaticism during her later years, probably received constant support from her reflecting on this papal argument with which she had been confronted as a girl of fifteen.) When she accepted the marriage, her family hesitated on account of James' religious position. But these doubts, too, were overcome with papal assistance, and on 30 Sept. the marriage was performed with Peterborough standing proxy. He then escorted the bride to England, arriving at Dover on 21 Nov. At Court the new Duchess was received warmly and, except with the Queen, found general favor. But she shared the unpopularity of her husband with the populace, who saw in the match an additional proof of York's subservience to France.

34. *without the aids of parliament:* James kept himself free from parliamentary interference but short of parliamentary supply by a series of prorogations which ended on 4 July 1687 with dissolution of his first and only parliament.

36. *turn'd:* Peterborough's conversion came at the end of March 1687 (Luttrell, *1*, 398). Ailesbury reported that when the Countess was complimented "by way of trouble that her lord and she were of two different communions, she replied, 'My Lord hath not changed, but he hath found a religion;' and when the Churchwardens of St. Margaret's, Westminster, asked his lordship if they might dispose of his pew in the church, 'No, no,' he said, 'one doth not know what may happen'" (*Memoirs, 1,* 153).

But 'twas to please his daughter Mary;   40
And she to make retaliation
Is full as lewd in her vocation.
 The next, a caravanish thief,
A lazy mass of damn'd rump beef;
Prodigious guts, no brains at all,   45
But very rhinocerical;
Was marri'd ere the cub was lick'd,
And now not worthy to be kick'd;
By jockies bubbl'd, forc'd to fly,
To save his coat, to Italy,   50
Where Haines and he, that virtuous youth,

40. *to please his daughter Mary:* There is no evidence that Peterborough undertook to become a convert at her behest. Satirically, the line allows the poet opportunity to attack Peterborough's daughter who, as Duchess of Norfolk, was scandalously involved with John Germain (see below, *A Faithful Catalogue*, &c. 72 n).

43. *a caravanish thief:* Identified in Firth b. 21 as James Cecil (1666–93), fourth Earl of Salisbury, who became a convert while in Rome on a diplomatic mission for James (see 49 n.). News of his conversion reached London early in April 1687 (Luttrell, *1*, 400). He returned to England by the end of the year and soon undertook the construction of a Catholic chapel at Hatfield (Luttrell, *1*, 426, 433). Macaulay describes him as "foolish to a proverb. His figure was so bloated by sensual indulgence as to be almost incapable of moving, and his sluggish body was the abode of an equally sluggish mind" (2, 848). The following squib probably appeared about the time of his conversion, purportedly fixed "Over the Lord Salisbury's Door" at his house in the Strand:

 If Cecil the wise
 From his grave should arise
 And look the fat brat in the face,
 He'd take him from mass
 And turn him to grass
 And swear he was none of his race. (*POAS*, 1697, continuation, p. 150)

46. *rhinocerical:* "Full of money" (*DCC*). According to the *OED* this is the earliest known use of the word.

47. *marri'd ere the cub was lick'd:* In 1683 Salisbury married the 13-year-old Frances, daughter and coheiress of Samuel Bennet of Beechampton, Buckinghamshire (Luttrell, *1*, 269).

49. *By jockies bubbl'd:* As an obscure cant phrase either "duped by James" or, literally, by "jockies," i.e. riders or fraudulent characters. The latter suits the context best. James sent Salisbury on perfectly legitimate diplomatic business, though he could have requested the opportunity to leave England for a time. Macaulay read these lines similarly: "He was represented in popular lampoons as a man made to be duped, as a man who had hitherto been the prey of gamesters . . . " (2, 848).

51. *Haines:* Joseph Haines (d. 1701), the actor. "In the reign of the late King James he travelled in my Lord Castlemaine's retinue, when he went Ambassador to Rome,

Equal in honor, sense, and truth,
By reason and pure conscience urg'd,
Past sins by abjuration purg'd.
But 'tis believ'd both rogue and peer   55
More worldly motives had to veer:
The scoundrel plebeian's swerving
Was to secure himself from starving,
And that which made the peer a starter
Was hope of a long-wish'd-for Garter.   60

  Next comes a peer who sits at helm
And long has steer'd the giddy realm
With tailor's motion, mien, and grace,
But a right statesman in grimace—
The sneer, the cringe, and then by turns,   65
The dully grave, the frowns, and scorns—
Promises all, but nought performs;
But howe'er great he's in promotion,
He's very humble in devotion:
With taper light, and feet all bare,   70

---

where he professed himself a member of that church (which was the first time he ever
pretended to any religion) and there he made use of his skill in gaming, by which he
got considerable sums from the cautious Italians; and being for some misbehavior
left behind at my Lord Castlemaine's return, he was obliged to make use of all his
wit and sharping to support himself there, and in his passage home to England"
(Theophilus Lucas, *Lives of the Gamesters, 1714*, English Library edn., 1930, p. 194).

  60. *Garter:* Salisbury was never elected Knight of the Garter.

  61. *a peer who sits at helm:* MS. note in Firth indicates this is Robert Spencer (1640–
1702), second Earl of Sunderland and President of the Privy Council. Most authorities
date Sunderland's conversion from his public declaration in Council on 24 June 1688,
when his position had become seriously undermined by the Jesuit faction at Court, and
he sought by this demonstration to regain his full share of the royal favor. This date
seems late in relation to *The Converts.* Some evidence, however, suits well with the
narrative of 70–80, that Sunderland became a convert in 1687 and made the renun-
ciation of 1688 "without any solemn abjuration, because he had the year before
secretly performed that ceremony to Father Petre." Indeed, Petre had been forced on
that occasion "to say two masses in one morning, because Lord Sunderland and Lord
Mulgrave were not to know of each other's conversion" (see Sir James Mackintosh,
History of the Revolution in England, 1835, *1,* 374; see also Clarke, *Life, 2,* 74; Dalrymple, Chap. 2, App., p. 123). There is no evidence of Mulgrave's conversion suggested also below by the author of *The Paradox,* 53–6. The whole story may have been
a fabrication. Possibly more than one such tale was current (see 77). The validity of
the story scarcely affects the dating of this poem. If the story were current in 1687, it
would probably find its way into anti-Catholic verse. Macaulay's description of
Sunderland's conversion (*2,* 1019–20) paraphrases 70–80.

He to the temple did repair,
And knocking softly at the portal,
Cried, "Pity, fathers, a poor mortal,"
And "for a sinner make some room,
A prodigal returned home."   75
Some say that in that very hour
Convert Mall Megs arriv'd at door;
So both with penitent grimace,
Statesman and bawd, with humble pace
Enter'd and were receiv'd to grace.   80
   The next, a knight of high command
'Twixt London Bridge and Dover Sand,
A man of strict and holy life,
Taking example from his wife;
He to a nunnery sent her packing,   85
Lest they should take each other napping.
Some say L'Estrange did him beget,
But that he wants his chin and wit;
Good-natur'd, as you may observe,
Letting his tit'lar father starve;   90
A man of sense and parts, we know it,
But dares as well be damn'd as show it;
Brib'd by himself, his trusty servant
At King's Bench Bar appear'd most fervent
Against his honor for the Test: 95
To him 'twas gain, to all mankind a jest.
   Blue-bonnet lords, a num'rous store,

77. *Mall Megs:* A cant phrase meaning "prostitute." The reference here seems to point to a particular conversion, but see 61 n.; also see above, *The Town Life,* 64 n.

81. *a knight of high command:* Sir Edward Hales (d. 1695), titular Earl of Tenterden. Educated at University College, Oxford, under the tutorship of Obadiah Walker, himself later a convert, Hales was early inclined toward Roman Catholicism but not converted until 11 Nov. 1685. Under James, Hales was sworn to the Privy Council, made one of the Lords of the Admiralty, Deputy-warden of the Cinque Ports, and Lieutenant of the Tower and Master of the Ordnance. The imputations in 83–90 seem to lack foundation.

88. *his chin and wit:* Cf. *Absalom and Achitophel,* 648; perhaps the sage's chin is long with pulling.

93–6. For details see above, *The Trial of Godden v. Hales.*

97. *Blue-bonnet lords:* Scottish lords. The "blue-bonnet" was the round, flattened cap of blue woolen material generally worn by Scotsmen at this time. The foremost converts were John and James Drummond, Earls of Melfort and Perth, respectively.

Whose best example is they're poor;
Merely drawn in in hopes of gains,
And reap the scandal for their pains;   100
Half starv'd at Court with expectation,
Forc'd to return to their Scotch station,
Despis'd and scorn'd by every nation.
   A paltry knight not worth a mention
Renounc'd his faith for piteous pension;   105
After upon true Protestant whore,
He'd spent a large estate before.
   A thick, short colonel next does come,
With straddling legs and massy bum:
With many more of shameful note,   110
Whose honor ne'er was worth a groat.
   If these be pillars of the church,
'Tis fear'd they'll leave her in the lurch.
If abler men do not support her weight,
All quickly will return to forty-eight!   115

With advancement their motive, Perth embraced Roman Catholicism in the autumn of 1685, Melfort in Feb. 1686.

104. *A paltry knight:* According to MS. note in Firth, Charles Middleton or Myddelton, husband of the beautiful Jane Middleton (1645–92), whose affections had been sought by the Duke of York. She had also for a time rivalled the Duchess of Portsmouth and thus could reasonably be called a "Protestant whore," though the epithet correctly belongs to Nell Gwynne. When James came to the throne, she received a pension of £500 from the secret service money. Her husband had held a minor post in the prize office, but died insolvent in 1691.

108. *A thick, short colonel:* Col. Thomas Stradling, appointed sergeant porter to the King and knighted in Jan. 1687 (Luttrell, *1*, 391).

115. *forty-eight:* 1648—one of the key years of the Civil War and, by old style, the year of Charles I's execution.

[CHARLES MONTAGU]

THE MAN OF HONOR

Occasioned by the Postscript of Penn's Letter

Not all the threats or favors of a crown,
A prince's whisper, or a tyrant's frown,
Can awe the spirit, or allure the mind
Of him who to strict Honor is inclin'd;
Though all the pomp and pleasure that does wait   5
On public places and affairs of state
Should fondly court him to be base and great,
With even passions and with settled face
He would remove the harlot's false embrace;
Though all the storms and tempests should arise   10
That church-magicians in their cells devise
And from their settled basis nations tear,
He would unmov'd the mighty ruin bear,
Secure in innocence contemn 'em all
And, decently array'd in Honors, fall.   15

For this brave Shrewsbury and Lumley's name
Shall stand the foremost in the list of fame,

Subtitle: For an explanation of the connection between this poem and Penn's "post-script," see headnote. William Penn (1644–1718), "the oddest person in the royal entourage" (Ogg, p. 180), has since Macaulay been both bitterly attacked and staunchly defended by historians of the reign of James II (see Charles Firth's *Commentary on Macaulay's History of England*, 1938, pp. 269–73). "He was, in fact, a sanguine optimist, destitute of the penetration into human nature and capacity for determining the limits of the ideal and the practicable which mark the statesman" (*DNB*). "Penn . . . was optimistic or dense enough to believe that his sovereign was at heart clement and tolerant" (Ogg, p. 180). Penn spoke of himself on one occasion as not a Papist but a "dissenting Protestant" (see below, headnote to *The Progress of Popery—II*). Whatever side one takes, there is little doubt that the majority of the opponents to James' policy saw Penn as a despicable sycophant. For an example of their treatment of him, see the pamphlet cited above under *Dryden's Ghost*, 106 and n.

16. *Shrewsbury and Lumley:* Charles Talbot (1660–1718), Duke of Shrewsbury, and Richard Lumley (d. 1721), first Earl of Scarborough, opponents to James' plans as early as Dec. 1685 (*HMC, Rutland*, 2, 97). In Jan. 1687 they were deprived of their cavalry commissions and in August of their lord-lieutenancies. Both, born Catholic—Talbot changed to Protestantism in 1679 during the Popish Plot, Lumley in 1687—were among the seven who signed the invitation to William in 1688 (Reresby, p. 442; Luttrell, *1*, 393).

Who first with steady minds the current broke,
And to the suppliant Monarch boldly spoke.

"Great sir, renown'd for constancy, how just   20
Have we obey'd the Crown and serv'd our trust,
Espous'd your cause and interest in distress,
Yourself must witness, and our foes confess!
Permit us then ill fortune to accuse
That you at last unhappy counsels use,   25
And ask the only thing we must refuse.
Our lives and fortunes freely we'll expose;
Honor alone we cannot, must not, lose:
Honor that spark of the celestial fire,
That above Nature makes mankind aspire,   30
Ennobles the rude passions of our frame
With thirst of glory and desire of fame,
The richest treasure of a generous breast
That gives the stamp and standard to the rest.
Wit, strength, and courage are wild, dangerous force,   35
Unless this softens and directs their course;
And would you rob us of the noblest part,
Accept a sacrifice without a heart?
'Tis much beneath the greatness of a throne
To take the casket when the jewel's gone: 40
Debauch our principles, corrupt our race,
And teach the nobles to be false and base!
What confidence can you in them repose,
Who, ere they serve you, all their value lose;
Who once enslave their conscience to their lust   45
Have lost the reins and can no more be just.
Of Honor men at first like women nice
Raise maiden scruples at unpractic'd vice;
Their modest nature curbs the struggling flame
And stifles what they wish to act with shame;   50
But once this fence thrown down, when they perceive
That they may taste forbidden fruit and live,
They stop not here their course, but safely in,
Grow strong, luxuriant, and bold in sin;

29. ff. Cf. Dryden, *Absalom and Achitophel*, 305–14.

True to no principles, press forward still,   55
And only bound by appetite their will;
Now fawn and flatter while this tide prevails,
But shift with every verring blast their sails;
Mark those that meanly truckle to your power,
They once deserted and chang'd sides before   60
And would tomorrow Mohammed adore!
On higher springs true Men of Honor move:
Free is their service and unbought their love;
When danger calls, and Honor leads the way,
With joy they follow and with pride obey.   65
When the rebellious foe came rolling on
And shook with gathering multitudes the throne,
Where were the minions then? What arms, what force,
Could they oppose to stop the torrent's course?
Then Pembroke, then the nobles, firmly stood,   70
Free of their lives and lavish of their blood,
But when your orders to mean ends decline,
With the same constancy they all resign."

    Thus spake the youth who open'd first the way
And was the Phosph'rus to the dawning day;   75
Follow'd by a more glorious splendid host
Than any age or any realm can boast:
So great their fame, so numerous the train,
To name were endless and to praise in vain;
But Herbert and great Oxford merit more,   80

62. *springs: fig.,* "motives."

70. *Pembroke:* Thomas Herbert (1656–1733), eighth Earl of Pembroke. As Lord Lieutenant of Wiltshire, he had raised the county militia against Monmouth in the summer of 1685, but in 1687 he was dismissed his office.

80. *Herbert:* Arthur Herbert (1647–1716), Earl of Torrington and commander of the navy, was deprived of his posts early in 1687, when he refused to vote for the repeal of the Test (Luttrell, *1*, 396–8).

Oxford: Aubrey de Vere (1626–1703), twentieth Earl of Oxford. At the end of Feb. 1688, Reresby records that, "My Lord of Oxford, first earl of the realm (but low in his fortune), being commanded by the King to use his interest in his lieutenancy for the taking off the penal laws and the Test, told the King plainly he could not persuade that to others which he was averse to in his own conscience, for which the King took from him his regiment of horse and gave it to the Duke of Berwick" (p. 487). He also lost his lord-lieutenancy of Essex (Luttrell, *1*, 431). Though these dates place this poem and *The Advice to the Test-Holders* (see below) in Feb. or March, 1688, instead of the

Bold is their flight, and more sublime they soar:
So high, their virtue as yet wants a name,
Exceeding wonder and surpassing fame.
Rise, glorious Church, erect thy radiant head!
The storm is past, th'impending tempest fled!   85
Had fate decreed thy ruin or disgrace,
It had not giv'n such sons, so brave a race.
When for destruction Heav'n a realm designs,
The symptoms first appear in slavish minds;
These men would prop a sinking nation's weight,   90
Stop falling vengeance and reverse e'en fate.
Let other nations boast their fruitful soil,
Their fragrant spices, their rich wine and oil;
In breathing colors and in living paint
Let them excel; their mastery we grant.   95
But to instruct the mind, to arm the soul
With virtue which no dangers can control;
Exalt the thought, a speedy courage lend,
That horror cannot shake, or pleasure bend:
These are the English arts, these we profess,   100
To be the same in mis'ry and success;
To teach oppressors law, assist the good,
Relieve the wretched and subdue the proud.
Such are our souls; but what doth worth avail,
When kings commit to hungry priests the scale?   105
All merit's light when they dispose the weight,
Who either would embroil, or rule, the state,
Defame those heroes, who their yoke refuse,
And blast that honesty they cannot use;
The strength and safety of the crown destroy,   110
And th'King's power against himself employ;
Affront his friends, deprive him of the brave,
Bereft of these he must become their slave.
Men like our money come the most in play

---

fall of 1687, it seems more likely that Oxford's defiance of the King occurred in Nov. 1687, when James ordered the lords-lieutenant to canvass their countries on their feelings regarding the removal of the Test and penals (see headnote below, *The Progress of Popery—II*).

107. Cf. *Absalom and Achitophel*, 174.

For being base and of a coarse allay;   115
The richest metals and the purest gold
Of native value and exactest mold,
By worth conceal'd, in private closets shine,
For vulgar use too precious and too fine,
Whilst tin and copper with new stamping bright,   120
Coins of base metal, counterfeit and light,
Do all the business of the nation's turn,
Rais'd in contempt, us'd and employ'd in scorn;
So shining virtues are for courts too bright,
Whose guilty actions fly their searching light;   125
Rich in themselves, disdaining to aspire,
Great without pomp they willingly retire;
Give place to fools, whose rash misjudging sense
Increases the weak measures of their prince;
Prone to admire and flatter him in ease,   130
They study not his good but how to please;
They blindly and implicitly run on,
Nor see those dangers which the others shun,
Who, slow to act, each business duly weigh,
Advise with freedom and with care obey;   135
With wisdom fatal to their interest strive
To make their monarch lov'd, and nation thrive—
Such have no place where priests and women reign,
Who love fierce drivers, and a looser rein.

THE MEN OF HONOR MADE MEN WORTHY

Si natura negat, facit indignatio versum. Juvenal.

[What, shall the honest silently permit
The daily treasons that hid rebels spit?
Read the blasphemous libels of the times,
Where the best King's traduc'd in nauseous rhymes?
Where knaves and fools from honor disengage   5

139. *fierce drivers:* Cf. "Jehu" in connection with Shaftesbury and Monmouth: see, for example, *The Western Rebel,* 48 and n.
Epigraph: Juvenal, *Sat.,* I. 79: "If Nature could not, anger would indite" (Dryden's translation).

And set up for the patriots of the age?
While men of virtue are expos'd to shame,
Ungrateful villains pass for men of fame!
But I more just, more reasonable far,
Will show these worthy men, men worthy are—   10
Though 'tis a task too great for me, unknown
To Court or Camp, or to the subtler town,
But so much to my country's good I owe
To sacrifice my silence, and speak now.]
    Honor, thou sacred name, how misappli'd   15
When base apostate Shrewsbury shall provide
Thy glorious veil his infamy to hide!
Unsulli'd virtue, make no more pretense
To glory, honor, or to excellence,
When such a prostitute as he is dress'd   20
With the false titles of just, good, and best;
While like a harden'd coward he could bear,
Nay, and caress his father's murderer;
With silent dullness could the scandal smother,
'Till Heaven reveng'd it on his bastard brother.   25
That last of the great race of Buckingham,
And the first witness of thy mother's shame,
So like his father duke, that none could tell
Which did in wit or lewdness most excell;
The youth to satisfy thy father's ghost   30
Fell to redeem that honor thou had'st lost;
Though justly, yet a piti'd sacrifice,
To make atonement for thy cowardice.
Where was thy honor then? or after this,
When thou could'st live with the adulteress,   35
In peaceful infamy to sit thee down
And be a slave to every stallion's frown?
Oh, dearth of honor! oh, ignoble blood!
How justly thou art styl'd "the great and good."
Not so the noble demi-god of old,   40

16. ff. Charles Talbot, Duke of Shrewsbury, was brought up a Roman Catholic but turned to the Church of England in 1681, at the height of the Popish Plot. For details of the other scandals connected with his name, see the above *Song*, "The widows and maids," 43–8 n.

The fam'd Orestes, could those arms behold
Whose lustful twins so often did embrace
The black Aegisthus in his father's place;
Nor could he hear that tongue that once had said,
"We can't live free till Agamemnon's dead!"   45
An act of justice and of honor, too,
For your example did the hero do.
   Where's this mistaken honor then? This fame,
Which amongst fools has got thee such a name?
To your forefathers' dictates and your God   50
You have long since in opposition stood,
Turn'd like a needy slave, condemn'd to fears,
And honorably damn'd your ancestors!
Think you're inform'd, of all your race, most right?
Your eyes were open'd to reforming light   55
When angry Heaven, your folly to deride,
Did in one night deprive you of your boasted guide.
   And yet as if your unrepenting mind
Were, than your body, more deprav'd and blind,
Disdaining loyalty and allegiance, too,   60
Or to be half Heav'n's friend and half its foe,
Basely abandon his anointed now—
There lies your honor! That celebrates your name!
(Oh, everlasting thirst of hated fame!)
You spurn all properties except your own   65
And those maintain, though you destroy the throne;
And when the best, the most indulgent Prince
Would have all taste the sweets he does dispense,
And like kind Heav'n would show'r upon the plain
To all the manna of his peaceful reign,   70
Would have us live like men, not beasts to prey
On one another's vitals, but enjoy
Each his own vine and his paternal field,
And what his honest industry does yield;
And with a father's providential cares,   75
For our succeeding happiness declares;
While all true patriots he would fain engage
To make our heirs, too, taste this Golden Age.

66. ff. Alluding to the Declaration of Toleration.

You, the faux-braves of honor, would oppose
(Whom good men ought to shun as common foes),   80
His pious meaning with the clamorous noise
Of honor, and religion's new-found voice.
But where is honor's fountain? where her spring?
Her only rise but streaming from the King?
What then? Can honor against honor go?   85
Shall springs disdain the source from whence they flow?
    Old Oxford, whose untainted family
So long have boasted noble loyalty,
The fool in all his actions has express'd
But ne'er till now the fool and knave confess'd.   90
The spending his estate, marrying his whore,
Suffering his son to perish at his door,
Are things that may with honor be perform'd:
No crime but taking off the Test is scorn'd.
So Oxford, last of all his race, will now   95
Prove himself last of all their honor, too.
    Lumley that renegade yet farther runs,
He saves himself but yet will damn his sons,
Obliging them still constant to abide
To faith from whence himself is slipp'd aside.   100
Fear of the Plot first made him turn his strain;
Fear keeps him still from turning back again:
He saves his bacon for another reign.
    But who can hold from laughing when they see
Incestuous Herbert in this company;   105

79. *faux-braves:* Not in *OED*. This, a made-up form like the obs. "faux-prude,"
would mean "men who simulate bravery."

87. *Oxford:* Although "the noblest subject in England, and indeed . . . the noblest
subject in Europe" (Macaulay, 2, 967), his character was more than a little tarnished.
A compulsive gambler, he "lost most of his estate at gaming before he died" (Theophilus
Lucas, *Lives of the Gamesters,* English Library edn., 1930, p. 166). In about 1671 he
married Diana Kirke, reputed to have had affairs with the Duke of York and Harry
Jermyn (see *POAS, 3,* 1704, 68). By her, Oxford had a son who predeceased him, and
three daughters (see below *A Faithful Catalogue,* 339 ff.).

97. *Lumley:* Converted to Anglicanism in 1687 and not during the Popish Plot (the
confusion appears also in Dartmouth's note to Burnet, *1,* 763). I find no evidence to
corroborate the suggestion that Lumley advised his sons to remain constant in their
faith.

105. *Herbert:* His unsavory character is well illustrated in Pepys' *Tangier Papers,* ed
Edwin Chappell, 1935, *Navy Records Society, 73:*

Who could have thought an admiral such a sot
To lose his all for the new creed o'th'Plot;
A slave bred up inhumanly in blood,
By whom no morals e'er were understood,
And for a whore would crucify his God; 110
Whose brutal mercenary life has been
Through its lewd course but one continu'd sin.
Witness Tangier: his honor there was shown
Not in heroic service for the Crown,
But drinking, pox, and whores of high renown. 115
Murders and rapes his honor can digest—
Boggles at nought but taking off the Test.
    But in what fitting words shall we express
The height of ignorance, folly in excess?
The Devil himself did surely ne'er beget 120
Ingratitude like that in Somerset!
Alike their obligations, and the same
Be their just fate—and equal be their shame!
What had'st thou in thy life that e'er was good,
Dull blockhead, both unmannerly and rude? 125
Tell me, what wert thou when this Royal Sun
Upon thy mean, thy humble, fortune shone?
Thy better part, thy wife; thy noblest show,
Thy Garter; places, all to him you owe:
This sacred, this too-much-offended King 130
Warm'd in his bosom the poor, frozen thing,
'Till on thy life's preserver, now, thou turn'st the sting.

W. Hewer tells me of captains submitting themselves to the meanest degree of servility to Herbert when he was at Tangier [1679–82], waiting at his rising and going to bed, combing his perruque, brushing him, putting on his coat for him, as the King is served; he living and keeping a house on shore and his mistresses visited and attended one after another, as the King's are (p. 138).

The story of Herbert's interview with James early in 1687 is given by both Burnet (*1*, 671) and Clarke (*Life*, *2*, 204), with some disagreement as to the particulars of the discourse which passed between the two men, though both make it clear that each man objected to the other's pleading honor and conscience in the conduct of his life.

128–9. *thy wife . . . Thy Garter:* Somerset married the beautiful, 15-year-old Elizabeth Percy, widow of the Earl of Ogle and of Thomas Thynne, on 30 May 1682. Appointed a gentleman of the bedchamber in 1683, Somerset was installed Knight of the Garter the next year, 8 April 1684. (For details of his refusal to introduce the Papal Nuncio, see above, *Diplomatic Relations with the Vatican*.)

Poor pop'lar ass, live scorn'd, contemn'd, abhorr'd,
And only be by wretched rogues ador'd;
Boast of the point you gain'd when you durst say   135
To your dread sovereign, "Lord—I can't obey;"
What was your master's hard command, I pray?
Men must expect some horrid, unjust thing,
When one so much oblig'd denies his King;
Behold, your expectations dwindle thus—   140
The Popish Nuncio he won't introduce!
Did ever mountain bring forth such a mouse?
These are the men whose judgments still are right,
And who profess a conscience out of spite.
These are the men such honor have express'd;   145
These are the glorious patrons of the Test!
    [Crawl on your knees, you stigmatized crew!
Humble your stubborn necks, ungratefuls, do;
Ask the King's pardon, and your country's, too.
You that would brother against brother fire,   150
And, for a poor opinion, damn your sire,
In hope to have your name by th'rabble spread;
And be in time of Wappingers the head,
Till like your predecessors in the West
Your forfeit, politic pates are fix'd northeast.]   155

153–5. *Wappingers:* Inhabitants of Wapping, but more particularly here Shaftesbury's "brisk boys" from Wapping, as they symbolized the lawless rout: and further,
Monmouth and the defeat of his forces in the west in the summer of 1685.

northeast: The heads of traitors were commonly set on pikes atop the Tower or
London Bridge, locations considerably "northeast" of the counties where Monmouth's
cause died.

The Summer Encampment
(June–July 1687)

The muster of James' army on Hounslow Heath in June and July
1687 substantially defined the particular threat of Popery and the
temper of Englishmen in face of that threat. This was the third time
during the reign that James had put on such a military display. On
23 July 1685 "six thousand of his Majesty's forces, horse and foot"
were reviewed on the Heath (Luttrell, *1, 355*). The next summer
he held his first full encampment. Though always fascinated by military pomp, he sought in these musters to intimidate the city of London. Initially, the encampment of 1686 may have awed the populace,
though inclement weather and illness reduced its effectiveness
(Evelyn, *4, 513*). But it soon became a place of diversion for most
Londoners, as shown by these lines describing the ghost of Charles II
on a nocturnal inspection:

> Thrice with majestic pace he walks the round,
> Surveying the pavilion's utmost bound,
> And useless grandeur everywhere he found.
> Philippi, nor the fam'd Pharsalian field,
> Did not more signs of glorious action yield;
> But this was all for show, not terror made,
> 'Twas Hounslow farce, a siege in masquerade.
>   More near he views it yet, and found within,
> All the degrees of luxury and sin;
> Alsatia's sink into this common shore *
> Did all its vile and nasty nuisance pour;
> Fat sharpers, broken cuckolds, gamesters, cheats,
> What Newgate disembogues, find here retreats;
> The groom and footman from their liv'ry stripp'd,
> With scarf, gay feather, and command equipp'd,
> Promotion gives to sauciness pretense,
> And greatness is mistook for insolence;

common shore: sewer.

And to evince their valor every hour,
Bamboo ** the slaves that bow beneath their pow'r;
Yet to the country ladies these appear
So novel, witty, *beau en cavalier,*
That scarce a tender heart is left behind:
Pray God a maidenhead you chance to find!
(*Caesar's Ghost, POAS, 1,* continuation, 1703, pp. 162–71)

The "third campaign" (see Evelyn, *4, 533,* and Luttrell, *1, 405–06*) encountered less fear and more familiarity. In attempting to cow his subjects by a show of force, James had as a precedent Charles' encampment on the Heath in 1678, of which he had not accurately assessed the impact. Charles' attempt to bully Parliament in 1678 had been futile, yet James may have seen that display as a moment of monarchical strength among years of complacency. He seems never to have understood the use of passive resistance to turn opposition back upon itself. It was a lesson Charles had early learned and effectively reaffirmed in the muster of 1678.

In addition to a jibe at Dryden and a mocking account of the re-enactment of the siege and capture of the Hungarian city of Buda, wrested from the Turks in September 1686, the following satire attacks James with bitter irony. With each new phrase of acclaim, the poet manages more thoroughly to condemn the King and points to the discrepancy not only between the image and the man, but also between that man's past and his present self. As Duke of York, James had been renowned for his courage and "his constant keeping of his word." Now these qualities had apparently vanished, to be replaced by an awesome, if slightly clownish, truculence which threatened havoc even while it invited ridicule.

HOUNSLOW HEATH

Upon this place are to be seen
Many rare sights: God save the Queen!

Near Hampton Court there lies a common
Unknown to neither man nor woman,
The Heath of Hounslow it is styl'd,

** *Bamboo, v.* "To beat or 'cane' with bamboo." The *OED* records no use of this verb earlier than 1816.

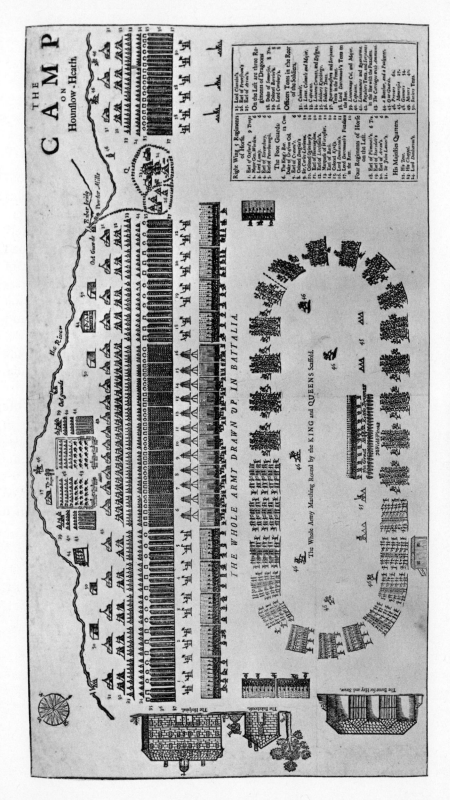

The Royal Encampment on Hounslow Heath, 1686

Which never was with blood defil'd,
Though it has been of war the seat   5
Now three campaigns almost complete.

Here you may see great James the Second
(The greatest of our kings he's reckon'd),
A hero of such high renown
Whole nations tremble at his frown,   10
And when he smiles men die away
In transports of excessive joy.
A prince of admirable learning!
Quick wit! of judgment most discerning!
His knowledge in all arts is such   15
No monarch ever knew so much.
Not that old blust'ring King of Pontus,
Whom men call learned to affront us,
With all his tongues and dialects
Could equal him in all respects;   20
His two and twenty languages
Were trifles, if compared to his;
Jargons which we esteem but small:
English and French are worth 'em all.
What though he had some skill in physic,   25
Could cure the dropsy or the phthisic,
Perhaps was able to advise one
To 'scape the danger of rank poison,
And could prepare an antidote

---

14. *Quick wit!:* James' slowness of wit had become almost proverbial, due both to his phlegmatic nature and to such well-known remarks as Catherine Sedley's on the reasons for the Duke's passion for her: "It cannot be my beauty, for he must see I have none; and it cannot be my wit, for he has not enough to know that I have any."

17. *King of Pontus:* Mithridates VI (c. 131–63 B.C.), King of Pontus and enemy of Rome. See Nathaniel Lee's play *Mithridates . . . King of Pontus,* 1678, for which Dryden wrote the epilogue. The figure of Mithridates was elaborately glorified by ancient authorities: "His courage, his bodily strength and size, his skill in the use of weapons, in riding, and in the chase, his speed of foot, his capacity for eating and drinking, his penetrating intellect and his mastery of 22 languages are celebrated to a degree which is almost incredible" (*EB*).

26. *phthisic:* A wasting disease of the lungs.

28–29. Mithridates was said to have inured himself to the effects of poisons by their constant use—hence mithridatism.

Should carry't off—though down your throat!   30
These are but poor, mechanic arts,
Inferior to great James's parts.
Shall he be set in the same rank
With a pedantic mountebank?
He's master of such eloquence,   35
Well chosen words, and weighty sense,
That he ne'er parts his lovely lips,
But out a trope or figure slips;
And, when he moves his fluent tongue,
Is sure to ravish all the throng;   40
And every mortal that can hear
Is held fast pris'ner by the ear.

His other gifts we need but name,
They are so spread abroad by fame:
His faith, his zeal, his constancy,   45
Aversion to all bigotry!
His firm adhering to the laws,
By which he judges every cause
And deals to all impartial justice,
In which the subject's greatest trust is!   50
His constant keeping of his word
As well to peasant as to lord;
Which he no more would violate,
Than he would quit his regal state!
Who has not his least promise broke,   55
Nor contradicted what he spoke!
His governing the brutal passions
With far more rigor than his nations
Would not be sway'd by's appetite
Were he to gain an empire by't!   60
From hence does flow that chastity,
Temperance, love, sincerity,
And unaffected piety,
That just abhorrence of ambition,
Idolatry, and superstition,   65
Which through his life have shin'd so bright
That nought could dazzle their clear light!

These qualities we'll not insist on,
Because they all are duties Christian;
But haste to celebrate his courage,   70
Which is the prodigy of our age:
A spirit which exceeds relation
And were too great for any nation
Did not those virtues nam'd before
Confine it to its native shore,   75
Restrain it from the thirst of blood,
And only exercise't in good!

   The tedious Mithridatic War—
The noise whereof is spread so far—
Was nothing to what's practic'd here,   80
Though carri'd on for forty year
'Gainst Pompey, Sulla, and Lucullus—
High-sounding names, brought in to gull us—
In which the Romans lost more men
Than one age could repair again,   85
Who perished not by sword or bullet
But melted gold pour'd down the gullet.
Heroes of old were only fam'd
For having millions kill'd or maim'd,
For being th'instruments of fate   90
In making nations desolate,
For wading to the chin i'th'blood
Of those that in their passage stood;
And thought the point they had not gain'd
While any foe alive remain'd.   95
Our monarch, by more gentle rules,
Has prov'd the ancients arrant fools:
He only studies and contrives,
Not to destroy, but save, men's lives;

81. *forty year:* Mithridates actively opposed the Romans for less than twenty years.

82. *Pompey, Sulla, and Lucullus:* L. Cornelius Sulla (138–78 B.C.), L. Lucullus (114–57 B.C.), and Pompey the Great (106–48 B.C.) successively commanded the Roman forces which waged the interminable struggle against Mithridates. Possibly more than 80,000 Roman citizens were slaughtered in Asia by the Persians.

87. *melted gold pour'd down the gullet:* See Lee's play, I.i., for Mithridates' method of punishing "Souls made up of avarice."

Shows all the military skill,   100
Without committing ought that's ill.
He'll teach his men, in warlike sport,
How to defend or storm a fort,
And in heroic interlude
Will act the dreadful scene of Bude: 105
Here Lorraine storms, the Vizier dies,
And Brandenburg routs the supplies;
Bavaria there blows up their train,
And all the Turks are took or slain.
All this perform'd with no more harm   110
Than loss of a simple gunner's arm;
And surely 'tis a greater good
To teach men war than shed their blood.

Now pause, and view the army royal,
Compos'd of valiant souls and loyal;   115
Not rais'd (as ill men say) to hurt ye,
But to defend, or to convert ye;
For that's the method now in use,
The Faith Tridentine to diffuse.
Time was the word was powerful,   120
But now 'tis thought remiss and dull,
Has not that energy and force
Which is in well-arm'd foot and horse.
Thus, when the faith has had mutation,
We change its way of propagation;   125
So Mohammed with arms and terrors
Spread over half the world his errors.

Here daily swarm prodigious wights
And strange variety of sights,
As ladies lewd and foppish knights,   130
Priests, poets, pimps, and parasites,

106–07. Charles, Duke of Lorraine, with the aid of the electors of Brandenburg and
Bavaria, recovered Buda from the Turks in 1686.

119. *Tridentine:* The Council of the Roman Catholic Church sat, with considerable
intervals, from 1545–63 at Trent to organize the church in opposition to the Reformation.

120. Presumably a play on John 1:1 and on the Bible as the Word.

Which now we'll spare and only mention
The hungry bard that writes for pension:
Old Squab—who's sometimes here, I'm told—
That oft has with his Prince made bold,   135
Call'd the late King a saunt'ring cully
To magnify the Gallic bully;
Who lately put a senseless banter
Upon the world with *Hind and Panther,*
Making the beasts and birds o'th'wood   140
Debate what he ne'er understood,
Deep secrets in philosophy
And mysteries in theology,
All sung in wretched poetry;
Which rambling piece is as much farce all   145
As his true mirror, *The Rehearsal,*
For which he has been soundly bang'd
But hain't his just reward till hang'd.

Now you have seen all that is here
Have patience till another year.   150

134. *Old Squab:* See, *To Mr. Dryden, Upon His Declaring Himself a Roman Catholic,* 26 n.

136. *a saunt'ring cully:* A leisurely dupe. The adjective "sauntering" was originally applied to Charles by Mulgrave in his *Essay on Satire,* commonly thought to have been written by Dryden, and probably worked on by him. Cf. another attack on Dryden, *The Laureate,* by Robert Gould (*Popery, 1,* 1689, 17–18):

> Nay, e'en the Royal Patron was not spar'd,
> But an obscene, a saunt'ring wretch declar'd. (68–69)

137. *Gallic bully:* Louis XIV.

146. *The Rehearsal:* The popular farce, probably written by Buckingham in collaboration with other, lesser wits in 1671, satirizing the heroic tragedies of the time and chiefly those of Dryden, the laureate "Bays" of the play.

147. *soundly bang'd:* In the Rose Alley ambuscade; see *To Mr. Dryden,* &c., 37 n.

The Progress of Popery—II
(Fall–Winter 1687)

Henry Clerke, president of Magdalen College, Oxford, died on 24 March 1687. A week later notice of the death was given the fellows assembled in the college chapel, and it was determined "to proceed to the election of a president on Wednesday, the 13th of April, following, "a citation to this effect being affixed to the chapel door." (See Rev. J. R. Bloxam, *Magdalen College and King James II*, Oxf. Hist. Soc., *6*, 1886, which is arranged chronologically.) Even before the fellows had met, however, news of the death reached James, and his plans were made. On 5 April the King's mandamus was sent down to Oxford, greeting the fellows and charging them with the election of the convert Anthony Farmer, a young debauchee disqualified by the statutes of the college. Disregarding the mandamus, on 15 April the fellows elected John Hough, a senior, and thus joined battle with the King in a struggle which lasted until the college had been reduced to the status of a Popish seminary, its rightful fellows dismissed and deprived of all church preferments (Bloxam).

Before this came about, however, the summer and fall had been spent in maneuver. During June the president-elect and fellows appeared before the Ecclesiastical Commission. After considerable humiliation, on 22 June they were cited for their independent action and the election of Hough declared void. In August, dropping the candidacy of Farmer, James required the fellows to elect Samuel Parker, a moderate, though called by the prejudiced Burnet one of the "fittest instruments that could be found among all the clergy to betray and ruin the church" (*1*, 696; Parker had been the object of Marvell's derision in *The Rehearsal Transpros'd*, 1672–73). This, too, the fellows refused to do, arguing that they had already made their decision. Matters remained thus deadlocked until early in September when the King stopped at Oxford on his way south from his progress through the western and northwestern counties. At one point during the several sharp exchanges which followed, the King exclaimed, "Is this your Church of England loyalty? . . . Go home and show yourselves good members of the Church of England . . . and admit the Bishop of Oxford head" (Bloxam, p. 85; see above *Dr. Wild's Ghost,* 41 n.). Early in October William Penn received a deputation of fellows at his house in Windsor. Assuring them "that however people were pleased to call him Papist . . . he was a dissenting Protestant," Penn dismayed the deputation by making it clear that he felt "two or three colleges" would content the Papists (Bloxam, pp. 104–05). Amid continued resistance, the proceedings were put back into the hands of the Commission which installed Parker on 25 October. In mid-November twenty-five recalcitrant fellows were dismissed; two weeks later they were deprived of all church preferment. On December 31, Parker was ordered to appoint twelve new fellows, of whom at least six were known Roman Catholics. Parker himself died on 21 March 1688, following an illness apparently brought on by James' final demands:

> A confidential servant was with him when he received the last mandate to admit nine more Roman Catholics as Fellows. "I am sure," said [the witness], "I never saw him in such a passion in the sixteen years I lived with him. He walked up and down the room, and smote his breast and said, 'There is no trust in man. There is no trust in Princes. Is this the kindness the King promised me? To set me here to make me his tool and his prop! To place me with a company of men, which he knows I hate the conversation of!' So he sat down in his chair, and fell into a convulsive fit, and never went down stairs more till he was carried down." (Bloxam, p. 240)

Parker was replaced by Bonaventura Giffard, one of the four Catholic Vicars-General; only one or two Protestant fellows remained at Magdalen.

Of more far-reaching consequence was James' attempt during the last months of 1687 to achieve sufficient control over local constituencies to ensure the election of a new parliament which would comply with his design to abolish the Test. On about 25 October letters were sent to this end by Sunderland, the Lord President of the Council, to the lords-lieutenant, requiring them to put the following questions to their deputies, sheriffs, and justices of the peace:

1. If in case he should be chosen knight of the shire, or burgess of a town, when the King shall think fit to call a parliament, whether he will be for taking off the penal laws and the Tests.

2. Whether he will assist and contribute to the election of such members as shall be for taking off the penal laws and the Tests.

3. Whether he will support the King's Declaration for Liberty of Conscience by living friendly with those of all persuasions, as subjects of the same Prince and good Christians ought to do. (Sir George Duckett, *Penal Laws and Test Act,* 1882, p. 29)

Answering as evasively as possible, most of James' lieutenants sent back returns of little real value. But Sunderland and the King worked diligently over these for most of the next year, selecting those who could be counted on for support and winnowing out those others who, in fact, represented the majority of opinion. Their places were filled with Roman Catholics or Dissenters. Most of these were reputable men, but they lacked the support and confidence of their constituents.

James' activities against the universities and the corporations are chronicled in the following poems. With these victories, ironically, the progress of Popery halted its forward movement. The results were:

> . . . the creation of a certain national unity. Party distinction and even family rivalry were still subordinate to the ancient principle that the local defenders of the royal dignity and authority were to be found in the landed classes. That royal dignity and authority had now, for the first time, been brought into grave disrepute by wholesale eviction of men who assumed, without question, a vested and hereditary right to power and pre-eminence in those parts of England where they had their estates. (Ogg, p. 189)

To the Haters of Popery

By what Names or Titles soever Dignified or Distinguished

Thus 'twas of old; then Israel felt the rod,
   When they obey'd their kings and not their God;
When they went whoring after other loves,

To worship idols in new-planted groves,
They made their gods of silver, wood, and stone,   5
   And bow'd and worshipp'd them when they had done;
And to complete their sins in every way,
   They made 'em things call'd priests! Priests, did I say?
   A crew of villains more profane than they!
Hence sprung that Romish crew, first spawn'd in hell,   10
   Who now in vice their pedagogues excel;
Their church consists of vicious popes; the rest
   Are whoring nuns and bawdy, bugg'ring priests:
   A noble church, daub'd with religious paint—
   Each priest's a stallion, every rogue's a saint!   15
Come, you that loath this brood, this murd'ring crew,
   Your predecessors well their mercies knew.
Take courage now, and be both bold and wise;
   Stand for your laws, religion, liberties;
You have the odds, the law is still your own;   20
   They're but your traitors, therefore pull 'em down.
They struck with fear for to destroy your laws—
   There, raving mad, you see them fix their paws—
Because from them they fear their fatal fall,
   And by them laws they know you'll hang 'em all.   25
Then keep your laws, the penal and the rest,
   And give your lives up ere you give the Test.
And thou, great Church of England, hold thy own;
   Force you they may, otherwise give up none:
   Robbers and thieves must 'count for what they've done.   30
Let all thy mighty pillars now appear
   Zealous and brave, void both of hate and fear,
That Popish fops may grin, lie, cheat, and whine,
   And curse their faith, while all admire thine.
And thou, brave Oxford, Cambridge, and the rest,   35
   Great Hough and Fairfax, that durst beard the beast,

35. *Cambridge:* On 15 Feb. 1687 Luttrell recorded that "a mandamus is gone down to the University of Cambridge to constitute a Romish priest [Alban Francis] of the Benedictine Order, a master of arts." The University refused James' order and was called before the Ecclesiastical Commission. In May that body deprived Dr. John Pechell, Vice Chancellor, of his offices, and "the other heads . . . were severely checked and ordered to go home . . ." (Luttrell, *1, 403*).

36. *Hough:* Dr. John Hough (1651–1743). Formerly chaplain to the Duke of Ormonde, he was made prebendary of Worcester and received the living of Dempsford in 1685.

Let all the just with thanks record your name
On standing pillars of immortal fame!
    Let God arise, and his enemies perish!

ADVICE TO THE TEST-HOLDERS

We, father Godden, Gregory, and all
The pious priests that on the saints do call,
To the blest Virgin make it our request
That you Test-holders would abjure the Test,
By Christian liberty to heal our sins,   5
And not lay stumbling blocks to break our shins.
Such rich returns can your allegiance bring,
Is this your interest to oblige the King?
He that by's liberty has giv'n you scope
Enough to hang yourselves in your own rope,   10
And would you have him to exclude the Pope?
 What got that looby duke that did oppose
Our soul advice, but pious checks and blows?
The holy priest he o'er the temple smote,

He was presented to the visitor of Magdalen, the Bishop of Winchester, by the fellows on 16 April 1687, being formally admitted and sworn that day (Bloxam, pp. 34–5).

 Fairfax: Dr. Henry Fairfax (1634–1702), fellow of Magdalen and later Dean of Norwich. Daring to question Lord Chancellor Jeffreys' authority, "he was severely reprimanded and told he was fitter for a madhouse" (Bloxam, p. 61).

 Title: This poem purports to be an address to the most notable of James' antagonists by his priests, entreating them "to oblige the King" and win "rich returns" for their submissiveness. The irony depends on an awareness of the truculence with which James' advisors had pursued the supremacy they sought and of the fickleness with which James himself had handled former friends and allies, although not all the satiric ire is reserved for him and his priests. More than a few of the "Test-holders" are also held up to ridicule.

 1. *Godden, Gregory:* Thomas Godden (1624–88), almoner to the Queen Dowager and, with Francis Gregory (1625?–1707), chaplain to the court.

 5. *our sins:* The state of "sin" the priests are held in under the Test.

 12. *looby duke:* Henry Fitzroy (1633–90), first Duke of Grafton, "who when a priest came to him to turn his religion beat him soundly, at which the King James was very angry" (marginalia in Harleian 7317). "Looby", meaning awkward or clumsy, hardly fits Grafton except as a general appellation thought suitable for Charles' illegitimate offspring.

 13. *soul advice:* A pun on advice designed to save one's soul, the sole advice that priests give.

'Twas well that beating sav'd his grace's throat. 15
   So Albemarle, whether i'th'wrong or right,
For his religion can like Grafton fight;
Let learned doctors arraign by the word,
He knows no syllogism but his sword.
   The haughty peer fam'd for the conference, 20
Although his lordship made a stout defense,
What got he by't? He baffled us, and we
Blew up his lordship from the treasury.
And Clarendon, that Whig, from Ireland come,
For all his sense receiv'd no better doom; 25
The brothers now may strut, since he came hither,
Like the two Brentford Kings, and reign together.
   For Norfolk, Suffolk, Lumley, Shrewsbury—
They were our own, and so again shall be.

16. *Albemarle:* Christopher Monck (1653–88), Duke of Albemarle. Appointed governor of Jamaica in April, Monck left England in Sept. 1687 to take up his post abroad, where he remained until his death. A prominent Protestant, Monck may have received the appointment less as a reward than as a device for removing him from court. In Aug. 1685, Luttrell reports, "The Duke of Albemarle, on his return out of the west, finding himself to be represented otherwise than he thought he deserved, has laid down all his commissions . . . all which since ('tis said) are conferred on the Earl of Feversham" (*1*, 356).

18. *arraign:* Employed here with much of its Latin meaning of "to reason".

20. *haughty peer:* Laurence Hyde, Earl of Rochester and, until Jan. 1687, Lord Treasurer.

24. *Clarendon:* Henry Hyde (1638–1709), Earl of Clarendon and the elder brother of Rochester. He returned to England from Ireland in Feb. 1687 humiliated and disillusioned by the appointment of the Roman Catholic Richard Talbot (1630–91), created Earl of Tyrconnel in 1685. Though Talbot was appointed lieutenant of the army in Ireland in the spring of 1686, on his arrival in Dublin in June he saw that he was expected to undermine Clarendon's position as Lord Lieutenant and to replace Protestant officers in the army with Roman Catholics. As part of this plan, the parish priests had been instructed "to give an exact list of all the men in every of their parishes . . . fit to bear arms" (Clarendon *Correspondence*, *1*, 223–24).

27. *Brentford Kings:* See *The Rehearsal* by George Villiers, second Duke of Buckingham, especially II.ii.

28. *Norfolk:* Henry Howard (1655–1701), seventh Duke of Norfolk, resigned his regiment of foot in June 1686.

   Suffolk: James Howard (1619–88), third Earl of Suffolk. Little is known of Suffolk's activities during James' reign. In March 1681, he had been discharged from the lord-lieutenancy of Suffolk and Cambridgeshire and banished from attendance in the King's bedchamber (Luttrell, *1*, 69).

   Lumley, Shrewsbury: See above, *The Men of Honor Made Men Worthy*, 16, 97 and nn.

Though one hath sworn he will not tack about,   30
Till he's quite blind, and t'other eye be out.
And for the Gallic peer with golden key
We have on a sure lock as well as they,
With Peterborough, Moray, Mulgrave—all
The peers in pay in th'circuit of Whitehall.   35
But Somerset's lost state we all condole,
For we have a compassion for his soul;
The King may send such orders as he list,
But he'll receive no orders from a priest;
His grace's orders his dragoons secures   40
To kick the holy fathers out of doors.
But with that turncoat marquis it was worse,
Who while we pray'd began to swear and curse,
(Whilst not his soul we aim'd at but his money),
To toss the fathers over the balcony.   45

32. *Gallic peer:* Louis Duras (1640?–1709), Earl of Feversham, born of French nobility and naturalized in 1665. He had commanded the royal forces during the Monmouth Rebellion and been made a member of the Privy Council.

    golden key: Feversham was Lord Chamberlain to the Queen Dowager.

33. Feversham professed Protestantism, though "his religion was not much trusted to" (Burnet, *1*, 643).

34. *Peterborough, Moray, Mulgrave:* Henry Mordaunt, second Earl of Peterborough, a convert in March 1687 (see *The Converts*, 36, 40 and nn.); Alexander Stewart (d. 1701), fifth Earl of Moray; and John Sheffield (1648–1721), Earl of Mulgrave. All were members of James' Privy Council. Moray was also one of the two secretaries of state in Scotland. Of Mulgrave the hostile Burnet says: "He was apt to comply in everything that he thought might be acceptable; for he went with the King to mass and kneeled at it. And, being looked on as indifferent to all religions, the priests made an attack on him. He heard them gravely arguing for transubstantiation. He told them he was willing to receive instruction. He had taken much pains to bring himself to believe in God, who made the world and all men in it. But it must not be an ordinary force of argument that could make him believe that man was quits with God and made God again" (*1*, 683). For rumors of his conversion see *The Converts*, 61 and n.

36. *Somerset:* Charles Seymour (1662–1748), sixth Duke of Somerset, "who, when the priests came to him to preach Popery to him, beat them out of doors, for which and for his refusing to introduce the pope's nuncio when the King commanded him was turned out of all his places" (Harleian 7317).

39–40. The syntax of these lines is very difficult, if not garbled. The difficulty probably arises from the pun on the various meanings of "orders", i.e. directions, 36; ecclesiastical orders, 37; and institutional or political orders, 38.

42. *turncoat marquis:* George Savile (1633–95), Marquis of Halifax. Though he had fought attempts to exclude James from the throne, Halifax could not tolerate the Catholic policies adopted by James as King and particularly opposed any attempts at repeal of the Test. In Oct. 1685, he was removed from the Privy Council (Luttrell, *1*, 361). According to marginalia in Harleian 7317, he "threw one of the priests over his balcony into the streets." The statement remains uncorroborated.

In vain poor Harry strives against the tide,
He suffers penance for his brother's pride;
As Newport late, who did the court control,
First lost his office, and then lost his soul.

Herbert, whose fall a greater blow did feel 50
From topmast pennant to the lower keel,
Whose courage boundless as the seas before
Undaunted stood at the loud cannon's roar,
Now ducks at a false firing on the shore;
The admiral may now turn common seaman, 55
Or Ferrers-like, from court to country yeoman.

Preston, in France who pass'd for such a saint,
Since he came o'er has danc'd the same courante;
French breeding sure would teach a man more sense
Than to be lost in point of conscience. 60

Wise Montagu the wardrobe best does fit,
Boast you your loyalty, he has the wit;
For he with ev'ry side can change his strain—

46. *poor Harry:* Identified in Folger v. b. 94, Henry Savile (1642–87), brother to the Marquis of Halifax, had served in various minor capacities under the Duke of York, and was re-appointed Vice-Chamberlain on James' accession to the throne (Luttrell, *1*, 330). The King's favor was often strained as a result of Savile's disreputable activities and of James' extreme antipathy for his brother Halifax. Henry died following a surgical operation in Paris early in Oct. 1687, leaving his brother an accumulation of debts.

48. *Newport:* Francis Newport (1619–1708), Viscount Newport, afterwards Earl of Bradford, had been Comptroller of the Household and a member of the Privy Council under Charles. For a time, at least, he seems to have continued to hold some offices under James (see Luttrell, *1*, 330), but in 1687 he lost them (ibid., *1*, 394, 413).

50. *Herbert:* Arthur Herbert (1647–1716), Earl of Torrington and commander of the navy, was deprived of his posts early in 1687. For notice of his unsavory character, see *The Men of Honor Made Men Worthy*, 105 n.

56. *Ferrers-like:* Robert Shirley (1650–1717), Lord Ferrers. His regiment was taken from him in Jan. 1687. Early in Nov. 1687, he was turned out of his post as Lord Lieutenant of Staffordshire for refusing to comply with James' order to petition his officers concerning the Test and penal laws (Luttrell, *1*, 393, 419; Reresby, p. 478).

57. *Preston:* Richard Graham (1648–95), Viscount Preston and envoy extraordinary to the court of Louis XIV from 1682–85, where he was held in high esteem by the French King. As a member of James' Privy Council he was a moderate.

61. *Montagu:* Ralph, Duke of Montagu (1638?–1709), a notorious turncoat. He had plotted to install Monmouth on the throne, but swore his allegiance to James on his accession. In 1688 he was one of the first to welcome William of Orange. He had held the office of Master of the Wardrobe under Charles, but lost the post in favor of Preston (see above). In 1689 Montagu brought an action against Preston to recover the profits of the office, for which he held a life patent.

Such policy will build his house again.
Dartmouth we had forgot, but 'twas his prayer   65
When all were turn'd that he might 'scape the snare;
For this the powers and all the saints, we pray—
Fair Winifred and sweet Cecilia—
When all the purgatorian flames have pass'd,
For penance grant that he may be the last.   70
   Now for advice, which if you would pursue,
Would save your souls and your employments, too,
Dissemble, and take pensions, as we do.
   Who'd be like Oxford stiff, or Kendall shy,
To lose a regiment or company;   75
Who pities the Test-holders, or affords
Compassion to the disobliged lords.
But neither closet nor advice can win
To change th'obdurate Ethiopian skin.
The Durhamite and timber knight may strain   80

64. *his house:* "His house in Bloomsbury, one of the finest in England, was burnt down to the ground: value £150,000" (Harleian 7317). The fire broke out at midnight on 19 Jan. 1686. The damage was estimated at £60,000 by Luttrell (*1*, 369–70).

65. *Dartmouth:* George Legge (1648–91), first Baron Dartmouth. He succeeded Lord Herbert (see 48) as admiral of James' fleet. Turner says of him: "Dartmouth had a long record of faithful service to James, in particular he had stood by him in the period of his exile [in Brussels and Scotland, 1679–82] when his fortunes were at their lowest; he was not a man of outstanding ability or intelligence, but he was an ardent Protestant, . . . one of the few Protestants of respectable position who remained true to the King without equivocation" (p. 438).

68. *Fair Winifred . . . sweet Cecilia:* Since the festivals of these saints fall on Nov. 3d and 22d, the poem was probably written about Nov. 1687. Toward the end of August, during his progress, James had visited St. Winifred's Well in Flintshire, where he offered prayers for a son and received from the local inhabitants a purse which contained £100 in gold (*HMC, Rep.* X, app., pt. 4, p. 376). Protestant tracts of the period often used the still-revered St. Winifred's Well as an example of Popish superstition.

74. *Oxford:* See above, *The Man of Honor,* 80 and n.

Kendall: James Kendall, a needy retainer at court, made captain in the Coldstream regiment. He was M.P. for West Looe in the packed corporation of Cornwall. When he failed to support the King in a vote to take up matters of supply (*Commons' Journals,* 13 Nov. 1685), the Earl of Middleton said to him: " 'Sir, have not you a troop of horse in his majesty's service?' 'Yes, my lord,' says the other, 'but my brother died last night and has left me £700 a year' " (Burnet, *1*, 666, Speaker Onslow's note).

shy: The preceeding anecdote lends point to the variant reading "sly" found in Firth c. 16 and Stowe 305.

80. *Durhamite:* Identified in Folger v.b. 94, as Nathaniel Crew, third Baron Crew of Stene and Bishop of Durham (see *The Entry of the Pope's Nuncio,* 20 n.).

timber knight: According to Folger v.b. 94 Sir Richard Temple (1634–97), M.P. for

For golden proselytes, but all in vain,
All our endeavors cannot gain a man,
They will be obstinate, do what we can,
And will with Kirke first turn Mohammedan.
And why all this, to see the land oppress'd   85
With Bess's acts and Ashley Cooper's Test,
Which to repeal we have such strong directions,
Windings and turnings and daily transmigrations,
You cannot err if you oblige the court,
Or if you do, we can absolve you for't.   90

Stowe, Buckinghamshire, in Oct. 1679; he "had offered a present of timber for the town-hall, which his enemies misrepresented as a bribe" (*Roxburghe Ballads, 4,* 618). His adherence to the principals of exclusion won him the nickname of the "Stowe monster," and of course lost him his posts on James' accession.

84. *Kirke:* Percy Kirke (1646?–91). In 1681, as colonel of the Tangier regiment, he had visited the Emperor of Morocco, after which when pressed to become a convert, he "replied briskly that he was already pre-engaged, for he had promised the King of Morocco, that, if ever he changed his religion, he would turn Mahometan" (Burnet, *1,* 684).

86. *Bess's acts:* The penal measures against Catholics were instituted during Elizabeth's reign.

Ashley Cooper's Test: Shaftesbury staunchly supported the Test Act of 1672.

1688

A Faithful Catalogue of Our Most Eminent Ninnies
(February 1688)

"Nothing has been more fatal to men and to great men than the letting themselves go to the forbidden love of women. Of all the vices it is most bewitching and harder to be mastered if it be not crushed in the very bud." Thus James in advice bequeathed his son in 1692 (Clarke, 2, 622). He knew whereof he spoke. The list of his mistresses is long; the prospect, for the most part, dreary. Not "exact of taste," concerning the delights of the flesh he was a gourmand rather than a gourmet. He had sought the love of beautiful and witty women, courting Hamilton and Jennings among others, but he lacked the grace and verve by which to attract them. Moreover, James early was forced to accept the frustrations of having a brilliant older brother. In his love affairs, as in all things, he had to take what he could get, following a course of suppression and unwilling humility, which to a man of strong convictions could only end in a dangerous narrowing of vision and response.

This path proved the real penance. It may have been aggravated by an advanced syphilitic condition that could have brought James to the throne, as Turner thinks, "suffering from premature mental decline." In fairness to James, however, it must be said that there is no real proof of this. Though contemporaries found evidence for it in the early death of so many of his children and traced the disease back to his affair in 1668 with Lady Carnegy (see below, headnote to *The Birth of the Prince*). James' own "health and vigor . . . continued unbroken throughout his reign . . ." (Turner, p. 234).

In addition to the real penance of long years in the shadow of his brilliant brother, James undoubtedly suffered as well from the torments of spiritual malaise, that "great punishment God inflicts on such as have had the misfortune to be led away by the unlawful love of women" (Clarke, 2, 631). After the Sedley affair, James handled his romantic liaisons with more discretion, but he continued to have reason to employ the flail given him by his irate Queen with priestly approval to castigate himself. (The flail was among the possessions

189

the Queen bequeathed to the Monastery of St. Marie of Chaillot on her death; see Macaulay, 2, 728).

"There is another great inconvenience (which I think I have not yet mentioned) which attends kings and great men having of mistresses, which is the children they have by those fair ladies, who will never be at quiet till they are owned [and] have great titles given them . . ." (Clarke, 2, 631). With this "inconvenience" Dorset's *Faithful Catalogue* ostensibly concerns itself. Here Dorset presents us with the host of "eminent ninnies" and their accomplices, which the royal brothers had spawned. Himself noted for the profligacy of his youth, for nights of drinking with Sedley and "running up and down . . . with their arses bare through the streets and, at last, fighting and being beat by the watch and clapped up all night" (Pepys, *Diary, 8,* 129), Dorset had both the vulgar knowledge and the poetic talents to carry off this satire in the manner of Juvenal, lashing out with indignation at the follies and crimes of his age. *A Faithful Catalogue,* however, is more than a display of gross abuse. Written sometime early in 1688, it appeared when James still remained awesome enough to dismay all who opposed him. The poem rehearses, with considerable accuracy for its kind, all that by nature would tend to reduce James and his courtiers to the level of buffoons acting out an absurd low comedy. Circulated in manuscript, the poem was written for those among gentry and court who could understand the numerous allusions to contemporary scandal and, as political opponents, would welcome the reduction of their enemies.

The poem is ascribed to Dorset in the eighteenth-century editions of his works. Though Dorset's biographer, Brice Harris, feels that the poem "is very likely his" (see *Charles Sackville,* Illinois Studies in Language and Literature, *26,* [1940], nos. 3–4, p. 238), it must be admitted that there is little real evidence to support the claim. The wit and poetic excellence, however, suggest a man of Dorset's talents, and the absence of such prominent figures as Nell Gwynne, the Northamptons, and, of course, Dorset himself points to him as author. His antagonism to James, his mistress, and his policy, had caused Dorset to withdraw from court early in the reign. By 1688 he had determined on an active role, however, in opposition to James. This poem may be one manifestation of that role, just as was his later public support of the Seven Bishops and of the invitation to William to intervene in England.

A Faithful Catalogue of our most
eminent Ninnies.
Six Sheets.   Florat. serm. 1°
                               Viros omne
Virgins oderunt, Noti, Pueri, atqz Puellæ.

First of those dull unpointed doggrel Rhymes,
Whose harmless Rage has Curst our Impious Times.
Rise thou, my Muse, and with the sharpest Thorn,
Instead of peaceful Bays, my Brows adorn.
Inspir'd with just Disdain and mortal Hate,
Who long have bin my Plague may shall feel thy weight.
I scorn a giddy and unsafe Applause,
But they (ye Gods) if Trifling in your Cause:
Let Sodom great and let Gomorrha tell
Of their curs'd lewdly deserv'd their Ruin so well.
Go on, my Muse, and with bold voice proclaim
The vicious Lives and long delight'd Fame
Of Scoundrel Lords, and their lewd wive's Amours
Pimp-Statesmen, Bugg——g Priests, Court-Bawds, &
                                          Catamites.
Exalt'd Vice its own vile name does send
To Climes remote and distant shores renown'd,
Thy Trumpets (Clarke) have scap'd no Nation's Ear,
Holland the Dane and Ports mouth led the Rear;
A Bract of Clerks of as base a Breed
As ever was produc'd of Human Seed.
To all but thee the Punks were ever kind,
Free as loose Air and generous as the Wind;
Both steer'd thy Pego and the Nation's Helm,
And both betray'd thy P——tle and thy Realm.
The Barbary! thy execrable Name
Is sure embalm'd with everlasting Shame.
Cou'd not the numerous Host thy Lust suffice
Which in Lascivious Shoals adorn'd thy Eyes,
When their bright Beauty were thro' our Orb display'd,
And Kings each Morn their Persian Homage payd.

Detail from Phillipps Manuscript 8301, Showing Directions for Copyist

[CHARLES SACKVILLE, EARL OF DORSET]

A FAITHFUL CATALOGUE OF OUR MOST EMINENT NINNIES

(*Quos, omnes*
Vicini oderunt, noti, pueri atque puellae.)
Horace, *Serm.* I.i.84–85.

Curs'd be those dull, unpointed, dogg'rel rhymes,
Whose harmless rage has lash'd our impious times.
Rise thou, my muse, and with the sharpest thorn,
Instead of peaceful bays, my brows adorn;
Inspir'd with just disdain and mortal hate,   5
Who long have been my plague, shall feel thy weight.
I scorn a giddy and unsafe applause,
But this, ye gods, is fighting in your cause;
Let Sodom speak, and let Gomorrah tell,
If their curs'd walls deserv'd their flames so well.   10
Go on, my muse, and with bold voice proclaim
The vicious lives and long detested fame
Of scoundrel lords, and their lewd wives' amours,
Pimp-statesmen, bugg'ring priests, court bawds, and whores.
    Exalted vice its own vile name does sound   15
To climes remote and distant shores renown'd.
Thy strumpets, Charles have 'scap'd no nation's ear;
Cleveland the van, and Portsmouth led the rear:

Epigraph: "Whom everyone hates, neighbors and acquaintances, boys and girls."

9. *Sodom . . . Gomorrah:* Though the reference (Gen. 13:18–19) is natural enough in the context of this poem, Dorset probably intended his readers to recall, here and elsewhere in the poem, the obscene play *Sodom,* a burlesque on the court of Charles II and its relations with that of Louis XIV. Whether *Sodom* was ever acted at court, certainly it was freely circulated in MS. and would have been well-known to Dorset's audience.

18. *Cleveland . . . Portsmouth:* Barbara Villiers, Countess of Castlemaine (1641–1709), created Duchess of Cleveland in 1670, but completely supplanted a year later by Louise-Renée de Kéroualle (1649–1734), the Breton maid known as Madam Carwell, who was created Duchess of Portsmouth in 1673.

A brace of cherubs of as vile a breed
As ever was produc'd of human seed.   20
To all but thee the punks were ever kind,
Free as loose air and gen'rous as the wind;
Both steer'd thy pego and the nation's helm,
And both betray'd thy pintle and thy realm.
Ah, Barbary! thy execrable name   25
Is sure embalm'd with everlasting shame.
Could not that num'rous host thy lust suffice,
Which in lasciv'ous shoals ador'd thy eyes,
When their bright beams were through our orb display'd,
And kings each morn their Persian homage paid?   30
Now (Churchill, Dover), see how they are sunk
Into her loathsome, sapless, aged trunk!
And yet remains her c———'s insatiate itch,
And there's a devil yet can hug the witch.
Pardon me, Bab, if I mistake his race,   35
Which is infernal, sure, for though he has
No cloven foot, he has a cloven face.

19-22. Cf. Sheffield's *Essay Upon Satire* (*POAS*, Yale, *1*, 404-05):

> Yet saunt'ring Charles, between his beastly brace,
> Meets with dissembling still in either place,
> Affected humor or a painted face.
> In loyal libels we have often told him
> How one has jilted him, the other sold him;
> How that affects to laugh and this to weep;
> But who can rail so long as he can keep?
> Was ever prince by two at once misled,
> False, foolish, old, ill-natur'd and ill-bred? (65-73)

21. *punks:* Harlots.

23-4. *pego . . . . pintle:* The penis.

25. *Barbary:* Barbara Castlemaine. The epithet is probably meant to suggest her "heathenish or barbarous" sexual nature. See Marvell's treatment of her in *Last Instructions to a Painter*, 79-104 (*POAS*, Yale, *1*, 104-05).

31. *Churchill, Dover:* John Churchill (1650-1722), afterwards Earl of Marlborough, had an affair with Cleveland which produced a daughter, Barbara, in 1672. Henry Jermyn (1638-1708), created Baron Dover in 1685, had been intimate with Cleveland in 1667. Among the "num'rous host" who had succeeded them were Ralph Montagu and William Wycherley.

34. *a devil:* Sometime late in 1684 Castlemaine took for her lover Cardonnell Goodman, the actor-adventurer, for whom see Theophilus Lucas, *Lives of the Most Famous Gamesters*, 1714, pp. 256-60. She was said to have had a son by him in March 1686 (*Song*, "The widows and maids," 8 n.). There are frequent references in the *State Poems* to his "cloven," or "pock-fret" face.

Oh, sacred James! may thy dread noddle be
As free from danger as from wit 'tis free!
But if that good and gracious Monarch's charms   40
Could ne'er confine one woman to his arms,
What strange, mysterious spell, what strong defense,
Can guard that front which has not half his sense?
Poor Sedley's fall e'en her own sex deplore,
Who with so small temptation turn'd thy whore.   45
But Grafton bravely does revenge her fate
And says, thou court'st her thirty years too late;
She scorns such dwindles, her capacious arse
Is fitter for thy scepter, than thy tarse.
  Old Dover, Shrewsbury, and Mordaunt know   50

39. *as from wit 'tis free:* Reminiscent of Catherine Sedley's oft-quoted appraisal of her royal lover's attentions to her: "It cannot be my beauty, for he must see that I have none; and it cannot be my wit, for he has not enough to know that I have any."

46. *Grafton bravely does revenge her fate:* Presumably, a reference to the "bravery" with which Isabella, Duchess of Grafton, carried on her own affairs (see the following lines), although it is certainly possible that she had made some such jibe about James' age at the time of Sedley's advancement as Countess of Dorchester. James was then 52.

49. *tarse:* The penis.

50. *Old Dover, Shrewsbury, and Mordaunt know:* Here the attack shifts to the Duchess of Grafton herself. This beauty, of whom Evelyn spoke so admiringly and whose character Mrs. Jameson found "irreproachable" (*Memoirs of the Beauties of the Court of Charles the Second*, 1837, *1*, 85), certainly received her share of notoriety. "Counted the finest woman in town" (*HMC, Rutland, 2*, 99), she was repeatedly associated in libels of the day with Dover and Charles Mordaunt (1658–1735), afterwards third Earl of Peterborough; see, e.g., *Madam le Croy (POAS*, 1703, *2*, 152):

> Grafton with jealousy oppress'd
> She adds a crescent to his crest;
> No planet-mount his brow adorns,
> Saturn and Venus turn to horns:
> His grace is but an independent,
> Whilst Mordaunt rules in the ascendant. (23–28)

For her supposed affair with Dover see *To Julian* ("Dear friend, I fain would try once more," Harleian 7317, pp. 117 ff.):

> Just so it's with her little grace,
> Whose charms lie only in her face—
> That face though none can praise too much,
> Her shape and understanding's Dutch—
> Who else but she would for a lover
> Accept of antiquated Dover,
> Long since drain'd by her husband's mother; *
> And with him every day repair

Why in that stately frame she lies so low;
And who but her dull blockhead would have found
Her window's small descent on rising ground?
Through the large sash they pass, like Jove of old,
To her attendant bawd, in showers of gold.   55
Mordaunt that insolent, ill-natur'd bear,
From the close grotto, when no danger's near,
Mounts, like a rampant stag, and ruts his deer.
But when by dire mischance the harmless maid
In the dark closet with loud shrieks betray'd   60
The naked lecher, what a woeful grief
It was, th'adult'ress flew to his relief

> In vizard mask to Smithfield Fair,
> For which her husband doth not care. (120–29)

[* Isabella was the daughter of Henry Bennet, Earl of Arlington, by Isabella, daughter of Henry de Nassau, Lord of Auverquerque in Holland. The Duke of Grafton's mother was, of course, Cleveland, whose earlier affair with Jermyn was well-known (see Gramont).]

Grafton's liaison with Charles Talbot, Earl of Shrewsbury, is cited by the satirist responsible for *An Answer to the Poem to Captain Warcup* (Harleian 7319):

> Mordaunt's young Lord, the knowing say,
> Did first find out the happy way
> To conquer Grafton's honor;
>
> By strong persuasions did remove
> The fatal enemy to love,
> Then threw himself upon her.
>
> Shrewsbury now supplies his place;
> In constant waiting on her grace,
> Outgoes her formal lover [sic]

51–53. Apparently anyone should have been able to see and enter such a window. Her residence was Arlington House, built in St. James' Park in 1674, on the present site of Buckingham Palace. "The site of the Mulberry Garden adjoining his house was granted Lord Arlington by Charles II" in 1672. Later, it was reported that "His Majesty has been pleased to give my Lord Arlington the ground at the farther end of the Park, where the deer-harbor is, which is walled in as you go towards Hyde Park," *The Loyal Protestant and True Domestic Intelligencer,* 11 March 1682 (see Wheatley, *1,* 60–1, and 2, 565–7).

52. *blockhead:* A common, derisive name for Charles' natural children; here refers to the Duke of Grafton.

found: Perhaps "established."

55. *her attendant bawd:* Possibly the Duchess' mother-in-law, the Countess of Castlemaine.

in showers of gold: Enamored of Danae, Zeus came to her in a shower of gold. Perseus was their son.

And sav'd his being murder'd for a thief!
Defenseless limbs the well-arm'd host assail'd;
Scarce her own pray'rs with her own slaves prevail'd.   65
Though well prepar'd for flight, he mourn'd his weight
And begg'd Actaeon's change to 'scape Actaeon's fate;
But wing'd with fear, though untransform'd, he bounds,
And swift as hinds outstripp'd the yelling hounds.

    Beware, adulterers, betimes beware   70
You fall not in the same unhappy snare;
From Norfolk's ruin, and his narrow 'scape,
Swive on, contented with a willing rape
On a strong chair, soft couch, or side of bed,
Which never does surprising dangers dread;   75
Let no such harlots lead your steps astray,
Her clitoris will mount in open day;
And, from St. James's to the land of Thule,
There's not a whore who spends so like a mule.
Yet who, to tell the truth, could less have swiv'd,   80
Whose c——— was from such lech'rous stoats deriv'd?
For 'twas the custom of her ancient race
To f——— with any fool, in any place.
And yet her blund'ring dolt deserves a worse,
Could man be plagu'd with a severer curse?   85
A meeter couple never sure were hatch'd;

72. *Norfolk's ruin, and his narrow 'scape:* One of the most notorious scandals of the reign occurred in Oct. 1685 and involved Mary, Duchess of Norfolk, daughter and heiress of Henry Mordaunt, second Earl of Peterborough, and John Germain, the Dutch adventurer whose mother was said to have been mistress to William II. Reresby (pp. 392–93) gives a full account of the affair:

> There seemed to be a strange fatality to attend that family at this time in relation to their wives. The young Duke of Norfolk . . . being told that [his wife] was in league with one St. Germain, a Dutch gentleman, he was not willing to believe it till pretending to go from Windsor to Winchester with the King this very summer, he returned the same evening and surprised them so near that St. Germain, being in bed with the Duchess when the Duke came to the chamber door, was forced to leap out of the window to save himself, and the Duchess was found in all the confusion that so black a guilt could occasion. However, the Duke had the temper not to hurt her, but sent her some days after into a monastery in France.

In 1700 the Duke of Norfolk obtained a divorce (*State Trials, 13,* 1283–1370), and she married Germain in 1701. The affair is satirized often in the *State Poems,* see in particular *Norfolk's Fall* (Harleian 6914).

79. *mule:* Strumpet or concubine (?), obs.

Some marri'd are, indeed, but they are match'd.
The sodomite complains of too much room
And for an arse disdains her spacious womb;
A common bulker is his chief delight,   90
And they in conscience ought to do him right;
And, as c——— spends, arse when well pleas'd should
    sh———!
But, seeing they are lawful man and wife,
Why should the fool and drazel live in strife,
While they both lead the same lasciv'ous life?   95
Or why should he to Meg's or Southcot's roam,
When he may find as great a whore at home?
    Mulgrave, who all his summons to big war
Safely commits to his wise Prince's care,
Lords it o'er all mankind, and is the first   100
By woman hated, and by man accurs'd.
Well has his staff a double use suppli'd,
At once upheld his body, and his pride.
How haughtily he cries, "Page, fetch a whore!
Damn her! She's ugly! Rascal, fetch me more!   105
Bring in that black-ey'd wench. Woman, come near.
Rot you, you draggl'd bitch, what is't you fear?"
Trembling she comes, and with as little flame
As he for the dear part from whence he came;
But, by the help of an assisting thumb,   110
Squeezes his chitterling into her bum;
And if it prove a straight, well-sphincter'd arse,
Perhaps it rears a little his feeble tarse;
But if one drop of vital juice it shed,

90. *common bulker:* A common whore, who will lie down to a man on a bulk, or stand, in front of a shop.

94. *drazel:* A slut.

96. *Meg's or Southcot's:* Brothels kept by well-known bawds. The latter is known to have kept a "quality bawd house" near Old Dunkirk Square (see *The Last Night's Ramble,* Harleian 7317). I have adopted "Southcot's" from the various MS. readings, as the most plausible in light of our present knowledge of such establishments in 17th-century London. That a Madam Circut's existed, however, as several MSS. suggest, is certainly possible, if not highly probable.

98. *Mulgrave . . . his summons:* John Sheffield, third Earl of Mulgrave, Rochester's Lord All-Pride. MSS. gloss: "He carried Lord Peterborough's challenge to the King."

102. *his staff:* The white staff; Mulgrave was Lord Chamberlain.

Help him, good Jove, for both sides then are dead. 115
   Thine, crafty Seymour, was a good design,
For sure his issue ne'er will injure thine;
But thou, thyself, must needs confess that she
Does justly curse thy politics and thee.
Her noble Protestant has got a flail 120
Young, large, and fit to feague her briny tale;
But now, poor wretch, she lies as she would bust,
Sometimes with brandy, and sometimes with lust;
Though prime as goats, she courts in vain her drone:
The frigid he, and she the torrid zone. 125
Both friend and foe he with vast ruin mauls,
Who, at first thrust, before both sexes falls.
   Had I, oh, had I his transcendent verse,
In his own lofty strains I would rehearse
That deep intrigue, when he the princess woo'd, 130

---

116. *Seymour:* Charles Seymour, sixth Duke of Somerset, in May 1682 married the 15-year-old Elizabeth Percy, widow of Henry Cavendish, Earl of Ogle, and of Thomas Thynne.

119. *Does justly curse thy politics:* Somerset was dismissed from his places in 1687 upon his refusal to introduce the Papal Nuncio. One of his losses was the lord-lieutenancy of Somerset.

120. *Protestant . . . flail:* Besides the obscene reference, a pun on the hinged and weighted wooden flail of this name invented in the late 1670s by Stephen College. (For a picture of the flail in use, see *POAS*, Yale, 2, opp. p. 12.)

121. *feague:* To beat or whip.

122. *poor wretch:* Mulgrave married Ursula, widow of Edward, first Earl of Conway, in March 1686, though it was said that she perferred the suit of Northampton (see above, *Song,* "The widows and maids"). Her proclivity for drink is stressed by satirists; see, e.g., *The Session of Ladies* (Taylor 2):

> Pert Mulgrave, well fluster'd with brandy and sack,
> To Cupid in passion her story appli'd . . .

> But Cupid repli'd in Adonis's praise,
> Though he had esteem for a lecherous punk,
> The pox or the plague he could freely embrace,
> But could not dispense with a whore would be drunk.

124. *her drone:* Mulgrave, said to have "grown feeble and weak in the back" by the satirist of *The Session of Ladies.*

130. *when he the princess woo'd:* In Nov. 1682 Mulgrave was in disgrace at court "for making some applications to my Lady Anne Stuart, the Duke of York's daughter, and suspicion of adhering to the Duke of Monmouth's interest. He had great employments at Court, which were disposed of after this manner . . . his lieutenancy of the East Riding to the Duke of Somerset . . . " (Reresby, p. 281).

But lov'd adult'ry more than royal blood.

Young Ossory, who lov'd the haughty peer,
Her mother's darling sins could best declare,
But to her memory we must be just;
'Tis sacrilege to rob such beaut'ous dust.   135

Oh, Wharton, Wharton, what a wretched tool
Is a dull wit, when made a woman's fool!
Thy rammish, spendthrift buttock, 'tis well known,
Her nauseous bait has made thee swallow down,
Though mumbled and spit out by half the town.   140
How well (my honest Lexington) she knows
The many mansions in thy f———ing house;
How often prais'd thy dear, curvetting tarse,
Which thou rid'st curb'd, like an unruly horse!

132. *Young Ossory, who lov'd the haughty peer:* The beautiful Lady Anne, daughter
of Laurence Hyde, Earl of Rochester, and his wife, Henrietta Boyle. She had been
married in July 1682, not yet fifteen, to the Earl of Ossory, grandson to the Duke of
Ormond. She died prematurely on 25 Jan. 1685. She was said to have been pursued by
Mulgrave, the proverbially "haughty" King John. See *To Julian:*

> Now Mordaunt Grafton's virtue tries
> More than King John does Ossory's.

136. *Wharton:* Thomas Wharton, afterwards first Marquis of Wharton. Lady Mary
Wortley Montagu described him as the "most profligate, impious, and shameless of
men." His first wife, Anne, daughter of Sir Henry Lee, fifth Baron of Ditchley, died in
Oct. 1685, after an unhappy and fruitless marriage.

137. *a woman's fool:* Wharton was apparently involved in an affair with Sophia Bulkeley, widow of Henry Bulkeley, master of the household under Charles and James (the
exact date of his death is unrecorded). Sophia, the sister of Frances, La Belle Stuart,
was a Jacobite and acclaimed in verse a most "religious" whore. A lady of the bedchamber to Queen Mary, St. Evremont wrote of her: "[Elle] faisoit la prude et affectoit
de paraître dévot quoi-qu'elle ne fut point ennemi de la galantrie."

141. *honest Lexington:* Robert Sutton (1661–1723), second Baron of Lexington (?).
Why he should be addressed here remains a mystery. His "honesty" showed itself in
1686 when he laid down his commission (Luttrell, *1*, 381).

142. *many mansions:* John 14:2.

144. *thou rid'st curb'd:* The metaphor is appropriately derived from Wharton's in-
tense interest in horse racing, an interest he probably combined as often as possible
with his amorous concerns:

> In the Grove, or Wilderness, on the eastern verge of the gardens, is a small turreted
> brick building, originally erected by Thomas, Marquis of Wharton, for the residence
> of a favorite lady. Its situation, though solitary, commanded a remarkably fine view,
> embracing the racecourse in Quainton meadow, and the adjacent fields, about two
> miles' distance (Lipscomb, *Hist. and Antiq. of Bucks.*, *1*, 167, cited by J. P. Hore,
> *The Hist. of Newmarket*, 1886, *3*, 163).

That crooked martyr, which most c———s would flout,   145
Turns her lascivious matrix inside out;
Pleas'd with the novelty, she freely spends,
And turns and winds which way soe'er it bends.
How big with joy she went with thee to th'church,
When thou, false varlet! left her in the lurch;   150
E'en Elliot, who refus'd none before,
Scorn'd to pronounce the banns with such a whore.

   To Pancras, Tom, there such as she resort
(That mother church, too, does all sinners court);
As she has been thy strumpet all her life,   155
'Tis time to make her now thy lawful wife,
That Bulkeley's spouse may pride it in the box,
With face and c——— all martyr'd with the pox;
In some deep sawpit both your noddles hide,
For 'tis hard guessing which has the best bride.   160
Ah, Tom, thy brother, like a prudent man,
Has chosen the much better harridan;
She, a good-natur'd, candid devil, shows
Him all the bawding, jilting tricks she knows.
Thy rook some trivial cheats her blockhead learns,   165
While he the master hocus ne'er discerns.

151. *Elliot:* "Parson of Duke's place" (MSS. gloss). "St. James' Church, Duke's Place, Aldgate . . . acquired notoriety towards the close of the 17th century for clandestine and irregular marriages, and Adam Elliot, the incumbent, was in February 1686 suspended for three years for solemnizing marriages without bans or license; but three months later it was decided that the Church of St. James being extra-parochial was not subject to the ordinary. The suspension was therefore void, and the weddings went on more merrily than ever. Thirty or forty couples were sometimes married in a day . . . " (Wheatley, 2, 278).

153. *Pancras:* MSS. gloss, "Pancridge, Mother of St. Paul's." St. Pancras-in-the-Fields, for a great many years the chief burial place for Roman Catholic residents in London. Its popularity is variously attributed, but one tradition makes it the last church in London where mass was said. Originally, it was a prebendal manor in Middlesex, which belonged to the Dean and Chapter of St. Paul's (Wheatley, 3, 16 ff.).

159. *In some deep sawpit:* Philip, fourth Baron Wharton and father of Thomas, was said by royalist satirists to have hidden himself in a sawpit when his regiment was routed at Edgehill (*Rump Songs,* pp. 91, 103).

161. *thy brother:* Although Wharton had three brothers, this is almost certainly Henry, or Harry, who died in Ireland in 1689. Contemporary gossip linked him with "Norfolk's lewd Moll," i.e. Mary, Duchess of Norfolk (*POAS, 2,* 1703, 157).

165. *rook:* A swindler.

166. *hocus:* Trickery, or deception.

To pox and plague, oh, may she subject be,
As she's from childbed pain and peril free!
Her actual sins invalidate the first,
With ease she teems, and brings forth unaccurs'd;   170
To thee, Lucina, she need never call,
Like ripen'd fruit her mellow bastards fall;
And what with needless labor I disclose,
Her well-stretch'd c————— and rivell'd belly shows.

    Whoever, like Charles Dering, scorns disgrace,   175
Can never want, although he lose his place;
That toothless murd'rer, to his just reproach,
Pimps for his sister, to maintain a coach;
And, let what will the church or state befall,
One fulsome, crafty whore supports 'em all.   180
    Scarsdale, though loath'd, still the fair sex adores,
And has a regiment of horse and whores.
Amid the common rout of early duns,
For mustard, soap, milk, small coal, swords, and guns,
Two reverend officers, more highly born,   185
Wait on his stinking levy every morn
And in th'full pomp his palace gates adorn;
But which is most in vogue is hard to tell,
The public bawd or private sentinel
That blubber'd oaf, for two, dull, dribbling bouts,   190

    169. *invalidate:* I.e. by miscarriage, punning on *v.* "invalid," "to affect with disease or sickness."

    171. *Lucina:* The Roman goddess who watched over and eased childbirth.

    175. *Charles Dering:* Probably, one of the three sons of Sir Edward Dering of Surrenden Dering, Kent (d. 1684). His mistress may have been Elizabeth Villiers (1657?-1733), first cousin to Barbara, and mistress of William III, see *POAS,* Yale, 2, 233, where his toothlessness is also mentioned:

> Never, till Dering Villiers does embrace,
> His false teeth printing in her falser face . . . (122–3)

Dering had one sister. I know of no reason to call him a murderer, but the title may refer to a duel he fought in this period.

    180. *crafty whore:* Probably Elizabeth Villiers, though the pronoun may refer as well to Dering's sister.

    181. *Scarsdale:* Robert Leeke, third Earl of Scarsdale. In Nov. 1687 he was dismissed from his regiment and later deprived of his place as Groom of the Stole to the Prince of Denmark (Luttrell, *1,* 422–3, 425).

    184. *small coal:* Charcoal

Maintains two bastards made of Jenny's clouts.
Ere it could fetch, 'twas, like pox'd Eland, spoil'd;
Yet it can't touch a wench, but she's with child.
But who can think that pestilential breath
Should raise up life that always blasts with death? 195
    'Tis strange, Kildare, that refin'd *beau garçon,*
Was never yet at the Bell Savage shown,
For 'tis a true and wonderful baboon.
It therefore wisely was at first design'd
He ne'er should like to propagate his kind; 200
But the dull, venom'd draught in vain employ'd,
Like the false serpent's, was itself destroy'd.
With foul corruption sure he first was fed,
And by equiv'cal generation bred;
An honest solan goose, compared to him, 205
Is a fine creature, and of more esteem.
No learn'd philosphers need strive to know
Whether his soul's *extraduce,* or no;

191. *Jenny:* Jenny Cromwell, a notorious bawd (MS. gloss).
    clouts: Underlinen or sanitary napkins.
192. *pox'd Eland:* Henry Savile (1660–88), styled Lord Eland from 1679, the eldest son of Lord Halifax. He married Esther de la Tour, daughter of the Marquis de Gouvernet (Evelyn, *4,* 517–18). Rumor had it that he had been forced to undertake the marriage to preserve her honor (see *The Lady's Mistake,* Taylor 2):

> Had she not so long stay'd,
>   She had still been a maid;
> She by keeping its secret was only betray'd;
> A Marquis's daughter and a Marquis's son [Lord Eland]
> By concealing a brat and a pox are undone. (41–45)

196. *Kildare:* John Fitzgerald (1661–1707), eighteenth Earl of Kildare. His second wife was Elizabeth, daughter and coheir of Richard Jones, third Viscount and first Earl of Ranelagh, whom he married on 12 June 1684. She brought with her a fortune of £10,000 and the reputation of having been one of the mistresses of Charles II.
    beau garçon: A fop.
197. *Bell Savage:* An inn at Ludgate Hill. Originally, a place at which dramas were played, it continued for some time a place of various minor entertainments. At the turn of the last century Bankes had exhibited the feats of his famous horse Marocco at the inn (Wheatley, *1,* 154–56).
205. *solan goose:* Cf. Cleveland, *Rebel Scot,* 125–26, and Butler, *Hudibras,* III. ii. 655, for the curious belief, or spoof on belief, that barnacles hanging from trees contained little, perfectly-formed sea fowls, like the gannet.
208. *extraduce:* Derived as from a parent stock—the theory that held the soul was begotten with the body by the father (4 syllables).

He has none yet, nor never will, I fear—
No soul of sense would ever enter there;   210
Though Talbot, that young sodomite, they say,
With tarse and carrot well enlarg'd the way.
With painful look he grins, as if the fool
Were always squeezing for a costive stool.
I wonder he dares speak, for fear we firk   215
His lazy bones and make the monkey work;
Swive on, my fair adult'ress, you do well,
For who would not loath him much more than Hell?
F——— with some true wild Irish fool, or brim
With savage boars, rather than lie with him.   220
If aged Devonshire has left the trade
And had enough of costly masquerade,
With renew'd flames your old amour pursue,
Now Rochester has nothing else to do.
Well done, old Hyde! we all thy choice adore;   225
She is the younger and much better whore.
    But Hales has sure, to his eternal curse,
Left his own strumpet and espous'd a worse;
That blazing star still rises with the sun
And will, I hope, whene'er it sets, go down.   230
St. Peter ne'er deni'd his Lord but thrice,

211. *Talbot:* Jack Talbot, brother of Charles, twelfth Earl of Shewsbury. He danced
in a shroud at Devonshire's masquerade and was later killed in a duel with the Duke of
Grafton (see *Song,* "The widows and maids," 43–48 and n.).

219. *brim:* Of swine, to copulate.

221. *aged Devonshire:* Presumably Elizabeth, wife of William Cavendish, third Earl of
Devonshire. She outlived her husband, who had died in 1684 at the age of 67, by five
years. Her son, William, first Duke of Devonshire, "a Corydon among the ladies," according to Walpole, had married Mary, daughter of James Butler, first Duke of
Ormonde, in 1662. For an account of a "great masquerade" given by Devonshire in the
winter of 1685–86, see *HMC, Rutland,* 2, 99–106 *passim.*

224. *Rochester:* Laurence Hyde, first Earl of Rochester, was left with "nothing else to
do" after his dismissal as Lord Treasurer in Jan. 1687. He had married Henrietta Boyle
in 1665.

227. *Hales:* Sir Edward Hales (d. 1695), titular Earl of Tenterden, married Frances,
daughter of Sir Francis Windebank, kt., of Oxfordshire, by whom he had five sons and
seven daughters. The references here are almost certainly political and religious, however. For his proselytizing see above, *The Trial of Godden v. Hales.* His "star" rose
with James' "sun." He was made a member of the Privy Council, appointed one of the
Lords of the Admiralty, Deputy Warden of the Cinque Ports, Lieutenant of the Tower,
and Master of the Ordnance.

But good St. Edward scorns to be so nice;
He every mass abjures what he before
On Tests and sacraments so often swore.
His mother-church will have a special son   235
Of him, by whom his father was undone.
He turn'd, because on bread alone he'd dine
And make the wafer save his meat and wine;
Mammon's the god he'll worship, anyway,
And keeps conviction ready to a day.   240
Forbid it, heav'n, I e'er should live to see
Our pious monarch's gorgeous chapel be
Fill'd with such miscreant proselytes as he!
   Miserere Domine! Ave Maria!
Poor Father Dover has got a gonorrhea.   245
Was e'er, dread James, so much affection shown?
He'd save thy soul, but cares not for his own.
How Sedley prays, the old adult'rous fop
May find it a Carnegan-swinding clap!
And sure 'twill in the bones and marrow stick,   250
And must be damnable to soul and pr——— —
The pocky jade was a damn'd heretic!

236. *his father:* Hales' father, a zealous Royalist, died in France shortly after the Restoration.

237–38. With the ironic inversion of Matt. 4:4: "Man shall not live by bread alone," and the introduction of Mammon, "the least erected spirit," the satirist attempts to mock transubstantiation while seeing Hales' conversion as a purely venal act.

242. *chapel:* Shortly after his accession James had the oratory attached to his old lodgings as Duke of York splendidly fitted out for his use. In 1686 the Privy Gallery near the Banqueting House at Whitehall was demolished and replaced by a group of apartments, offices, and a magnificent chapel. Designed by Christopher Wren, the buildings were completed by the end of the year and the chapel was opened for Roman Catholic services on Christmas Day (Turner, p. 246).

245. *Father Dover:* Presumably an ironic reference to Henry Jermyn, Lord Dover (1636–1708), one of the Catholic members of James' Privy Council and a commissioner of the treasury.

247–48. James was constantly under pressure from Mary and the more radical Catholic faction to dismiss Catherine Sedley. For an account of such importuning, see Burnet, *1*, 683.

249. *Carnegan-swinding:* A reference to the supposed revenge taken against James by Robert Carnegie, Earl of Southesk, said to have purchased a "twenty-guinea clap" in order to convey it to James by means of his inconstant wife, Lady Southesk. His "revenge" was held responsible for James' inability to produce a healthy heir (see below, headnote to *The Birth of . . . Prince of Wales*).
   swinding: Wasting away.

"Odzons, ods blood, our family's besh————,"
Quoth Winchester, "but I'll be drunk at night;"
Unhappy maid, who man has never known,   255
And yet, with per'lous pangs, brought forth a son!
Rejoice, ye slavish tribe of later Jews;
Sound in your synogogues the blessed news;
A new messiah is at last arriv'd
From an unspotted womb that ne'er was swiv'd.   260
Our chiro-medico did'mist nothing smelt,
Till he the sprawling prophet heard, and felt;
And now it surely cannot be deni'd
By him, who cur'd the King of what he di'd.
    Now Herbert boasts that his wise King's Head crew   265
Foretold the dismal times we all should rue!
Curs'd be the screech owls! that rebellious crowd
Presag'd, indeed, Rome's swift approach, as loud
As wise Cassandra's boding voice of old
The wretched fate of ancient Troy foretold.   270
But why is he against the bringing in
Any religion that indulges sin?
He, who his other charges can retrench,

254-55. *I'll be drunk at night:* Charles Paulet, sixth Marquis of Winchester, wrote this "in a letter to Charles Duncombe" (MS. gloss). His daughter Mary's disgrace is considered in *The Lady's Mistake* (Taylor 2):

> All ye that know men and for virgins would pass,
> To your mothers and midwives make known your condition;
> And learn by my young Lady Mary's* disgrace [*Paulet]
> There is no such a coxcomb as is the physician.

It was said in June 1686 that she was to marry a Lord Spencer (*HMC, Rutland, 2,* 110)—perhaps Robert, eldest son of Sunderland. A profligate, he died, apparently unmarried, in 1688.

261. *chiro-medico:* "Dr. King," MSS. gloss. Edmund King (1629–1709), see Evelyn, *4,* 406: "if . . . Dr. King (that excellent chirurgeon as well as physician) had not been accidentally present [to let him blood] (with his lancet in his pocket) his Majesty had certainly died that moment. . . ."

did'mist: Didymist, a doubter, from the surname of St. Thomas. Perhaps an obscure pun is also intended on "didymis," or "testicles."

265. *Herbert:* Identified by MSS. as Henry Herbert (1654–1709), created Baron Herbert of Cherbury in 1694. He was a staunch opponent of the Crown throughout James' reign and joined William III in Holland in 1688.

King's Head: Marginal note, "[In] Chancery Lane and where the Whigs' [Green Ribbon] Club was kept." See Wheatley, *2,* 345.

To save ten guineas for a handsome wench;
Or be content to part with twenty pound,   275
If Mrs. Wright insure her being sound.
That idiot thinks the tawdry harlot's glad
To serve him now, for favors she has had;
But who, dear Hally, ever heard before
Of gratitude in any common whore?   280
She mounts the price and goes half-snack herself,
And well knows how to cully such an elf.
Poor Jenny I must needs much more applaud,
A better whore, and truer friend and bawd.
Like the French King, he all his conquests buys,   285
And pow'rful guinea still subdues their eyes;
How his smug, little black-ey'd harlot gaz'd
On his broad gold and fine apartments prais'd!
But f————'d, not trusting to the miser's truth,
Like Joseph's sacks, with money in her mouth.   290
Sometimes he'll venture for himself to trade,
With awkward grace, at balls and masquerade;
But what was the proud coxcomb e'er the near,
Unless he got my Lady Gerard there?
Her qualities to all the world are known: 295
Fair as his kin and honest as her own.
She makes the brothel worse than common stews,
And loves to swive in her own tribe, like Jews;
Incest with nearest blood, adult'ry, all
Her darling sins, we may well deadly call.   300
Whate'er in times of yore she may have been,
Her lust has now parch'd up her rivell'd skin.
    Thou, town of Edmonton, I charge, declare

276. *Mrs. Wright:* A well-known bawd.
281. *half-snack:* Half-shares.
282. *cully:* To deceive, or cheat.
283. *Jenny:* Jenny Cromwell again? See above, 191 n.
290. *Joseph's sacks:* Gen. 42, especially 25–27.
293. *e'er the near:* i.e. "ever nearer."
294. *Lady Gerard:* Elizabeth (d. 1699), widow of Digby, fifth Lord Gerard of Bromley. She was the daughter of Charles Gerard, Earl of Macclesfield, and thus distantly related to her husband (see 289).
303. *Edmonton:* A village—now part of London—about nine miles directly north of the Tower.

What she and Wolseley did so often there;
That scribbling fool, who writes to her in meter,   305
And only speaks his songs to make 'em sweeter.
Great Virgil's true reverse in sense and fate!
For what another writ, procur'd his hate;
To be but thought a wit, he lost his place,
And yet, to show he is not of that race,   310
Will write himself and add to his disgrace.
His *Valentinian*'s learned preface shines
Like Memphis' siege or Bulloigne's radiant lines.
Among the Muses all his time he spends,
And his whole study tow'rds Parnassus bends;   315
Yet, if for his, one handsome thought be shown,
Stop the dull thief, I'll swear 'tis not his own.
Satire's his joy, but, if he don't improve,
Give me his hate, and let her take his love.
That fop she, Herbert, more than thee admires;   320
He oft'ner quenches her lascivious fires.
In vain poor Harry, with ridic'lous joy,
Shows her and every whore his hopeful boy;

304. *Wolseley:* Presumably Robert Wolseley (1649–97), chiefly remembered for a preface in 1685 to Rochester's play *Valentinian* and for a duel with Harry Wharton in 1692
in consequence of a "poetical quarrel," which resulted in Wharton's death. Wolseley
supposedly died unmarried (*DNB*), but 329 suggests that he was a widower.

305–17. *scribbling fool:* According to the gloss in most MSS., Wolseley borrowed "from
the 'divine' Mr. [Thomas] D'Urfey" (1653–1723), the poet and dramatist, author of
The Siege of Memphis, or the Ambitious Queen, 1676, "an insufferably bombastic heroic
play" (*Songs,* ed. C. L. Day, 1933, p. 5). Two examples of Wolseley's amorous verse are
preserved in *Examen Miscellaneum* (1702) a fair sample of which are these lines addressed to "Cloris":

> . . . think not, Cloris, Heav'n design'd
> The fairest creatures, most unkind;
> Those who may boast the brightest eyes,
> Can claim but hearts for sacrifice;
> And when you proudly would make life your prey,
> Like an ambitious tyrant you will fall,
> Fear'd and admir'd, but envy'd by us all;
> You, like the sun, your glories should display:
> Though in one clime a greater heat you give,
> You nowhere should refuse enough to live.

312. *Bulloigne's radiant lines:* Edward Fairfax translated Tasso's *Gerusalemme Libe-*
rata as *Godfrey of Bulloigne, or the Recoverie of Jerusalem* (1600).

323. *his hopeful boy:* Cf. MacFlecknoe, 61. Herbert had only one child, Henry, afterwards second Baron Herbert of Cherbury, by his wife Ann, whom he had married in 1678.

His city songstress says he keeps such pother
He'll scarce be able e'er to get another.   325
   Join then, propitious stars, their widow'd store,
And make them happy, as they were before;
That is, may the decay'd, incestuous punk
Swill like his spouse; and he, like hers, die drunk.
   Why, Houghton, has the good old Queen the grace   330
To see thy bear-like mien and baboon face?
Her court, ye gods be prais'd, has long been free
From Irish prigs and such dull sots as thee.
The wakeful gen'ral, conscious of thy charms,
Dreads thine as much as Monmouth's fierce alarms;   335
Yet sure there is a greater ditch between
A greasy Whiggish dolt and Charles's Queen.
There is, and Houghton soars not yet so high;
His ogling pigsnies gloat on Lady Di.
That gudgeon on soft baits will only bite,   340
For easy conquests are his sole delight;
And none can say but that his judgment's good,

329. *die drunk:* Digby, Lord Gerard of Bromley, died suddenly on 10 Oct. 1684, aged 22, "of a drinking match, and fell down on the spot" at the Rose Tavern, Covent Garden. He was known to be "a great swearer, drunkard, and very debauched," and had been imprisoned before he was 15 for having killed an apprentice. (For these and other notices, see Cokayne, *Peerage*).

330. *Houghton:* John Holles (1662–1711), Lord Houghton, afterwards Duke of Newcastle.

332–33. *free From Irish prigs:* Deliberately ironic. For the Irish influence at Court, see *The Town Life,* 122–27.

334. *the wakeful gen'ral:* Louis Duras, Earl of Feversham. In command of James' troops at the battle of Sedgemoor, he was said to have been asleep after an overly festive banquet when Monmouth's troops attacked.

336. *a greater ditch:* The allusion is to the unexpected Bussex Rhine, which confronted Monmouth's men as they were about to fall upon the King's army, destroying any chance of surprise and success the rebels might have had. The reference here related figuratively, as well, to the Dowager Queen's religion.

337. *Whiggish dolt:* Houghton was a staunch Protestant and Whig. In 1681 Dryden dedicated *The Spanish Friar* to him, recommending "a Protestant play to a Protestant patron."

339. *Lady Di:* Diana Kirke, daughter of George Kirke (d. 1675?), Gentleman of the Robes to Charles I, and Groom of the Bedchamber and Keeper of Whitehall Palace under Charles II, by his second wife, Mary, daughter of the poet Aurelian Townshend. For Diana Kirke's marriage to Aubrey de Vere, twentieth Earl of Oxford, see below, 369 ff. and n.

340. *gudgeon:* "A small European fresh-water fish . . . much used for bait;" fig. "One that will bite at any bait or swallow anything: a credulous, gullible person."

For all the Kirkes are made of flesh and blood.
    Vernon, the glory of that lustful tribe,
Scorns to be meanly purchas'd with a bribe;   345
To fame and honor hates to be a slave,
And freely gives what nature freely gave;
Like heirs to crowns, with sure credentials born,
Her hasty bastards private entries scorn;
In midst of courts, and in the mid of day,   350
With little peril force their easy way.
    But Woodford is, methinks, a better seat,
And for distended wames a safe retreat;
'Twas well advised, old Kirke, no danger's fear'd,
No groans nor yelling cries can there be heard.   355
In this lewd town and these censorious times,
Where every whore rails at each other's crimes,
Fair Theodosia, thy romantic name
Had sure been blasted with eternal shame;
But thy wise stratagems so well were laid,   360

344. *Vernon:* Mary Kirke, Diana's older sister, married Sir Thomas Vernon in Paris in May 1677. Previously, she had been mistress to the Duke of York, Monmouth, and Mulgrave, all of whom were receiving her favors at the same time (*HMC, Rutland, 2,* 27 and Elizabeth D'Oyley, *James, Duke of Monmouth,* 1938, pp. 100–01). For her marriage with Vernon, see Jesse, *Memoirs,* 1846, *4,* 362–6. Some of the confusion in Jesse's account is cleared up in *N&Q,* 12 Nov. 1853, pp. 461–63.

349–50. *Her hasty bastards . . . . :* For a long time the lady was identified as Gramont's Miss Warmestry, "quietly brought to bed in the sight of all the Court" (Gramont, pp. 143–44). It is clear, however, that Mary Kirke was another who suffered a similar public discomfiture (ibid. p. 118 n.).

352. *Woodford:* Perhaps the town of Woodford, about nine miles northeast of London in Essex, the Veres' county (see 369 n).

353. *wames:* "The belly, abdomen," or "womb."

354. *old Kirke:* Mary Townshend, wife of George Kirke (see 339 n. and *The Men of Honor Made Men Worthy,* 87 n.), lived on through the reign of James (*Moneys Received and Paid for Secret Services of Charles II and James II,* ed. J. Y. Akerman, Camden Society, 1851, pp. 204, 212). In *Queries and Answers from Garraway's Coffee House, POAS, 3,* 1704, 76, she is vulgarly characterized:

    Q. How often has Mrs. Kirke sold her daughter Di's maidenhead before the Lord of Oxford married her?
    A. Ask the Prince and Harry Jermyn.

358. *Theodosia:* Diana Kirke? Possibly a mistake for Theodora, however, the notorious wife of Justinian, said to have been "an incessant and tyrannical match-maker, forcing men to accept wives and women to accept husbands at her caprice. She constituted herself the protectress of faithless wives against outraged husbands, yet professed great zeal for the moral reformation of the city . . . " (*EB*).

I'd almost swear thou art a very maid.
Go on, and scorn our common swiving rules,
Let Warcup make th'incest'ous uncles fools,
Impregnate more and more thy seedy loins;
While prudence pimps, and such a bawd combines,   365
Thou still art safe, though thy large womb should bear
Like hers who teem'd for every day o'th'year.

    Proud Oxford justly thinks her Dutch-built shape
A little too unwieldy for a rape;
Yet, being conscious it will tumble down,   370
At first assault surrenders up the town;
But no kind conqueror has yet thought fit
To make it his belov'd imperial seat;
That batter'd fort, which they with ease deceive,
Pillag'd and sack'd, to the next foe they leave;   375
And haughty Di in just revenge will lig,
Although she starve, with any senseless Whig;
Not that to any principle she's firm,
But is debauch'd by damn'd seducing sperm;
Sidney well knew the banning hour, when sev'n   380

363. *Warcup:* Capt. Edmund Warcup, mentioned by Anthony Wood (*Fasti Oxonienses,* ed. Bliss, 1820, 2, 325). Apparently he took over the duties of Robert Julian, the Muses' Secretary, after the latter's imprisonment (*CSPD,* 1685, pp. 124, 233), and purveyed scandalous gossip and obscene poetry among the coffee-shops (see the *Letter to C*[aptain] *W*[arcup] in *POAS,* 2, 1703, 143. There is an answer to this poem in Harleian 7319, p. 398, entitled *In Answer to the Poem to Capt. Warcup*). Warcup had a daughter, Mrs. Price, whom he had the vanity to believe Charles II would marry. "There were letters of his, wherein he mentioned that 'his daughter was one night and t'other with the King, and very graciously received by him'" (Granger, *4,* 437–8).

th'incest'ous uncles: On her mother's side, Aurelian Townshend, the poet and profligate, was an uncle to Diana Kirke. She was also related to the Killegrews both through her father's first wife and through her husband, Sir Thomas Vernon.

367. *who teem'd for every day o'th' year:* Unidentified.

368. *Proud Oxford:* Diana Kirke married Aubrey de Vere (1626–1703), twentieth Earl of Oxford, about 1671.

Dutch-built: Opprobrious combination, presumably both in reference to her "unwieldy" frame and in mocking allusion to Dutch prowess.

376. *lig:* "Lie," in the sense, "to lie with or have sexual intercourse with," obs.

380. *Sidney:* Henry Sidney (1641–1704), Earl of Romney. "His later years were pestered by acrimonious letters on behalf of the numerous children for whom he refused to provide" (*DNB*). One such case involved Diana Kirk, Oxford's wife, and Grace Worthley, for 20 years Sidney's mistress. The latter, writing to her cousin Lord Brandon in Sept. 1682, threatened to "pistol him and be hanged for him, which I had rather do than sit still and starve or be any longer a laughing-stock for any of Mrs. Kirke's bastards"

" 'Od's wounds" throws out, or else " 'Od's blood" elev'n,
When her decrepit, spendthrift, troopless rook
Is meek as Moses hid in fire and smoke.
    Our sacred writ does learnedly relate
For one poor babe two mothers' hot debate;   385
But our two doughty heroes, I am told,
Which is the truest father fiercely scold:
Both claims seem just and great, but gen'rous Hales
(Who always is on the right side) prevails.
He will not only save its life, but soul;   390
So poor Phil Kirke is fobb'd off for a fool.
But 'tis all one—Sir Courtly Nice does swear
He'll go to Mistress Grace of Exeter.
    But why to Ireland, Braithwait? Can the clime,
Dost thou imagine, make an easy time?   395

[i.e. "the common Countess of Oxford and her adulterous bastards"], see *The Diary of the times of Charles the Second by the Honorable Henry Sidney*, ed. R. W. Blencowe, 1843, *1*, xxx–xxxi.

380–81. *Sidney well knew the banning hour . . . :* Several ideas run through these lines. Sidney knows when Oxford, a compulsive gambler (Theophilus Lucas, *Lives of the Gamesters*, pp. 165–66), will be out throwing dice and swearing home the winning rolls of seven and eleven. There is as well a play on the idea of the "banns" and on the obs. form of "bane," which also meant "to poison, ruin, or destroy."

382. *troopless:* In Feb. 1688 Vere lost his regiment, when he failed to comply with James' command "to use his interest in his lieutenancy for the taking off the penal laws and the Test." He replied to the King that "he could not persuade that to others which he was adverse to in his own conscience" (Reresby, p. 487).

rook: Probably in the sense of "sharper" at cards or dice, with a pun on "chess piece."

384–85. *mothers' hot debate:* Judging between the two harlots who sought the right to one child (I Kings 3:16–28), Solomon decided to cut the live child in half and give each woman a portion. The real mother offered to give up the child rather than see it put to death.

386. *two doughty heroes:* Sir Edmund Hales was a convert to Catholicism in Nov. 1685 (see above, 227 ff. and nn.). Phil Kirke was a colonel under Percy Kirke in the Queen Dowager's Regiment of Foot (Charles Dalton, *English Army Lists and Commission Registers (1685–89)*, 1960, *2*, 25, 91). A Phil Kirke, Esq., is cited in *Angliae Notitia*, 1687, pp. 169, 213, as housekeeper at Whitehall and as Groom to the Bedchamber to Prince George of Denmark. The relation of this man, or these men, to Percy Kirke remains undetermined.

392. *Sir Courtly Nice:* The pompous fool in John Crowne's comedy of the same name, produced in 1685.

393. *Mistress Grace of Exeter:* Presumably a daughter of John Cecil, fifth Earl of Exeter (1638?–1700; married 1670), or of his father, John, fourth Earl (d. 1678).

394. *Braithwait:* I have been unable to discover any data on this woman or on her affairs with Kirke and "Ned" Hales.

Ungratefully, indeed, thou didst requite
The skillful goddess of the silent night
By whose kind help thou wast so oft before
Deliver'd safely on thy native shore.
Thy belly shin'd, and an unusual load   400
Made thee believe Kirke's shoulders were too broad.
And thou'dst be sure we should not hear thee roar,
And, if poor tuzzy-muzzy should be tore,
Wisely resolv'd Ned should ne'er see it more.
But, since all's well, return, that we may laugh   405
At Irish c———s, which in all climes are safe.
    Justly, false Monmouth, did thy Lord declare
Thou should'st not in his crown nor empire share;
Indeed, dear Limp, it was a just design,
Seeing he had so small a share of thine.   410
Brave Feversham, that thund'ring son of arms,
With pow'rful magic conquer'd both your charms:
Virtue, thy weak lieutenant, ran away,
Just like that curs'd, miscreant coward, Grey.
And as poor James from his new subjects did,   415
At last from thy fair breast the Gen'ral fled.
His conversation, wit, and parts, and mien
Deserv'd, he thought, at least a widow'd queen.

397–99. *skillful goddess:* A play on Diana, goddess of the moon and of chastity, and on Diana as Lucina, the goddess of childbirth. Both "deliver" her safely and skillfully on her "native," i.e. local and habitual, shore.

403. *tuzzy-muzzy:* Jocularly the pudendum.

406. *in all climes are safe:* A humorous reference to the absence of poisonous beasts in Ireland.

407. *false Monmouth:* Anne Scott, Duchess of Monmouth and Buccleuch. The Duke of Monmouth had deserted her for his mistress Henrietta Wentworth in 1674 or 1675.

409. *dear Limp:* An opprobrious epithet for the Duchess of Monmouth?

411. *Feversham:* See above, 334 n. No evidence of a liaison between Feversham and the Duchess of Monmouth has been uncovered.

414. *Grey:* Forde, Lord Grey of Wark. For his cowardice during the Monmouth Rebellion see *supra* the poems on that campaign.

415. *poor James:* Monmouth—James Scott.

    his new subjects: Monmouth allowed himself to be proclaimed King on 20 June 1685 in the market place at Taunton.

418. *a widow'd queen:* Catherine of Braganza, the Queen Dowager. Feversham was her Lord Chamberlain. "From his intimacy with the Queen Dowager, and having the management of her affairs, he was commonly called the 'King Dowager'" (Jesse, *3,* 412–13). For the anecdote about his "keeping the bank" for the Dowager Queen when she played basset, see below, *Ballad,* "Come, come, great Orange, come away," 29 n.

Nor wert thou sorry, since most seeds are found
To flourish better when we change the ground;   420
He, struck in years and spent in toils and war,
Could please thee less than did the strong Dunbar.
Ne'er was a truer stallion, to his cost;
He, as he was most able, lov'd thee most;
But politic Monmouth thought it too much grace   425
For one t'enjoy so long so great a place.
Cornwallis next succeeds the lovely train
And round his neck displays a captive's chain.
He, greater fool than any of the rest,
They say, will marry with the trimming beast;   430
Which, if he does, oh, may his blood be shed
On that high throne where her last traitor bled!

Mysterious powers! what wond'rous influence
Governs (ye ruling stars) poor mortals' sense?
What unknown motive our dread King persuades   435
To make lewd Ogle mother of the maids?
The gracious Prince had sure much wiser been,
Had he made Stamford tutress to the Queen;
And then perhaps her chaste instructions would

---

422. *Dunbar:* Robert Constable, Viscount Dunbar. He was one of Monmouth's companions who killed the Beadle, Peter Vernell, during a night of debauchery in 1671 (see *POAS,* Yale, *1,* 172 ff.). In *The Session of Ladies,* found in most of the MSS. containing the present poem, he is noticed along with the Duchess' other suitors:

> Another grave widow, in sables' deep veil,
> Did send in by proxy her claim to the court;
> She pleaded, since Monmouth his project did fail,
> None could but Adonis make recompence for 't.

> But she was soon answer'd that she had her choice
> Of Stamford, Cornwallis, and brawny Dunbar;
> Or take 'em all three, if one could not suffice . . .

427. *Cornwallis:* Charles Cornwallis (1655–98), third Baron Cornwallis of Eye, married the Duchess early in March 1688 (Clarendon, *Diary,* 2, 54–55).
    the lovely train: i.e. the suite of her lovers.
430. *trimming:* Accommodating according to expediency.
432. *her last traitor:* The Duke of Monmouth, beheaded on 15 July 1685.
436. *lewd Ogle:* Probably Anne Ogle, sister of "mad Jack" Ogle, the gamester. A gentlewoman to the Countess of Inchiquin and mistress to the Duke of York (*DNB*). She was one of the Duchess' maids of honor (*Angliae Notitia,* 1673, p. 235), but apparently never "mother of the maids."
438. *Stamford:* Elizabeth, the notorious wife of Thomas Grey, second Earl of Stamford; see *The Ladies' March,* "Stamford's countess led the van" (Taylor 2, pp. 97–102).

Have sav'd a world of unbegotten blood. 440
But pious James, with profound parts endu'd,
Will prefer none but whom he knows are lewd:
Sophia Belasyse, all the court breed,
Ladies of wond'rous honor are, indeed!

Ye scoundrel nymphs, whom rags and scabs adorn 445
(Than that small paltry whore more highly born),
If you are wise apply yourselves betimes;
None highly merit now but by their crimes,
And the King does whate'er he's bid by Grimes.

Which made the wiser choice, is now our strife; 450
Hoyle his he-mistress, or the Prince his wife.
Those traders, sure, will be beloved as well
As all the dainty tender birds they sell.
The learned advocate, that rugged stump
Of old Nol's honor, always lov'd the Rump; 455
And 'tis no miracle, since all the hoiles
Were given, they say, to raise intestine broils.
But seeing, to the upright jurors' praise,
We are return'd to ignoramus days,

443. *Sophia Belasyse:* The wife of John, Baron Belasyse, one of James' Roman Catholic privy councillors and first lord commissioner of the treasury. Sophia came in for her share of abuse at the hands of the court satirists, but she is not to be confused with her sister-in-law Susan Armine, once mistress of James.

446. *small paltry whore:* Anne Ogle?

449. *Grimes:* "He got Mrs. Ogle the reversion of Mrs. Cooper's place" (MS. gloss). Possibly Robert Graham or Grimes (d. 1701), the libertine who became a Trappist monk toward the end of his life. He became a particular favorite at the fugitive court in St. Germaine (Duke of Manchester's *Court and Society from Elizabeth to Anne*, 1864, 2, 93 ff.). A Mrs. Cooper was mother of the maids to Anne, Princess of Denmark, in 1687 (see *Angliae Notitia*, 1687, p. 217, according to which she still held the position in 1692, but changes were made slowly in the text of *Angliae Notitia*, if at all).

451. *Hoyle:* John Hoyle, the friend of poetess Aphra Behn. On 26 Feb. 1687 Luttrell recorded that the "sessions began at the Old Baily the 23rd and held till the 26th . . . And at the . . . sessions one Mr. Hoyle, a lawyer of the Temple, had a bill preferred against him to the grand jury for buggery, which the jury found ignoramus, so he was discharged."

the Prince: Northumberland (MSS. gloss). For details of his marriage to Capt. Lucy's widow, see above, *Song,* "The widows and maids," 6 n.

452. *traders:* "Poulterers both" (MSS. gloss). Capt. Lucy's widow was said to have been the daughter of a poulterer.

455. *Nol:* Cromwell.

the Rump: A pun on the Long Parliament and on the buttocks.

456. *hoiles:* holes, obs.

459. *ignoramus days:* The time of Shaftesbury's acquittal in 1681 (see above, *Salamanca Doctor's Farewell,* 20 n.).

The lawyer swears he greater hazard runs   460
Who f———s one daughter than a hundred sons.
    Preposterous fate! while poor Miss Jenny bawds,
Each foreign fop her mother's charms applauds.
Autumnal whore! to every nation known!
A curse to them and scandal to her own.   465
Forgive me, chaster Hinton, if I name
Her stinking toes, with thine of sweeter fame;
Thou wond'rous pocky art and wond'rous poor,
But, as she's richer, she's a greater whore;
What with her breath, her armpits, and her feet,   470
Ten civet cats can hardly make her sweet.
From all the corners of our noisome town
The filth of ev'ry brute ran freely down
To that insatiate strumpet's common shore,
Till it broke out and poison'd her all o'er.   475
Poor Buckingham, in unsuccessful verse
And terms too mild, did her lewd crimes rehearse.
Bold is the man that ventures such a flight;
Her life's a satire which no pen can write.
And therefore cursed may she ever be,   480
As when old Hyde was catch'd with *rem in re.*

Cætera desunt.

462. *Miss Jenny:* Jane, daughter of Jane Middleton or Myddleton, the famous beauty of the court of Charles II. The elder Middleton had been one of James' mistresses and received a pension of £500 on his accession. Her daughter was born in 1661, when her mother was 16. A poem generally ascribed to Dorset entitled *Colin* (*POAS,* Yale, 2, 170) has these lines about her:

> Next Middleton appear'd in view,
> Who straight was told of Montagu,
> Of baits from Hyde, of clothes from France,
> Of armpits, toes, of suffisance;
> At which the court set up a laughter,
> But then she pleaded for her daughter:
> A buxom lass fit for the place*
> Were not her father in disgrace. . . .

[* i.e. that place "abdicated" by the Duchess of Portsmouth.]

466. *Hinton:* Moll Hinton, a well-known bawd during the reign of Charles II.

474. *common shore:* Sewer.

476. *Buckingham:* George Villiers, second Duke of Buckingham, one of Middleton's lovers. I do not know the poem here referred to, unless it is *Colin,* cited above.

481. *old Hyde:* Laurence Hyde, Earl of Rochester. "Lord Montagu found her, in fact, with my Lord Rochester" (MSS. gloss).

The Trial of the Seven Bishops
(June–July 1688)

No single event did more to precipitate James' fall than the imprisonment and subsequent trial of the Seven Bishops. After nearly two years of some patience and more cynical forbearance, a great many Englishmen had come to see the need for active resistance to James' policies. Indications of their willingness actively to oppose the Crown were manifest in the determined stand of the fellows of Magdalen College and in the more circumspect checks from the lords-lieutenant (see *The Progress of Popery, II*). Had James been astute in interpreting the signs of resistance, he might have avoided the impasse with the bishops.

Early in 1688 a letter was printed, nominally by Gaspard Fagel, Grand Pensionary of Holland, which set forth "An Account of the Prince and Princess of Orange's Thoughts Concerning the Repeal of the Test and the Penal Laws." Though William and Mary concurred with the concept of toleration, the letter made it clear that they felt strongly the need to restrain Catholics:

> . . . their highnesses cannot agree to the repeal of the Test, or of those other penal laws . . . that tend to the security of the Protestant religion, since the Roman Catholics receive no other prejudice from these than the being excluded from parliaments, or from public employments. And that by them the Protestant religion is covered from all the designs of the Roman Catholics against it, or against the public safety . . . plain reason, as well as the experience of all ages, the present as well as the past, shows that it will be impossible for Roman Catholics and Protestants, when they are mixed together in places of trust and public employments, to live together peaceably, or to maintain a good correspondence together. (*Somers' Tracts, 9,* 183–88)

The letter presented an accurate statement of William's position, long clear to James. In the summer of 1686 during several interviews at the Hague with William Penn, the Prince of Orange made it clear that "no man was more for toleration in principle than he was. He thought that conscience was subject only to God. And as far as a general toleration, even of papists, would content the King, he would concur in it heartily." The real issue was the Test Act. The Prince "would enter into no treaty" on this point, the Test was the only "real security" in maintaining the Protestant religion (Burnet, *1*, 693–94). The printing of Fagel's letter in 1688 made public the Prince's position, clarifying any uncertainty about the differences between him and his father-in-law concerning religious toleration. James might have ignored the letter publicly while heeding it privately as an indication that restraint was required in the pursuance of his policies. Had he done so, all might still have been well. Instead, he chose—in face of the letter, as it were—to reissue the Declaration of Indulgence on 27 April 1688, explaining his actions by saying:

> Our conduct has been such in all times as ought to have persuaded the world that we are firm and constant to our resolutions. Yet, that easy people may not be abused by the malice of crafty, wicked men, we think fit to declare that our intentions are not changed since the 4th of April 1687, when we issued out our declaration for liberty of conscience. . . . (Reprinted in *EHD, 8*, 399–400)

The second Declaration, like the first, concluded with the hope that parliamentary ratification could be obtained by the autumn, at the latest. Again, as in 1687, addresses poured in, filling the *London Gazette* for weeks after the event. As if in response to the general show of enthusiasm on the side of dissent, James ordered that the Declaration be read on two successive Sundays from pulpits throughout the realm. (The Order in Council was issued on 4 May; the Declaration was to be read in London on 20 and 27 May, elsewhere on 3 and 10 June: *London Gazette*, 7 May 1688.)

Royal declarations were often disseminated in this fashion, but the method was normally reserved for secular matters. Now, James was asking his clergy by implication to approve what, in their eyes, "would make them accomplices in the destruction of their Church" (Turner, p. 396). Reaction to the order was swift. A group of the London clergy met at the suggestion of Bishop Compton, long de-

The Seuen Stars are yͤ angels of yͤ Seuen Churches. and yͤ Seuen golden Candlesticks which thou Sauvest. are yͤ Seuen Churches. reuelation chap 1 υ 20

Les sept estoiles sont les anges des sept Eglises. et les sept Chandeliers dor que tu as veus. sont les Sept Eglises. apocalipse chap 1 υ 20

HIS GRACE WILLIAM Lͩͩͩͩ Arch Bᵖᵖ of Canterbury

William Lͩ Bᵖᵖ of St Asaph.

Thomas Lͩ Bᵖᵖ of Bath & Wells.

Jonathan Lͩ Bᵖ of Bristol.

Johnn Lͩ Bᵖ of Chichester.

Francis Lͩ Bᵖᵖ of Ely.

Thomas Lͩ Bᵖ of Peterborow.

S. Gribelin. inu: et sculp   Sold by P. Vansomer. in newport street near leicester-fields.   Iune 1688

SECOND STATE

1168

The Seven Bishops

nied the court, and sent round a letter proscribing the order (see *The Clerical Cabal*). A more formidable force gathered on 12 May at Lambeth Palace, in the presence of Archbishop Sancroft, but perhaps at the instigation of Compton. The group decided to petition the King against the reading of the Declaration. A second meeting was arranged to allow others to join in formulating the protest, and on the evening of 18 May the Bishops Ken (Bath and Wells), White (Peterborough), Turner (Ely), Lloyd (St. Asaph), Trelawney (Bristol), and Lake (Chichester) presented James with their petition, written out in Sancroft's hand. The brief document challenged the dispensing power in these words:

> the declaration is founded upon such a dispensing power as has been often declared illegal in parliament . . . and is a matter of so great moment and consequence to the whole nation, both in church and state, that your petitioners cannot in prudence, honor, and conscience, so far make themselves parties to it, as the distribution of it all over the nation, and reading it even in God's house. . . . (*Somers' Tracts, 9,* 116)

Startled by the rebuff from men he considered would remain loyal to their doctrine of Non-Resistance, James called the petition "a standard of rebellion." In James' eyes

> the great mark of insincerity in this affair was that, either designedly or indiscreetly, [the Bishops] had put it out of his . . . power to consult about and, by consequence, to grant what they required. The Declaration for Liberty of Conscience was no new thing. It had been published above a year before, and this reiteration of it had been since the 27th of April, which was time enough to have considered the matter. And yet the Bishops made no scruple till the 18th of May about ten o'clock at night (at which time they gave their petition) and the 20th it was appointed to be read. They could not believe the King would depart from an opinion and resolution he was settled in without consultation, and what time was there for that, much less for countermanding his orders (had he altered his mind) in the compass of one day? This looked, therefore, as if they had been numbering the people, to see if they would stick by them, and finding it in their power to whistle up the winds were resolved

to raise a storm, though they seemingly pretended to lay it. (Clarke, *Life, 2,* 155–6)

James' wrath might have been quelled but for the clandestine publication of the petition on the same evening. "In the King's closet the petition was not, as James said it was, 'a standard of rebellion,' but, dispersed in the streets, that is exactly what it became" (Turner, p. 400). James felt forced to act, forced to make an example of his antagonists. On 8 June the bishops were ordered to appear before the privy council and, following a tempestuous hearing, they were committed to the Tower. A week later they appeared before the four judges of the King's Bench, and after a plea of "not guilty" were released to await trial.

The date of the trial was set for the 29th of June. The prosecution was entrusted to a battery of James' minions, chief among them Sir William Williams, a renegade from the Whig cause. Attorney General Sir Robert Sawyer was chief counsel for the defense.

> The 29th being the day appointed for the trial of the seven bishops at the Court of King's Bench, it accordingly came on. The court was filled with noblemen and other persons of quality, and all the hall below and galleries as full as possible . . . the trial held till six in the evening; and the jury went away, and lay together till six the next morning, when they agreed. . . . They would give no privy verdict, but came into court, and being called they found all the defendants not guilty, at which there was a most mighty huzzah and shouting in the hall, which was very full of people. And all the way they came down people asked their blessing on their knees. There was continued shoutings for one-half an hour, so that no business could be done; and they hissed the solicitor. And at night was mighty rejoicing, in ringing of bells, discharging of guns, lighting of candles, and bonfires in several places, though forbid, and watchmen went about to take an account of such as made them. A joyful deliverance to the Church of England. (Luttrell, *1,* 446, 448)

James heard the news of the verdict while he was visiting the encampment at Hounslow Heath. His comment, oft repeated, was "so much the worse for them" (Dutch Dispatches, B.M. Add. 34510, f. 139; Mazure, 2, 472). But he must have recognized that the toil of several years was culminating in frustration. The dispensing power, which at great pains had been confirmed to him in the trial of God-den *v.* Hales in 1686, was now impugned and a major weapon successfully denied him.

The poems which follow are interesting in light of the writers' less than enthusiastic feelings toward the bishops. There were, of course, many poems of the unqualified praise of *A New Catch,* but the strongly ironic, anti-clerical view taken in *The Clerical Cabal* and *The Sentiments* presents the position of men who had seen and understood the implications of shifting allegiances all too well and too often in the previous decade. *The Sentiments* is particularly noteworthy for its play on such ominous words as "principles" and "heretics"—words which would be recalled within the year as five of the seven bishops became non-jurors at the outset of William's reign. *The Paradox* presents the injustice of James' own position, which sought to uphold religious toleration by imprisoning the chief clerics of the land. *The Church of England's Glory* is, on the other hand, a strong sectarian, pro-Catholic attack on the Anglican church, issued immediately after the acquittal of the bishops. With *The Story of the Pot and the Kettle,* it indicates how strongly the Dissenters had rallied to James. It is one of the last important satiric statements directly in James' behalf.

The Dissenters' Thanksgiving for the Late Declaration

For this additional declaration,
This double grace of dispensation,
For liberty and toleration
Against anti-Christian violation:

Title: This mock-address parodies prayers of thanksgiving offered in church or at home. For a similar riposte, but in prose, see "The Humble Address of the Atheists, or the Sect of the Epicureans," 1688 (reprinted in *Somers' Tracts, 9,* 46–7), which observes that James' "universal indulgence hath introduced such unanswerable objections towards all religion, that many have given over the troublesome enquiry after truth and set down easy and happy inference that all religion is a cheat." It bears the following imprint: "From the Devil Tavern, the fifth of November, 1688. Presented by Justice Baldock and was graciously received." Sir Robert Baldock (d. 1691) was "one of the counsel employed by the crown in the prosecution of the Seven Bishops, and showed himself so thorough-paced a stickler for prerogative" that on 6 July he was named justice of the King's Bench (Edward Foss, *Bio. Dict. of Judges,* 1870, p. 51).

Whatever zeal-misguided passion   5
Persuades the sons of reformation,
'Tis but a sly insinuation
To work a popish inundation.
We of the new regeneration,
The well affected of the nation   10
That will be useful in our station,
Do offer up our due oblation
And make our humble supplication:
While Test and penals are in fashion,
We be not brought in tribulation   15
By the next synod of the nation.

The Clerical Cabal

When lately King James, whom our sovereign we call,
For reasons of state and the good of the nation,
By advice of his Council commanded that all
Should read in their churches his last Declaration;
As soon as it was to the clergy reported,   5
To a place in the City they in private resorted
To advise on the matter and gravely debate
Whether conscience should truckle to reasons of state;
Which though we must own was most prudently done
Yet some think they'd better have let it alone,   10
Since 'twill no small suspicion to schismatics give
That they're not quite so loyal as they'd make us believe;
For if conscience be thought a sufficient pretense,
Why should it not salve the Dissenters' offense,

16. *the next synod:* The second Declaration, like the first, expressed the hope that toleration would be confirmed by parliament, which James resolved to call "in November next at furthest."

6. *a place in the City:* Prior to the meeting of the bishops at Lambeth Palace, 15 of the London clergy assembled to consider what action, if any, should be taken on James' order. They agreed not to read the Declaration, drawing up and signing a resolution to that effect, which was then circulated round the city and signed by 85 clerics (James Johnstone's correspondence, letter of 23 May 1688, *Jerviswoode Correspondence,* Bannatyne Club; the meeting is discussed by Macaulay, 2, 992–4).

14–15. This points with considerable irony to the double standard that the bishops condoned by raising the question of conscience. The bishops had long enforced the penal laws with rigor against the scruple of conscience held by Dissenters.

When refusing to bow to their Common Pray'r idol,   15
They were forc'd to take quarters in Newgate and Bridewell?

But the case is now alter'd, th'ecclesiastical club
Met with countenance solid and wond'rous meek,
Consulting like coopers to mend an old tub,
Which for want of good hooping does now spring a leak.   20
Each man in his order began to dispute:
Some few would submit, but the rest would not do't;
Some boldly alleg'd that the Tests were the thing
That secur'd them now from the lash of the King,
"And should we comply, the gentry would say   25
We had virtually given our safeguard away.
And if we displease them, whom can we expect
Should hereafter our cause and our persons protect?
Besides the great loss of our princely dominion
Might serve one would think t'enforce this opinion,   30
That should we submit to his Majesty's order,
The world would regard our church thunder no further."

"That's true," says another, "and when the King's dead
You know that the Princess of Orange comes in,
And then this denial may stand us instead   35
To purchase her favor and fix us again.
Though of Passive Obedience we talk like the best,
'Tis prudence, when interest sways, to resist.
What though Jupiter thunder, and Juno do scold,
We'll still our true int'rest and principles hold.   40
Our livings alone supply us with treasure,
When those are once gone, we may starve at our leisure.

16. *Newgate and Bridewell:* London prisons.

17. *th'ecclesiastical club:* Probably the London clerics, and not the ecclesiastical commission. The "old tub" would then refer to the doctrine of Passive Obedience.

22. *Some few would submit:* Those bishops who either demurred or were not asked to sign were Chester (Cartwright), St. David's (Watson), Durham (Crew), Hereford (Croft), Exeter (Lamplugh), Coventry and Litchfield (Wood), and Lincoln (Barlow); York was vacant (see *HMC, Le Fleming,* p. 210).

32. *thunder:* Traditionally figurative for the exercise of the Church's harshest powers, e.g. excommunication.

34. *Princess of Orange:* Mary, James' eldest daughter and William of Orange's wife. She was a Protestant and next in line, if there were no male heir.

No argument better than this can convince us
How much 'tis our duty to please the Dutch Princess;
But some will now say, since the Queen is with child,   45
If a male should be born, our project is spoil'd:
We've a salvo for that, too, if he lives to be man,
Like true Vicars of Bray we'll retract all again."

Their ponderous reasons when put in the scale,
With duty and manners did quickly prevail,   50
For a churchman's civility never is seen
Till preferment appears as a medium between.

Straight orders are issu'd t'enjoin the young fry
That on pain of ejectment they should not comply,
Which were strictly observ'd, such respect do they bear   55
To the wretched allowance of ten pounds a year
That for fear of displeasing a stingless old drone
They disgrace their religion and incur the King's frown.

What they get by the bargain will soon be made plain,
'Twill be well if their Godliness turns to their gain.   60

45. *the Queen is with child:* The prince was born on 10 June 1688, about three weeks after this meeting took place.

47. *salvo:* A saving clause; reservation.

48. *Vicars of Bray:* Refers to the time-serving parson of Bray in Berkshire who, though variously identified, was probably Simon Aleyn. During the reigns of Henry VIII, Edward VI, Mary, and Elizabeth, he was twice a Papist and twice a Protestant to preserve his choice living. The well-known ballad dates from the 18th century and places the vicar's apostacies from the Restoration through the reign of George I (Chappell, 2, 652).

56. *ten pounds a year:* The stipend which went with most minor clerical posts was notoriously small even for that time.

57. *a stingless old drone:* Presumably, Archbishop William Sancroft (1617–93), characterized by Trevelyan as "by nature a shy and retiring man," belonging "to the strictest school of High Churchmen, who had hitherto taught that the King's will was the guide for all true subjects and Christians." Up to the publishing of the second Declaration, he "had been hesitating and backward in resistance to James, much as he regretted his policy" (*The English Revolution, 1688–1689,* 1939, p. 92).

THE SENTIMENTS

To the Bishops

1.

Ye miter'd fathers of the land,
Is your obedience at a stand?
   Now does your conscience boggle?
That nicety was laid aside,
Canon and common law deni'd,   5
   When you i'th'House did juggle?

2.

What prince could doubt you'd not go on,
Whom you had plac'd upon the throne,
   Whose principles you knew;
The consequence of which each man   10
That has but common sense might scan;
   There's no excuse for you!

3.

Who puts a sword in's enemy's hand
And weaponless denies command,
   May strive, but 'tis in vain;   15
Had you the first great evil waiv'd,
You by the last had ne'er been brav'd,
   Nor in the Tower lain.

4

In Holy Writ you're conversant,
In Romish maxims ignorant;   20
   Good men I mourn your case:
They'll plight their faith and give their oath,

Title: Sentiments: Here presumably, "what one feels with regard to something; . . .
an opinion or view as to what is right or agreeable. . . ."
  6. *i'th'House:* As members of the House of Lords, the bishops had supported James
during the Whig attempts in 1679–81 to exclude him from the throne.

Keep either, neither, rarely both,
    If interest does give place.

5.

To heretics no faith is due,   25
Would you expect it then to you,
    When you are in the role?
Promises are only words,
'Tis binding when the heart accords—
    They're licens'd to cajole.   30

6.

Passive Obedience you did preach,
A virtue which we all must reach,
    And now you're to it brought;
For when the nail you'd no more drive,
Straight to remove you they contrive,   35
    Though they lost the point they sought.

7.

You see the judges of the land
Are listed in the Roman band,
    And what they're bid they do;
Hope of preferment does o'erawe   40
Both conscience, justice, and the law—
    Faith and religion, too.

8.

Sacred engagements are but vain
Your rights and properties to maintain;
    They are but words, of course,   45
And not obliging any more
To heretics than to a whore,
    Nor valid, nor of force.

9.

'Tis obvious now to every one,
Since Romish measures are begun,   50
    What we must all expect;

Those sheep are in a woeful stead,
Where wolf and shepherd are agreed
   To kill without respect.

10.

Stick to your principles, howe'er,   55
And neither axe nor faggot fear:
   That is the worst can come;
But e're to those they shall you bring,
Though justly we will serve our King,
   We'll try a tug with Rome.   60

THE PARADOX

Upon the Confinement of the Bishops and Their Bailing Out

Let Cynics bark, and the stern Stagirite,
At Epicurus' precepts vent their spite;
Let Churchmen preach their threadbare paradox,
Passive Obedience, to their bleeding flocks.

Let Stoics boast of a contented mind,   5
The joy and pleasure of a life confin'd,
That in imprisonment the soul is free—
Grant me, ye gods, but ease and liberty!

That there is pleasure in a dirty road,
A tired horse that sinks below his load,   10
No money, and an old, inveterate pox—
This I'll believe without a paradox.

But to affirm 'twas the dispensing pow'r
That did decree the prelates to the Tow'r,
And such confinement's for the propagation   15
O'th'faith and doctrine of the Reformation;

That to remove the candlesticks from sight
Is to enlarge the Gospel and the light;

52–53. Traditionally, of course, sheep are "believers," wolves "heretics," and shepherds "priests."

17. *candlesticks:* See illustration facing p. 216.

And the seven angels under sequestration,
To guard the church from pagan innovation;   20

To say that this is keeping of our word,
The only means we have to be secur'd;
Supporting of the English Church and cause
In all its privileges, rights, and laws:

Pardon my faith, for sooner I'll believe   25
The subtle serpent was deceiv'd by Eve;
Rome shall with heretics her promise keep,
And wolves and bears protect the straggling sheep!

That Powis shall be mild and moderate,
Not out of mere regard to his estate;   30
And for a hopeful heir invoke the saints
Out of his tender love to Protestants.

That this young heir, great Orange to prevent,
Being assign'd to the next parliament,
Shall be brought up i'th'Protestant profession   35
To ratify a Catholic succession.

That Father Petre's counsel shall prevail
To quit their guiltless lordships without bail;
And Giffard beg, i'th'name of the young Prince,
Dispensing pow'r may with their crimes dispense.   40

19. *sequestration:* The bishops are compared to the dispossessed Anglican clergy during the years of the Commonwealth.

21. *our word:* From his accession James had promised to maintain the government in Church and State according to the laws of the realm. From the beginning he had insisted, as well, that his word was all the security necessary, though he felt it conditional upon the support of the Establishment.

29. *Powis:* William Herbert (1617–96), first Marquis and titular Duke of Powis, was leader of the moderate Catholic party and a member of James' Privy Council.

33. *this young heir:* Prince of Wales.

35. For attempts to have the Prince brought up a Protestant, see the *DNB* account of his life and Trevelyan, "The Peace," *England Under Queen Anne,* 1934, *3,* 268–69.

37. *Petre:* Father Edward Petre, the Jesuit confessor of James and an influential member of the Privy Council.

39. *Giffard:* Bonaventure Giffard, Bishop of Madaura. One of the four vicars-apostolic of England, he had been installed as President of Magdalen College, Oxford, by James early in 1688.

That Condom with the Jesuits shall side
To beg their lordships never may be tri'd,
Chiefly old Sancroft, the dear hopes to shun
Of being England's metropolitan.

That Durham shall propitiate for his Grace,   45
And Chester shall with Chichester change place;
And Hereford, when made a cardinal,
Shall make a learn'd apology for all.

That for old Ely, Bristol, Bath and Wells,
The Jesuits shall pawn their beads and bells;   50
For Lloyd and Peterborough to be bail
Good Rochester will lie himself in jail.

That Mulgrave's pride and lust, in Dryden's rhymes,
Shall make atonement for their lordship's crimes;

41. *Condom:* Jaques Bénigne Bossuet, Bishop of Condom and Meaux (1627–1704), he sought to reconcile Protestants with the Roman Catholic position, particularly in his *Exposition of the Doctrine of the Catholic Church,* first published in England in 1672, re-issued in 1685, 1686, and 1687. His hatred of the Jesuits was underlined early in the 1680s during the Gallican controversy by his *Defensio Cleri Gallicani.*

43. *Sancroft:* Identified in Firth c. 16. The point of these lines appears to be that being Metropolitan, i.e. Bishop of London, under the Pope, is a greater honor than being Primate.

45. *Durham:* Nathaniel Crew, Bishop of Durham and a staunch supporter of James' policies. Luttrell records that he "hath taken an account of his clergy that have read his Majesty's Declaration and those who have not" (1, 449).

his Grace: Sancroft.

46. *Chester:* Thomas Cartwright, the sycophantic Bishop of Chester, was appointed to that see by James in Dec. 1686.

Chichester: John Lake, Bishop of Chicester.

47. *Hereford:* Identified by Firth c. 16 as Herbert Croft (1603–91), Bishop of Hereford. Though "generally energetic in his efforts to prevent the growth of 'Popery' in his diocese" during Charles' reign (*DNB*), in 1688 he was one of the bishops mentioned by Luttrell "for reading the King's Declaration" (*1*, 440).

49. *Ely, Bristol, Bath & Wells:* Bishops Turner, Trelawney, and Ken.

52. *Rochester:* Thomas Sprat, Bishop of Rochester. A member of the ecclesiastical commission, which continued to function after the trial of the bishops. Sprat asked in August "that he might be dismissed that board, being unwilling to act against his brethren the clergy" (Luttrell, *1*, 455–56).

53–6. *Mulgrave:* John Sheffield, Earl of Mulgrave. He was Dryden's patron and had collaborated with him in writing *An Essay upon Satire* (see *POAS*, Yale, 1). Notoriously vain and proud, in 1686 he had married Ursula, widow of Edward, Lord Conway, who matched her husband's reputation for vanity with her own for drunkenness (see above, *A Faithful Catalogue,* &c., 122 and n.).

And wife's sobriety shall recompense   55
For their apostate disobedience.

Or that the Groom o'th'Stole, since he declar'd,
Should from his former luxury be debarr'd;
Or the grave President should reinstall
The English Church upon the bishops' fall.   60

That the Lord Chancellor should quit the purse
For their respective fines to reimburse;
Or that the judges should not all conspire
To find 'em guilty of a praemunire.

That Pemberton's sound counsel should prevail,   65
And Allibone should sue to be their bail;
Or Halifax, that lies upon the lurch,
Who left the charters, shall restore the Church.

That Melfort's Cross, erected at the Bath,
With Perth, an emblem of their new-got faith;   70

57. *Groom o'th'Stole:* Henry Mordaunt, second Earl of Peterborough. He became a
convert in March 1687.

59. *President:* Robert Spencer, second Earl of Sunderland and President of the
Privy Council.

61. *Lord Chancellor:* George Jeffreys.

64. *praemunire:* The charge of calling into question the supremacy of the English
Crown by resorting to a foreign court or authority, e.g. that of the Pope.

65. *Pemberton:* Sir Francis Pemberton (1625–97), counsel for the bishops. Luttrell
notes that during the trial "the dispensing power . . . was so strangely exposed and
so run down, even very boldly, especially by Pemberton and Finch, that it is hardly
credible" (*1*, 447).

66. *Allibone:* Sir Richard Allibone (1636–88), a Papist and one of the four judges of
the King's bench.

67. *Halifax:* George Savile, Marquis of Halifax, a staunch opponent in the 1680s of
all attempts to exclude James, had been out of favor since the autumn of 1685, lying
"upon the lurch," i.e. lying in wait, at Rufford Abbey, the family seat in Sherwood
Forest, for "the next probable revolution" which he predicted in his *Letter to a
Dissenter*. (The *OED* cites this poem in defining the phrase "to lie upon the lurch.")

68. *the charters:* As Lord Privy Seal, Halifax had assisted in the removal of corporation charters in the last year of Charles' reign.

69–70. *Melfort . . . Perth:* John Drummond (1649–1714), first Earl and titular Duke
of Melfort, and James (1648–1716), his elder brother, the fourth Earl and first titular
Duke of Perth, both converts to the Roman Catholic Church. "Melfort's Cross" was a
pillar erected at Bath by John Drummond in 1688 in memory of Queen Mary (for the
full inscription, see Wood, *Life, 3*, 268–9).

The cause o'th'Queen's conception do remain,
And will produce the same effects again.

That city treats with masquerades are grac'd,
To keep their wives upright, their daughters chast;
And court intrigues with balls are carri'd on   75
For virtue only to preserve the throne.

That she who lately took into her choice
The witty author of the brace of mice
Shall battle the old panther in her race,
And crown her husband with the laureate's bays.   80

All this I freely can believe and more,
But that the Lords are bail'd out of the Tow'r
With greater load to be sent there again,
For breach of laws they endeavor'd to maintain.

That they have guilt of disobedience,   85
In this you must excuse my diffidence;
Who plac'd upon the Monarch's head the crown:
Props of the Church, and Pillars of the Throne?

A NEW CATCH IN PRAISE OF THE REVEREND BISHOPS

True Englishmen, drink a good health to the miter;
Let our church ever flourish, though her enemies spite her.

77–80. In Feb. 1688, Charles Montagu, Prior's collaborator in *The Hind and the Panther Transversed to the Story of the Country Mouse and the City Mouse;* married Anne, daughter of Sir Christopher Yelverton and widow of Robert, third Earl of Manchester. She was thirty-three at the time of her second marriage and bore Montagu no children, though she had had nine by her first husband. Cf. *A Supplement to the Session of Ladies* (Firth c. 15):

> With confidence awkward and countenance pale,
> The old Lady Manchester loudly did bawl;
> If ugliness, fondness, and age could prevail,
> I have as good right as the best of you all.
> The court of young Montagu rung in her ear
> And bid her (since blest in so equal a choice),
> If she was too old to produce him an heir,
> Adopt for his issue a couple of mice.

> May their cunning and forces no longer prevail;
> And their malice, as well as their arguments, fail.
> Then remember the Seven, which supported our cause,   5
> As stout as our martyrs and as just as our laws!

THE CHURCH OF ENGLAND'S GLORY

or The Vindication of Episcopacy

> Now call to mind Edom, remember well
> Your cursed cries against God's Israel.
> Now who's disloyal, where's the obstinate
> And busy fops that talk of things of state?
> "A plot, a plot!" Who is't that now looks blue?   5
> Now where's sedition? Where's the factious crew?
> Now mock no more, go consecrate the room
> Where Essex di'd, and think on Russell's doom.
> Now who are they that cri'd, "ram us" and "damn us?"
> Who is't that now comes off with "ignoramus"?   10
> Now who's surmising fears and jealousies?

1. *Edom:* Esau, from the red color of the lentil pottage for which he sold his birthright. The Edomites remained generally hostile to the Israelites, refusing them the right to cross their land during the flight from Egypt and much later joining Nebuchadnezzar in his siege of Jerusalem (H. B. Hackett, *Dict. of the Bible*). This allusion to the Church of England and its "apostasy" was fairly common in controversialist tracts and sermons of the period. On 1 April 1688, Thomas Ken, Bishop of Bath and Wells, preached a sermon before Princess Anne, "describing the calamity of the reformed church of Judah under the Babylonish persecution," saying "she should certainly rise again and be delivered by him who would avenge her enemies, as God did upon the Edomites her apostate brother and neighbors" (Evelyn, *4*, 577–8).

5. *Who . . . now looks blue:* A pun on the blue of "True Blue Protestantism" and on the "blue look" of disappointment.

8. *Essex:* Arthur Capel, Earl of Essex. Accused of complicity in the Rye House Plot, he committed suicide in July 1683 while prisoner in the Tower.

Russell: Lord William Russell, executed in 1683 for his part in the plot.

9. *"ram us" and "damn us":* An ironic reference to Whig outcries against the Tories during the furor of plot and counterplot in 1679–83.

10. *ignoramus:* As in the previous reference to the Whigs' outcry during 1679–83, here the acquittal of the bishops is compared with that of Shaftesbury in 1681, when the Grand Jury found the evidence against him insufficient to constitute a "true bill." Shaftesbury's "escape" would have seemed to most of the Anglican clergy a miscarriage of justice. Throughout this passage the satirist deflates the present Anglican jubilation by likening it to the jubilation of their opponents of the 1680s.

Now who's malicious, fomenting of lies?
Now whose nice conscience pleads religion?
Nay, rather they that once swore they had none!
Now let's "huzza, huzza, huzza," examine   15
Now for the loyalty express'd by damning,
Roaring, and whoring—that—rotting and sinking:
"Hey boys! new healths with bumpers bravely drinking."
But say these are the worst, whose words are wind;
But mark our doctrines, and the more refin'd.   20
Now where's the doctrine made the pulpits ring?
'Twas all divine to love and laud the King!
Where's loyal sermons now? Where are they gone?
Hark, hark a while, and you shall hear anon.
Where's Non-Resistance now? Now where's compliance?   25
Why here, in this, to bid the King defiance!
In what, an edict? No, his declaration
For conscience liberty, to free the nation
From those accursed penal laws and Test,
That tender conscience ever might have rest.   30
But now 'tis "Popery, Popery," that's the song;
'Tis coming like a flood—But, pray, how long
Has fear of Popery been this dreadful tone?
Just since you let the Protestants alone.
'Tis fear of Papists—good lack!—sad's the case,   35
Since they've excell'd Episcopals in grace.
No sooner Clemency doth peace propose,
But Envy cries, "Take heed of Popish foes."
Was't not for fear of Popery once ago
You writ and printed, preach'd and raged so?   40
"Down with Dissenters"—thus with storm and thunder;
"Magistrates, mind your duty, seize and plunder,

15. *huzza:* The cry of Tory partisans in the 1680s.

18. *"Hey boys!* . . . : A parody on the typical opening line of a broadside rehearsing a popular event.

34. *Just since you let the Protestants alone:* i.e. just since the Anglican church turned its attention from the Dissenters to the Catholics, considering the latter, under James, a more serious threat to the Establishment.

41–50. Dissenters and Catholics alike had long suffered under acts nominally directed against Dissenters. A particular instance of this coincided in 1683 with the extra-legal attack on local self-government by Charles in 1683–84 in his attempts to extirpate Nonconformity (Ogg, *Charles II,* 2, 639–40; Trevelyan, pp. 424–25).

Fine and imprison, ruin—follow't hot!"
This was for fear of Popery, was it not?
Thus persecution echo'd from the pulpit;   45
But now look simply, say you cannot help it.
Law was not then so much as it is since,
But the King's pleasure, as you made pretense:
Yet though you've lost the spur, you'd hold the bridle—
With a straight rein, too. O! but that's as idle   50
As those that blame this Liberty of Conscience
And have the impudence to say 'tis nonsense.
Were they (which God forbid) but half so long
To feel the right that did Dissenters wrong,
They'd wiser be, kinder, and humbler, too,   55
Who're now so proud they know not what they do.
Now who are they that cannot be content
With regal right, but acts of parliament
Of their own choosing? Yet this will not do;
But must have also convocation, too.   60
Now who like toads spit venom, swell, and pant?
Now who are they that have the way to cant?
Now who's most busy to degrade the King?
And who knows what? With secret whispering,
And holding consults, who makes parties now?   65
For to rebel the malcontent knows how.
Fat benefits, and tithes, and bishoprics
Do not content you; O, these little tricks!
For Mordecai stoops not: here's the dispute;
You want the power still to persecute.   70
Whence comes this rule to lord it o'er the rest?

56. *they know not what they do:* Luke 23:34.

60. *convocation:* The general assembly of the clergy of the Church of England. Probably also a derisive allusion to the gatherings of the heads of the Church both in London and at Lambeth (see 65).

65. *consults:* Specifically (17th century), "a secret meeting for purposes of sedition or intrigue."

69. *Mordecai stoops not:* The foster father of Esther who, when Ahasuerus made Esther his queen, sat at the palace gates and would not bow to Haman, the King's chief minister. Whatever Mordecai's motive, here the context suggests religious scruples, and Mordecai becomes a type of religious dissent. The irony of the original story lies in the execution of Haman on the scaffold he had ordered built for Mordecai.

70. *You:* The Bishops.

From Tory-Gospel, penal laws, and Test—
Touch 'em in that, and they'll begin to wince,
And galled loyalty spurns at their Prince.
But poor Dissenters, now, as heretofore,   75
Thankful for peace, rejoice, and seek no more.
But now, 'tis well, your cursed power's subdu'd;
Here's peace, which others like—but let's conclude:
Here's your own language and the work of late
You glori'd in and still would vindicate.   80
Look in this glass and learn to blush for shame;
Be Christians once, and stain no more that name.

[CHARLES MONTAGU]

THE STORY OF THE POT AND THE KETTLE

As it was told by Colonel Titus the night before
he kissed the King's hand

As down the torrent of an angry flood
An earthen pot and a brass kettle flow'd,
The heavy caldron sinking, and distress'd
By its own weight, and the fierce waves oppress'd,
Slyly bespoke the lighter vessel's aid,   5
And to the earthen pitcher friendly said,

74. *spurns:* Kicks.

Ascription: It is likely that Montagu was, indeed, responsible for these rhymes. The ascription comes from a gloss in *An Epistle to . . . Charles Montagu, Baron of Halifax. Writ upon Occasion of the Signal Successes of Her Majesty's Arms in the Last Summer's Campaign,* 1707, p. 6. The note reads: "Your 'Fable of the Pot and the Kettle' kept the most prudent Dissenters from joining with Papists against the Church."

Subtitle: Colonel Titus: Col. Silius Titus (1623?–1704), a prominent Presbyterian and vigorous parliamentary opponent both of Papists and of the Catholic succession during the last years of the reign of Charles II. In July 1688, James put aside his own animosity for Titus and invited him to join the Privy Council. Titus attended the last meeting of the council but, within a few weeks openly declared for William.

2. *brass kettle:* Probably James himself. He was frequently fixed by his opponents with the word "brass" or "brazen," suggesting his hard-headedness.

"Come, brother, why should we divided lose
The strength of union and ourselves expose
To the insults of this poor, paltry stream,
Which with united forces we can stem?   10
Though different, heretofore, have been our parts,
The common danger reconciles our hearts.
Here, lend me thy kind arm to break this flood."
    The pitcher this new friendship understood
And made this answer, "Though I wish for ease   15
And safety, this alliance does not please.
Such different natures never will agree;
Your constitution is too rough for me.
If by the waves I against you am toss'd,
Or you to me, I equally am lost,   20
And fear more mischief from your harden'd side,
Than from the shore, the billows, or the tide.
I calmer days and ebbing waves attend,
Rather than buoy you up and serve your end
To perish by the rigor of my friend."   25

Moral

Learn hence, you Whigs, and act no more like fools,
Nor trust their friendship who would make you tools;
While empty praises and smooth flatteries serve,
Pay with feign'd thanks what their feign'd smiles deserve,
But let not this alliance further pass;   30
For know that you are clay, and they are brass.

The Birth of James Frances Edward, Prince of Wales
(10 June 1688)

Long before James came to the throne, fear of a papist dynasty had been working in the minds of the English. It led to the attempts by the parliaments of 1679 and 1680–81 at an Exclusion Bill, and the question became critical after the accession. Yet throughout most of the reign it operated not only to stir up the populace but also to pacify it. As long as a Protestant succession seemed secure in James' daughter Mary, the English were inclined to wait; without a male heir all the papist machinations would ultimately prove ineffectual. A Catholic heir would be disastrous to English Protestantism, because he would require a nation still strong in its beliefs in obedience and in the right of kings to take drastic action to free itself from the rule of popes. But a male heir seemed a virtual impossibility, and the people could willfully indulge themselves, even during the worst moments of papist encroachment, by rehearsing the popular tale of James and Mary's ability to produce only a "race of ninnies" whose life expectancy was very short indeed. Yet the impossible happened. On 10 June a prince was born.

Though the birth of the Prince is rightly regarded by historians as the catalyst which caused the ultimate reaction to James' policies, at the historical moment the imagination of the London mob was already seething with the spectacle of the bishops leaving the barge to pass along Tower Wharf and through Traitor's Gate, which three years before had received the Duke of Monmouth. As the summer progressed, however, the old fears grew in proportion, fed on the refuse of rumor and scurrility. On 10 June, Evelyn saw fit merely to remark, "a young Prince born," and to follow this with a brief description of the day's celebration. The event was "very surprising, it being universally given out that her Majesty did not look till the next month" (4, 586–87). Later Evelyn, perhaps in an attempt to appear a more acute judge of events, added to his entry that the birth "will cost dispute."

On the 29th of June the bishops were acquitted, and the people were again able to turn their full attention to the young Prince. Newsletters had been, as Luttrell said, "stuffed with nothing but rejoicings" for the birth (*1*, 444), ironically providing a continual reminder of the situation. Within a fortnight of the acquittal, Luttrell put down that there was "great liberty in discoursing about the young Prince, with strange reflections upon him, not fit to insert here" (*1*, 449). Over the next few months the reaction grew,

> the people therefore who too easily credit lies of their Prince, especially considering his religion, gave so roundly into this, that it was thought indispensably necessary to have the reality of the Prince's birth proved by those who were present at it. (Clarke, *Life*, 2, 193)

Late in October James assembled a council to hear evidence on the legitimacy of his son, once and for all to lay the spectre of popish fraud that filled the minds of nearly all his subjects. (As early as 26 July 1688, William's envoy, Zuylestein, wrote to the Hague that nine persons in ten believed the birth to be a deception: Dutch Dispatches.) But the absurdity of James' condescension in this matter, the apparent collusion of the witnesses making depositions, and the anxieties over Irish marauders, Dutch threats, and papist pretensions nullified any advantage James had hoped to gain. He had, however, made public record of the facts, and in his mind that was undoubtedly a gain.

From the beginning of this sordid affair the image of James and Mary as parents worked against acceptance of the facts of the birth. It had been five years since Mary had given birth. Twice since, in October 1683 and in April 1684, her delicate constitution had failed her, and she had miscarried. Her five previous children had died in infancy. The blame for these unfortunate occurrences, however, was largely shifted to James. In 1668 it was rumored, Lord Carnegy, Earl of Southesk, had sought a desperate remedy to avenge his wife's infidelity with James, and thus put an end to later hopes of a Catholic line. *A Catholic Hymn* opens with a lengthy allusion to the affair (the lampoon is in *Popery*, *3*, 1689, p. 20. Accounts of the affair are given by Pepys and Anthony Hamilton.):

> When enrag'd Southesk
> In his female's womb cast
> A clap, which cost twenty guineas,

A project he had
Of revenge on the dad,
And to blow up the race of the ninnies.

The "virulent distemper" James was thought thus to have contracted
made an heir improbable; for

The poison entail'd
So far had prevail'd,
'Twas high time to seek out a wonder;
Our case must be sad,
If a boy can't be had
To keep the heretics under.

Though this scurrilous tale could be shrugged off by most, the early
death of James' children might well have been the result of the ir-
regularities of his sexual conduct. Beyond this, it was known that
Mary Beatrice was not robust, a weakness underlined on 2 November
1687, when Luttrell recorded that "the Queen, two months gone with
child, had been let blood to prevent miscarriage."

On 23 December 1687, James issued a proclamation appointing a
time for public prayer and thanksgiving throughout the kingdom for
the Queen, "who (through God's great goodness) is now with child."
He ordered Nathaniel Crew, Thomas Sprat, and Thomas White,
Bishops of Durham, Rochester, and Peterborough, "to prepare a
Form of Prayer and Religious Service" to be celebrated in the London area on 15 January and elsewhere in the realm on 29 January
(A Form and Order of Thanksgiving and Prayer, 1687; London
Gazette, 5 Jan. 1688). The Council, once attributed to Swift, lampoons the preparations and adds another anti-Catholic calumny.
Abraham de la Pryme, the Yorkshire antiquarian who had noted
shorty after the proclamation that "no one scarce believes that she is
really with bairn," summed up one aspect of the imputation. It was
a common jest "that the Virgin Mary [had] appeared to her and
declared to her that the holy thing that shall be born of her shall be
a son. They say likewise that the Pope has sent her the Virgin Mary's
smock and hallowed bairn clothes" (Diary, ed. Charles Jackson, Surtees Society, 1869, p. 11). Anthony Wood noted that the Queen's
"breeding was occasioned, as the papists say, by the prayer of the
chaplain of Our Lady of Loreto to whom the Duchess of Modena,

mother of the said Queen, bequeathed a golden heart at her death [in July 1687], purposely to pray for her breeding a son." Wood adds that the "Protestants say 'twas by her being at the Bath last August" (*Life and Times,* ed. Andrew Clarke, 1894, *3,* 255). Imputations such as these support Turner's observation:

> It is difficult to believe that the doubts which were immediately cast on the genuineness of the birth arose spontaneously; the phenomenon of a fanatically held belief in what we now know to be utterly untrue in fact, is almost exactly a repetition of what happened ten years earlier in connection with the so-called Popish Plot . . . (p. 405).

The imprisonment of the bishops preoccupied the Londoner, whose decision about the baby had been made long before.

In May 1688, further rumors of a miscarriage forced James to hurry back from Chatham, where he had been viewing preparations against Dutch attack:

> Her Majesty having heretofore received advice that her illustrious brother the Duke of Modena was under some indisposition; being on Wednesday last in the evening surprised with a false report of his death, increased by the misapprehension of the first words of a letter at the same time received from Italy, through the excess of her natural affection fell into some swooning fits; of which expresses being immediately sent to his Majesty hastened his return, who arrived here the next morning and found her Majesty had rested pretty well. For upon the first recollection from the transports of her grief, it appeared that the very next words of the same letter assured her Majesty of her brother's good health. . . . (*Public Occurrences,* No. 13)

At the time, however, the people were ready to believe a miscarriage had occurred, if not then, certainly at some other point. This if, indeed, the Queen had ever really been pregnant.

The birth of the Prince took place earlier than expected—or so most believed—though the Queen herself had not been certain of the date to expect the arrival (see *The Deponents,* 217 and n.), and quite naturally the birth gave rise to hasty preparations. But the event which caused most speculation was the "last-minute" removal of the Queen from Whitehall to St. James' Palace for the delivery. At

St. James' a convent adjoined, "where a woman might be kept all the time of her bigness" and where her child could be safely carried through the passageways to the Queen's bedchamber. The Queen's quick removal had allowed no time for an official search of the lying-in chambers. The imprisonment of the bishops had aided the deception. In retrospect, it appeared to the royal antagonists that the bishops had conveniently been got out of the way "to distract all those who designed to watch the Queen" (*Answer to the Depositions*, &c., 1689, p. 7). The birth had been "staged" at a time, morever, when the Protestant Princess Anne was absent from Court. Luttrell had reported in the end of May, however, that the Queen had given up Windsor and Whitehall and was "resolved to lie in at St. James," adding that "the lodgings are making ready" (*1*, 441). Against the absence of the bishops must be set the more than forty witnesses actually in attendance at the birth, though James erred in not having more Protestants present. Anne's absence may have been self-imposed. James believed that she had gone to Bath purposely to avoid the royal birth, and that she later feigned fear of a miscarriage to excuse her absence from the October depositions (Clarke, *Life*, 2, 159, 201–02).

After the birth formal addresses came in from all parts of the kingdom, and special envoys arrived from neighboring countries to offer their monarchs' congratulations (see *The Audience*). Londoners remained skeptical. Their doubts were increased when in August a wet nurse was brought in for the young Prince, who lay ill at Richmond with "the gripes" (Luttrell, *1*, 453). Evelyn said of the illness:

> After long trials of the doctors to bring up the little Prince of Wales by hand (so many of her Majesty's children having died infants) not succeeding, a country nurse [named Cooper] (the wife of a tile-maker) is taken to give it suck (*4*, 597).

By October discontent had become so great that James felt himself compelled to answer back. He summoned an extraordinary council to give testimony on the birth. Forty-three witnesses gave evidence, but the deposition did not shake the story the mob wished to believe. They suspected collusion and, as it was pointed out in the *Answer to the Depositions*, p. 1, felt "the depositions themselves were made from inconclusive evidence." Morever, few of the opposite party had been present to attest to the truth of the affair.

Having rehearsed the events surrounding the birth of the Prince, it is difficult to avoid the conclusion drawn by G. N. Clarke in his study of *The Later Stuarts* (1949). "In the seventeenth century people would believe anything. The Catholics thought the birth was a miracle, and the Protestants said it was an imposture. It was neither" (p. 121). The truth remains that most Englishmen recognized the difficulties the birth put them in. Within three weeks Admiral Edward Russell, in the guise of an ordinary seaman, had left for Holland with the invitation to William in his care.

In addition to the host of satires on the birth, equally numerous and quite predictably fulsome ballads and panegyrics celebrated the event throughout June. Though most of these poems are of even less note than their satiric counterparts (see, for example, the Oxford collection, *Strenæ Natalitæ Celsissimum Principem*), one stands out above the rest both in artistry and in interest. On or about 23 June (the date given by Malone is probably derived from Luttrell's copy) appeared *Britannia Rediviva* from the pen of the Crown's great apologist, John Dryden. Written, as Scott points out, "in the character of a devout and grateful Catholic" and displaying "an enthusiastic faith in the mystic doctrines of the Catholic faith," the poem also adopts what was to be the last attempt at presenting an heroic view of the Stuart line. Dryden had returned poetically to the exalted high style of twenty-eight years before, when he celebrated the "happy restoration" of the Stuarts in the verses of *Astræa Redux*.

THE COUNCIL

To the tune of "Jamaica"

1.

Two Toms and Nat
In council sat
To rig out a thanksgiving,

Ascription: Sir William R. Wilde (*The Closing Years of Dean Swift's Life*, 1849. pp. 126–36) discovered a version of this poem in what he thought to be Swift's hand. On this evidence he suggested the poem might be ascribed to him. Harold Williams (Swift's *Poems*, 1937, *3*, 1058–63) refutes the supposition.

And make a prayer
For a thing in the air   5
That's neither dead nor living.

2.

The dame of Este,
As 'tis express'd
In her late, quaint epistle,
Did to our lady   10
Bequeath the baby
With coral, bells, and whistle.

3.

With this intent
She to her sent
Her gold and diamond bodkin,   15
That to conceive
She might have leave—
And is not this an odd thing?

4.

Then a pot of ale
To the Prince of Wales,   20
Though some are of opinion
That when 'tis come out
A double clout
Will cover his dominion.

9. *quaint:* "Ingeniously or cunningly designed or contrived," with a possible ana-
tomical pun.

10. *our lady:* The Queen.

15. *Her gold and diamond bodkin:* Wood recorded the rumor that the Duchess of
Modena had sent a golden heart to Loreto (see headnote). Such an offering was
not uncommon. Evelyn mentions a visit he made in Paris to the shop of Jacques
Sarrazin, where he watched the molding of a large gold madonna "to be sent by the
Queen Regent to Loreto as an offering for the birth of the Dauphine . . ." (2, 105–6).

23. *clout:* A pun on "swaddling clothes" and "a blow."

UPON THE KING'S VOYAGE TO CHATHAM
TO MAKE BULWARKS AGAINST THE DUTCH,
AND THE QUEEN'S MISCARRIAGE THEREUPON

When James, our great monarch, so wise and discreet,
Was gone with three barges to face the Dutch fleet,
Our young Prince of Wales, by inheritance stout,
Was coming to aid him and peep'd his head out;
But seeing his father, without ships or men,   5
Commit the defense of us all to a chain,
Taffy was frighted and skulk'd in again;
Nor thought, while the Dutch domineer'd in our road,
It was safe to come further and venture abroad.
Not Waldegrave, or th'epistle of Seigneur le Duke,   10
Made her Majesty sick, and her royal womb puke;
But the Dutchmen pickeering at Dover and Harwich,
Gave the ministers agues and the Queen a miscarriage.
And to see the poor King stand in ships of such need,

6. *Commit the defense of us all to a chain:* Late in April 1688, Luttrell writes:
"The King hath ordered a new platform of 50 guns at Sheerness, and a chain to be
laid over to block up the mouth of the River Medway that runs to Chatham, and a
fort to protect it." Another entry for this period reports that the "King is going
down to Sheerness to view that place, Chatham and others" (*1*, 438; and see *London
Gazette*, 10 May). Although sympathies were much different, the posture of James'
naval defenses would certainly have brought to mind the great naval defeat inflicted
on the English in 1667 by De Ruyter, when the Dutch broke through the chain and
fell upon the unprepared ships in the Thames and the Medway (see *POAS*, Yale, *1*,
97–139).

7. *Taffy:* A nickname for Welshmen, from the River Taff; the child was to be
the Prince of Wales.

10. *Waldegrave:* William Waldegrave, the Queen's first physician; he was knighted
by James shortly after the birth of the Prince.

th'epistle of Seigneur le Duke: On 11 May "the Queen, having received an
account that the Duke of Modena, her brother, was dead, fell into fits, which occasioned an express to his Majesty and brought him to town immediately" (Luttrell, *1*,
439; and see headnote to this section).

12. *pickeering:* Obs. or arch. "to forage, maraud, pillage," or "to skirmish, scout, or
reconnoiter."

14. *to see the poor King stand in ships of such need:* Feverish efforts were being
made by James to get his fleet in readiness (see J. R. Tanner, "Naval Preparations of
James II in 1688," *EHR*, *8* (1893), 272–83; and E. B. Powley, *The English Navy in the
Revolution of 1688*, 1928). Reports of the Dutch preparations for war had been coming
in since February; late in April word came that a Dutch fleet of 25 sail had put to
sea (Luttrell, *1*, 441).

Made the Catholics quake, and her majesty bleed.   15
I wish the sad accident don't spoil the young Prince,
Take off all his manhood and make him a wench;
But the hero, his father, no courage did lack,
Who was sorry on such a pretext to come back.
He mark'd out his ground, and mounted a gun,   20
And, 'tis thought, without such a pretense he had run;
For his army and navy were said to increase,
As appears (when we have no occasion) in peace.
Nay, if the Dutch come, we despise 'em so much,
Our navy incognito will leave 'em i'th'lurch;   25
And, to their eternal disgrace, we are able
To beat 'em by way of a post and a cable.
Why was this, sir, left out of th' wise Declaration
That flatter'd with hopes of more forces the nation?
'Twould have done us great good to have said you intended   30
The strength of the nation, the chain should be mended.
Though we thank you for passing so kindly your word
(Which never was broke) that you'd rule by the sword,
This promise we know you meant to fulfill,
And therefore you have reason (by Gad!) to take't ill   35
That the bishops, the bishops did throw out the bill.

19. *a pretext:* Antagonists viewed the alarm as such: ". . . the King's going to Chatham just before this pretended likelihood of a miscarriage, [was] for no real occasion known but the private one of designing to have her pretend a miscarriage and so send for him . . ." (*Answer to the Depositions,* &c., 1689, p. 5).

22–23. These lines refer to the general fears throughout the reign of James' efforts to increase the size of his standing army rather than remodel the trainbands as parliament had suggested in Nov. 1685.

28. *Declaration:* The Declaration of Toleration had appended to it remarks concerning the army and the fleet "which with good management shall be constantly the same, and greater, if the safety or honor of the nation require it."

33. *Which never was broke:* The King's word became a standing joke during the reign (see above, *The Paradox,* 21 and n.).

36. *the bishops:* The Seven Bishops.

JOHN DRYDEN

BRITANNIA REDIVIVA

A Poem on the Birth of the Prince

Di patrii indigetes, et Romule, Vestaque mater,
Quae Tuscum Tyberim et Romana palatia servas,
Hunc saltem everso *puerum* succurrere saeclo
Ne prohibete! satis jampridem sanguine nostro
Laomedonteae luimus *perjuria* Trojae.

Virgil, *Georgics* I.498–502

BRITANNIA REDIVIVA

A Poem on the Prince
Born on the 10th of June 1688

Our vows are heard betimes, and Heaven takes care
To grant, before we can conclude the prayer;
Preventing angels met it half the way,
And sent us back to praise, who came to pray.
   Just on the day, when the high-mounted sun   5
Did farthest in his northern progress run,
He bended forward, and e'en stretch'd the sphere
Beyond the limits of the lengthen'd year,

Epigraph: Thou father Romulus and mother Earth,
               Goddess unmov'd! whose gentle arms extend
               O'er Tuscan Tiber's course, and Roman tow'rs defend;
               With youthful Caesar your joint pow'rs engage,
               Nor hinder him to save the sinking age.
               Oh! let the blood already spilt, atone
               For the past crimes of curst Laomedon! (tr. Dryden)

In the epigraph Dryden has substituted *puerum* for *juvenem*. He has had *perjuria* set
off in italic type to call attention to the reference to the perjured witnesses against
Catholics in the days of the Popish Plot.

To view a brighter sun in Britain born;
That was the bus'ness of his longest morn; 10
The glorious object seen, 'twas time to turn.

    Departing spring could only stay to shed
Her bloomy beauties on the genial bed,
But left the manly summer in her stead,
With timely fruit the longing land to cheer, 15
And to fulfill the promise of the year.
Betwixt two seasons comes th'auspicious heir,
This age to blossom, and the next to bear.

    Last solemn Sabbath saw the Church attend,
The Paraclete in fiery pomp descend; 20
But when his wondrous octave roll'd again,
He brought a royal infant in his train:
So great a blessing to so good a King,
None but th'Eternal Comforter could bring.

    Or did the mighty Trinity conspire, 25
As once in council to create our Sire?
It seems as if they sent the new-born guest
To wait on the procession of their feast;
And on their sacred anniverse decreed
To stamp their image on the promis'd seed. 30
Three realms united, and on one bestow'd,
An emblem of their mystic union show'd;
The Mighty Trine the triple empire shar'd,
As every person would have one to guard.

    Hail, son of prayers! by holy violence 35
Drawn down from Heaven; but long be banish'd thence,
And late to thy paternal skies retire!
To mend our crimes, whole ages would require;
To change th'inveterate habit of our sins,
And finish what thy godlike Sire begins. 40

19. Textual note in all editions (hereafter designated *BR*): "Whitsunday."
21. *wond'rous octave:* "Trinity Sunday" (*BR*).
35–36. Cf. *Astræa Redux:*

> Yet as he knew his blessing's worth, took care
> That we should know it by repeated pray'r;
> Which storm'd the skies and ravish'd Charles from thence
> As Heaven itself it took by violence. (141–44)

37–40. Cf. Horace, *Odes* I.ii.43–49 (to Augustus).

Kind Heav'n, to make us Englishmen again,
No less can give us than a patriarch's reign.
  The sacred cradle to your charge receive,
Ye seraphs, and by turns the guard relieve;
Thy father's angel and thy father join,   45
To keep possession, and secure the line;
But long defer the honors of thy fate;
Great may they be like his, like his be late,
That James this running century may view,
And give his son an auspice to the new.   50
  Our wants exact at least that moderate stay;
For, see the dragon winged on his way,
To watch the travail, and devour the prey:
Or, if allusions may not rise so high,
Thus, when Alcides rais'd his infant cry,   55
The snakes besieg'd his young divinity;
But vainly with their forked tongues they threat,
For opposition makes a hero great.
To needful succor all the good will run,
And Jove assert the godhead of his son.   60
  O still repining at your present state,
Grudging yourselves the benefits of fate;
Look up, and read in characters of light
A blessing sent you in your own despite!
The manna falls, yet that celestial bread,   65
Like Jews, you munch, and murmur while you feed.
May not your fortune be, like theirs, exil'd,
Yet forty years to wander in the wild!
Or, if it be, may Moses live at least,

52. *the dragon:* "Alluding only to the Commonwealth Party, here and in other places in the poem" (*BR*). According to Scott, "The acquittal of the Bishops . . . two days before the poem was licensed, must have excited a prudential reverence for the Church of England in her moment of triumph. The poet fixes upon the Commonwealth party therefore, exclusively, the common reports which had been circulated during the Queen's pregnancy. . . ."

53. *the travail:* "Rev. 12:4" (*BR*). "And the dragon stood before the woman which was ready to be delivered, for to devour her child as soon as it was born."

55–60. On Hercules' feats at birth see Theocritus, xxiv.

65–66. Cf. Exod. 16. The image had become a commonplace for God's providence in face of man's ungratefulness and was employed to support the orthodox position of church-state, *de jure divino.*

69–70. Num. 27:12–18.

To lead you to the verge of promis'd rest! 70
    Though poets are not prophets to foreknow
What plants will take the blight and what will grow,
By tracing Heav'n, his footsteps may be found;
Behold, how awfully he walks the round!
God is abroad, and, wondrous in his ways, 75
The rise of empires, and their fall, surveys;
More, might I say, than with an usual eye,
He sees his bleeding Church in ruin lie,
And hears the souls of saints beneath his altar cry.
Already has he lifted high the sign, 80
Which crown'd the conquering arms of Constantine.
The moon grows pale at that presaging sight,
And half her train of stars have lost their light.
    Behold another Sylvester, to bless
The sacred standard, and secure success; 85
Large of his treasures, of a soul so great,
As fills and crowds his universal seat.
Now view at home a second Constantine
(The former too was of the British line);
Has not his healing balm your breaches clos'd 90
Whose exile many sought, and few oppos'd?

78. Cf. *The Hind and the Panther,* I.9–24.
80. *the sign:* "The Cross" (*BR*). Dryden refers to the vision of the luminous cross, inscribed *In hoc signo vinces,* that was said to have appeared to Constantine before his great victory over Maxentius in 312. Here James' adoption of the Roman Catholic religion is seen as a similar portent of a Christian victory over the Turk in the war then being fought on the Danube.
82. *The moon:* "The Crescent, which the Turks bear for their arms" (*BR*).
84. *Sylvester:* "The Pope in the time of Constantine the Great; alluding to the present Pope [Innocent XI]" (*BR*). For James' relations with him, see above, *Diplomatic Relations with the Vatican.*
88. *Constantine:* "King James the Second" (*BR*).
89. *of British Line:* Kinsley cites Gibbon, *Decline and Fall,* xiv, on the birthplace of Constantine "as well as the condition of his mother Helena. . . . Notwithstanding the recent tradition, which assigns for her father a British king, we are obliged to confess that Helena was the daughter of an innkeeper. . . . This tradition . . . was invented in the darkness of monasteries [and] has been defended by the antiquarians of the last age."
91. *Whose exile many sought:* During the Whig attempts to exclude James from the throne, Charles found it expedient to "exile" his brother, sending him to Brussels from March to Sept. 1679 and to Scotland from Nov. 1679 to Feb. 1680 and from Oct. 1680 to March 1682.

Or, did not Heav'n, by its eternal doom,
Permit those evils, that this good might come?
So manifest that e'en the moon-ey'd sects
See whom and what this Providence protects.   95
Methinks, had we within our minds no more
Than that one shipwreck on the fatal ore,
That only thought may make us think again,
What wonders God reserves for such a reign.
To dream that chance his preservation wrought   100
Were to think Noah was preserv'd for nought;
Or the surviving eight were not design'd
To people earth, and to restore their kind.
    When humbly on the royal babe we gaze,
The manly lines of a majestic face   105
Give awful joy; 'tis paradise to look
On the fair frontispiece of nature's book:
If the first opening page so charms the sight,
Think how th'unfolded volume will delight!
    See how the venerable infant lies   110
In early pomp; how through the mother's eyes
The father's soul, with an undaunted view,
Looks out, and takes our homage as his due!
See on his future subjects how he smiles,
Nor meanly flatters, nor with craft beguiles;   115
But with an open face, as on his throne,
Assures our birthrights, and assumes his own.
Born in broad day-light, that th'ungrateful rout
May find no room for a remaining doubt;
Truth, which itself is light, does darkness shun,   120
And the true eaglet safely dares the sun.
    Fain would the fiends have made a dubious birth,
Loath to confess the godhead cloth'd in earth;
But, sicken'd, after all their baffled lies,
To find an heir apparent of the skies,   125

94. *moon-ey'd:* Affected with intermittent blindness, supposedly caused by the influence of the moon.

97. *the fatal ore:* "The Lemmon Ore" (*BR*). The sandbank in the Yarmouth road on which James' ship was wrecked in the spring of 1682 on his voyage to "fetch the Duchess, big with child, out of Scotland" (Clarke, *Life, 1,* 730).

122-23. "Alluding to the temptation in the wilderness" (*BR*).

Abandon'd to despair, still may they grudge,
And, owning not the Savior, prove the judge.
  Not great Aeneas stood in plainer day,
When, the dark mantling mist dissolv'd away,
He to the Tyrians show'd his sudden face,   130
Shining with all his goddess mother's grace;
For she herself had made his count'nance bright,
Breath'd honor on his eyes, and her own purple light.
  If our victorious Edward, as they say
Gave Wales a Prince on that propitious day,   135
Why may not years revolving with his fate
Produce his like, but with a longer date;
One, who may carry to a distant shore
The terror that his fam'd forefather bore?
But why should James, or his young hero, stay   140
For slight pressages of a name or day?
We need no Edward's fortune to adorn
That happy moment when our Prince was born;
Our Prince adorns this day, and ages hence
Shall wish his birthday for some future prince.   145
  Great Michael, prince of all th'ethereal hosts,
And whate'er inborn saints our Britain boasts;
And thou, th'adopted patron of our isle,
With cheerful aspects on this infant smile!
The pledge of Heaven, which, dropping from above,   150
Secures our bliss, and reconciles his love.
  Enough of ills our dire rebellion wrought,
When to the dregs we drank the bitter draught;
Then airy atoms did in plagues conspire,
Nor did th'avenging angel yet retire,   155
But purg'd our still-increasing crimes with fire.
Then perjur'd plots, the still impending Test,
And worse—but charity conceals the rest.

128. "Virgil, *Aeneid*, I.[588–91]" (*BR*).
134. *victorious Edward:* "Edward, the Black Prince, born on Trinity Sunday" (*BR*).
146. *Great Michael:* "The motto of the poem explained" (*BR*).
148. *th'adopted patron:* "St. George" (*BR*).
152. *dire rebellion:* The Civil War.
154–56. *plagues . . . fire:* The plague of 1665 and the great fire of 1666.
157. *plots, the . . . Test:* The Popish Plot and the Test Act.

Here stop the current of the sanguine flood;
Require not, gracious God! thy martyrs' blood;   160
But let their dying pangs, their living toil,
Spread a rich harvest through their native soil;
A harvest ripening for another reign,
Of which this royal babe may reap the grain.
　　Enough of early saints one womb has giv'n,   165
Enough increas'd the family of Heav'n;
Let them for his and our atonement go,
And, reigning blest above, leave him to rule below.
　　Enough already has the year foreslow'd,
His wonted course, the seas have overflow'd,   170
The meads were floated with a weeping spring,
And frighten'd birds in woods forgot to sing;
The strong-limb'd steed beneath his harness faints,
And the same shiv'ring sweat his lord attaints.
When will the minister of wrath give o'er?   175
Behold him at Araunah's threshing-floor!
He stops, and seems to sheathe his flaming brand,
Pleas'd with burnt incense from our David's hand;
David has bought the Jebusite's abode,
And rais'd an altar to the living God.   180
　　Heaven, to reward him, makes his joys sincere;
No future ills nor accidents appear
To sully and pollute the sacred infant's year.
Five months to discord and debate were giv'n;
He sanctifies the yet remaining sev'n.   185
Sabbath of months! henceforth in him be blest,
And prelude to the realm's perpetual rest!
　　Let his baptismal drops for us atone;
Lustrations for offenses not his own:

165–66. For the early deaths of the Queen's former children, see the headnote to
this section.

169–72. "The year 1688, big with so many events of importance, commenced very
unfavorably with stormy weather, and an epidemical distemper among men and cattle"
(Scott).

176. *Araunah's threshing floor:* "Alluding to the passage in the 1st Book of Kings,
ch. 24, v. 20th" (*BR*). The reference should have been to II Kings (now II Sam.), the
first two books of Samuel being considered in the Vulgate the first two of Kings, which
was four books in all.

184. *Five months:* i.e. the first five months of 1688.

189. *offenses not his own:* "Original sin" (*BR*).

Let conscience, which is int'rest ill disguis'd,   190
In the same font be cleans'd, and all the land baptiz'd.
   Unnam'd as yet; at least unknown to fame;
Is there a strife in Heav'n about his name,
Where every famous predecessor vies,
And makes a faction for it in the skies?   195
Or must it be reserv'd to thought alone?
Such was the sacred Tetragrammaton.
Things worthy silence must not be reveal'd;
Thus the true name of Rome was kept conceal'd,
To shun the spells and sorceries of those   200
Who durst her infant majesty oppose.
But when his tender strength in time shall rise
To dare ill tongues, and fascinating eyes,
This isle, which hides the little Thund'rer's fame,
Shall be too narrow to contain his name: 205
Th'artillery of Heav'n shall make him known;
Crete could not hold the god, when Jove was grown.
   As Jove's increase, who from his brain was born,
Whom arms and arts did equally adorn,
Free of the breast was bred, whose milky taste   210
Minerva's name to Venus had debas'd;
So this imperial babe rejects the food,
That mixes monarch's with plebeian blood:
Food that his inborn courage might control,
Extinguish all the father in his soul,   215
And for his Estian race, and Saxon strain,
Might reproduce some second Richard's reign.
Mildness he shares from both his parents' blood;

190–91. Cf. *The Hind and the Panther*, III.823–4:

> Immortal pow'rs the term of conscience know,
> But int'rest is her name with men below.

192. *Unnam'd as yet:* "The Prince christened, but not named" (*BR*). See above, *An Excellent New Ballad*, 10 and n.

197. *Tetragrammaton:* "Jehovah, or the name of God, unlawful to be pronounced by the Jews" (*BR*).

199. *name of Rome:* "Some authors say that the true name of Rome was kept a secret: *ne hostes incantamentis deos elicerent*" (*BR*).

207. *Crete:* "Candia, where Jupiter was born and bred secretly" (*BR*).

208. *Jove's increase:* "Pallas, or Minerva; said by the poets to have been bred up by hand" (*BR*).

But kings too tame are despicably good:
Be this the mixture of this regal child,　　　　　220
By nature manly, but by virtue mild.
　　Thus far the furious transport of the news
Had to prophetic madness fir'd the muse;
Madness ungovernable, uninspir'd,
Swift to foretell whatever she desir'd.　　　　　225
Was it for me the dark abyss to tread,
And read the book which angels cannot read?
How was I punish'd, when the sudden blast
The face of Heav'n, and our young sun, o'ercast!
Fame, the swift ill increasing as she roll'd,　　　230
Disease, despair, and death, at three reprises told:
At three insulting strides she stalk'd the town,
And, like contagion, struck the loyal down.
Down fell the winnow'd wheat; but, mounted high,
The whirlwind bore the chaff, and hid the sky.　　235
Here black rebellion shooting from below,
(As earth's gigantic brood by moments grow)
And here the sons of God are petrifi'd with woe:
An apoplex of grief! so low were driv'n
The saints, as hardly to defend their Heav'n.　　240
　　As, when pent vapors run their hollow round,
Earthquakes, which are convulsions of the ground,
Break bellowing forth, and no confinement brook,
Till the third settles what the former shook;
Such heavings had our souls, till, slow and late,　245
Our life with his return'd, and faith prevailed on fate.
By prayers the mighty blessing was implor'd,
To prayers was granted, and by prayers restor'd.
　　So, ere the Shunammite a son conceiv'd,
The prophet promis'd, and the wife believ'd;　　250
A son was sent, the son so much desir'd,

228. *the sudden blast:* "The sudden false report of the Prince's death" (*BR*).
231. *reprises:* Occasions; renewals of Fame's report.
237. "Those giants are feigned to have grown fifteen ells every day" (*BR*). The twins, Otus and Ephialtes, were sired by Neptune on Iphimedia, wife of the giant Aloeus. They were reckoned to be nine fathoms tall when they reached nine years of age. (*Odyssey,* IX.305–20).
249–56. "In the second Book of Kings, chap. 4th" (*BR*).

But soon upon the mother's knees expir'd.
The troubled seer approach'd the mournful door,
Ran, pray'd, and sent his past'ral staff before,
Then stretch'd his limbs upon the child, and mourn'd,   255
Till warmth, and breath, and a new soul return'd.

    Thus Mercy stretches out her hand, and saves
Desponding Peter, sinking in the waves.

    As when a sudden storm of hail and rain
Beats to the ground the yet unbearded grain,   260
Think not the hopes of harvest are destroy'd
On the flat field, and on the naked void;
The light, unloaded stem, from tempest freed,
Will raise the youthful honors of his head;
And, soon restor'd by native vigor, bear   265
The timely product of the bounteous year.

    Nor yet conclude all fiery trials past,
For Heav'n will exercise us to the last;
Sometimes will check us in our full career,
With doubtful blessings, and with mingled fear,   270
That, still depending on his daily grace,
His every mercy for an alms may pass;
With sparing hands will diet us to good,
Preventing surfeits of our pamper'd blood.
So feeds the mother bird her craving young   275
With little morsels, and delays 'em long.

    True, this last blessing was a royal feast;
But where's the wedding-garment on the guest?
Our manners, as religion were a dream,
Are such as teach the nations to blaspheme.   280
In lusts we wallow, and with pride we swell,
And injuries with injuries repel;
Prompt to revenge, not daring to forgive,
Our lives unteach the doctrine we believe.
Thus Israel sinn'd, impenitently hard,   285
And vainly thought the present ark their guard;
But when the haughty Philistines appear,
They fled, abandon'd to their foes and fear;
Their God was absent, though his ark was there.

285-89. "Samuel 4th, v. 10th" (BR).

Ah! lest our crimes should snatch this pledge away,   290
And make our joys the blessings of a day!
For we have sinn'd him hence, and that he lives,
God to his promise, not our practice, gives.
Our crimes would soon weigh down the guilty scale,
But James and Mary and the Church prevail.   295
Nor Amalech can rout the chosen bands,
While Hur and Aaron hold up Moses' hands.

    By living well, let us secure his days,
Mod'rate in hopes, and humble in our ways.
No force the free-born spirit can constrain,   300
But charity, and great examples gain.
Forgiveness is our thanks for such a day;
'Tis godlike God in his own coin to pay.

    But you, propitious Queen, translated here,
From your mild Heav'n, to rule our rugged sphere,   305
Beyond the sunny walks, and circling year;
You, who your native climate have bereft
Of all the virtues, and the vices left;
Whom piety and beauty make their boast,
Though beautiful is well in pious lost;   310
So lost as star-light is dissolv'd away,
And melts into the brightness of the day;
Or gold about the regal diadem,
Lost, to improve the lustre of the gem—
What can we add to your triumphant day?   315
Let the great gift the beauteous giver pay;
For should our thanks awake the rising sun,
And lengthen, as his latest shadows run,
That, though the longest day, would soon, too soon be done.
Let angels' voices with their harps conspire,   320
But keep th'auspicious infant from the choir;
Late let him sing above, and let us know
No sweeter music than his cries below.

    Nor can I wish to you, great Monarch, more
Than such an annual income to your store;   325
The day, which gave this unit, did not shine
For a less omen, than to fill the trine.

296–97. "Exodus, 17, v. 8th" (BR).

After a Prince, an Admiral beget;
The *Royal Sov'reign* wants an anchor yet.
Our isle has younger titles still in store,   330
And when th'exhausted land can yield no more,
Your line can force them from a foreign shore.
   The name of Great your martial mind will suit;
But justice is your darling attribute:
Of all the Greeks, 'twas but one hero's due,   335
And, in him, Plutarch prophesi'd of you.
A Prince's favors but on few can fall,
But justice is a virtue shar'd by all.
   Some kings the name of conqu'rors have assum'd,
Some to be great, some to be gods presum'd;   340
But boundless pow'r, and arbitrary lust,
Made tyrants still abhor the name of Just;
They shunn'd the praise this godlike virtue gives
And fear'd a title that reproach'd their lives.
   The pow'r, from which all kings derive their state,   345
Whom they pretend, at least, to imitate,
Is equal both to punish and reward;
For few would love their God, unless they fear'd.
   Resistless force and immortality
Make but a lame, imperfect deity;   350
Tempests have force unbounded to destroy,
And deathless being e'en the damn'd enjoy;
And yet Heav'n's attributes, both last and first;
One without life, and one with life accurst;
But justice is Heav'n's self, so strictly he,   355
That could it fail, the godhead could not be.
This virtue is your own; but life and state
Are one to fortune subject, one to fate:
Equal to all, you justly frown or smile;
Nor hopes nor fears your steady hand beguile;   360
Yourself our balance hold, the world's our isle.

   329. *The Royal Sov'reign:* Described by Evelyn as "a monstrous vessel so called, being for burden, defense, and ornament the richest that ever spread cloth before the wind" (2, 30), the ship, rebuilt in 1659 and 1685, was accidentally burned in 1696.
   335. *one hero's due:* "Aristides; see his *Life* in Plutarch" (*BR*). He was known for his great justice.

An Excellent New Ballad Called the
Prince of Darkness

Showing how Three Nations may
be Set on Fire by a Warming Pan

As I went by St. James', I heard a bird sing,
"Of certain the Queen has a boy in the spring."
But one of the chairmen did laugh and did say,
"It was born overnight and brought forth the next day."
This bantling was heard at St. James's to squall,   5
Which made the Queen make so much haste from Whitehall.
"Peace, peace, little master, and hold up thy head;
Here's money bid for thee," the true mother said.
But nobody knows from what parish it came,
And that is the reason it has not a name.   10

1. The present ballad reworks a scurrilous song of 1666 attacking Margaret, wife of Sir John Denham and mistress of the Duke of York. Preserved in Harleian 7332, the song begins:

> As I went by St. James's, I heard a bird sing
> That Denham's fair wife was a miss for a King,
>
> But the King goes without her, as I have been told,
> And the Duke does enjoy her, though Nan pout and scold.

4. *It was born over night and brought forth the next day:* It was said that a child had been born at St. James' before the Queen went there for her lying-in, and that this child was later brought in, perhaps in a warming pan, and put into the Queen's bed. It was also commonly said that the Prince seemed a strong, healthy child, beyond his age. *A Catholic Hymn* (see headnote) put it this way:

> And now he's come out,
> A blessing no doubt,
> And an hero as sure as may be;
> As big and as bold
> As a babe a month old,
> More like than a new born baby.

6. *so much haste from Whitehall:* Burnet records that the Queen, though in haste, actually "by a sort of affectation" insisted on being "carried thither by Charing Cross through the Pall Mall," a route longer than her accustomed way through the park (*1,* 751). This, too, was viewed suspiciously in retrospect.

10. *it has not a name:* "Amongst these distractions and preparations for war, the King forgot not the ceremony of naming the Prince of Wales, which had not been done when he was christened, but on the 15th of October was performed in the King's chapel at St. James' with great solemnity, the Pope being godfather, represented by the Nuncio, and Queen Dowager godmother" (Clarke, 2, 191–92).

Father Petre, the Queen, and the Prince

Good Catholics all were afraid it was dying,
There was such abundance of sighing and crying;
Which is a good token by which we may swear
It is the Queen's own and the kingdom's right heir.
Now if we should happen to have a true lad 15
From the loins of so wholesome a mother and dad,
'Twere hard to determine which blood were the best—
That of Southesk, or the bastard of Est!
But now we have cause for thanksgiving, indeed,
There was no other way for mending the breed! 20

Tom Tiler, or the Nurse

Old stories of a Tyler sing
That did attempt to be a king.
Our age is with a tiler grac'd,
By more preposterous planets rais'd.
His cap with Jocky's match'd together, 5
Turn'd to a beaver and a feather;

11–12. Charles Middleton, second Earl of Middleton, and one of James' secretaries of state, deposed that he had stood near the bed's foot on the left side, from where he had heard the Queen's groans and several loud shrieks. The Lady Susanna Belasyse testified that when she did not hear the infant cry she was afraid it was in a convulsive fit, its skin seeming to her unnaturally dark.

Date: This ballad was "published some few days before Christmas 1688" (MS. note in Wood 417). Reference to the flight of the Queen and Prince (36–38) confirms the date.

Title: The nurse, a tilemaker's wife named Cooper, was brought in shortly after the Prince's illness at Richmond. The child was supposed to have a birth mark, by which several of the deponents claimed to know him as the King's son (see *A Poem on the Deponents,* 133–35 and n.). Lampoonists were quick to turn the wet-nurse's success with the baby to their own account, appropriating at the same time the story of the birth mark. In *Father Petre's Policy Discovered (Popery,* 2, 1689, 29) the satirist writes:

> They knew sweet babe from a thousand, they cri'd,
> 'Twas born with the point of a tile on his side.

1. *Tyler:* Wat Tyler, leader of the Peasants' Revolt of 1381.

5. *Jocky:* One of James' numerous nicknames.

6. *a beaver and a feather:* The beaver hat, worn chiefly by men, was looked on as expensively stylish. The Prince of Wales' emblem is three ostrich feathers, first adopted as a crest by the Black Prince. Also, the feather is a personal decoration and mark of honor, e.g. "to put a feather in one's cap."

His clay transform'd to yellow gilt,
And trowel to a silver hilt.

His lady from the tiles and bricks
Kidnapp'd to court in coach and six;   10
Her arms a sucking Prince embrace,
Whate'er you think, of royal race;
A Prince come in the nick of time
(Bless'd d'Adda!), 'tis a venial crime
That shall repair our breach of state;   15
While all the world congratulate,
Shall, like his Sire, suppress the just,
Raise knaves and fools to place of trust:
Titus and Vane, who sought his fate;
Tilers and Macs to chits of state.   20
But here, unhappy babe, alas,
I cannot but lament thy case.
That thou, fed up with Rome's strong meats,
Should long for milk of heretic teats.
Among the daughters was there none   25
Worthy to nurse a Monarch's son?
But if thy uncle, who before
Was always right, chang'd the last hour;
If thy undoubted Sire, so sage,
Declar'd i'th'evening of his age;   30
Why should'st not thou, Papist so soon,
Be a staunch Protestant ere noon?

7. *yellow gilt:* Gold, the metal of kings; here a play on the idea of "guilt."
8. *a silver hilt:* The scepter.

14. *d'Adda:* Count Ferdinand d'Adda, the Papal Nuncio, with a play on the baby-talk word for "father" (see *The Audience,* 30 and n.). Both d'Adda and Petre were slandered as responsible for the child.

15. *breach of state:* An obscene pun.

19. *Titus and Vane:* Col. Silius Titus and Christopher Vane (1653–1723), sworn to the Privy Council on 6 July (*London Gazette,* 9 July 1688). Both were Dissenters with reputations as opponents of the Crown.

20. *Macs:* Irishmen.

27–30. Charles II was said to have died a Roman Catholic (Evelyn, *4,* 407–8 and nn.); James' conversion took place in 1667, when he was 34, though it was not publicly admitted until 1676 (Turner, pp. 87, 125).

32. Ironically, attempts were made to bring the Prince up in the Protestant faith, but they failed (see *The Paradox,* 35 n.).

This said, the tiler laugh'd in's sleeve
And took his audience of leave.
The Prince, who answer'd ne'er a word,   35
That he should travel did accord;
To Paris sent to learn grimace,
To swear and damn with a *bonne grâce.*

[GEORGE STEPNEY]

THE AUDIENCE

The critics that pretend to sense
Do cavil at the Audience,
As if his Grace were not as good
To bow to as a piece of wood.
Did not our fathers heretofore   5
Their senseless deities adore?
Did not old Delphos all along
Vent oracles without a tongue?
And wisest monarchs did importune
From the dumb god to know their fortune.   10
Did not the speaking head of late

34. *audience of leave:* Farewell interview.

37. *To Paris sent:* Mary Beatrice fled with the Prince on 10 Dec., arriving in Calais
the next day.

Ascription: This poem is printed with Stepney's works in *Minor Poets, 3,* 1749. I
have found no corroborating evidence for the ascription.

11. *the speaking head:* A figure in puppet shows. A specific show may be intended,
however; cf. the prologue to Aphra Behn's *Emperor of the Moon* (1687), in which
Mr. Jevern, the speaker, is interrupted by a "speaking head" that

[. . . rises upon a twisted post on a bench from under the stage. After Jevern
speaks to its mouth.]
                    Oh! Oh! Oh!
                    Stentor. Oh! Oh! Oh!
[After this it sings *Sawney,* laughs, cries "God bless the King," in order.]

The tune *Sawney,* written by D'Urfey for his comedy *The Virtuous Wife* (1680), soon
became popular as a political ballad (Chappell, *2,* 618–20). In 1685 the tune was employed to sing of the downfall of *The Rebel Captive,* the Earl of Argyle, beheaded in
Edinburgh on 30 June 1685 (see *Roxburghe Ballads, 5,* 621).

Of matters learnedly debate?
And render'd without tongue or ears
Wise answers to his whisp'ring peers;
And shall we to a living Prince   15
Deny the state of Audience?
What though the bantling cannot speak?
Yet like the blockhead he may squeak,
Give audience by interpreter—
The wisest prince can do no more.   20
    Then enter, with a Prince's banner,
Sir Charles, after the usual manner:
"Great Sir, His Holiness from Rome
Greets your high birth." The Prince cri'd, "Mum!"
"The consecrated pilch and clout—   25
If you'll vouchsafe to hear me out—
And many other toys, I'm come
To lay them at your sacred bum.
So young, yet such a god-like ray!
Phoebus, your dad was priest d'Adda—   30
Great Prince, I have no more to say."
"Conducted next, there comes, Great Sir,
An envoy from the Emperor,
To gratulate your lucky fate,
That gives to England's throne new date.   35
We joy that any thing should reign
To baffle Orange and the Dane."
The youth, to see them thus beguil'd,

15–17. Protocol required envoys to have an audience with the infant, as well as with the King, Queen, and Queen Dowager.

17. *bantling:* A brat, or bastard.

22. *Sir Charles:* Sir Charles Cotterell, Master of the Ceremonies. He was in charge of court audiences.

25. *pilch and clout:* A pilch is a triangular flannel wrapper for an infant, worn over the diaper, or clout. The phrase suggests "king of clouts"—a mere doll in the garb of king.

30. *d'Adda:* Cf. *Tom Tyler,* 14. There is a note on the usage and pronunciation of this and the rhyme word "Mamma" (83), in *N&Q,* 4 June 1881, p. 456.

33. *envoy from the Emperor:* On 19 Aug. Count Hamilton, envoy extraordinary from the Elector Palatine, had his first audience with the Prince. (Notices of this and other interviews were carried by the *London Gazette.*)

37. *Orange and the Dane:* James' Protestant daughters, Mary and Anne, were married to William of Orange and George of Denmark.

In token of his favor, smil'd.
But at the Spaniard laugh'd outright,   40
As shamm'd again in eighty-eight.
Next, having pass'd the inward sentry,
The doubtful Monsieur made his entry:
"The King, my master, Sir, has sent
Your royal birth to compliment,   45
If you will make it but appear
That you are England's lawful heir."
Here Lady Powis took him short,
"Have you a King? Thank Maz'rin for't!"
FRENCHMAN: "Whoe'er the father was, the mother   50
Was France's Queen."
POWIS: "Who questions t'other?"
At this reproof he pawn'd a purse
And parting made his peace with nurse.
The Dane, the Swede, with other nations,   55
Come in with loud congratulations.
Upon the Swede so fam'd for battle,
He cast a frown and shook his rattle.
And for the Dane, who took the part

40. *the Spaniard:* Don Pedro Ronquillo was the Spanish Ambassador. I have found no record of his audience with the Prince. In Dec. 1688 his house near Lincoln's Inn Fields was pillaged by a mob of anti-Catholic demonstrators and his library burned (Evelyn, *4*, 610).

41. *eighty-eight:* "Eighty-eight" became a byword when the descent of William seemed imminent. Depending on the sympathies of the speaker, it could allude to the great victory in 1588 over another attacking force, or to the destruction of a Catholic threat.

43. *the doubtful Monsieur:* On 10 July, Count Philibert de Gramont, envoy from Louis XIV, had an audience with the Prince. He is "doubtful," presumably, as a result of James' constant vacillation in his dealings with Louis. He is also uncertain of the birth—its legitimacy and its ultimate bearing on the future (see 47).

48. *Lady Powis:* Elizabeth, Marchioness of Powis. She was appointed governess of the Prince on 10 June, while Lady Strickland, wife of the papist Sir Thomas Strickland, was named under-governess (Luttrell, *1*, 443).

49. *Maz'rin:* Jules Mazarin (1602–61) succeeded Richelieu as Prime Minister of France and was kept in that office by Anne of Austria, the Queen Regent, after the death of Louis XIII. He was largely responsible for governing France during the minority of Louis XIV and through the Fronde. Generally disliked by anti-government factions, he was often identified in lampoons as the father of Louis XIV.

52. *pawn'd a purse:* A reference to Louis' financial aid to both Charles and James.

54. *the Dane, the Swede:* Count de Reventlau and Baron Lyonberg.

Of good Prince George, he let a f———.
This put him in a sullen fit;   60
Nurse scarce could dance him out of it.
When an ambassador from Poland,
Knock'd at the door, and Veldt from Holland,
He crying suck'd, and sucking cri'd,
When Lady Governess repli'd,   65
"Peace, Prince, peace, Prince; peace, pretty Prince,
And let the States have audience."
DUTCHMAN: "From Holland I am hither sent,
To challenge, not to compliment;
Prepare with speed your twenty sail,   70
Your twice four thousand, on the nail,
Which by your senate was enacted
With Orange, when your Sire contracted."
The name of Holland did affright,
And make th'young hero scream outright.   75
But Orange nam'd, the royal elf,
The sweet, sweet babe besh—— himself.
Tyrconnel, who came o'er no less
Then to be made his governess,
To take her leave by luck came in;   80
She suck'd his nose, and lick'd him clean.
Last came the Lady Hales from play,

59. *Prince George:* Cf. 37. An early defector to William, going over to him before the end of November.

60. *a sullen fit:* Contemporary accounts indicate that the Prince suffered from fits (see Luttrell, *1,* 443).

62. *ambassador from Poland:* Not until the first week in October did Count de la Neville, envoy from Poland, arrive for his audience.

63. *Veldt from Holland:* Willem van Zuylestein was sent by William ostensibly to congratulate, but unofficially to sound the climate of opinion in England. "Veldt" is an abbreviation for veldt-marshal, Dutch equivalent of field-marshal.

70–71. For James' military preparations, see below, *Invasion Fears*.

71. *on the nail:* Immediately; at once.

78. *Tyrconnel:* Frances, wife of Richard Talbot, Earl of Tyrconnel and Viceroy of Ireland. She came over from Ireland to assist at the birth, and apartments were assigned her in Whitehall (*Public Occurrences,* 5 June 1688).

82. *Lady Hales:* Frances, wife of Sir Edward Hales, by whom she had had 12 children. Cf. *A Loyal Litany* (*Popery, 3,* 1689, 30–1):

> Grant it may be a Prince of Wales,
> Or if the smock and d'Adda fails,
> Adopt a brat of Neddy Hales.

Mov'd by instinct, he cried, "Mamma!"
And posted to the Queen away.

A POEM ON THE DEPONENTS

Concerning the Birth of the Prince of Wales

The mighty Monarch of this British isle,
Disturb'd to hear his subjects prate and smile
That he is so content to own a son
For to inherit the imperial throne
To please his Queen, and put by both his own;   5
But finding England not so credulous,
And clear-ey'd Orange more suspect than us,
By instigation of the Queen and P.
He summon'd all together, as you see,
And there declares his own sufficiency.   10
He says his subjects' minds now poison'd are,
They'll not believe God bless'd him with an heir;
But to convince them they are in the wrong
In come the swearers and depose as long
A narrative as perjur'd Oates could do;   15
What these depose unquestionably's true,

Despite its abusiveness, this poem gives a fairly accurate résumé of what the deponents did swear to. In fact, the lampoonist probably worked directly from the account published as *The Several Declarations, Together with the Several Depositions*, 1688 (reprinted in *State Tracts, 8,* 123–82), which may partially explain the stiltedness of several passages. The printing of these sordid declarations called forth this comment by the author of *The History of the Reign of James II,* 1689: "Now, boys and girls threw away their *Aristotle's Problems* and made that Book of Midwifery the delight of their candlelight studies" (p. 189).

5. *and put by both his own:* i.e. to deprive his daughters Mary and Anne of their place in the line of succession.

7. *clear-ey'd Orange:* In an official declaration, which circulated early in November, Orange voiced his concern over the legitimacy of the birth and promised to put the matter under parliamentary investigation (Kennett, *3,* 523–4). William's unofficial position had long been clear:

> The birth of the Prince, as it was an argument of the greatest joy to the King and Queen, and to all those who wished them well, so it gave the greatest agonies imaginable to the generality of the kingdom, but to none more than the Prince of Orange, however he was as forward as any with his congratulations (Clarke, *2,* 161).

8. *P.:* Father Edward Petre, confessor to the King and a member of his Privy Council.
15. *perjur'd Oates:* Titus Oates.

Our King says so, who dare say other now?
There's lords, knights, ladies, esquires, quacks, and all
The papal locusts that infect Whitehall.
They swear what King would have to gain their ends,   20
Since he's a Prince that ne'er forgets his friends;
But witness, bishops, for your loyalty
He makes you great; he did bestow on ye,
To keep you safe, his greatest, strongest fort;
While you were there, the Tower was the court.   25
All fled from James', to you for blessing came;
Imprisonment immortaliz'd your name:
Bishops of England's Church are men of fame.
And since his dire design in law has fail'd,
He seems to smile, you are to council call'd,   30
To hear the worthy loyal swearers swear
That at the birth of Wales's Prince they were.
    And first begins old England's barren Queen
That at her sister's labor was not seen
Till all was past, yet for the holy cause   35
She'll do what e'er she can to blind the laws
Of England, and doth there declare and say
She hasted to the Queen that very day,
And never stirr'd till this great Prince was born
For th'nation's glory, but he proves their scorn;   40
Except of those that on him daily wait,
Whose loyal love is only to be great.
    Next comes old Powis, who a story feigns
Of riff-raff stuff to fill the people's brains
Of what she saw and knew about the thing,   45

21. *a Prince that ne'er forgets his friends:* A claim James made constantly. His opponents were quick to remind themselves that he never forgot an enemy, as well.

26. *James':* St. James' Palace.

30. *you are to council call'd:* The council took place before "such of the peers of this Kingdom, both spiritual and temporal, as were in town." See Evelyn's account of the Archbishop of Canterbury's refusal to sit with papists. Halifax and the Earls of Nottingham and Clarendon refused to attend for the same reason (*4*, 602-3). Petre was also absent, but other Roman Catholics were in attendance.

33. *England's barren Queen:* Catherine of Braganza, the Queen Dowager.

43. *old Powis:* Elizabeth, Marchioness of Powis. Her tale of "riff-raff stuff" concerned the remedy employed to prevent the danger of fits in the new-born child: three drops of blood from the umbilical cord given the child in a solution of black cherry syrup.

And in a modest circumstance doth bring
Of something, which into the world he brought,
And by the doctors gave him, as she thought;
Now as a governess she tends his grace
And would not for all heaven quit her place;   50
So sweet a babe, so fine a hopeful lad,
The forward'st son the father ever had!
    Then Arran's Countess with her oath comes in
That at the Prince's birth her self had been,
And how she heard complainings from the Queen   55
Of little pains, and then the child was seen;
But oh! he did not cry! the Queen bawl'd out
For fear 'twas dead, but granny clear'd the doubt;
And further honor this great lady had,
She saw smock spoil'd with milk (the sign was bad!)   60
    And Peterborough could not be beguil'd,
Knowing the father's strength (at thought she smil'd),
She saw the smock and swears she was with child.
    While pious Sunderland to chapel went,
On purpose to receive the sacrament;   65
Devotion was so great she disobey'd
Her Majesty and said, when she had pray'd,
She'd wait on her; but hearing that the Prince
Was hast'ning to the world, this, this pretense
Soon brought our saint-like lady quick from thence;   70
And from her bended knees flew to the Queen,
And there saw all the sight was to be seen:
The bed was warm'd, and into it she went

53–57. *Arran's Countess:* Lady Anne Spencer, eldest daughter of the Earl of Sunderland, married James Douglas, Lord Arran, in Jan. 1688. According to her, the Queen said "Oh Lord, I don't hear the child cry, and immediately upon that this deponent did hear it cry."

60. *the sign was bad:* The meaning is unclear; could "glad" be meant?

61. *Peterborough:* Penelope, wife of Henry Mordaunt, second Earl of Peterborough. She was Groom of the Stole to Mary of Modena.

64. *Sunderland:* "Anne, Countess of Sunderland, deposeth, that June the 10th, 1688, being Trinity Sunday, the deponent went to St. James' chapel at eight o'clock in the morning, intending to receive the sacrament, but in the beginning of the communion service, the man which looks to the chapel came . . . and told her she must come to the Queen. The deponent said she would come as soon as prayers were done." The satirist turns her "obvious" piety to ironic account.

And ask'd the King if for the guests he'd sent;
A lingering pain she had and seem'd to fear   75
'Twould not be born till all the fools were there;
But by her midwife was assur'd one pain
Would bring the Prince into the world amain;
But, faithless Queen, the child did lie so high,
She'd not believe but Judith told a lie;   80
And such an honor to this deponent granted,
It's hardly more by th'Pope for to be sainted!
    Roscommon swears she stood by Sunderland,
Near the Queen's bed, just by the midwife's hand,
And saw his Highness taken out of bed,   85
Fit for a crown t'adorn his princely head.
    Fingel depos'd that in the Queen's distress,
She stood at the bed's feet, just by mistress,
And saw the Prince into the world did come
And by de la Baudie carri'd from the room.   90
    Then painted Bulkeley early in the morn
Came to St. James' to see his Highness born;
With all the haste she could, she up did rise,
Soon dress'd, she came by nine o'clock precise,
And found her Majesty was in the bed,   95
And groaning dismally, she further said;
Cri'd to the midwife, "Do not the child part!"
Old granny crav'd her leave with all her heart;
She granted what the beldam did desire;
And certain 'tis there was no danger nigh her.   100
Crying, "Oh King, where are you gone and fled?"

    79–82. The Countess of Sunderland's long deposition recounts how the Queen spoke
to the midwife and was assured "she wanted only one thorough pain to bring the
child into the world; upon which the Queen said, 'it is impossible, the child lies so
high,' and commanded this deponent to lay her hand on her Majesty's belly to feel
how high the child lay. . . ."

    80 *Judith:* Judith Wilkes, the midwife.

    83. *Roscommon:* Isabella Dillon, Countess of Roscommon.

    87. *Fingall:* Margaret Plunkett, Countess of Fingall.

    90. *de la Baudie:* Marie de la Baudie, the Queen's French dry-nurse. In the original
text the name is written "D—dy" and was perhaps meant to be pronounced as two
syllables only. See also line 131.

    91. *painted Bulkeley:* Lady Sophia Bulkeley, a Court beauty whose intrigues were
notorious.

He said, "I'm, madam, kneeling on your bed."
This plain deponent bellows bawdy forth,
To be exposed east, west, south, and north,
Without e'er fear or shame, bars modesty,   105
For to outface the world with such a lie.
    Then pocky Belasyse the next comes in
And says she saw the coach of Charles's Queen,
And hearing that the Queen in labor was,
She hurri'd in without a call or pass   110
With this excuse—she knew she was forgot;
Where she talks bawdy, shows impudence, what not!
Expose herself in print to show her love,
Exalted by the King and one above;
She'll lie and swear, forswear, to prop the cause,   115
That baffles England's sound and wholesome laws.
    Then Lady Waldegrave, who was there before
This royal babe was launched from the shore,
And heard her Majesty cry out full sore.
    Then Crane and sottish Wentworth say the same,   120
With Sawyer, Waldegrave, Dawson, that they came
And saw this wonder, which the world won't own,
And blames their little faith, to think this son
Is spurious and not in truth proceeding
From majesty, when they all saw him bleeding;   125
Nay! gave him of his blood squeez'd from the string
That did the royal babe into the world bring!

103–106. Lady Sophia's deposition, though long and detailed, is not particularly bawdy. It was enough for the satirist, presumably, that a woman of her reputation would be heard on a matter of this nature.

107. *Belasyse:* Susanna, Lady Belasyse, "seeing the Queen Dowager's coaches in St. James' at an unusual hour, went and asked the occasion, and was told the Queen was in labor."

114. *one above:* i.e. the Pope.

117. *Lady Waldegrave:* Henrietta, wife of Henry, first Baron Waldegrave, and natural daughter of James by Arabella Churchill.

120–121. *Crane . . . Wentworth . . . Sawyer, Waldegrave, Dawson:* Mrs. Mary Crane, Gentlewoman of the Bedchamber to the Queen Dowager; Dames Isabella Wentworth, Catherine Sawyer, Isabella Waldegrave, and Mrs. Margaret Dawson, all Gentlewomen of the Bedchamber to the Queen.

126. See note to 43.

127. Pope revised this line in his copy of *POAS* to read: "That to the world the Royal Babe did bring."

Then Bromley, Turini, and Nan Cary, too,
Swear they saw all the work that was to do;
And more by half is sworn, than they'll prove true.   130
Then comes de la Baudie, the great nurse,
Who with the Queen is all in all in trust,
And swears that Danvers, maid to Princess Anne,
Was joy'd to see this little royal man,
With former mark on eye that us'd to be   135
On all Queen Mary's royal progeny.
James seem'd to doubt that which before he knew
And fear'd this treach'rous nurse not told him true,
But he must peep and see the royal elf,
And joy'd as if he'd got him his own self!   140
For Mrs. Wilks, who doubts but she would say
She brought the Prince to town that very day,
And told the King the trembling Queen did fear
'Twould be hard labor, though no child was there;
Explains most impudently those concerns   145
That follow women, when they bear their bairns;
But what cares she, the heretics she'll blind
And then, no fear, the King will prove most kind
To all those wretches that swear to his mind.
Then comes the washer-woman, Mrs. Pierce,   150
Who says that to the Queen she is laundress,
And there declares a story of hot linen
That us'd to come just from child-bearing women.

128. *Bromley, Turini . . . Cary:* Mrs. Elizabeth Bromley, Mrs. Pelegrina Turini, and Mrs. Anna Cary, Gentlewomen of the Bedchamber; the last to the Queen Dowager.

131. For question of meter, see above, line 90 and n.

133–135. *Danvers . . . Was joy'd:* In her deposition Marie de la Baudie remarked "that Mrs. Danvers, one of the Princess of Denmark's women and formerly nurse to the Lady Isabella, coming to see the Prince, she told this deponent she was glad to see the same marks upon his eye, as the Queen's former children had."

137–140. *James seem'd to doubt:* Mrs. de la Baudie said that the King asked her what the child was. She replied, "what he desired," but James wished to see for himself and caused her to open the receiver and show the babe to him. The innuendo of 137 refers, of course, to James' supposed previous knowledge of the nurse and the ruse which they were perpetrating.

148–149. *King will prove most kind:* James presented 500 guineas to Mrs. Wilkes for her services at the birth (Luttrell, *1*, 442).

150. *Mrs. Pierce:* Elizabeth Pierce, or Pearse, laundress to the Queen, claimed to have taken "away all the foul linen hot, as they came from the Queen."

Richmond and Litchfield, and brave Marischall,
Though not at labor, they believe it all,   155
And fain would be believed, if these tools,
By swearing falsely, could make us such fools;
They give such demonstrations, which do lie
As much aside as they do modesty.

    Then comes great George, of England Chancellor,   160
Who was with expedition call'd t'th'labor;
The Queen cri'd out as women us'd to do,
And he believes the Prince is real, too;
But not so certain nor, 'tis fear'd, so true
As he wears horns that were by Mountfort made—   165
Them and his noise makes all the fools afraid;
Tongue runs at random and horn pushes those
That are so learn'd his lordship to oppose;
He fears to act no wretched villainies,
He dreads no torments for inventing lies;   170
For he of Heav'n is sure, when e'er he dies,
Thanks to the care of fond, indulgent wife;
To make atonement for his wicked life,
Damns her own soul and whores with all she could,
T'allay impetuous sallies of her blood!   175
    Lord President comes next that's now cashier'd
For only speaking of the truth, 'tis fear'd,

154. *Richmond and Lichfield . . . Marischall:* Frances, Duchess of Richmond and
Lennox, Charlotte, Countess of Lichfield, and Anne, Countess of Marischall, testified to
the Queen's condition prior to the birth.

160. *great George:* Jeffreys. In *On the Deponents* ("Hold, Madam Modena, you come
too late") Jeffreys is also castigated:

> There's the lewd Lord of Wem,
> Whom all men hate and equally contemn;
> Who to the splendor of commanding awe
> Waded through innocent blood and breach of law;
> Yet with brazening of ten carted mobs
> Wears rogue in face and peerage in his robes.
> His oath, he would have lent it Caiaphas,
> Had he then liv'd, to save his purse and mace. (Taylor 2)

165. *Mountfort:* William Montford, the actor. For his relations with Jeffreys, see
above, *Song,* "The widows and maids," 72 and n.

176. *Lord President:* Sunderland, relieved of his office as President of the Privy Council a few days after the depositions (see *Clarendon Correspondence, 2,* 195–6, and
Evelyn, *4,* 602).

Yet he, for to be great again at court,
Would be forsworn, though he is damned for't.
     Then Arundell of Wardour, Privy Seal,   180
Was so concern'd that he her pains did feel,
And 'tis believ'd this tender-hearted man
Did feel as much as majesty did then;
He show'd so great concern to mighty Wem,
Who knew too much to have concern for him   185
But satisfi'd the fool it would be past,
And wonder'd much her pains so long did last.
     Then in comes my Lord All-Pride with modesty,
And seems unwilling to affirm a lie;
With stately gesture, he did himself excuse,   190
But setting hand to paper can't refuse.
     Then foolish Craven comes and doth depose,
A mark he has that he the Prince well knows;
If't be his lordship's mark, he must ne'er rule,
For Europe knows that he's mark'd out a fool.   195
     Then in comes Feversham, that haughty beau,
And tells a tale of "den" and "dat" and "how,"
Though he's no more believ'd than all the rest;
Only, poor man, he fain would do his best
And be rewarded, as when come from th'West.   200
     Earl of Moray, that Alexander great,
He doth believe 'twas King that did the feat,

180–83. *Arundell:* Henry, third Baron Arundell of Wardour, "could not forbid himself the being concerned for her great pain, which the deponent expressing to the Lord Chancellor, he told the deponent it was a sign her Majesty would the sooner be delivered."

188–91. *Lord All-Pride:* John Sheffield, Earl of Mulgrave, Lord Chamberlain, whose haughtiness was made proverbial by Rochester's poem *My Lord All-Pride*. At the deposition he protested that it was "not to be expected one of his sex should be able to give full evidence in such a matter," but followed this with a brief statement confirming the birth.

192–95. *Craven:* William, Earl of Craven, "took that particular mark of this child, that he may safely aver that the Prince of Wales is that very child that then was so brought out of the Queen's great bedchamber."

196–97. *Feversham:* Louis Duras, Earl of Feversham, Lord Chamberlain to the Queen Dowager. According to the satirist, he had lost neither the accent nor manner of his French birth and upbringing.

200. *come from th' West:* Feversham led the campaign against Monmouth in the summer of 1685.

201. *Moray:* Alexander Stewart, Earl of Moray, a secretary of state for Scotland.

And that his son is true and not a cheat;
Then Middleton and Melford both explain'd
The business, which they from the King had gain'd;   205
As knowing men, his Majesty did trust
His Consort's secret, hoping they'd be just
To his endeared son, our mighty Prince,
That, as he thought, would hide his impotence;
Godolphin, too, with confidence pretends   210
It is true-born, but 'tis for his own ends.
    And Fox a story tells of God knows what,
To fool the nation's all he would be at;
He keeps in favor with his princely grace,
He fawns and flatters for to keep his place.   215
    Then famous Scarborough and Witherley,
With Waldegrave, Brady, and Amand do lie,
And bring their circumstances to convince
The world that 'tis a real, high-born prince;
Thus they stick out at nothing that will do   220
The Nation's wrong and bring to England woe.
Base mercenary slaves! for a King's smile
Would spurious issue rear, and us beguile;
That fawn on him and more observe a nod,
Then fear the vengeance of an angry God;   225
And on the turn of times would all fly back,

204. *Middleton:* Charles, Earl of Middleton, one of James' secretaries of state. The King had confided in him since, as a married man, he might "know these matters."
    Melfort: John Drummond, Earl of Melfort, a convert and, like Moray, a Scottish secretary of state.
210. *Godolphin:* Sidney Godolphin, Lord Chamberlain to the Queen.
212. *Fox:* Sir Stephen Fox, a commissioner of the treasury. He had missed the birth, being concerned that "there might not be anything wanting of household provisions and necessaries," but managed to see the child "before he was dressed."
216–219. *Scarborough and Witherley . . . Waldegrave, Brady, and Amand:* Sir Charles Scarborough, Principal Physician to the King; Sir William Waldegrave, Principal Physician to the Queen; Sir Thomas Witherley and Dr. Robert Brady, Physicians-in-Ordinary to the King; and James St. Amand, Royal Apothecary. Scarborough made the following deposition, corroborated by Waldegrave: "Now for the time of the Queen's conception, she often told the deponent and others that she had two reckonings: one from Tuesday, the 6th of September, when the King returned from his progress to the Queen then at Bath, and the other from Thursday, the 6th of October, when the Queen came to the King at Windsor; but for some reasons the Queen rather reckoned from the latter. . . ." Waldegrave was knighted by James shortly after the birth of the Prince (Luttrell, *1*, 443).

And let his Highness' interest go to wrack!
Two depositions more to Council sent,
Asham'd t'appear to further the intent
Of Popish principles and perjuries—   230
None but the devil could invent such lies.
Then after this, the King himself declares
He don't design with England to make wars,
But he such aggravations hath of late
That he must needs be angry with the state;   235
A specious prologue to conclude withal,
But all the Protestants, he vows, shall fall
A sacrifice to Rome, and his revenge;
Then, soldiers, fear not fools, but scorn to cringe,
Be resolute and stout, and scorn to sell   240
Your souls to Rome, but send the Pope to hell!

228. *Two depositions more:* William Herbert, Earl of Huntingdon, and Henry Mordaunt, Earl of Peterborough, arrived too late to make their depositions before the Council. Accordingly, they submitted their testimony in writing after the close of the hearing.

236. *A specious prologue to conclude withal:* James closed the hearing by saying:

And now, my Lords, although I did not question but every person here present was satisfied before in this matter, yet by what you have heard, you will be better able to satisfy others. Besides, if I and the Queen could be thought so wicked as to endeavor to impose a child upon a nation, you see how impossible it would have been. Neither could I myself be imposed upon, having constantly been with the Queen during her being with child, and the whole time of her labor. And there is none of you but will easily believe me, who have suffered so much for the conscience' sake, incapable of so great a villainy, to the prejudice of my own children. And I thank God that those that know me well that it is my principle to do as I would be done by, for that is the Law and the Prophets. And I would rather die a thousand deaths, than do the least wrong to any of my children.

Invasion Fears
(Spring–Summer 1688)

For most Englishmen the first ten months of 1688 were a period of extraordinary tension. Tension so great that the anticlimactic nature of William's November campaign was an almost inevitable result of it. From the end of February when the country received the first reports of Dutch military preparations (Luttrell, *1*, 433), until 5 November when William finally landed at Tor Bay, a state of near-crisis prevailed. During this time, Luttrell records no fewer than twenty-one separate reports of the Dutch build-up and of the imminence of invasion. At first these reports were officially denied through such "unofficial" organs as Henry Care's newssheet *Public Occurrences,* which as late as 15 May dismissed reports of the Dutch fleet putting to sea, calling the activities merely those normally connected with the spring convoys. But rumors persisted and became more welcome as the events of June and July confirmed the possibility of a papist dynasty and gave evidence of the kind of suppression it would lead to. These fears were to some extent counter-balanced by the Englishmen's abiding animosity for the Dutch, while James' own military preparations and the hint of a few reforms in his Romanizing policy provided some further stimulation to patriotic zeal. Even these elements heightened the tension, however, and by 3 November defection had become so common that one writer remarked "for everybody that's missing but two or three days, we say here, is gone" (*HMC, Rutland, 2*, 122). When, two days later, news of the invasion reached the nation, it must have come almost as a relief, even to the King.

Throughout the months which led up to William's landing, James pursued three distinct courses of action in his attempt to maintain his position. Foremost were his military preparations. In the fall of 1687 disaffection in the army and stiffening resistance to his policies first caused him to consider recalling the English and Scottish troops serving in Holland in the pay of the States General. The Queen's pregnancy made it seem even "more imperative that the dynasty should, if necessary, be preserved by military force" (Ogg, p. 191). Not until February 1688, however, did he finally determine to recall the troops. In March a proclamation was issued, but to James' consternation the States General refused to comply with it and held the troops from him. Only a few officers reached England from the Continent. Commissions were granted for the raising of five new regiments, but these James found difficult to staff. By August he was desperate for soldiers on whose loyalty he could depend. An obvious, but unwise, solution offered itself. In August and September he ordered Irish and Scottish troops mustered in England for his defense.

Similar preparations were carried out to refit the navy. Early in January the first orders were sent down from the Admiralty to the dockyards (Luttrell, *1*, 429). Throughout the spring the yards were unusually busy, and the press boats made frequent trips down the Thames seeking seamen. By June a fleet of twenty ships sailed for the Downs under Sir Roger Strickland. In August and September activities increased, leave was refused officers, the dockyards at Chatham and Portsmouth were put in a state of defense, the fleet was divided into three squadrons to patrol all waters in the Channel and to the south, and an ingenious plan was actually carried out to mislead a possible attack up the Thames by removing the buoys in the river and by replacing the lights at Harwich with a fake lighthouse "made of canvas streached upon poles" which would "lead the enemy upon the ridge" (for these and other details see J. R. Tanner, "Naval Preparations of James II in 1688," *EHR*, *8* [1893], pp. 272–83; and Edward B. Powley, *The English Navy in the Revolution of 1688*, 1928).

The second step James took involved the stricter enforcement of censorship (see Luttrell, *1*, 431, 434, 472–3; *HMC, Portland, 3*, 420; *Le Fleming*, p. 214) and the wider dissemination of anti-Dutch propaganda. Rumor was so strong in and around London that "each graver Sir Pol unfolded his sheet" of computations and prognostications (see below, *All Shams*), and little else was talked of after the beginning of August. James' counter activities were so numerous during these months that it was said his declarations were as common as ballads (*HMC, Leeds*, p. 25).

Finally, toward the end of August James undertook a series of reforms, or concessions, to win support in his struggle to retain the throne. On August 24 the King ordered that writs be issued for the calling of parliament for the end of November (*London Gazette*, 27 Aug.). The writs went out in mid-September though they were recalled on the imminent threat of invasion. James began, as well, openly to court the Anglican Church. In September and October he disbanded the Ecclesiastical Commission and restored the Bishop of London and the Fellows of Magdalen College. Early in October he ordered Jeffreys to return the corporation charters—a move met like the others with unreserved skepticism, as evident from the following, widely-circulated squib, *Made upon the Lord Chancellor when He Carried the Charter Home:*

> A thief that bravely bears away his prize
> Proclaims his valor in the enterprize,
> But he that basely steals and brings it home,
> Let Heer van Brush, or Tyburn be his doom.

In general, it was thought that the "King began now to find his error, but too late" (Reresby, p. 516), and most, like Luttrell, attributed the reforms to the "rare invasion" which occasioned "so many gracious acts in restoring things to their old, legal foundation, which hath been the work of some years past to unhinge!" (*1*, 468; see also Evelyn, *4*, 599–600).

TO THE PRINCE OF ORANGE

A Packet of Advice, with the
Packet Boat Returned

ADVICE: The year of wonder now is come,
    A jubilee proclaim at Rome;
    The Church has pregnant made the Crown!
PACKET: No more of your admired year,
    No more your jubilees declare;   5
    All trees that blossom do not bear.
ADVICE: Orange, lay by your hope of crowns,

Ascription: This poem, like *The Council* (see above), is ascribed incorrectly to Swift by W. R. Wilde, *The Closing Years of Swift's Life*, 1849, pp. 136–8.

3. The Queen's conception was popularly attributed either to divine intervention or to the physical assistance of Petre or d'Adda.

Give up to France your Belgic towns,
And keep your fleet out of the Downs.
PACKET: We'll wait for crowns, not int'rest quit,   10
Till Louis take what he can get;
And do not you proscribe our fleet.
ADVICE: You boast you've eighty men of war,
Well-rigg'd and mann'd, you say they are;
Such news can't fail of welcome here.   15
PACKET: Well may the sound of eighty sail
Make England's greatest courage fail,
When half the number will prevail.
ADVICE: Now we have some upon our stocks,
And some are laid up in our docks,   20
When fitted out, will match your cocks.
PACKET: Talk not as you would match our cocks,
But launch your few ships on the stocks,
And, if you can, secure your docks.
ADVICE: Besides, we have our men call'd home,   25
Which in your fleet and army roam,
But you, 'tis said, won't let 'em come.
PACKET: Your subjects in our camp and fleet,
Whom you with proclamation greet,
Will all obey when they think fit.   30
ADVICE: Soldiers and seamen both we need,
Old England's quite out of the breed,
Feather and scarf won't do the deed.

---

8. *Belgic towns:* Probably the towns given up to France by Spain under terms
of the Treaty of Nijmwegen (1678), among them the fortress towns of Cambray, St.
Omer, and Ypres, which became a constant source of irritation to William.

9. *the Downs:* The waters off the east coast of Kent. A normal place of rendezvous
for ships.

21. *cock:* A small ship's boat; perhaps also an obscene pun.

33. *Feather and scarf:* Designations of an officer. James had staffed as many of his
regiments with Catholic or pro-Catholic officers as he could, but he was fairly sure he
could not rely too heavily on the average fighting man's loyalty. His desire for more
soldiers caused him in the early summer to dispatch "agents to Liege and Antwerp to
offer money and employment to Englishmen in the garrisons of Maestricht and French
Flanders; with these, and some Roman Catholic English officers who succeeded in getting out of Holland, he formed the nucleus of three new regiments" (Ogg, p. 192). The
need for men, however, particularly seamen, remained strong throughout the summer.
On 27 Aug., Luttrell reported, "the drums beat up for seamen, and . . . the press boats
went down the river to press seamen, the want of which is the general complaint. . . ."

PACKET: Of men of arms never despair,
    The civiliz'd, wild Irish are   35
    Courageous, e'en to massacre.
ADVICE: But if victorious you'd be made,
    Like us, in Hounslow masquerade,
    Advance your honor and your trade.
PACKET: Then take this counsel back again,   40
    Leave off to mimic in campaign
    And fight in earnest on the main.
ADVICE: Buda we storm'd and took with ease,
    Pursue such grandeur on the seas
    And fight us so when e'er you please.   45
PACKET: Your taking Buda does declare
    That you the glorious off-spring are
    Of them who made all Europe fear.
ADVICE: Such warlike actions will, at least,
    Inspire each neighb'ring monarch's breast,   50
    Till Louis shall complete the rest.
PACKET: Such camps, such sieges, and such shows,
    Make each small state your pow'r oppose,
    And Louis lead you by the nose.

ALL SHAMS

To the tune of "Packington's Pound"

1.

An invasion from Dutchland is all the discourse,
An incredible tale of incredible force!
While each graver Sir Pol unfolded his sheet,
An exact computation of army and fleet,

35–36. Fear of the Irish troops brought over to bolster James' position gave rise to many wild rumors of atrocities; see below, *All Shams,* 22 and n.

38. *Hounslow masquerade:* Military drill at the encampments held on Hounslow Heath; for the mock storming of Buda (46), see above, *Hounslow Heath,* headnote and 105.

39. *Advance your honor, &c.:* Refers to the "exercise," or drills practiced at the encampment (see plate facing 170), an obscene parody of which is in Osborn Box 89 #3, entitled *The Blackguard's Exercise at the Camp* ("Silence,/Gentlemen troopers").

3. Cf. *Volpone,* the character of Sir Politic Would-be.

Of their horse and their foot   5
And their great guns, to boot,
Each fire-ship, each tender, and flat-bottom'd boat;
The time of their landing and place can reveal,
But that, as a secret, as yet he'll conceal.

2.

While each busy-brain'd coxcomb, mechanic, and fool,   10
Each chattering barber, each apron and rule,
Let his private concern be of ne'er so much weight,
And nought but his trade, he can call his estate;
   Yet straight he declares
   It has long been his fears,   15
He dreaded this business for several years;
Nay, the future events he could eas'ly relate,
But 'tis dangerous, neighbors, and touches the state.

3.

Now while we are hearing and telling of lies,
A cloud from the west does quite darken the skies;   20
All Egypt's ten plagues do at once on us fall,
For in naming the Irish, it comprehends all.
   To what purpose they come
   Is no secret to Rome,
And to guess at the consequence we may presume: 25
Old England was ne'er so unhappy before,
While the scum of three nations for aid we implore.

4.

Now lay by chimeras of fleets and armados,
And, if you can, fairly march off to Barbados,
Jamaica, Virginia, or any plantation,   30
Except that of Will Penn, the disturber o'th'nation;

22. *the Irish:* A few scattered incidents and many rumors gave rise to an exaggerated
fear of the Irish troops. Evelyn says, for example, "The popish Irish soldiers commit
many murders and insolences; the whole nation disaffected and in apprehensions" (*4*,
596–7). See also, Luttrell, *1*, 449, and *Ellis Correspondence*, *2*, 139, 255–6. For reports
of Scottish troop movements see Luttrell, *1*, 465, 467–68, and Reresby, p. 518.

31. *Will Penn:* For details of Penn's activities during the reign, see above, *The Man
of Honor.*

To Lapland or Greenland,
Nay, sail into Finland,
To Presbyter John or the islands within land;
And leave both your honors' estates and your wives,   35
On condition that you may depart with your lives.

THE STATESMAN'S ALMANAC

Being an excellent new ballad, in which the
qualities of each month are considered; whereby it
appears that a parliament cannot meet in any of the
old months. With a proposal for mending the calendar,
humbly offered to the packers of the next parliament.

To the tune of "Cold and raw, the North did blow"

PROLOGUE

1.

The talk up and down
In country and town
Has been long of a parliament's sitting,
But we'll make it clear
Ne'er a month in the year   5
Is proper for such a meeting.

2.

The judges declare it,
The ministers swear it,
And the town as a tale receives it;
Let 'em say what they can,   10
There's never a man,
Except God's Vicegerent, believes it.

3.

If the critics in spite
Our arguments slight

34. *Presbyter John:* Prester John, the fabulous medieval Christian king and priest, whose vast domains originally were placed in Asia, though from the 15th century on he was usually identified with the King of Ethiopia. Contemporary satirists were wont to play on the meanings of priest and Presbyterian suggested by his title.

the islands within land: Perhaps the fabulous lands of Prester John.

12. *God's Vicegerent:* The King.

And think 'em too light for the matter,   15
    It has often been known
    That men on a throne
Have harangu'd the whole realm with no better.

4.

    For in times of old,
    When kings were less bold   20
And made for their faults excuses;
    Such topics as these,
    The Commons to please,
Did serve for most excellent uses.

5.

    Either Christmas came on,   25
    Or harvest begun,
And all must repair to their station;
    'Twas too dry or too wet
    For the Houses to sit,
And "Hey" for a prorogation.   30

6.

    Then sir, if you please,
    With such reasons as these,
Let's see how each moon is appointed;
    For though it be strange,
    In all her change   35
She favors not God's anointed.

The Almanac

JANUARY.   1.

    The first is too cold
    For Popery to hold,
Since southern climates improve it;
    And therefore in frost   40
    'Tis odds but it's lost,
If they offer to remove it.

FEBRUARY.   2.

The next does betide,
Though then the King died,
Ill luck, and they must not be tamp'ring;   45
   For had not Providence quick
   Cool'd his head i'th'nick,
'Fore God they were all a scamp'ring.

MARCH.   3.

The month of old Rome
Has an omen with some,   50
But the sleeping wind then rouses;
   And trust not the crowd
   When storms are so loud,
Lest their breath infect the houses.

APRIL.   4.

In this by mishap   55
Southesk had a clap,
Which pepper'd our gracious master;
   And therefore i'th'spring
   He must physic his thing
And venture no new disaster.   60

MAY.   5.

This month is too good,
And too lusty his blood
To be for business at leisure;
   With his confessor's leave
   Honest Bridget may give   65
The fumbler Royal his pleasure.

46–48. Meaning, had Charles not died when he did, he would soon have put the Catholics to rout.

56. *Southesk:* Robert Carnegy, Earl of Southesk. For a brief account of the "pernicious . . . piece of revenge" (Pepys, 7, 396) that he allegedly undertook against James, see headnote to *The Birth of the Prince.*

64. *confessor:* Father Edward Petre, James' confessor.

65. *Bridget:* Presumably used generically for a country wench.

66. *fumbler:* "An impotent man, generally old; an unperforming or inadequate husband" (Partridge).

JUNE.   6.

> The brains of the state
> Have been too hot of late,
> They have manag'd all business in rapture;
> And to call us in June   70
> Is much to the same tune,
> Being mad to the end of the chapter.

JULY.   7.

> This season was made
> For camp and parade,
> Where with the expense of his treasures,   75
> Of much sweat and pains,
> Discreetly he trains
> Such men as will break all his measures.

AUGUST.   8.

> This month did advance
> Their projects in France,   80
> As Bartholomew remembers;
> But, alas, they want force
> To take the same course
> With our heretical members.

SEPTEMBER.   9.

> They cannot now meet   85
> For the progress was set,
> But they find it a scurvy fashion,
> To ride and to ride,
> To be snubb'd and deni'd,
> By every good man in the nation.   90

72. *to the end of the chapter:* "Always; to the end; until death" (Partridge).

74. *camp and parade:* The muster held each summer at Hounslow Heath.

80–81. The St. Bartholomew Day's Massacre of Huguenots in France took place on 24 August 1572, beginning more than a century of intermittent "projects" against them (see Evelyn, *4*, 574–5).

86. *the progress:* August and September were the usual months for a royal progress, though none was planned for 1688 because of the danger of invasion. James had been poorly received by many during his progress in 1687 through the west and northwest of England, areas perhaps selected as least loyal and therefore most in need of the stimulus of a royal tour.

OCTOBER.   10.

Now hunting comes in,
That license for sin,
That does with a cloak befriend him;
   For if the Queen knows
   What at Graham's he does,   95
His divine right can hardly defend him.

NOVEMBER.   11.

November might do
For aught that we know,
But that the King promis'd by chance, sirs,
   And his word before   100
   Was pawn'd for much more
Than e'er 'twill be able to answer.

DECEMBER.   12.

The last of the year
Resemblance does bear
To their hopes and fortune declining;   105
   Ne'er hope for success,
   Day grows less and less,
And the sun once so high has done shining.

EPILOGUE

1.

You gypsies of Rome
That run up and down,   110
And with miracles people cozen;
   By the help of some saint
   Get the month that you want,
And make thirteen of the dozen.

91. James, an ardent hunter, was probably one of those chiefly responsible for the
development of fox-hunting as an aristocratic pastime in England, the stag and hare
having been the chief prey for gentlemen before the Restoration.

95. *Graham's:* Col. James Graham (1649–1730), Keeper of the Privy Purse and Master
of the Harthounds and Buckhounds. In 1687 he was given a 31-year lease of the lodge
at Bagshot Park, part of Windsor Forest. For description of the lodge and of Graham's
first wife, the beautiful Dorothy Howard, a Maid of Honor to Catherine of Braganza,
see Evelyn, *4,* 467–8.

99. On 24 Aug. James ordered writs issued for a parliament to be convened on 27 Nov.

2.

You see the old year   115
Won't help ye, 'tis clear,
And therefore to save your honor
Get a new sun and moon,
And the work is half done,
And faith I think not sooner.   120

September the 1st
From the Imperial Camp before Belgrade, to Chevalier Janco Don
Lazarillo.

IN DEFIANCE TO THE DUTCH

Robb'd of our rights, and by such water-rats?
We'll doff their heads, if they won't doff their hats.
Affront too Hogen Mogen to endure!
'Tis time to box these butter-boxes sure.
If they the flag's undoubted right deny us,   5
Who won't strike to us, must be stricken by us.

Inscription: For news of the siege of Louis XIV's secret allies the Turks in Belgrade by the imperial forces of the Holy Roman Emperor, see Luttrell, *1,* 456, 458.

Lazarillo: Spanish for "a small boy who guides a blind man," i.e. James as leader of England.

Date: The first part of this poem originally appeared in the spring of 1672, shortly after the outbreak of the Third Dutch War, ascribed to "Mr. Benjamin Willy, sometime master of the Free School of Newark-upon-Trent" (*Political Recreations,* 1685). Willy was greatly indebted to Marvell's *Character of Holland* both for the particular allusions cited below and for the general tone and method employed.

On or about "13 November 1688," according to Luttrell's MS. notes on the Harvard broadside, the revised version of this poem "Against the Dutch" was published with an envoy to the King. The broadside was probably circulated as a last-minute endeavor on the part of the Crown to stir Englishmen to stand with their King against an old and common enemy.

3. *Hogen Mogen:* A corruption of *Hoogmogendheiden,* "High Mightinesses," the official designation of the States General. Here, properly "high and mighty;" see Marvell, *Character,* 80.

4. *butter-boxes:* Contemptuous for Dutchmen; cf. *Character,* 94.

6. *strike:* To lower sail, or haul down one's flag in surrender. By tradition, the English claimed that all ships salute their flag in "British seas," see below, 20, 70, and nn.

A crew of boors and sooterkins that know
Themselves they to our blood and valor owe;
Did we for this knock off their Spanish fetters,
To make 'em able to abuse their betters?   10
If at this rate they rave, I think 'tis good
Not to omit the fall, but let them blood.
    Rouse then, heroic Britains, 'tis not words
But wounds, must work with leather-apron lords.
Since they are deaf, to them your meaning break   15
With mouths of brass, that words of iron speak;
I hope we shall to purpose the next bout
Cure 'em, as we did Opdam, of the gout.
And when i'th'bottom of the sea they come,
They'll have enough of *Mare Liberum*.   20
    Our brandish'd steel, though now they seem so tall,
Shall make 'em lower than Low Country fall.
But they'll ere long come to themselves, you'll see,
When we in earnest are at snick-a-snee;
When once the boors perceive our swords are drawn,   25
And we converting are those boors to brawn.
    Methinks the ruin of their Belgic banners,

---

7. *boors:* A peasant or rustic, particularly a Dutch peasant; 17th century spelling allowed a clear pun with "boar." Again, cf. Marvell's *Character,* 80.

    sooterkins: A chimerical kind of afterbirth associated with Dutch women; see above, *The Tragi-Comedy of Titus Oates,* 38 and n.

14. *leather-apron lords:* An imputation on the Dutch as tradesmen.

17. *bout:* "A round of fighting;" cf. *The Reward of Loyalty,* 39 and n.

18. *Opdam:* Jacob Wassenaer, Baron von Opdam, Admiral of the Dutch fleet, killed during the Second Dutch War at the battle of Lowestoft, 3 June 1665.

    gout: Cf. Marvell's *Second Advice to a Painter (POAS,* Yale, *1, 38):*

> Then in kind visit unto Opdam's gout,
> Hedge the Dutch in only to let them out. (45–46)

20. *Mare Liberum:* A short treatise by Hugo Grotius (1583–1645), Dutch publicist and statesman, in which he maintained that the seas were free to all nations. The treatise was first printed in 1609 and referred to Portuguese claims of possession of eastern waters. It did not become important until the 1630s, however, when Anglo-Dutch rivalries for the freedom of the seas, particularly in relation to fishing rights, became severely aggravated. Cf. Marvell's *Character,* 26.

24. *snick-a-snee:* Obs. variant of "snick and snee," i.e. "a combat with cut and thrust knives." The phrase was derived from the Dutch *steken and snijen.* Cf. Marvell's *Character,* 96.

Last fight almost as ragged as their manners,
Might have persuaded 'em to better things,
Than be so saucy to their betters, kings.   30
Is it of wealth they are so proud become?
James has a wain, I hope, to fetch it home,
And with it pay himself his just arrears
Of fishing tribute for this hundred years,
That we may say, as all the store comes in,   35
The Dutch, alas, have but our factors been.
They fathom sea and land; we, when we please,
Have both the Indies brought to our own seas.
For rich, and proud, they bring in ships by shoals,
And then we humble'em to save their souls.   40
   Pox of their pictures! if we had 'em here,
We'd find 'em frames at Tyburn, or elsewhere.
The next they draw, be it their admirals
Transpeciated into fins and scales;
Or, which would do as well, draw if they please,   45
Opdam, with th' seven sinking provinces;
Or draw their captains from the conquering main,
First beaten home, then beaten back again;

28. *Last fight:* Originally, the Second Dutch War, and, more specifically, the English victory at Lowestoft in 1665, during which the Dutch suffered heavy casualties both in ships and men (cf. *POAS,* Yale, *1,* 20–53).

32. *a wain:* A wagon or cart. The original version read "Charles" for "James," of course, and thus included a not particularly noteworthy pun on Charles' Wain, the Big Dipper.

34. *fishing tribute:* In March 1636, the English imposed tribute on the Dutch fishing fleet for the right to fish in British waters. To be paid yearly, it succeeded in little more than establishing a precedent productive of future irritation to Anglo-Dutch relations.

36. *factors:* Commercial agents.

41. *Pox of their pictures:* Cf. Dryden's prologue to *Amboyna* (1673):

> No map shows Holland truer than our play;
> Their pictures and inscriptions well we know;
> We may be bold one medal sure to show. (26–28)

"The war being thus resolved on, some pretenses were in the next place to be sought out to excuse it. . . . Some medals were complained of that seemed dishonorable to the King; as also some pictures. And though these were not made by public order, yet a great noise was raised about them" (Burnet, *1,* 305).

44. *Transpeciated:* Transformed.

46. *seven sinking provinces:* The seven states of the United Provinces, with a pun on the sinking of their ships and on the failure of their political and military prowess.

And after this so just, though fatal strife,
Draw their dead boors again unto the life.   50
Lastly, remember, to prevent all laughter,
Drawing goes first, but hanging follows after.
If then lampooning thus be their undoing,
Who pities them that purchase their own ruin?
Or will hereafter trust their treacheries,   55
Until they leave their heads for hostages?
For, as the proverb has of women said,
"Believe 'em not, nay, though you'd swear they're dead."
The Dutch are stubborn, and will yield not fruit,
Till, like the walnut tree, ye beat 'em to't.   60

To the King

I see an age when, after some few years,
And revolutions of the slow pac'd spheres;
These days shall be 'bove others far esteem'd,
And like the world's great conquerors be deem'd.
The names of Caesar, and feign'd Paladin,   65
Grav'n in Time's surly brows, in wrinkled Time,
Shall by this Prince's name be pass'd as far
As meteors are by the Idalian star;
For to Great Britain's Isle thou shalt restore
Her *Mare Clausum*, guard her pearly shore;   70
The lions passant of th' Dutch bands shalt free,

52. *Drawing goes first:* A pun on the "drawing" or dragging of a criminal "at a horse's tail, or on a hurdle or the like to the place of execution," and, of course, on the artist's "drawing," or delineation of a figure.

59–60. Cf. Marvell's *Second Advice to a Painter* (*POAS*, Yale, *1*, 49):

> The Dutch armada yet had th'impudence
> To put to sea to waft their merchants hence;
> For, as if their ships of walnut were,
> The more we beat them, still the more they bear; . . . (289–92)

See the English proverb, "A woman, ass, and walnut tree, the more you beat the better be" (Tilley, W644).

68. *the Idalian star:* Venus (as the "morning star," called Phosphorus, as the "evening star," Hesperus).

70. *Mare Clausum:* The title of a treatise by John Selden, which was written as a rejoinder to Grotius' *Mare Liberum* (20). Though written almost 20 years earlier, the treatise was not published until 1632.

71–72. *lions passant . . . lilies three:* Heraldic devices of England.

To the true owner of the lilies three.
The seas shall shrink; shake shall the spacious earth,
And tremble in her chamber, like pale death.
Thy thund'ring cannons shall proclaim to all   75
Great Britain's glory, and proud Holland's fall.
   Run on, brave Prince, thy course in glory's way;
The end the life, the evening crowns the day.
Reap worth on worth, and strongly soar above
Those heights which made the world thee first to love.   80
Surmount thyself, and make thy actions past
Be but as gleams or lightnings of thy last.
Let them exceed those of thy younger time,
As far as autumn doth the flow'ry prime;
So ever gold and bays thy brow adorn,   85
So never Time may see thy race out-worn;
So of thine own still mayst thou be desir'd,
Of Holland fear'd, and by the world admir'd;
Till thy great deeds all former deeds surmount:
Thou'st quell'd the Nimrods of our Hellespont.   90
So may his high exploits at last make even
With earth his honor, glory with the Heaven.

William's Campaign
(5–27 November 1688)

During October tension grew. James' show of reform, according to Evelyn, "gave no satisfaction to the nation but, increasing the universal discontent, brought people to so desperate a pass" that they seemed "to long for and desire the landing . . . praying incessantly for an easterly wind" (*4*, 600). Much of the month, however, the wind remained in the north and William's fleet was "damnified" by its harshness (*Ellis Correspondence*, 2, 237–44). On 19 October his ships had put to sea only to be scattered and driven back again by storm. The insignificant losses were apparently magnified by the time James received word of them. It was thought "that the whole armament was lost. James received the news at dinner and, with an appearance of great devotion, remarked, 'It is not to be wondered at, for the Host has been exposed these several days!' " (Dalrymple, pt. I, bk. VI, p. 192). Within two weeks, however, Orange received that "Protestant wind" for which he and his well-wishers in England had so patiently waited. He set sail on 1 November. Between his fleet and its landfall lay the English ships of the line, fifty-two strong, anchored in the Gunfleet on the northern shore of the Thames estuary, commanded by the Protestant George Legge, Lord Dartmouth, who had remained faithful to his Prince even during the days of disfavor in Charles' reign. Dartmouth had replaced Sir Roger Strickland, whose open Catholicism had brought his seamen to mutiny. The fleet was now felt once again to be fit for the King's service, but as Ogg has pointed out, "other influences" undermined the morale:

> It has been said that harbors corrupt men and ships. The sailors in Dartmouth's fleet were receiving pamphlets and newsletters from ashore, and were caballing among themselves; indeed, the situation at the Gunfleet was not unlike that on Hounslow Heath (Ogg, p. 214).

Moreover, despite Pepys' attempts to rebuild the navy, a great want of good, reliable equipment and armaments remained. After some prodding by James, Dartmouth ventured out of the Gunfleet on 30 October, only to meet an easterly wind which forced him to ride at anchor off Longsands Head for the next five days, during which time he sighted Orange's fleet passing to the south of him on its way westward. On 5 November 1688, William landed without incident at Torbay, near where three years earlier Monmouth had planted his Protestant standard. This time, however, James' campaign would be futile and not a little absurd. (For full details of the events leading up to William's landing see Dartmouth's papers in *HMC, Rept. 11*, App. pt. 5; Edward B. Powley, *The English Navy and the Revolution of 1688*, 1928.)

During the week immediately following word of Orange's landing in Devon, fear and suspicion of the Catholics in general and of the Irish troops in particular produced numerous disturbances in London, and "reports as various as those who report" them kept agitation feverish (*HMC, Le Fleming* no. 3315). On 11 November, for example, the rabble assembled

> in a tumultuous manner at St. John's, Clerkenwell, the popish monastery there, on a report of gridirons, spits, great caldrons, etc., to destroy Protestants. They began some outrageous acts, till the horse and foot guards were sent to suppress them. 'Tis said they killed some first (Luttrell, *1*, 474).

When James determined to go to the west on 17 November, he was compelled to leave an entire regiment behind to guard London at night (*Le Fleming*, no. 3317).

William had established his headquarters in Exeter, where he remained until 21 November, awaiting the gentry's support. Although several men of eminence had already determined to join Orange, the defection of Clarendon's eldest son, Edward, Lord Cornbury, with a portion of his command, on 14 November, represented the first important loss sustained by the King's forces. When James reached Salisbury on the 19th, however, he might still have achieved a decisive victory, had he been able to summon the kind of forceful leadership for which he had been known in his youth. But in a council of war on 22 November, he allowed the dull-witted Feversham, General of the Army, to prevail over the younger officers' urgings for attack. The meeting broke up determined on retreat to London even though

James' forces outnumbered William's by almost two to one. The King abandoned the original plan of attack which would

> march his horse and dragoons as far as Axminster, Chard, and Lamport, to prevent the country's coming in to the Prince of Orange, and close him up in the corner of the kingdom; and then have advanced the foot as fast as possible to their support, where the highways being narrow and the hedges and ditches exceeding great would have been as good as retrenchments to whosoever had first possessed them. (Clarke, 2, 222)

It was a plan strikingly similar to that which had effectively bottled up Monmouth in the summer of 1685, and the reasons given for abandoning it are unconvincing, although faulty intelligence contributed to the decision (ibid.).

During two of the five days James spent at Salisbury, he was incapacitated by severe nosebleeds which kept him from going to Warminster to review the troops under the command of Col. Percy Kirke. Later it was rumored that Kirke and some of his officers had plotted to seize James on his tour, and the nosebleeds suddenly seemed providential. On the 23d, however, the eve of James' departure for London, Providence must have seemed more than a little indifferent to a King's plight. That night he learned that Churchill and the Duke of Grafton had gone over to Orange. Upon returning three days later, he was dismayed to learn that Princess Anne had left the city for Nottingham, escorted by the Bishop of London. Her husband, Prince George, had already defected at Andover during the retreat. The losses, most certainly influenced by Churchill, proved mortifying for James at this crucial time. A much-chastened King, within a few hours of his arrival back in London, met with the members of his Privy Council to reopen discussion of the petition from nineteen peers of the realm calling for a free parliament, which had been received on the 17th with astonishment and had been given "a very short answer" (Clarendon, *Correspondence*, 2, 205). Now it elicited a much more conciliatory response from James.

THE ADVICE

Would you be famous and renown'd in story,
And, after having run a stage of glory,

Go straight to Heav'n, and not to Purgatory?
　　　　　　　　　　　　　This is the time.
Would you surrender your dispensing power,   5
And send the Western Hangman to the Tower,
From whence he'll find it difficult to scour?
　　　　　　　　　　　　　This is the time.
Would you send Father Penn and Father Lobb,
Assisted by the Poet Laureate Squab,   10
To teach obedience passive to the mob?
　　　　　　　　　　　　　This is the time.
Would you let Reverend Father Peters know
What thanks the Church of England to him owe
For favors past, he did on them bestow?   15
　　　　　　　　　　　　　This is the time.
Would you with expedition send away
Those four dim lights made bishops t'other day,

4. *This is the time:* The refrain recalls a speech given in the Commons by Sir Heneage Finch, Lord Chancellor to Charles II, at the opening of the Third Parliament, 6 March 1679:

> Would you secure religion at home, and strengthen it abroad, by uniting the interest of all the Protestants in Europe? This is the time. Would you let the Christian world see the King in a condition able to protect those who shall adhere to him, or depend on him? This is the time, etc . . . (Richard Chandler, *History and Proceedings of the House of Commons*, 1742, *1*, 328–9).

Poetically, the refrain had been employed in *On the Lord Chancellor's Speech to the Parliament* ("Would you send Kate to Portugal"), *POAS*, 2, 1689, 14.

5. *dispensing power:* The royal prerogative, by which a sovereign could exempt individuals from the operation of the penal laws. James had won a legal decision for his rights in the Godden *v.* Hales trial of 1686; the decision in the trial of the bishops was, essentially, a vote against his prerogative.

6. *Western Hangman:* Jeffreys, who conducted the Bloody Assizes of 1685.

7. *scour:* Cant for "run away."

9. *Father Penn and Father Lobb:* William Penn, the Quaker, and Stephen Lobb, called "the Jacobite Independent," had both attempted to win dissenters to James' cause in 1687 and had fully endorsed the Declaration of Indulgence.

10. *Poet Laureate Squab:* Rochester's nickname for Dryden, see above, *To Mr. Dryden, &c.*, 26 and n.

12. *Father Peters:* Edward Petre, Jesuit confessor to the King and a member of the Privy Council.

18. *Those four dim lights:* Bonaventure Giffard (1642–1734), Philip Ellis (1652–1726), James Smith (1645–1711), and John Leyburn (1620–1702). The first three men were made bishops by James in Feb. 1688 (Luttrell, *1*, 430); Leyburn was elected vicar-apostolic of England on 6 Aug. 1685 and first vicar-apostolic of the London district in Jan. 1688. All four men were Roman Catholics.

To convert Indians in America?

                           This is the time.   20

Would you the rest of that bald-pated train
No longer flatter with thin hopes of gain,
But send them to Saint Omer's back again?

                           This is the time.

Would you (instead of holding birchen tool)   25
Send Pulton to be lash'd at Busby's school,
That he in print no longer play the fool?

                           This is the time.

Would you that Jack-of-all-religions scare,
Bid him for hanging speedily prepare,   30
That Harry Hills may visit Harry Care?

                           This is the time.

Would you let Ireland no more fear Macdonell,
And all the rabble under Philem O'Neill,
And Clarendon again succeed Tyrconnel?   35

                           This is the time.

Would you court-earwigs banish from your ears,

---

23. *Saint Omer's:* The seminary for English Roman Catholics at Pas-de-Calais, France, irrevocably associated with the name of Titus Oates.

26. *Pulton:* Father Andrew Pulton, master of the Jesuit school at the Savoy and a prominent controversialist. In *Remarks of A. Pulton . . . upon Dr. Thomas Tension's Late Narrative,* 1688, he says that "having been eighteen years out of his own country, [he] pretends not yet to any perfection of the English expression or orthography; wherefore for the future he will crave the favor of treating with the doctor in Latin or Greek, since the doctor finds fault with his English."

Busby's school: Westminster School, of which Richard Busby, famous for his canings, was headmaster.

29. *Jack-of-all-religions:* Henry Hills, Sr. (1641–89). He was printer to Cromwell, Charles, and James, and became a convert to Roman Catholicism. On 12 Dec. 1688, a mob attacked his establishment in Blackfriars, "spoiled his forms, letters, &c., and burnt 200 or 300 reams of paper, printed and unprinted" (*English Currant,* 12–14 Dec. 1688; see Plomer, 1668–1725). Hills fled to St. Omer, where he died within a few weeks.

31. *Harry Care:* Henry Care (1646–88), the much despised journalist and pamphleteer, best known for his *Weekly Packet of Advice from Rome* and for *Public Occurrences.* Care died on 8 Aug.

33–5. *Macdonnell . . . O'Neill . . . Clarendon . . . Tyrconnel:* Alexander, or Alaster, Macdonnell and Phelim O'Neill were leaders of the Irish Rebellion, 1641–42. Henry Hyde, Earl of Clarendon, was Viceroy of Ireland under Charles and James, until replaced in Feb. 1687 by James' tool, the Roman Catholic Richard Talbot, Earl of Tyrconnel.

Those carpet knights and interested peers,
And rid the kingdoms from impending fears?

>   This is the time.   40

Would you at once make all the Hogen Mogens yield,
And be at once their terror and our shield,
And not appear by proxy in the field?

>   This is the time.

Would you no more a woman's counsel take,   45
But love your kingdoms for your kingdoms' sake,
Make subjects love, and enemies to quake?

>   This is the time.

BALLAD

To the tune of "Couragio"

1.

Come, come, great Orange, come away

38. *carpet knights:* Though subservience is here implied, the term "knight of the carpet" normally distinguishes knights dubbed by the king in court from those dubbed as soldiers in the field.

41. *Hogen Mogens:* The Dutch.

45. *a woman's counsel:* Queen Mary of Modena's, hence Roman Catholic counsel.

The popularity of this poem was great enough to occasion a re-writing of it early in December which brought allusions up to date. Much more general than its predecessor, this second poem, *The Prince of Orange's Triumph,* alludes to the escape of Petre, the first of James' supporters openly to flee (Luttrell, *1,* 480–1), but otherwise contents itself with general exclamations on William's "glorious cause." The poem is printed in *Pepys Ballads, 3,* 325–28. I cite here a few of the more interesting stanzas by way of comparison with the present text:

> Now Orange is on British shore,
> Come from his long voyage-o;
>
>   . . .   .
>
> We now shall have no masses more
> But will pull down their scarlet whore;
> Couragio, couragio, couragio.

2.

> Now all her brats we understand,
> Does weep at this voyage-o,
> And forced are to quit the land,
> For fear of a strong hempen band . . . .

On thy august voyagio;
The church and state admit no stay,
And Protestants would once more say,
Couragio, couragio, couragio.   5

2.

Stand east, dear wind, till they arrive
On their design'd voyagio,

3.

While here they sung their antic song,
  Before the brave voyage-o,
The best of subjects they did wrong,
But now they run away ding-dong . . . .

4.

The London lads was much concern'd
  At Friars in this age-o,
Therefore their wooden gods they burn'd
And trinkets into ashes turn'd . . . .

5.

They never stood to count their cost,
  They being in a rage-o;
Their beads and crucifix they lost—
Was ever Jesuits so cross'd?
          . . .

9.

Now welcome to our English shore,
  And now we will engage-o,
To thump the Babylonish whore
And kick her trumpery out of door . . . .

10.

A short and merry life they led,
  Before this rare voyage-o,
But now old Petre, he is fled,
  And some in Newgate hide their head . . . .
          . . .

13.

Now let us all united be,
  And then I will engage-o,
In little space we soon shall free
This land from Popish tyranny. . . .

2. *august voyagio:* Probably no pun on the month of August. The poem appeared
within a few days of William's landing and after Sunderland's dismissal from the
Presidency of the Council (26 Oct.).

And let each noble soul alive
Cry loud "Qu'il Prince d'Aurange vive!"
Couragio, couragio, couragio.   10

3.

Look sharp, and see the glorious fleet
    Appear in their voyagio!
With loud huzzas we will them greet,
And with both arms and armies meet;
    Couragio, couragio, couragio.   15

4.

Then, welcome to our English shore;
    And now I will engage—o,
We'll thump the Babylonish whore,
And kick her trump'ries out of door;
    Couragio, couragio, couragio.   20

5.

Poor Berwick! how will thy dear joys
    Oppose this brave voyagio?
Thy tallest sparks will be mere toys
To Brandenburg and Swedish boys;
    Couragio, couragio, couragio.   25

6.

Dumbarton sputters now like mad,
    Against this great voyagio;

18. *the Babylonish whore:* Catholicism.

21. *Berwick:* James Fitzjames (1670–1734), natural son of James by Arabella Churchill, created Duke of Berwick in March 1687. In Feb. 1688, he had been given Aubrey de Vere's place as colonel of the royal horse guards, the Blues. In September, Reresby writes that "fifty Irishmen and Papists had been sent for from Ireland by the Duke of Berwick to be put into his regiment, and every captain to have some." The captains refused and were brought "up to Windsor in custody, where they were to be tried by a council of war" (p. 509).

dear joys: Cant for Irishmen.

24. *Brandenburg and Swedish boys:* Mercenaries in William's employ. In a play entitled *The Late Revolution,* 1690 (Wing L558), the "Swiss, Swedes, and Bradenburgers" are "all six foot high, at least."

26. *Dumbarton:* George Douglas (1636?–92), Earl of Dumbarton, a Roman Catholic, was one of the three generals James named to meet the invasion: "the army will be commanded under him [i.e. the King] by 3 Lieutenant Generals, Lord Feversham, Lord Dumbarton, and the Count du Croy" (Luttrell, *1,* 464).

Old Craven, too, in sable's clad,
And Feversham looks monstrous sad;
   Couragio, couragio, couragio.   30

7.

But Solms has took a glorious cause
   In this warlike voyagio,
To guard us from their ravening paws
And to protect our lives and laws;
   Couragio, couragio, couragio.   35

8.

Nassau will ridicule the fop
   By this Belgic voyagio,
And make their gaudy feathers drop—
Their slaughter's but a harvest-crop;
   Couragio, couragio, couragio.   40

9.

Stirum, advance the Buda Blades
   Thou'st brought in this voyagio;
And, since thy laurel never fades,
Send our foes to the Stygian shades;
   Couragio, couragio, couragio.   45

10.

Schomberg thunders hero-like
   In this stormy voyagio;

28. *Craven:* William (1606–97), Earl of Craven, Lieutenant General of the Coldstream regiment, and a member of James' Privy Council.

29. *Feversham:* James' general gave rise to constant humor both for his foreign manners and his military ineffectiveness. In December he was taken into custody by William at Windsor while seeking a conference for James. Injudiciously enough he was travelling without a safe-conduct. "He was released a fortnight later, 1 Jan. 1688–9, on the Queen Dowager's representing to William that she could not indulge in her favorite game of basset without her Lord Chamberlain to keep the bank" (*DNB*).

31. *Solms:* Heinrich Maastrict, Count of Solms-Braufels, one of the generals in the Dutch service.

36. *Nassau:* William of Orange-Nassau.

41. *Stirum:* Vice-admiral van Stirum who, according to this poem, transported Hungarian mercenaries—the "Buda Blades"—in his ship.

46. *Schomberg:* Frederick Herman, Duke of Schomberg, second in command of William's fleet.

His very name does horror strike
And will slay more than gun or pike;
　　Couragio, couragio, couragio.   50

11.

Thus they the victory will gain,
　　After their brave voyagio;
And all our liberties maintain,
And settle church and state again;
　　Couragio, couragio, couragio.   55

12.

Then 'twill be just, and no extreme,
　　To see by this voyagio,
That Wem should have th'effect of's dream
For driving headlong with the stream;
　　Couragio, couragio, couragio.   60

13.

The judges too, that traitors be,
　　Must truss by this voyagio;
'Twill be a noble sight, to see
Dispensing Scarlet on a tree!
　　Couragio, couragio, couragio.   65

14.

The monks away full swift will hie
　　On their dismal voyagio;
Ten pounds a post-horse then they cry,
And all away to Calais fly;
　　Couragio, couragio, couragio.   70

15.

Sunderland has shot the pit
And is on his voyagio;

58. *Wem:* Jeffreys.

62. *truss:* To be hanged.

64. *Scarlet:* The ceremonial gown of a judge.

71–2. Sunderland did not leave England until 7 Dec., when he escaped to Rotterdam disguised as a woman. He had been in hiding at Althorp, however, for some time before his actual flight (Campana, 2, 373), and as far as the satirist knew he had gone from the country on his first being missed.

71. *shot the pit:* Flown from the pit, cockpit, or enclosure.

D'Adda must no more hatching sit,
And Petre, too, the board must quit;
    Couragio, couragio, couragio.   75

16.

Old Arundell does hang his ears
    Because of this voyagio;
And miser Powis stews in tears;
Belasyse roars and damns and swears;
    Couragio, couragio, couragio.   80

17.

When all is done, we then shall hope
    To see by this voyagio
No more Nuncio, no more Pope,
Except it be to have a rope;
    Couragio, couragio, couragio.   85

THE PLOWMAN

  As Ralph and Nick i'th'field were plowing,
One of the oxen fell a-lowing
With such a strange and uncouth voice,
As if the beast seem'd to rejoice;
Which put the youths in consternation   5
To see the creature in that passion,
But, after they had gaz'd awhile,
The wonder turn'd into a smile.
Says Ralph to Nick, there's more in this
Than either thou or I can guess,   10
And was old Father Ant'ny here,
That does all dreams and riddles clear,

---

73. *d'Adda:* Count Ferdinand d'Adda, Papal Nuncio. "Hatching" presumably refers to his supposed part in the birth of the Prince, though it may, of course, refer to his "plotting" the overthrow of the Anglican Church.

74. *Petre:* Father Edward Petre.

76–9. *Arundell . . . Powis . . . Belasyse:* Three Catholic lords, members of James' Privy Council.

76. *hang his ears:* "To be cowed, discouraged."

He could prognostic, being a scholar,
What put old Brindle in that choler;
For I have drove him fifteen year   15
And never yet so much did hear.
    But, Nick, to pass the time along,
I prithee, sing the Irish song;
The tune I like, the story's base—
And so is all that cursed race;   20
Each bears the mark of Cain in's face.

NICK: Thou bidd'st me sing, I'd more need pray
    To keep our enemies away,
    Who now are landed in the west—
    The thing's too true to make a jest.   25
RALPH: Our enemies, you simple lurdan!
    They're come to ease us of our burden,
    To free us from the Popish brood
    That never did to England good.
    Why prithee, I have read my book,   30
    On which poor Papists never look;
    Thy ignorance does move my pity—
    All are not destin'd to be witty;
    Come, come, you fool, mind you your singing,
    I hope ere long to see some swinging.   35
NICK: No, I will never sing again,
    Unless the meaning you explain.
RALPH: Nay, if thou wilt not sing before
    Thou hear'st my tale, thou'lt ne'er sing more,
    For I shall tell thee such a story   40
    Will make thee laugh, and yet be sorry.
    Along the road the soldiers pass
    Like herds of cattle going to grass
    Or droves of sheep to Smithfield fair,
    In the same pickle, too, they are,   45

13. *prognostic:* Obs. form of "prognosticate."
18. *the Irish song: Lilli burlero,* see below.
24. *landed in the west:* William landed at Torbay in southeast Devon.
26. *lurdan:* "A general term of opprobrium . . . implying either dullness and in-
capacity, or idleness and rascality."
44. *Smithfield fair:* The cattle market.

And with like cheerfulness each goes.
Poor men, their hearts are in their hose!
Where one is silent, ten do curse;
None goes by choice, but all perforce;
When the road's dirty, or if't rain,   50
Aloud on Popery they complain,
And all declare they'll never fight
'Gainst that Church they believe the right—
Rome ne'er shall bring their conscience under,
(Conscience in soldiers made me wonder!)   55
Then rail'd on some whom I'll not name.
But, faith, I doubt they are to blame,
Yet I have nought to do with that,
Still let the mouse beware the cat.
But if you'd trust a London parson,   60
A Popish priest's a very whoreson,
A wolf that's in sheep's clothing dress'd,
A saint without, within a beast.
For when I thither went last week,
The people did not stick to speak   65
Such horrid stories of the Papists
That I believe 'em worse than Atheists.
Nay, worse than devils, I'm afeard,
If all be true that I have heard;
They say the Jesuit priests have order'd   70
That all the Protestants must be murder'd;
The faithless Irish with 'em join
As partners in their black design,
And though we now do plow and sow,
They are come o'er to reap and mow.   75
NICK: They reap and mow! They suck the sow!
Zoons, though I'm born to hold the plow
And never bred to read and write,

---

47. *their hearts are in their hose:* Afraid, extremely dejected; an early form of "one's heart in one's boots" (Partridge).

76. *suck the sow:* To become drunk.

77. *Zoons:* A form of the oath "zounds;" cf. Farquhar, *Love and Bottle* (1699), II.ii, "'Zoons' is only us'd by the disbanded officers and bullies; but 'zauns' is the beaux' pronunciation."

By the Lord Harry! I can fight;
And if the Irish are but men,   80
Why thou and I can master ten.
Ne'er fear 'em, Ralph, we country boys
Will piss on their belov'd dear joys;
And if we're forc'd to make an head,
'Od's heart! we'll stave the vermin dead.   85
When once we're vext they'll find us sour;
Rome and its rubbish soon will scour.

RALPH: Nay, boy, we don't the country fear,
I for poor London take such care;
There in each house they sculk and lurk,   90
But naturally do hate to work.
Though, as that Parson did declare,
They've Jacob's voice and Esau's hair,
Their conscience base, religion worse;
Their conversation is a curse;   95
'Tis more than time they were remov'd.
They neither love nor are belov'd,
Folk shun them like infected men;
There's not a grain of sense in ten;
Yet all the while good Catholics—   100
None closer to religion sticks—
Such as their church is, such are they.
Then never 'gainst preservers pray,
But let our bullocks bellow still,
And Pro. Prince act Heaven's high will.   105
If this be still the year of wonder,
Or they or we must truckle under;

---

79. *By the Lord Harry:* Perhaps jocular, apparently derived from "old Harry," the devil (Partridge).

83. *dear joys:* Cant for Irishmen.

84. *to make an head:* To make head; to advance or press forward, especially in opposition to some one or thing.

85. *'od's heart:* God's heart—an oath.

87. *scour:* Flee.

105. *Pro. Prince:* William, the Protestant Prince.

106. *the year of wonder:* Cf. *To the Prince of Orange: A Packet of Advice, &c.;* the "original" year of wonder was, of course, 1666, proclaimed in Dryden's *Annus Mirabilis.*

107. *truckle:* Submit, yield obsequiously.

Therefore unyoke, let's home to dinner,
There'll be two losses for one winner.

Song

To the tune of "Men in Fashion"

Would you be a man in power?
Would you have the nation kind?
Be a traitor and a coward,
You'll have all things to your mind.

If the Dutch cannot reform you,   5
English faith will do the thing;
There's a Churchill to inform you
How to quit your friend and King.

That great knave and greater dastard,
With van [ordmd] and [oij dei],   10
And the dull kidnapping bastard,
Would to force the King betray.

109. *two losses:* The MS. is difficult to decipher at this point, reading either "looses,"
an obs. form of "losses," or "looser," i.e. "losers," the terminal "s" having been omitted
by the scribe whose hand throughout the MS. is careless. I have chosen the least sup-
positious of the two possibilities. The meaning of the line would appear to be that
there will be two lost dinners if they keep on talking.

7. *Churchill:* John Churchill (1650–1722), later Lord Churchill and Duke of Marl-
borough. James and his sympathizers viewed his defection as the darkest of treacheries.
Reresby remarked that "this ungrateful Lord Churchill was raised from page to the
King to the degree of viscount of England and had got a great estate with it by the
King's bounty" (p. 534). On 7 Nov. Churchill had been appointed Lieutenant General
of James' army and had vowed to shed the last drop of his blood for his royal master
(Clarke, *Life,* 2, 219). On the night of 23 Nov., claiming that zeal for the Protestant
religion prompted the action, Churchill left Salisbury and joined William at Axminster.
He was met at William's camp by Marshall Frederick de Schomberg, who was said to
have remarked merely "that he was the first lieutenant general he had ever heard of
that had deserted from his colors" (ibid. p. 224; Churchill's letter to James giving his
motives for deserting is in Kennett, *3, 530*).

10. The poor scribal hand throughout this MS. is here almost impossible to decipher
because of cancellation and contraction of what are apparently proper names. Any
reading would be purely conjectural.

11. *kidnapping bastard:* The Duke of Grafton, who fled with Churchill. Though the
reference could be to his part in the plan to surrender the King to William, more likely
the satirist refers to Grafton's past activities, when he spirited away the widow of
Tom Lucy (see above, *Song,* "The widows and maids," 6 and n.).

But their plot was disappointed
By his bleeding at the nose,
And then was the Lord's annointed   15
Freed from his and heaven's foes.

But why should not we tell a jest
Of Kirke, Langston, Cornbury,
Trelawney, Berkley, and the rest
Now so fam'd for treachery?   20

They for religion's fiery zeal
All religion's laws transgress'd,
As he that did a Bible steal
By his reading to be blest.

Would you see an army low'ring,   25
Pall'd with conscience and with fear,
And their officers a-scouring,
When the danger first drew near?

England to its lasting glory
Brought such men and deeds to light,   30
And all ages shall in story
Tell their faith and truth and might.

But how came men that had so long
Been finely trained, clad, and fed

13–16. James was wont to describe the nosebleed, which prevented him from going
to Warminster to review his troops, as an act of Providence (Clarke, 2, 222–23).

18. *Kirke, Langston, Cornbury:* In mid-November Clarendon's son, Edward Hyde
(1661–1724), styled Lord Cornbury, deserted to William. Luttrell records the defection:
"the Lord Cornbury, with his regiment of dragoons; the Duke of St. Alban's regiment
of horse, commanded by Colonel Langston, and the royal regiment of horse of the
Duke of Berwick's, commanded by Sir Francis Compton" have largely "gone over to"
William (*1*, 475). Langston and George Kirke were implicated in the plot to hand over
James to William. Kirke was apprehended before he could desert (Luttrell, *1*, 480, 483).

19. *Trelawney . . . Berkley:* "His Majesty, when he left Salisbury, came thence in a
great hurry and consternation upon the news of the Prince of Denmark, and the Dukes
of Ormonde, Grafton, and Northumberland, Lord Churchill, Colonel Trelawney, Colonel Berkley, Sir John Laveer, and several other officers and common soldiers, to the
number of four or five thousand, being gone over to the Prince of Orange . . . " (Luttrell, *1*, 479).

23. *he that did a Bible steal:* I am unable to identify the person referred to here,
if indeed a specific reference is intended.

Thus from their King to run "ding-dong," 35
As if by the Furies led?

Whilst instead of being a soldier
Each turn'd lawyer or divine,
And the case being scann'd with rigor,
None to fighting did incline. 40

Thus the Non-Resistance Doctrine,
Follow'd by the Theban band,
Is become an art of bart'ring
Princes into traitors' hands.

Then let the Church of England be 45
The sole mistress of the juggle,
For no Church else that we can see
Can their King so neatly bubble.

MATTHEW PRIOR

THE ORANGE

1.

Good people, I pray,
Throw the Orange away;
'Tis a very sour fruit, and was first brought in play
When good Judith Wilk

35. "ding-dong": Vigorously.
42. Theban band: An ironic comparison of the seven bishops who turned against
James on the question of toleration to the seven against Thebes.
48. bubble: Arch., to cheat, deceive, or swindle.

The popularity of this ballad form, set to a tune called "A Pudding" (Chappell, 1,
235), and of its scant motif on the Orange, is attested by two earlier poems (Pepys
Ballads, 3, 333, 336). Rehearsing the events of November and early December, respectively, these poems provided Prior with a readymade satiric vehicle.
4. Judith Wilk: The Queen's midwife. Among the many rumors about the birth,
some suggested that the Queen had used cushions to counterfeit pregnancy, and that
the pretender had been introduced into the Queen's bed by means of a warming-pan
brought in by the midwife.

In her pocket brought milk,   5
And with cushions and warming-pans labor'd to bilk
                                   This same Orange.

                                        2.

When the army retreats
And the parliament sits
To vote our King the true use of his wits,   10
    'Twill be a sad means
    When all he obtains
Is to have his calves' head dress'd with other men's brains,
                                   And an Orange.

                                        3.

The sins of his youth   15
Made him think of one truth,
When he spawl'd from his lungs and bled twice at the mouth,
    That your fresh sort of food
    Does his carcass more good,
And the damn'd thing that cur'd his putrefi'd blood   20
                                   Was an Orange.

                                        4.

This hopeful young son
Is surely his own,
Because from an Orange it cri'd to be gone,
    But the heretics say   25
    He was got by d'Adda,
For neither King nor the Nuncio dare stay
                                   Near an Orange.

13. *calves' head:* On 30 January, the anniversary of the beheading of Charles I, the Calves' Head Club held dinners, which featured this dish in disrespect to the "royal martyr."

15. *The sins of his youth:* In particular, the story of James' affair with Lady Southesk and the revenge her husband supposedly wrought on James (see headnote to *The Birth of the Prince*).

17. *spawl'd:* Spit copiously, or coarsely.

26. *d'Adda:* The Papal Nuncio, said to have sired the young Prince, fled early in December under the protection of the envoy of the Duke of Savoy (Campana, 2, 373).

England's Memorial

5.

Since Louis was cut
From his breech to the gut   30
France fancies an open-arse, delicate fruit;
We wiser than so
Have two strings to our bow
For we've a good Queen that's an open-arse, too,

And an Orange.   35

6.

Till Nanny writ much
To the rebels, the Dutch,
Her mother, good woman, ne'er ow'd her a grutch,
And the box of the ear
Made the matter appear   40
That the only foul savor the Queen could not hear

Was an Orange.

7.

An honest old peer
That forsook God last year,
Pull'd off all his plasters, and arm'd for the war;   45
But his arms would not do,
And his aches throbb'd, too,

29. *Since Louis was cut:* In November and again in Dec. 1686, Louis XIV had under-
gone surgery for *fistula in ano* (see Luttrell's notices, *1, 373, 388, 390*).

31. *open-arse:* A medlar. Applied to the Queen (34), the phrase also refers to the
suspiciously easy birth of her son.

36. *Nanny:* Princess Anne of Denmark had written to her sister, Mary of Orange,
concerning the validity of the birth of the Prince, which she had investigated "nar-
rowly." Her conclusion was that "it is wonderful if it is no cheat," and she assured her
sister that she had taken "all the care" possible "that the King and Queen might not
be angry" (*The Letters of Queen Anne,* ed. Beatrice Curtis Brown, 1935, pp. 39–43). On
25 Nov. she fled the palace with Lady Sarah Churchill, under the protection of Lord
Dorset and Bishop Compton. The numerous rumors as to the cause of her flight suggest the ill-will between the Queen and her step-daughter (Clarke, *Life, 2, 226*).

38. *grutch:* Obs., complaint, or grudge.

43. *An honest old peer:* Henry Mordaunt (1624?–97), second Earl of Peterborough.
For his conversion, see above, *The Converts,* 11 and n. His "arming" took the form of
flight. He was apprehended in Kent in mid-December and confined in the Tower on
the 24th.

That he wish'd his own pox and his Majesty's, too,

On an Orange.

8.

Old Tyburn must groan,   50
For Jeffreys is known
To have perjur'd his conscience to marry his son;
And Devonshire's cause
Will be tri'd by just laws,
And Herbert must taste a most damnable sauce   55

With an Orange.

9.

Lobb, Penn, and a score
Of those honest men more
Will find this same Orange exceedingly sour;
The Queen to be seiz'd   60
Will be very pleas'd,
And so will King Pippin, too dry to be squeez'd

By an Orange.

48. *his Majesty's* [*pox*]: It seems unlikely that Prior could have intended "Mistress's" in this instance, as the text of *POAS, 3*, 1704, has it. The story of Southesk's infamous revenge on James was so widely circulated and so generally believed to be the cause of James' inability to produce a healthy male heir that it would naturally be cursed as contributing to the ultimate ruin of the Catholic cause.

51–2. *Jeffreys . . . perjur'd his conscience:* Jeffreys, never a convert, worked hard to achieve a Catholic liaison, marrying his son John to the Catholic heiress, Lady Charlotte, daughter of the deceased Earl of Pembroke. Luttrell notes the marriage in mid-July 1688, and adds, "she is said to be worth £70,000. They were married by a Church of England man and by a Romish Bishop . . . " (*1*, 451).

53. *Devonshire's cause:* William Cavendish (1641–1707), first Duke of Devonshire. In July 1687, he had quarrelled with and struck Colonel Thomas Colepepper on provocation from the latter (Evelyn, *4*, 453–4). At Jeffreys' instigation, Devonshire was fined £30,000 and imprisoned until he had agreed to sign a bond for the money. The unfair treatment of Devonshire was generally attributed to his opposition to James' policies. His case was reviewed after the Revolution, the Lords finding in his favor (Luttrell, *1*, 406, 417–18, 522).

55. *Herbert:* Sir Edward Herbert (1648?–98), succeeded Jeffreys as chief justice of the King's bench on 23 Oct. 1685. He fled soon after James himself and became his Lord Chancellor in exile.

57. *Lobb, Penn:* Stephen Lobb, "the Jacobite Independent," and William Penn, the Quaker; see above, *The Advice*, 9 n.

Lilli burlero
(October–December 1688)

The question of the significance of verse satire in shaping events constantly confronts the student of this period. Though many proofs of influence could be adduced, perhaps none is as convincing as the doggerel ballad *Lilli burlero* with its numerous progeny.

With the approach of William's fleet, as the previous pages show, the satirist warmed to his task knowing that the simplest ideas or the rudest jargon might excite. Into the emotionally charged atmosphere late in October the first broadside copies of *Lilli burlero* were introduced (Luttrell purchased his copy on the 25th, according to his MS. note). Written two years earlier by Thomas Wharton against the then new administration in Ireland of Richard Talbot, Earl of Tyrconnel, the ballad was set to a brisk march rhythm by Henry Purcell and swept the country like a tune from Tin Pan Alley. Burnet said of it, "a foolish ballad was made at that time treating the papists and chiefly the Irish in a very ridiculous manner, which had a burden said to be Irish words 'lero lero, lilli burlero' "—words which Swift in his *Marginalia* on Burnet called "not Irish . . . but better than Scotch." Burnet went on to say that it "made an impression on the [King's] army that cannot be imagined by those who saw it not. The whole army and at last the people, both in city and country, were singing it perpetually" (*1*, 792). The tune which, as Wharton boasted, "sung a deluded Prince out of three kingdoms" (*A True Relation . . . of the Intended Riot and Tumult of Queen Elizabeth's Birthday, &c.*, 1712, p. 5), became so popular that a host of new poems was set to it. Recognizing the impact of the tune, government satirists unwisely wrote their own lines to the tune and circulated them about, vainly hoping thus either to compromise the effectiveness of the original or to capture for their own cause some of its magic. Below appear several poems which employ the tune to their own purposes. Numerous others were set to the music (cf. Chappell, 2, 568–71, 786) but the following poems record both the growth of the song's importance and the tempo of the days and weeks surrounding William's landing.

Written in an Englishman's concept of the Irish brogue, *Lilli bur-*

lero was composed shortly after the appointment of Tyrconnel to succeed the Earl of Clarendon as governor of Ireland in January 1687. Set to Purcell's tune (see illustration, facing p. 312), it achieved little if any popular success before October 1688, when the presence of Irish troops in England to bolster James' weakening position produced the immediate cause for its revival. Fortuitously, the poem contained a few phrases that lent themselves well to the present situation, particularly the reference to a "Protestant wind," which, while it had originally referred to the storms faced by Tyrconnel in 1687 (Clarendon, 2, 137), now quite obviously stood fair for William.

Almost immediately the second part of *Lilli burlero* was published (the publication may, indeed, have been simultaneous). It bears directly on the events of late October, giving the verses an immediacy lacking in the first part. Like those of part one, the new verses purport to be the conversation of two Irish soldiers in England who, having had more than enough of the English hatred for them and the Catholics, wish to go home before it is too late.

In an attempt to counteract the success of *Lilli burlero*, government balladists composed a song against the Dutch, introducing the refrain "Sooterkin, Hogen, Herring, Van Dunk" in place of the mock-Irish phrases of the original ballad. The format of the second part of *Lilli burlero* was adopted, this time with two Englishmen in the act of disparaging the Dutch. Just as *Lilli burlero* sought to arouse the fears and animosity of the English for the Irish, so here like feelings toward the Dutch were played upon. Luttrell bought a copy of the broadside when it first came out and felt it to be "against the Dutch." So, too, in all probability, did his contemporaries.

The government's attempt to employ the tune to its own ends apparently had scant success. It was countered by another version, circulated in MS. At best the government ballad provided a momentary backwash in the historical tide on which William rode. The sense of forward surge dominates the remaining poems of this section. In "Our history reckons some kings of great fame," James' kingship is considered, as news of the Dutch landing is expected momentarily. He receives a nickname massive in its disrespect, combining his Scots ancestry, his Catholic religion, and his dullness in the refrain "Ninny Mack Nero, Jemmy Transub." In the final poem disrespect for James turns to jubilation at his defeat. It is difficult to avoid the sense of full-circle which the opening lines of the poem convey:

The pillars of Popery now are blown down,
One thousand, six hundred, eighty and eight.

In the poems that follow I have not repeated the refrain lines after
the first verse.

[THOMAS WHARTON]

A NEW SONG

Ho, brother Teague, dost hear de decree,
    Lilli burlero, bullen a-la;
Dat we shall have a new debittie,
    Lilli burlero bullen a-la,
    Lero lero, lero lero, lilli burlero, bullen a-la;   5
    Lero lero, lero lero, lilli burlero, bullen a-la.

Ho, by my shoul, it is a Talbot,
And he will cut de Englishman's troat.

Though, by my shoul, de English do prat,
De law's on dare side, and Chreist knows what.   10

Author: Thomas Wharton (1648–1715), afterwards first Marquis of Wharton. One of
the greatest profligates of his time (see above, *A Faithful Catalogue,* &c., 136 and n.),
Wharton was a staunch Whig throughout James' reign, corresponding with Orange in
1688 and joining him at Exeter. No evidence challenges Wharton's claim in *A True
Relation . . . of the Intended Riot and Tumult of Queen Elizabeth's Birthday,* &c.,
1712, that he wrote this ballad.

Date: The broadside in the Firth collection bears the following MS. notes in Luttrell's hand: "2d. Made upon the Irish upon Tyrconnel's going deputy thither. 25 Oct.
1688." Luttrell has also filled in the blanks within the body of the poem. The broadside
is reproduced in Macaulay, *3,* 1075. Wood notes that he bought his copy of the poem
in "December 1688."

1. *Teague:* Cant name for an Irishman.

3. *debittie:* Opposition to the appointment of Tyrconnel in place of Clarendon was
very great. James' only concession to it, however, was to call Talbot Lord Deputy instead of Lord Lieutenant. Talbot never attained the higher title.

5. *Lero, lero . . . :* There have been several suggestions concerning the meaning of
the refrain, none of them satisfactory. The phrases are probably meaningless, as the *OED*
says, but see *The Historical Songs of Ireland* (The Percy Society), ed. T. Crofton Croker,
1841, pp. 1–2.

But if dispense do come from de Pope,
Weel hang Magno Cart and demselves on a rope.

And the good Talbot is made a lord,
And he with brave lads is coming aboard.

Who'll all in France have taken a swear,   15
Dat day will have no Protestant heir.

Oh, but why does he stay behind,
Ho, by my shoul, 'tis a Protestant wind.

Now Tyrconnel is come a-shore,
And we shall have commissions gillore.   20

And he dat will not go to mass,
Shall turn out and look like an ass.

Now, now, de heretics all go down,
By Chreist and St. Patrick, the nation's our own!

[THOMAS WHARTON]

AN IRISH PROPHECY

There was a prophecy lately found in a bog,
That Ireland should be rul'd by an ass and a dog;

13. *Talbot is made a lord:* On 20 June 1685 Talbot was elevated to the Irish peerage with the titles Baron of Talbotstown, Viscount Baltinglass, and Earl of Tyrconnel.

16. *Protestant heir:* Originally a reference to the hope that James' Protestant daughters could be excluded from the throne. This phrase was particularly inflammatory in the autumn of 1688, since the birth of the Prince had in fact accomplished the "Protestant exclusion."

18. *Protestant wind:* When Orange's departure from Holland for England was every day expected, James "caused a lofty vane to be erected" on the roof of the banquetting house across from his apartments at Whitehall, "which he is said to have regarded daily with extreme interest" (Croker, ed. cit., p. 11).

Ascription: Although this is a separate poem, it occurs as a part of the previous ballad often enough (see textual notes) to warrant the conclusion that it was also written by Wharton. There is, however, no direct evidence of this.

A New SONG.

Ho Brother *Teague* doſt hear de Decree, Lil‑‑li Burlero Bullen a‑‑la, Dat we ſhall have a

new Debittie, Lil‑li Bur‑le‑ro Bullen a‑la, Le‑ro, La‑ro, La‑ro Le‑ro, Lil‑li Bur‑le‑ro,

Bullen a la, Le=ro, La=ro, La‑ro, Le‑ro, Lil‑li Burlero Bullen a la,

Ho by my *Shoul* it is a T——t,
  Lilli Burlero, &c.
And he will Cut all de *Engliſh* Troat,
  Lilli, &c.
  Lero, Laro, &c.
  Lero, Laro, &c.

Though by my ſhoul de *Ingliſh* do Prat,
  Lilli, &c.
De Law's on Dare ſide, and *Chreiſt* knows what,
  Lilli, &c.
  Lero, Laro, &c.
  Lero, Laro, &c.

But if Diſpence do Come from de Pope,
  Lilli, &c.
Weel hang *Magno Carto* & demſelves in a Rope,
  Lilli, &c.
  Lero, Laro, &c.
  Lero, Laro, &c.

And the good T——t is made a Lord,
  Lilli, &c.
And he with brave Lads is coming aboard,
  Lilli, &c.
  Lero, Laro, &c.
  Lero, Laro, &c.

Who'! all in *France* have taken a ſwear,
  Lilli, &c.
Dat day will have no Proteſtant h——s

  Lilli, &c.
  Lero, Laro, &c.
  Lero, Laro, &c.

O but why does he ſtay behind,
  Lilli, &c.
Ho by my ſhoul 'tis a Proteſtant wind,
  Lilli, &c.
  Lero, Laro, &c.
  Lero, Laro, &c.

Now T——l is come a‑ſhore,
  Lilli, &c.
And we ſhall have Commiſſions gillore,
  Lilli, &c.
  Lero, Laro, &c.
  Lero, Laro, &c.

And he dat will not go to M——ſs,
  Lilli, &c.
Shall turn out and look like an Aſs,
  Lilli, &c.
  Lero, Laro, &c.
  Lero, Laro, &c.

Now now de Hereticks all go down,
  Lilli, &c.
By *Chreiſt* and *St. Patrick* the Nation's our own,
  Lilli, &c.
  Lero, Laro, &c.
  Lero, Laro, &c.

Lilli Burlero

This prophecy's true, and now come to pass,
For Talbot's a dog, and Tyrconnel's an ass.

THE SECOND PART OF LILLI BURLERO BULLEN A-LA

By Chreist, my dear Morish, vat maukes de sho' sad?
    Lilli burlero bullen a-la.
The heretics jear us and mauke me mad.
    Lilli burlero bullen a-la,
    Lero lero, lero lero, lilli burlero bullen a-la,   5
    Lero lero, lero lero, lilli burlero bullen a-la.

Pox take me, dear Teague, but I am in a rage,
Poo', what impidence is in dish age?

Vat if Dush should come as dey hope,
To up hang us for all de dispense of de Pope?   10

Dey shay dat Tyrconnel's a friend to de mash,
For which he's a traitor, a pimp, and an ass.

Ara', plague tauke me now, I make a swar,
I to Shent Tyburn will mauke a great prayer.

Oh, I will pray to Shent Patrick's frock,   15
Or to Loreto's sacred smock.

Now, a pox tauke me, what dost dow tink,
De English confusion to Popery drink.

And, by my shoul, de mash house pull down,
While dey were swearing de Mayor of de town.   20

16. *Loreto's . . . smock:* A common jest in reference to one of the various prayers
supposedly offered up for the Queen's "breeding a son"; see above, headnote to *The
Birth of the Prince.*

19. *de mash house pull down:* In October several times the London mobs attacked
various Catholic establishments; for examples, see Luttrell, *1, 472,* and *HMC, Le Fleming,* no. 3276.

20. *de Mayor:* Sir John Eyles was sworn in as Lord Mayor on 8 Sept. 1688 to fill
the vacancy caused by the death of Sir John Shorter. Eyles, a haberdasher, was termed

Oh, fait and be, I'll mauke de decree,
And swar by de Chancellor's modesty;

Dat I no longer in English will stay,
For be Goad, dey will hang us out of de way.

A New Song upon the Hogen Mogens

D'ye hear the news of the Dutch, dear Frank,
  Sooterkin, Hogen, Herring, Van Dunk;
That they intend to play us a prank,
  Sooterkin, Hogen, Herring, Van Dunk;
  Hogen Mogen, Hogen Mogen, Sooterkin, Hogen, Herring,
    Van Dunk;
  Hogen Mogen, Hogen Mogen, Sooterkin, Hogen, Herring,   5
    Van Dunk.

But if they boldly dare come ashore,
Some may repent themselves full sore;

For the brave English, Irish, and Scotch,
Will in their guts make such a hotch-potch,   10

Better they'd stuck to the herring trade,
For in pickle themselves shall be laid;

What though they have laid their heads together,
No Orange can thrive if't prove bad weather.

---

a "fanatic" by Luttrell, *1*, 457, 459 and the Rev. Alfred Beaven, *The Aldermen of the City of London*, 1908, 2, 114-15.

  22. *de Chancellor's modesty:* Jeffreys was, of course, anything but modest.

  Date: Luttrell's copy of the broadside, now in the Harvard collection, is completely engraved—the second broadside edition is set in type—and bears the following MS. notes in his hand: "Id. 17 Nov. 1688. Against the Dutch."

  2. *Sooterkin, Hogen, Herring, Van Dunk:* A mixture of cant words and phrases supposed to typify the Dutch. "Sooterkin" was a chimerical kind of afterbirth (see *Tragi-Comedy of Titus Oates*, 38 and n.); "Hogen," i.e. Hogen Mogen, was a corruption of *Hoogmogendheiden*, "high mightiness," the designation of the States General of the United Provinces; "Herring" was a staple of Dutch food, and "Van Dunk" a jocularly typical Dutch name.

Woe be to them if Dartmouth the great,   15
Should fall upon them with his whole fleet;

Pass not Port-bay for fear it should freeze,
For then, i'fegs, your Orange we'll squeeze!

A New Song

To the tune of "Lilli burlero"

1.

Our history reckons some kings of great fame,
   Ninny Mack Nero, Jemmy Transub;
But none before this who deserved the name
   Of Ninny Mack Nero, Jemmy Transub;
   Nero Nero, Nero Nero, Ninny Mack Nero, Jemmy Transub,   5
   Nero Nero, Nero Nero, Ninny Mack Nero, Jemmy Transub.

2.

He pick'd up a parcel of fools and knaves,
And made them all judges to make us all slaves;

---

15. *Dartmouth:* George Legge, Lord Dartmouth, admiral of James' fleet.
17. *Port-bay:* Portsmouth Harbor or Torbay?
18. *i'fegs:* Obs., a trivial oath: "in faith," "by my faith."
A reply to this poem, with the same refrain, is in B.M. Add. 29497, a portion of which follows:

> Now, now, the brave Dutch are all coming o'er,
> And all the English wish them ashore,
>
> For hither the brave Nassau doth come,
> Our Church to preserve from the errors of Rome;
>
> And he and the rest have solemnly swore,
> Our laws and our liberties they will restore;
>
>   · · ·   · · ·   · · ·
>
> And swears he will ne'er any more cross the main,
> Till he's fix'd the Succession, then for Holland again.
>
> And if their design of coming be such,
> God save the King, and preserve the Dutch.

3.

Then for the Church he solemnly swore,
He took as much care as his brother before.   10

4.

To Durham the dapper, and Chester the tall,
He added Tom Watson and Timothy Hall;

5.

Yet, for all this, the heretic clowns
Have set out a fleet to ride in the Downs.

6.

And General Schomberg fierce as a bear,   15
Is coming aboard—let him come if he dare!

7.

For now our brave King has fitted his arms,
And all our dear joys are landing in swarms.

8.

What though the Dutch are so impudent grown,
To swear the King's son is none of his own?   20

9.

What need they make such a deal ado,
Is not our King a chitterling too?

10.

As long as he bought him with his French pence,
For matter of getting the Pope will dispense.

11. *Durham . . . and Chester:* Thomas Cartwright and Nathaniel Crew, the servile bishops of Durham and Chester.

12. *Watson:* Thomas Watson (1637–1717), Bishop of St. David's, zealously promoted the Declaration of Indulgence. In 1699 he was convicted of simony and deprived of his offices.

Hall: Timothy Hall (1637?–1690), titular Bishop of Oxford, "who was looked upon as half a Presbyterian, yet because he read the Declaration was made Bishop of Oxford" (Burnet, *1*, 740; see also Luttrell, *1*, 457).

15. *Schomberg:* Frederick Herman, Duke of Schomberg, William's second-in-command, held to be without equal in Europe in the art of war.

18. *dear joys:* Irishmen.

22. *chitterling:* Diminutive of "chit," a person considered no better than a child.

Song

To the tune of "Lilli burlero"

1.

The pillars of Popery now are blown down,
    One thousand, six hundred, eighty and eight;
Which has frighted our Monarch away from his crown,
    One thousand, six hundred, eighty and eight.
For myn heer did appear, and they scamper'd for fear,   5
    One thousand, six hundred, eighty and eight;
For myn heer did appear, and they scamper'd for fear,
    One thousand, six hundred, eighty and eight.

2.

That mirror of mothers and wonder of wives,
With her joy of three titles are fled for their lives.   10

3.

George Jeffreys, who boasted his face was of brass,
Is now metamorphos'd into a Welsh ass.

2. *eighty and eight:* Throughout 1688 the impending crisis was likened to the struggle with Catholic Spain one hundred years before, which culminated in the defeat of
the Armada.

9–10. At 2 A.M. on Monday, 10 Dec., the Queen left Whitehall in disguise, taking with
her the Prince, exactly six months old that morning. The various chronicles of the escape rival in drama the flight of Louis XVI and Marie Antoinette to Varennes in 1791.
The most detailed accounts are given in French in Campana (2, 379 ff.). The flight is
briefly described in Clarke, *Life, 2,* 245–7:

> Separation therefore being at last resolved on, the Queen, disguising herself, crossed
> the river . . . taking only the Prince, his nurse, and two or three persons more
> along with her to avoid suspicion, and had sent to have a coach ready prepared
> on the other side, in which she went down to Gravesend and got safe aboard the
> yacht; which considering that the rabble was up in all parts to intercept and
> plunder whoever they thought were making their escape, was such a providence
> that nothing but a greater danger could excuse from rashness and temerity in at-
> tempting. . . . Otherwise for the Queen to cross the river in a tempestuous night
> with the Prince . . . to wait in the open air for a considerable time till the coach
> was ready, and not only being exposed to the cold but to the continual danger of
> being discovered, which at the least cry of the Prince might have done . . . how-
> ever it pleased God to bring them through all these dangers, and . . . the wind
> proving fair they had a quick passage and landed next day at Calais.

11–12. Jeffreys remained with James to the end. On 11 Dec., only a few hours after
the King's flight with Sir Edward Hales, Jeffreys quit his quarters at Whitehall and in

4.

That curse of three kingdoms, damn'd Peters, is fled,
Who, with Rome's *ignis fatuus,* our Monarch misled.

5.

Great d'Adda, whose presence made pregnant the Queen,   15
Now she has withdrawn, is no more to be seen.

6.

Old Mordaunt's good service shall doubly be paid,
For his fetching the Queen now his Lordship is stay'd.

7.

That sink of sedition, the wise *Observator,*
Shall receive the just merit that's due to a traitor.   20

8.

Our renegade rhymer, the cudgell'd and lick'd,
For his *Hind* and his *Panther* shall once more be kick'd.

---

disguise—he was dressed as a sailor and, according to one report, had shaved off his heavy eyebrows—made this way to Wapping. On the 12th he was recognized as he was passing along Anchor and Hope Alley toward the docks. He was later placed in the Tower, largely for his own protection, where he died on 18 April, 1689 (Seymour Schofield, *Jeffreys of "the Bloody Assizes,"* 1937, pp. 259–65).

13. *damn'd Peters is fled:* Late in Nov. 1688, Luttrell records that "Father Petre hath packed up several great chests from Whitehall and sent them away," adding in another entry that he "is now quite gone and retired beyond sea" (*1,* 480–81).

14. *Rome's ignis fatuus:* Pope Innocent XI.

15. *Great d'Adda:* For rumors that Papal Nuncio, Count Ferdinand d'Adda, was responsible for the Prince of Wales, see *Tom Tiler, or the Nurse,* 14 and n. He escaped among the entourage of the minister of the Duke of Savoy, disguised as a lackey (see Macaulay, *3,* 1212, from a letter of d'Adda's dated 9 Dec. among the B.M. transcripts).

17. *Mordaunt:* Henry, second Earl of Peterborough, was proxy for James in his marriage to Mary of Modena in 1673 and escorted the bride to England, where they arrived on 21 Nov. (see above, *The Converts,* 11–28 and nn.). Impeached on a charge of high treason on 26 Oct. 1689 for "departing from his allegiance and being reconciled to the Church of Rome," he was released on bail the next October as a result of the intervening dissolution.

19–20. *sink of sedition:* Roger L'Estrange, author of the Tory newssheet *The Observator,* was confined to Newgate on 16 Dec. 1688 for "writing and dispersing treasonable papers against the government" (*HMC, Kenyon,* p. 211). His enemies not only would see his newssheet as a "sink," or receptacle, of sedition, but would recognize the man himself as the fabulist of plots and counterplots (see Kitchin, p. 368).

21. *renegade rhymer:* For Dryden's cudgelling in Rose Alley, see above, *To Mr. Dryden, Upon his Declaring himself a Roman Catholic,* 37 and n.

9.

Now old Obadiah quits Ava Maria,
To sing lamentations worse than Jeremiah.

10.

That wittol and worse, who commanded the Tower,   25
With that shrimp of a soldier, sweet Cecil, did scour.

11.

All our priests are gone back with our Jesuits and monks,
And our nuns to their former profession as punks.

12.

'Twould tire your patience to number the rest,
You may guess by the paw at the bulk of the beast.   30

23. *Obadiah:* Obadiah Walker, the Catholic Master of University College, was arrested on 12 Dec. at Sittingbourne, Kent, with Bonaventure Giffard, Bishop of Madaura, and Andrew Poulton, Master of the Jesuit School in the Savoy (*London Mer-
cury,* 15 Dec. 1688).

25. *wittol and worse:* Sir Edward Hales accompanied James on his first flight, 11–12
Dec. Turner points out that "Sir Edward was thoroughly hated throughout Kent, and
it was unfortunate that James had chosen him as a companion" (p. 446). When it was
learned that Hales had been seen in the area, a search was undertaken, which over-
took the royal party at Faversham. There seems to be no truth in the imputation that
he was a "wittol," i.e. "a contented cuckold" (see *A Faithful Catalogue,* &c., 227 ff. and
nn.).

26. *sweet Cecil:* The adjective is ironic. James Cecil (d. 1693), fourth Earl of Salisbury, was generally considered beneath contempt by the balladists of the day (see below,
The Scamperers, 37–8 and n.). Luttrell records his capture in Kent with Peterborough
on 14 Dec. (*1,* 487), possibly the date Luttrell heard the news. Cecil did not accompany
Hales, but *like* him he fled.

30. *You may guess by the paw at the bulk of the beast:* A version of the proverb "a
lion is known by his paw" (Tilley, L313).

The Scamperers
(27 November–23 December, 1688)

On 27 November, after his return from Salisbury, James met with the peers who sought to mediate a compromise between him and his son-in-law. Agreeing to their demands that a free parliament be called, James ordered the issuance of writs setting 15 January as the date of parliament's convening. Acting on another demand from the group of peers, James dispatched Godolphin, Halifax, and Nottingham as commissioners to treat with William and apprise him of the King's willingness to call a parliament, thus to remedy one of the chief grievances which had determined William's intervention. The deputation was well enough received at the Prince's camp at Hungerford, and after considerable deliberation with members of his staff, William replied that he

> desired a parliament might be presently called, that no men should continue in any employment who were not qualified by law and had not taken the tests, that the Tower of London might be put in the keeping of the city, that the fleet and all the strong places of the kingdom be put in the hands of Protestants, that a portion of the revenue might be set off for the pay of the Prince's army, and that during the sitting of parliament the armies of both sides might not come within thirty miles of London. (Burnet, *1*, 795)

Though the conditions were reasonable and, indeed, caused some anxiety among the Whigs as too liberal, James found them overly hard.

There can be little doubt, however, that even before this James had determined upon the course already taken by many of his closest adherents. Reports of flight circulated daily, and Catholic refugees from all the neighboring counties poured into London to seek safety (Luttrell, *1*, 484). Among James' advisors Petre had been the first to leave. On 3 December the Scottish convert, John Drummond, Earl of Melfort, left for France. Four days later Sunderland departed for

The Scamperers

This Dutch engraving entitled "The Flight of Popedom Out of England" shows (1) Louis XIV drawing his sword against (2) the Belgic lion, protecting the English rose, thistle, and the Irish harp. The Dauphin (3) rides a wolf, while James (5), Mary (6), and the Prince (8) are in a cart drawn by a dog with a holy-water spout round his neck (9). Father Petre (4) flogs the dog forward and receives evil counsel from a devil with a pair of bellows (7). In the background are (10) monks, nuns, and friars fleeing England and (14) Jesuits being expelled from a Romish chapel to the great content of Englishmen (13), while the Papal sun sets in the west (17). Other numbers refer to the Pope (15) and a cock (12) being attacked by the German eagle (11).

Holland, followed shortly by Thomas Cartwright, Bishop of Chester
(Campana, 2, 373). As soon as he heard that the Queen and Prince of
Wales had got safely on board "the yacht and that they were gone
off with a fair wind . . . the King prepared to follow them" (Clarke,
Life, 2, 249).

On the night of 10 December, having promised to answer the conditions put to him by William the next morning, James retired to
his chambers and wrote Feversham a letter discharging him from
his military obligations to the Crown and intimating, or so Feversham and his staff thought, that he disband the army. Next James
set about burning the writs which had not yet gone out and invali-
dating those which had, thinking "it necessary to perplex his enemies
also in the civil, as he had done in their military affairs" (Clarke, 2,
251). Shortly after midnight he arose and slipped out of his apartments to a coach that awaited him, driving to the Thames where he
crossed to Lambeth. During this passage James threw the Great Seal
into the Thames, either to discomfit his adversaries still further, or
to lighten his own baggage for the trip on horseback to the coast.
Once on horse, the King, Sir Edward Hales, a servant, and a guide
who could lead the party by back roads, travelled better than fifty
miles in eight hours, reaching Little Marston on the Swale on the
morning of the 11th. There the customs hoy was hired to take them
to France:

> The wind was fair and it blew a fresh gale, but it seems the vessel
> wanted ballast, and the master telling the King he durst not
> venture to sea as it was, his Majesty consented to have him
> stay to take some in, being sensible himself she could not carry
> sail without it. So falling down to Sheerness at the west end of
> Sheepway, ran ashore at half ebb and, having taken some in, in-
> tended at half flood . . . to set sail for the nearest part of France
> they could make; but about eleven o'clock at night, just as the
> hoy began to float, the King was boarded with three small fisher
> boats of Faversham, having some fifty or sixty men in them, their
> captain with his sword and pistol in his hands jumped down
> into the cabin where the King and the two gentlemen were . . .
> seizing on them as suspect persons. . . . The King finding he
> was not known by any that came into the cabin, thought best
> not to discover himself, hoping still to find means to get from

them, and as the captain, whose name was Amis, sat examining them in the cabin, Sir Edward Hales took a time when none of his men looked that way to clap fifty guineas into his hand and told him in his ear he should have a hundred more if he would get him and his two friends off before they were carried to Faversham. He took the money and promised to do it. . . . The captain left them pretending it was to find means to get them off . . . [Later], it now being light, several of the seamen lept down into the cabin saying they must search them. . . . The King and the other two gentlemen bid them search if they pleased, imagining by that readiness to persuade them they had nothing more; but they not satisfied with that, fell a-searching their pockets and opening their breeches felt all about in a very rude manner, and the more because they found nothing. . . . By this time the coach was come to the shore side, so getting into the small boat, they landed and were guarded up to the town by one Edwards and some of the rabble and brought to an inn, where, as the King went upstairs, notwithstanding his disguise and black periwig, he perceived several people knew him (Clarke, 2, 252–4).

After considerable discomfort, James, having made contact with the Lords who had consituted themselves an unofficial commission acting as regent (*The Declaration of the Lords Spiritual and Temporal, &c.,* 11 December 1688), was escorted by Ailesbury and a suitable guard back to London (Ailesbury, *Memoirs, 1,* 202 ff.). On his entrance into the city he was greeted by acclamation in what seemed to him "liker a day of triumph than humiliation" (Clarke, 2, 262). The reception was in large measure a result of the fear and confusion that his flight had caused. Having made no provision for anyone to govern in his stead, James had left the city, indeed the nation, in a state of agitation that threatened anarchy, a situation only partially lessened by the action of the Lords. Momentarily sustained by his reception, James resumed the role of King, but he soon realized that his position had in no way changed. Messages from William "now began to take the air of commands rather than requests" (Clarke, 2, 262–63), and with hostile troops guarding St. James', the King "perceived he was absolutely the Prince of Orange's prisoner" (Clarke, 2, 265).

William was, however, clearly upset by the capture of James at Faversham. Burnet had told Clarendon that "it was foolishly done of those who stopped him . . . and that his coming back to Whitehall would very much disturb things" (Clarendon *Correspondence,* 2, 227). Accordingly, William sent Halifax, Delamere, and Shrewsbury to demand his departure from the city. The deputation arrived shortly after midnight on the morning of the 18th, caused the King to be awakened, and presented him with Orange's ultimatum. After some debate it was settled that the King should depart for Rochester by ten the same morning. It was raining heavily when James set out and, according to Bevil Higgons, whose account is colored by his Tory sympathies:

> The King was carried down the river . . . not without some danger; and while the poor old King was thus exposed to the mercy of the elements and an actual prisoner under guard of Dutchmen, that very moment his daughter Denmark, with her great favorite (Lady Churchill), both covered with Orange ribbons, in her father's coaches and attended by his guards, went triumphant to the playhouse. (*Short View of English History, &c.,* 1723)

That night the King spent at Gravesend under strict guard. The next day he arrived at Rochester, where he took up residence at the house of Sir Richard Head. Here, James noticed, the guards "were not so exact, which confirmed him in the belief . . . that the Prince of Orange would be well enough contented should he get away" (Clarke, 2, 267). On the morning of 23 December, therefore, James slipped off, observing an unnecessary degree of secrecy, but perhaps feeling the need to accommodate himself to a role which William apparently desired he should play.

A New Song

On the Calling of a Free Parliament
January 15, 1689

A parliament with one consent
 Is all the cry o'th'nation,
Which now may be, since Popery

Is growing out of fashion.
The Belgic troops approach to town,   5
  The Oranges come pouring,
And all the lords agree as one
  To send the Papists scouring.

The Holy Man shall lead the van,
  Our Father and Confessor;   10
In robes of red the Jesuit's fled,
  Who was the chief transgressor.
In this disguise he thought t'escape
  And hop'd to save his bacon,
But Herbert he has laid a trap,   15
  The rat may be retaken.

The Nuncio, too, the day may rue
  That he came o'er the ocean,
I'th'English Court, to keep's resort,
  And teach his blind devotion.   20
The Prelates Ellis, Smith, and Hall
  Have sold their coach and horses
And will no longer in Whitehall
  Foment their learn'd discourses.

The Groom o'th'Stool that play'd the fool   25
  Full sorely will repent it;

9–10. *Holy Man:* Petre had fled toward the end of Nov. 1688.

15. *Herbert:* Arthur Herbert, Earl of Torrington, and admiral of William's fleet. He stayed with the fleet at Torbay until the last week in December (John Ehrman, *The Navy in the War of William III, 1689–97*, 1953, p. 248).

17–20. *Nuncio:* D'Adda, the Papal Nuncio, had been an influence towards moderation.

21. *Ellis:* Philip Michael Ellis (1652–1726), one of the four vicars-apostolic created by James upon Innocent's dividing England into ecclesiastical districts (30 Jan. 1688). Ellis was consecrated Bishop of Aureliopolis at St. James' Palace on 6 May 1688 and became the first vicar-apostolic for the western region of England. Early in Dec. 1688 he was sent to Newgate (Luttrell, *1,* 486).

Smith: James Smith (1645–1711), vicar-apostolic of the northern region of England, consecrated Bishop of Callipolis at Somerset House on 13 May 1688.

Hall: Timothy Hall, titular Bishop of Oxford, for whom, see above, *A New Song* ("Our history reckons some kings of great fame"), 12 and n.

25. *Stool:* Presumably simply a variant spelling "Stole" (see *OED,* "*stool,*" *sb.* 6), I have retained the original spelling to indicate the possible pun. Peterborough was Groom of the Stole.

And Sunderland, did barefoot stand,
  For penance shall lament it.
Melfort and the Scotch are fled,
  Whom hopes of int'rest tempted.   30
Those lords did turn for want of bread
  And ought to be exempted.

But Salisbury, what cause had he
  To fear his Highness' landing?
Who by his arse and legs might pass   35
  For one of understanding.
To take up arms at such a time
  Against the rules were gave him,
His head must answer for the crime,
  His pardon will not save him.   40

The friars and monks, with all their punks,
  Are now upon the scamper;
Tyrconnel swears, and rants, and tears,

27. *Sunderland:* For the story of Sunderland's conversion, see above *The Converts,* 61 and n. He fled for Holland on 7 Dec.

29. *Melfort:* For his flight, see headnote. He and his brother James Drummond, the Scottish Earls of Melfort and Perth, held the offices of Secretary of State and Chancellor, respectively. Both had become converts in the winter of 1685–86 to gain favor and overthrow their rival William Douglas, first Duke of Queensbury; or so, at least, most of their contemporaries thought (Burnet, *1,* 652–3; for a modern appraisal, see Turner, p. 369 ff.).

33. *Salisbury:* See above, *Song,* "The pillars of Popery now are blown down," 26 and n. He received a pardon, along with Melfort, early in December, only to have it revoked a few days later and a charge of high treason entered against him for turning Catholic. Apparently he attempted an escape after this, was captured in Kent and committed to the Tower (Luttrell, *1,* 482, 483, 487, 493).

43. *Tyrconnel swears, and rants:* Cf. *Tyrconnel's Distracted Readings upon his Irish Forces in England. In allusion to Mr. Cowley's Pindaric Ode upon Destiny,* &c., *Muses Farewell,* 1689:

Me from the womb Midwife Pope Joan did take;
  She cut my navel, wash'd me, and my head
With her own hands she fashioned.
  She did a covenant with me make,
And circumcis'd my tender soul, and thus she spoke:
  "Thou Bigot of my Roman Church shall be.
  Hate and renounce," said she,
"Sense, reason, laws, and Test, justice and truth for me;
  So shalt thou great at Court be, but in war

And Teague does make a clamper.
The foreign priests that posted o'er   45
   Into the English nation
Do now repent that on that shore
   They laid their weak foundation.

'Twould be a sight would move delight
   In each obdurate varlet,   50
To see the graves that made us slaves
   Hang in dispensing scarlet;
And every Popish counsellor
   That for the same cause pleaded
Shall all turn off, at the same score,   55
   Be hang'd, or else beheaded.

Thy flight from Dublin gallows will thee bar;
   Boast thou of thy great fertile praise,
   Thy design'd massacre will raise,
Although thou liv'st not to enjoy the bays."
   She spoke, and all my years to come
   Bewitch'd took their unlucky doom.
Their several ways of life let others choose,
   Their several pleasures let them use:
But I was born for hate and to abuse.

With Fate what boots it to contend?
Such I began, such am, and so must end.
   The star that did my being frame
      Was but a lambent flame,
And some small light it did dispense,
   But neither wit nor sense,
      Nor heat nor influence.
No matter Talbot, let the blind goddess see
   How grateful thou can'st be
For all her eligible gifts conferr'd on thee
   (Specific essences of Popery),
As folly, lust, and flattery,
   Fraud, extortion, calumny,
Murder, self-will, and infidelity,
   Cowardice, and hypocrisy.
Do thou rejoice, not blush to be,
   As all th'inspir'd disingenuous men,
And all thy damn'd fore-fathers were, from Martell down to Penn.

44. *Teague:* Cant for Irishman.
   clamper: A botched-up argument or charge (?).

THE SCAMPERERS

To the tune of "Packington's Pound"

1.

When the joy of all hearts and desire of all eyes,
In whom our chief refuge and confidence lies,
The Protestant bulwark against all despair,
Has depriv'd us at once of herself and her heir:
    That hopeful young thing   5
    Begot by a King
And a Queen, whose perfections o'er all the world ring;
A father whose courage no mortal can daunt,
And a mother whose virtue no scandal can taint;

2.

When Jeffreys resigns up the purse and the mace,   10
Whose impudent arrogance gain'd him the place,
When like Lucifer thrown from the height of his pride,
And the knot of his villainy's strangely unti'd.
    From the Chancery bawling
    He turns a tarpaulin—   15
Men still catch at anything when they are falling—
But to hasten his fate, before he could scour,
He was tak'n at Wapping and sent to the Tow'r;

3.

When Confessor Petre does yield up the game,
And proves to the worst of religion a shame,   20
When his cheating no more o'er our reason prevails
But is blasted like that of his true Prince of Wales;
    Which was his contrivance,
    And our wise King's connivance,
To establish the Papists, and Protestants drive hence;   25
But their cobweb conception is brought to the test,
And the coming of Orange has quite spoil'd the jest.

15. *tarpaulin:* Jeffreys attempted to escape disguised as a sailor.

4.

When Peterborough, noted for all that's ill,
Was urg'd by his wife to the making his will,
At the hearing which words he did stare, foam, and roar,   30
Then broke out in cursing and calling her whore:
    And for two hours at least
    His tongue never ceas'd;
He rail'd on religion and damn'd the poor priest,
And his friends, who had hope to behold him expire,   35
Are afraid by this bout they shall lose their desire.

5.

Young Salisbury fam'd in this great expedition,
Not for going to war but obtaining commission;
It's no mystery to me if his courage did fail,
When the greatest of Monarchs himself did turn tail: 40
    So that if he took flight
    With his betters by night,
I am apt to believe the pert spark was i'th'right;
For the Papists this maxim do everywhere hold,
"To be forward in boasting, in courage less bold."   45

6.

Nor should Belasyse, Powis, and Arundell throng,
But each in due place have his attributes sung.

28–36. Henry Mordaunt (1624?–1697), second Earl of Peterborough. Though the story alluded to here is unconfirmed, it recalls stories of his conversion in March 1687 (see *The Converts*, 36 and n.).

37–38. On 5 Nov. 1688 Salisbury obtained his commission to raise one of five regiments of horse, to be added to James' army. The regiment was broken early in Jan. 1689 (*English Army Lists and Commission Registers*, ed. Charles Dalton, 1960, 2, 197). The following anecdote was recorded of him by Abraham de la Pryme in his *Diary*, Surtees Society, 1869, p. 94:

> [Salisbury] had the ill luck to turn Papist just two or three months before that the Prince of Orange came in, and became a mighty fat, unwieldy man, so that he could scarce stir with ease about, though he was not over thirty-nine or forty years old. When the rumor was that the Prince was coming, he would almost every hour be sending his man to Whitehall to hear the news there was. Then, when he heard that the Prince was coming and landed, and how he was received, he lamented sadly, and cursed and damned all about him, crying, "Oh, God! Oh, God! Oh, God! I turned too soon, I turned too soon."

He was captured in Kent with Peterborough early in December.

46–54. John, Baron Belasyse (1614–89), William Herbert, Earl of Powis (1617–96), and

Yet since 'tis believ'd by the strange turn of times,
They'll be call'd to account for their treas'nable crimes,
    While the damn'd Popish Plot   50
    Is not yet quite forgot,
For which the Lord Stafford went justly to pot;
And to their great comfort I'll make it appear,
They that gave 'em their freedom themselves are not clear.

7.

Wi. Williams, that friend to the Bishops and laws,   55
As the Devil would have it, espous'd the wrong cause;
Now loath'd by the Commons and scorn'd by the Peers,
His patent for honor in pieces he tears.

Henry, Baron Arundell of Wardour (1606?–94), three of "the five Popish lords" accused by Oates in 1678 of planning the military overthrow of England; the others were
William Howard, Viscount Stafford (1614–80), and the Irish peer, William Petre, fourth
Baron Petre (1622–84). Proceedings were undertaken first against Stafford who, on being found guilty, was beheaded on 29 Dec. 1678. At this point the trials were halted.
Petre died in the Tower in 1683. The others remained prisoners until the commence-
ment of James' reign, when the charges against them were officially annulled.

54. *clear:* Safe.

55. *Wi. Williams:* Sir William Williams (1634–1700) had fought for Exclusion and
had acted as counsel for the defense in several trials of prominent Whigs. In 1687 he
was brought to submission by James who then employed him as his own tool. His services were rewarded with the post of solicitor-general and with a knighthood in Dec.
1687. His unpopularity at that time was underscored by the following lampoon:

> Williams, thy tame submission suits thee more
> Than thy mean payment of thy fine before.
> Poor wretch! who, after taking down thy arms,
> Had a court smile! Strange, over-ruling charms!
> Bankrupt in honor, thou art tumbled down
> Below the abject'st creature of the gown.
> Wert thou the man whom the wise world did wait on?
> Worthily now the very spew of Peyton!
> What will Sir Trevor Williams, Barnardiston,
> And Arnold say but that thou should'st be piss'd on?
> Is this Wi. Williams who made such a noise,
> Dreadful to all the lewd abhorring boys?
> Is this Wi. Williams, spark of resolution,
> Who was so fierce for bill of damn'd Exclusion?
> Is this Wi. Williams who spoke the thing so strange,
> "Great Sir, your commons are not given to change"?
> Is this Wi. Williams now at last set right?
> Is't so, then drawer light me down to sh——.

In Oct. 1688, his "chamber windows in Gray's Inn were broken . . . and reflecting in-
scriptions fixed over his door" (Luttrell, *1,* 468).

Both our Britains are fool'd,
Who the laws overrul'd,   60
And next parliament each will be plaguily school'd;
Then try if your cunning can find out a flaw
To preserve you from judgment according to law.

8.

Sir Edward Hales' actions I shall not repeat,
Till by ax or by halter his life he complete;   65
Penn's history shall be related by Lobb,
Who has ventur'd his neck for a snack in the job.
All their priests and confessors,
With their dumb idol-dressers,
Shall meet that reward which is due to transgressors,   70
And no Papist henceforth shall these kingdoms inherit,
But Orange shall reap the reward of his merit.

[HENRY MILDMAY]

THE PROGRESS

In former days, when men had sense,
And reason rul'd both peer and prince;
When honesty no crime was thought,
And churchmen no sedition taught;
When soldiers for their pay would fight,   5
Without disputing wrong or right;

66. *Penn . . . Lobb:* For William Penn, the Quaker, and Stephen Lobb, the "Jacobite Independent," see above, *The Advice,* 9 and n.

67. *a snack:* A share (*in* something).

In tone and technique *The Progress* resembles *Nostradamus' Prophecy* (*POAS,* Yale, *1,*
185–9).

Ascription: The abbreviation "Md-may," which appears in the table of contents in
POAS, 1689, presumably stands for Mildmay, who may be Henry Mildmay (*d.* 1692) of
Graces, in Baddow, Essex, the "implacable political enemy" of Sir John Bramston (see
Bramston's *Autobiography,* Camden Society, 1845, *32,* 122 ff.). For more than a century
the Mildmay family had been militantly anti-Catholic.

5–10. For a similar account of popular interest in "affairs of state," cf. *All Shams,*
particularly 3–18.

When each mechanic kept his trade,
Ere tailor's yards were scepters made;
Before each coffee club durst prate,
Or pry into affairs of state;   10
When Quaker was a name unknown,
And ere the Bull and Mouth could groan;
Before each Anabaptist brother
To cheat the church baptis'd each other;
Ere Nonconformists belch'd forth lies,   15
Or sisters turn'd up white o'th'eyes;
Ere Levi's tribe were useless made
By preachers of a foreign trade;
Before each cobbler's dirty paw
Sulli'd the Gospel and the Law;   20
Ere women had the gift to preach,
And to their cuckolds patience teach;
Ere it was heard a Queen did bear
In Protestant land a Popish heir,
And ere at eight months' end 'twas known   25
A child was born without a groan;
Ere thirty thousand Englishmen
March'd out of town and in again;
And, ere an enemy appear'd,
Scamper'd the child by goblin scar'd;   30
Ere three fair realms were thrown away
And lost without one scarlet day;
And ere two millions by the year

8. *tailor's yards:* Normally a cloth yard, but here his measuring-rod.

9–10. Early in Oct. 1688 an order went out "that no coffee or public house keep any written or any other news, save the *Gazette*" (*HMC, Le Fleming,* no. 3276).

12. *Bull and Mouth:* A noted meeting house of the Quakers in St. Martin's-le-Grand, afterwards called the Queen's Hotel (Wheatley, *1,* 300).

16. *sisters:* Cf. Dekker and Webster, *Westward Ho,* II.ii: "The serving-man [had] his punk, the student his nun in Whitefriars, the Puritan his sister."

whites o'th'eyes: Implying both the religious zeal or enthusiasm of the group, and sexual frenzy.

17. *Levi's tribe:* Priests.

18. *foreign:* i.e. Catholic or, specifically, priests from the continent.

27. *Thirty-thousand:* This figure tallies with that given by Charles Dalton in his edition of *English Army Lists, &c.,* 1960, 2, xviii.

33. *two million:* James' revenues amounted to about £1,900,000 per annum (*Journals of the House of Commons,* 1 March 1689).

Was deem'd not worth a monarch's care;
Ere kings would quit so great revenue,   35
T'indulge a Queen brought not a penny;
Or leave his grandeur, court and state,
And for a tyrant's favor wait,
To be a fugitive declar'd,
Is such a frolic ne'er was heard;   40
When, like the King of Gypsies, we
Covet to live on charity,
And think another's scraps more sweet
Than our own table's choicest meat;
To be in fear of giving offense,   45
Lest they should compliment us thence;
Ere any of these things were known,
In ages that are past and gone;
When kings were kings, and men were men
(Will ever be such days again?),   50
'Twas ere His Holiness's niece,
More infamous than her of Greece,
Completed England's Happiness;
When she was made the lawful mother
Of tiler's children's youngest brother,   55
Who was begot, or born, or made,
A Prince of Wales in masquerade,
Apparent heir to kingdoms three,
That never were nor e'er will be:
I say, ere all these things befell,   60
Which now long since, no tongue can tell;
Then were the Golden Days, if any,
But I believe there were not many;

36. *not a penny:* Louis XIV of France guaranteed Mary's dowry, settled by the marriage treaty at 300,000 crowns.

51. *His Holiness's niece:* Mary was the niece of Cardinal Rinaldo d'Este, later Duke of Modena, though "the common people . . . and even those of quality" said in 1673 that she was "the Pope's eldest daughter" (*Letters to Sir Joseph Williamson,* Camden Society, 1874, 2, 63).

52. *her of Greece:* Theodora, the notorious courtesan and wife of the Emperor Justinian.

53. *England's Happiness:* The title of not infrequent propagandistic ballads; cf. that of the same name printed above.

55. *tiler's children's youngest brother:* For the rumor that the Prince was the son of a tiler, see above, *Tom Tiler, or the Nurse.*

For to be sure, since woman was,
Man's character was but an ass;   65
That this is truth there needs no more
To prove what I have said before,
Than what we read in James's life,
And of his more renowned wife,
Who stood possess'd of power and wealth   70
And did abound in all but health,
Which was impair'd in days of yore,
When first we learn'd the art to whore;
When man was subject to mishap,
And woman had the gift to clap;   75
When *Morbus Gallicus* gave place
To that deriv'd from Scottish race;
And countesses were grown as common
And pocky as night-walking women:
These with another damn'd mischance,   80
Forc'd him of late to visit France,
Who conscious is of shedding blood
(His own 'tis always understood);
And though he ne'er had maw to fight,
Nor do his friends or country right,   85
Abounds both in revenge and spite;
And if he e'er regains this isle,
He'll turn it to one fun'ral pile.
Nor does he want in will, but pow'r,
To make both peer and peasant scour.   90
Pity has long since left his breast,
'Twas never there a welcome guest;
Such men are ne'er prepar'd to die,
And 'twas that motive made him fly;
Else none at such a time o'th'year,   95
When maggots work not, thus would steer,
Unless from Bedlam broken out,
And the most senseless of that rout;
For in no country, I remember,
A monarch's Progress in December.   100

71–3. Queen Mary's constant indisposition and James' youthful indiscretions, particularly with the Countess of Southesk, are discussed in the headnote to *The Birth of the
Prince*.

76. *Morbus Gallicus:* Syphilis, the French or great pox.

Textual Notes

Copy text: Ashmole G. 16 (A).

Collation: The Pepys Ballads, 3 (B).

Note: The copy text bears the imprint, "London. Printed for J. Huzzey. 1685." Plomer does not list the bookseller; D'Urfey gives the tune in *Wit and Mirth, 1, 300.* The last five stanzas of *A* are also found in *B* as part of a ballad called *London's Loyalty,* "Sound a trumpet, beat a drum."

44. *When*] Whom B.   45. *church religious*] true religions's B.   62. *with affairs of*] the Church or B.   70. *when thou'rt*] and keep B.   71. *what may*] what's to B.

A Trick for Tyburn 8-10

Copy text: Harvard broadside.

Note: Imprint, "London. Printed by G[eorge] C[room] for J. Cox at the Blueball in Thames-street. 1685." For printer and bookseller, see Plomer (1668-1725), pp. 84 and 87; for tune, see note to *Reward of Loyalty,* above.

The Humble Address 12-13

Copy text: Phillipps 8302.

The Salamanca Doctor's Farewell 15-20

Copy text: Yale broadside (*A*).

Collation: 180 Loyal Songs (B); Roxburghe Ballads, 5, (C).

Note: Imprint, "Printed for G[eorge] C[room] and sold by Randall Taylor near Stationers'-Hall, 1685." See Plomer (1641-67), p. 175, for Taylor; (1668-1725), p. 87, for Croom. The tune is in Chappell, *1, 123.* The text for *C* comes from a separate, unlisted, edition of this broadside printed in 1685 by Richard Butt, which I have been unable to locate. The variants in *C* are, however, presumably of 19th-century origin, resulting from editoral prudery.

The Tragi-Comedy of Titus Oates   20–23

Copy text: Harvard broadside.

Note: Imprint, "London, Printed by J. M. and Published by Randal Taylor, MDCLXXXV." For publisher, see Plomer (1641–67), p. 175.

Prologue and Epilogue to Albion and Albanius   25–27

Copy text: Albion, &c., 1685.

Collation: Albion, &c., 1687; 1691.

Note: Imprint, "London, Printed for Jacob Tonson, at the Judge's Head in Chancery-Lane, near Fleet-street. 1685." For Tonson, see Plomer (1668–1725), p. 291.

The Western Rebel   32–34

Copy text: Harvard broadside #1 *(A).*

Collation: Harvard broadside #2 *(B);* Ashmole G. 16 *(C); Roxburghe Ballads, 5, (D).*

Note: Broadsides *A, B,* and *C* represent three distinct states and at least two separate editions of this ballad. Witness *C* would seem to be an early, uncorrected copy of *A; B* is apparently a separate edition set from *A,* with a new subtitle: *The True Whiggish Standard Set Up, by the True-Blue Protestant Perkin.* This broadside may even have been circulated as a separate ballad in an attempt to capitalize on the great interest in events in the west. The text of *D* follows *C.* The copy text was licensed on 17 June by Roger L'Estrange and bears the imprint, "London. Printed for Nicholas Woolfe, at the Leopard in Newgate-street. 1685." The printer's inscription is missing in *B.* For the tune, see *The Salamanca Doctor's Farewell;* for printer, see Plomer (1668–1725), p. 320.

11. *madman*] madam *C, D.*   17. *his*] *Omit C, D.*   52. *the poor*] poor *C, D.*

Monmouth Degraded   35–37

Copy text: Harvard broadside *(A).*

Collation: 180 Loyal Songs (B); Roxburghe Ballads, 5 (C).

Note: Imprint, "London. Printed for James Dean, bookseller at the Queen's-head, between the Royal Grove and Helmet in Drury Lane; removed from

Cranborn Street in Leicester Fields. 1685." The text of *C* follows *B*. For tune, see *The Reward of Loyalty;* for bookseller, see Plomer (1668–1725), p. 102.

25. *look B, C:* looks *A*.   31. Takes care] Takes cares *B*.   41. *these mock kings*] theis mock King *B:* their mock King *C*.   48. *in Lyme*] alive *B, C*. 52. *honors*] honor *B, C*.

The Country's Advice 37–40

Copy text: Harvard broadside (*A*).

Note: Licensed by Roger L'Estrange on 30 June 1685, the copy text bears the imprint, "London: Printed by T.M. (for the Author) in the Year 1685." For printer, see Plomer (1668–1725), p. 194.

74. *too Ed.: Omit A*.

On . . . Burning the Duke of Monmouth's Picture 41–43

Copy text: POAS, 1697, continuation (*A*).

Collation: POAS, 1705 (*B*); *Minor Poets,* 1749 (*C*); *Roxburghe Ballads,* 5 (*D*). MSS.: B.M. Add. 21094 (*E*), 27408 (*F*); Dyce 43 (*G*); Portland PwV 46 (*H*), PwV 47 (*I*); Vienna Nat. Lib. 14090 (*J*); Phillipps 8302 (*K*).

Note: There is no significant variation between printed witnesses: *B* is a piracy of *A; C* follows *A*, and *D* is set from *C*. The MSS. offer no distinct lines of transmission to or from the printed texts. Insofar as grouping occurs, MSS. *E, G, H, I*, and *J* are related as scriptorium texts to one or more unknown MSS., with *G* and *J* normally the most reliable of these witnesses (*G* in my notes represents the group). MSS. *F* and *K* (corrected) are closer to the printed texts than are the scriptorium texts but vary significantly from each other.

1. *Yes, fickle*] Ungrateful *K* (*b.c.*). *Perkin's*] Perkin *All:* Monmouth *K* (*b.c.*). *this*] it *All but F, K*.   2. *your . . . your*] the . . . the *G:* your . . . our *F, K*.   3. *you*] they *G:* yee *K:* ye *F:* you *K* (*b.c.*).   4. *a*] the *All but F, K*. 7. *sends*] sent *E, H, I*.   12. *with . . . thoughts*] by . . . thought *All*.   17. *in comes*] comes *All but F, K. gravely*] bravely *All*.   18. *He'll*] He'd *All but J. can*] could *All*.   19. *But the man of Clare hall*] But the son of the church *All but F:* Bonny Blyth though this generous *K* (*b.c.*).   21. *ten*] the *All but F, K. bring*] fetch down *K* (*b.c.*).   22. *crowning*] the crowning *All but I*. 23. *swears*] says *K. he will*] that he'll *All but F, K*.   25. *The*] But the *All but K. praise All:* profit *A*.   26. *too lavish*] and lavish *All but F*.   27. *This*] His *All but K*.   29. *The*] For the *All*.   31. *Thus joining . . . stocks*] Having thus join'd . . . stock *All but F:* Having join'd . . . stocks *F*.   32.

they club for a] men club for *All but K.* 34. *hangman*] hangmen *All but K.* *townsmen*] tradesmen *E, I. and the*] and their *E, H:* with the *F.* 35. *country in mail All:* countries in all *A:* countries in ale *C.* 38. *Does*] Doth *All but F, K.* 39. *The*] She *All but F.* 40. *a*] the *All but F. had*] Omit *F, K.* 41. *The heads, who never could hope for*] The heads because they despair'd of *K (b.c.):* The heads though who never could hope for *F, K.* 43. *air*] mien *All but F, K.* 44. *traitor*] rebel *All.* 46. *Melt down their Sejanus to*] Of Sejanus' statute make *All but K:* of Sejanus' face made seven brass kettles *K (b.c.).*

Advice to the Painter 44–49

Copy text: Rawl. Poet. 19 (*A*).

Collation: POAS, 2, 1703 (*B*); *POAS,* 1705 (*C*); *Roxburghe Ballads, 5* (*D*): MSS.: Firth c. 15 (*E*), c. 16 (*F*); Wood 417 (*G*); B.M. Add 21094 (*H*), 29497 (*I*); Sloane 655 (*J*); *Longleat,* vol. xxviii (*K*); Portland PwV 42 (*L*); Folger m. b. 12 (*M*); Ohio State (*N*); Taylor 2 (*O*).

Note: The text follows that in the Wright-Spears edition of Prior, with which my own collations agree. The copy text is "a holograph, probably sent to Bishop Turner in 1685. . . . It is unlikely that P[rior] was responsible for the variants in any of the other manuscripts, but they have as much authority as the variants" of *POAS, 2,* 1703 (Wright-Spears). Witness *B* represents the printed texts *C* and *D,* the former of which is a piracy of *B,* and the MS. text *K,* which purports to be a transcription of *B.* MSS. *E, H, L, M, N,* and *O* are closely related scriptorium texts for which *E* is cited as representative of the correct state.

Title: the] a *All but B.*
Subtitle: On the Happy] Upon the *All but B.* 1. *piece is*] picture's *G.* 3. *Employ*] Renew *All.* 4. *King*] Prince *All.* 5. *thy*] his *G.* 6. *counted*] called *G.* 7. *Where*] Whose *B, F.* 8. *whose*] where *G.* 9. *the*] that *E, I, J.* *they*] it *G.* 10. *instinctive*] intestine *G. dread*] tread *E. the*] that *A.* 12. *counsels*] counsel *E. that close*] this black *B, E, I:* the black *G, J:* that black *F.* 13. *Draw*] Paint *E, I, J. misled, aspiring*] aspiring, misled *G, L.* 15. *Julian nigh*] perfidy *All but F:* Julian by *F. Following 16:*
> Three direful [dreadful *E:* mighty *F*] engines of a rebel's hate,
> Fit to perform the blackest work of fate *All but G.*

> The dreadful engine . . .
> . . . works of fate *G.*
17. *And*] But *All.* 21. *his*] that *All.* 22. *worse*] more *All but F, G.* 24. *Dutch*] dull *E.* 27. *helps*] help *E.* 30. *the blackest*] thy darkest *B, F, G, I, J:* thy blackest *E.* 31. *treasons*] treason *All.* 32. *mischief*] mischiefs *E, G.* 33. *the*] that *E, F, I, J.* 35. *prayer book*] Bible *B, F, G, I, J:* Bibles *E. their magistrate*] the magistrate *E, I.* 36. *his*] the *All.* 37. *Whilst*] While *All but L.* 38. *the*] that *All. which*] they *All.* 39. *plows*] fields *All but F.* 41. *these exalted*] this, erected *All but F:* these erected *F.* 42. *enemy*] enemies

E.   43. *his*] false *All.*   44. *our*] vile *All but F:* vild *F. defames*] defiles *E.*
46. Heav'ns sacred word profanely does expose *All.*   47. *long-ear'd*] large-
ear'd *B.*   48. *battles*] battle *All.*   49. *near*] nigh *All.*   50. *Draw*] Paint
All. a romantic] his old Roman *E, I:* the old Roman *G, J.*   54. *thy piece*]
thy face *B:* this piece *G.*   55. *his party*] all parties *B, E, I, G.*   57. *glorious*]
baneful *All but F. horrid*] rebel *E, I, J:* rebel's *G.*   58. *zealous lust*] zealous
rage *B:* lawless lust *E, I, J:* rampant lust *G.*   59. *a*] the *All.*   65. *Excited*]
Erect *G.* thus] then *All but F. their*] the *E, I, G.*   67. *Whilst*] While *All.*
black] vile *B:* sad *E, G, I, J.*   68. *or*] and *E, I, J.*   69. *The*] Their *E, I, J.*
72. *or*] and *All.*   74. *grove her innocent*] innocent grove her *All but I:*
innocent grove their *I.*   76. *Which*] Who *All.*   78. *the*] their *G. enlarged*]
sacred *G.*   79. *Soon as*] Straight when *All. comes*] was *E, I, J.*   80 *trembling*]
fading *All.*   81. *Not*] Nor *B. itself*] herself *B, E, G, I. would*] will *All.*
83. *Seditious*] Rebellious *All but G:* Rebelling *G. arms*] arm *B.*   84. *angry
Heav'n his good*] Heav'n and Israel his *All.*   85. *with*] by *All.*   86. *shrinks*]
shrunk *F.*   89. *tell*] show *E, I, J.*   90. The dismal exit this sham Prince
befel *A, G:* This tragedies last act the fatal blow *E, I, J:* How the great, stubborn,
pitied traitor fell *F.*   92. *His*] With *All.*   93. *labors . . . tortur'd*] pangs
. . . distract'd *All.*   94. *imag'ry*] labors *All but G:* colors *G.*   95. *vast*] strong
E, G, I, J.   97. *draw*] place *All. prelate*] prelates *E, I, J.*   98. *confound*]
depress *E, I, J.*   99. *thought*] thoughts *B, E, G, I.*   100. *powerful words
which*] Heavenly words that *All but E:* Heavenly works that *E.*   101. *the*]
each *E, I. man's*] men's *B, J.*   105. *the*] their *All.*   108. *O'er*] On *E.*
111. *Now*] Here *All. conceal*] disclose *E.*   112. *can*] will *All.*   113. *ill-
plac'd*] ill-tim'd *B, F, G:* ill-tun'd *E, I, J.*   114. *whilst*] while *All.*

A Poem on England's Happiness   55-57

Copy text: Harvard broadside (*A*).

Note: Imprint: "London. Printed for G.P. 1686." The ballad was licensed on 22
Feb. 1686 by Richard Pocock, who succeeded Roger l'Estrange as licenser
towards the end of 1685; Plomer, 1668–1725, p. 227, lists three printers with
the initials "G. P." who were working at this time.

7. *do Ed.:* does *A.*   43. *sea Ed.:* seal *A.*

Song, "What think you of this age now"   57-59

Copy text: POAS, 3, 1704 (*A*).

Collation: POAS, 3, 1689 (*B*).

Note: For tune, see Chappell, 2, 42; line division in *B* varies from that in *A* on
several occasions.

Title: Monmouth's Remembrance *B.*

2. *When*] *Omit B.*   4. *Slights not*] That slights *B.*   6. *all*] do *B.*   16.
Ketch's] Catch his *B.*   31. *now we do say*] we said *B.*   37. *And*] *Omit B.*
45. *And*] *Omit B.*   52. *They'd*] They had *B.*

The Town Life   62–67

Copy text: POAS, 1697 *(A).*

Collation: POAS, 1705 *(B).* MSS.: B.M. Add. 27408 *(C);* Rawl. Poet. 152 *(D),*
173 *(E);* Dyce 43 *(F);* Advocate 19. 1. 12 *(G);* Vienna Nat. Lib. 14090 *(H);*
Harvard Eng. 585 *(I).*

Note: B is a piracy of *A.* Witness *D* is a corrupt representative of the MS. version
of the poem. Its many variants of no value are not recorded.

10. *homely*] quiet *MSS.*   15. *and*] a *All but G.*   23. *transverse*] translate
I.   24–32. *Omit E.*   25. *Bee Chreest MSS.:* Be Christ *A, B see note.*   32.
my C, F, I: our *A, B:* the *G.*   37–40. *Omit H.*   45–48. *Omit E.*   47. *so wise
these men*] these men so wise *MSS.*   49. *day MSS.:* may *A,B.*   55–58. *Omit H.*
58. *fame*] name *E.*   59. *she slights*] they slight *H.*   61. *some vain*] some
late *C.*   66. *The*] Though *C, F, G, H.*   76–77 *Omit H.*   82–83. *Omit E.*
89. *find*] get *F, H, I: Omit G.*   92. *tassels*] tarsels *A.*   93. *breast Ed.:* beast *A.*
98. *in order*] do *E, I.*   99. *drawing-room*] dressing-room *F.*   106–7. *Omit H.*
106. *shipped away C, F, G, H, I:* slipped away *A, B:* stepped aside *E see note.*
110–15. *Omit E, H.*   116. *and play they all*] they call and play *MSS.*   138.
Some where] Somewhere *A.*   140. *play*] drive *MSS.*

Song, "The widows and maids"   67–72

Copy text: POAS, 3, 1704 *(A).*

Collation: POAS, 1705 *(B).* MSS.: B.M. Add. 29497 *(C);* Harleian 6914 *(D),* 7319
(E); Sloane 2332 *(F);* Firth c. 16 *(G);* Dyce 43 *(H);* Advocate 19. 1. 12 *(I);* Vienna
Nat. Lib. 14090 *(J);* Harvard Eng. 585 *(K);* Folger x. d. 197 *(L).*

Note: B is a piracy of *A.* The MSS. fall into two broad categories—independent
MSS. *(F,G,L)* agreeing basically with the printed texts; scriptorium MSS. containing one or both of the bracketed stanzas. Though the presence and position
of these stanzas further distinguishes between scriptorium texts, the stanzas
themselves may be interpolations. I record scriptorium variants from *J,* as
normally representative, and cite only those variants from the other texts which
are of special interest. I have not located the source of this tune.

7–12. *Omit A, B, F, G, L.*   12. *always*] ever *D, K.*   13. *could*] would *J.*
15. *the*] that *J.*   16. *just*] fit *G.*   20. *at*] in *J.*   21. *counsel*] advice *F.*
22. *And*] But *G. may now*] now may *J.*   23. *go*] be *D, F, K:* do *C.*   26.
kept] keeps *G.*   28. *'Twas*] 'Tis *J.*   30. And it saves a world of nonsense *F:*
For then the town's free of his nonsense *C.*   31–36. *Omit A, B, F, G, L: Following 42 D, E, H, I, K: Following 24 C.*   39. *the best*] a safe *G.*   49.
Thus] *Omit J.*   54. *could*] can *J.*   55–60. *Omit C.*   59. He gained his renown *G.*   62. *That*] *Omit G.*   64. *'Tis*] And 'tis *J.*   65. *Tyrconnel*]
Talbot *J.*   66. *Was*] Is *G.*   69. *And*] But *J.*   70. *Though*] If *J. priest*]
priests *J.*   71. *that*] the *J.*   73. *fortunate*] happy *F.*   74. *canst*] can *J.*
76. *pleasures*] pleasure *J.*

To Mr. Dryden   75–78
Upon his Declaring himself a Roman Catholic

Copy text: *POAS*, 2, 1703.

To Mr. Bays   79–80
Copy text: Folger v. b. 94 (*A*).

Collation: Bodleian Eng. Poet d. 152 (*B*), Firth c. 16, #1 (*C*), #2 (*D*), Tanner
306 (*E*); Sloane 2332 (*F*).

Note: The variants to the copy text provide an unusually good picture of how
far a text could be corrupted by careless or ignorant transcription. I give a
sampling of these errors.

2. *changeling*] changing *MSS.*   3. *disgrace*] embrace *D.*   6. *proselyte*] prostitute *C, D.*   11. *express'd*] confess'd *MSS.*   14. *disus'd to truth*] to truths
disus'd *B, E, F.*   15. *fanciful*] fabulous *D.*   17. *old*] own *All but F.*   19.
There] Thence *MSS.*   22. *well we may*] we may well *B, E. distrust*] suspect *D.*
23. *to thy*] of thy *C, E.*   25. *prove*] be *B, E. gods*] God *E.*   26. *your*] thy
MSS.   28. But *B, C, F:* By *A, D, E. metalogic*] mythologic *MSS.*   32. *from*]
from from *A.*   33. *Why, 'tis*] It is *B, E.*

A Heroic Scene   80–90
Copy text: *Popery*, 2, 1689 (*A*).

Collation: Muses Farewell, 1689 (*B*); *POAS, 3,* 1704 (*C*); *POAS,* 1705 (*D*). MSS.:
Firth c. 16 (*E*); B.M. Add. 29497 (*F*); Advocate 19. 1. 12 (*G*).

Note: Title from *B.* As usual *B* normally follows *A* for its text; *D* is a piracy of *C.*

Title: Omitted in A, D, C, E, F: Oliver's Porter *G.*

6. *While*] Why *C, D:* When *E.*   7. *Johnny*] Poet *Throughout E.*   11. *god we adore*] the God w'adore *G.*   22. I to old Nol my utmost skill did show *F.* 27. *Baltinglass C, D, E, F, G:* Balt Gl-ss *A, B. could ne'er*] could not *G:* did not *C, D, E.*   32. *concern'd*] employ'd *C, D. greatest*] greater *G.*   33–4. *Ascribed to Hodge in E.*   35. *Ascribed to poet in E.*   45. *I'm still*] I am *G.* 51. *inferior*] infectious *F. I*] *Omit G.*   54. *what*] where *G:* as *E.*   57. *aside G: Omit all others.*   58. *to interrupt*] to rob me of *E. Following 68:* The flannel drawers I bare within my mind *F.*   69. *turn*] tack *F.*   78. *roar B, E, F, G:* war *A, C, D.*   79. *parson C, D, E, F, G:* person *A, B.*   88. *the infernal*] from the infernal *B, G:* Oh, th'infernal *C, D.*   100. Men 'gainst known foes themselves do best defend *G.*   110. Hold, did Coston th'inscription blunder out *F.*   126. *sped*] shed *F.*   129. *Stage direction:* scoffingly *E, G.*   134. *wag*] Whig *G.*   141. *Omit ascription E, G. lie*] die *E.*   149. *are*] were *G.*   152. *obtain'd*] receiv'd *E.*   175. *With*] Brass *F.*   177. *witless*] wither'd *F.*   188. *spend*] spout *E, F.*   194. *these*] the *G.*   198–99. *Omit E.*   199. *tortures*] torments *F.*   200. *very words All:* words *A.*   212. *decline*] encline *F.*   213. *delators did G:* delators *Others*   226. *yet*] *Omit G.* 231. *With . . . that*] By . . . who *G.*

A Stanza Put on Westminster Hall Gate   93

Copy text: Popery, 2, 1689 (*A*).

Collation: POAS, 3, 1704 (*B*).

7. *is't*] was't *B. ye*] you *B.*   8. *again*] once more *B.*   9,10. *ye*] you *B.*

To the Respective Judges   93–94

Copy text: Harvard broadside (*A*).

Collation: Popery 1, 1689 (*B*); *Muses Farewell,* 1689 (*C*); *POAS, 3,* 1704 (*D*). MSS.: Firth c. 16 (*E*); Advocate 19. 1. 12 (*F*).

Note: The poem was first printed in 1688, with *The Hieroglyphic* ("Come, painter, take a prospect from this hill"), in a broadside headed *More Lampoons.* As usual, *C* and *B* agree substantively, the latter set up from *A,* and the former following it.
Title: To the Ten Dispensing Judges *C, F:* To the Judges *D:* The Salutation to the Judges *E.*

4. *a D, E: Omit All others.*   5. *the*] you *E.*   9. flow *F:* flows *All others.* 10. *you must not her*] you, you must not *F.*   13. *brutes and*] brutish *E.*

20. *And*] Where *D:* There *E.*   27. *the*] that *E.*   28. *or*] and *D.*   30. *wise*] wild *D.*

An Epitaph on Lamentable Lory   98–99

Copy text: Advocate 19. 1. 12 [1684] (*A*).

Collation: POAS, 1698 (*B*); *POAS,* 2, 1703 (*C*). MSS.: Firth c. 15 (*D*); B.M. Add. 21094 (*E*), 27408 (*F*); Harleian 6914 (*G*); Dyce 43 (*H*); Vienna Nat. Lib. 14090 (*I*); Folger m. b. 12 (*J*); Wentworth (*K*); Taylor 2 (*L*); Phillipps 8301 [1684?] (*M*); Osborn, Box 89 #3 (*N*).

Note: There are no variant readings of particular significance. All MSS. but *A* and *M* are dated or appear to date from 1687; all MSS. but *A, J, M, N* ascribe the poem to Dryden.

3. *Elijah Ed.:* Elias or Elisha *Most MSS., see note.*   4. *regions All:* region *A.*

An Elogy   99

Copy text: Firth c. 15 (*A*).

Collation: POAS, 1698 (*B*). MSS.: Firth c. 16 (*C*); B.M. Add. MS. 27408 (*D*); Folger m.b.12 (*E*); Wentworth (*F*); Taylor 2 (*G*); Osborn, Box 89, #3 (*H*).

Note: The variant readings to the title or text are of no particular significance and thus have not been cited.

5. *th'yielding Ed.:* the yielding *Most MSS.*   6. *new*] fresh *C, H.*

A Poem Occasioned by His Majesty's Most Gracious Resolution, &c.   102–104

Copy text: Yale broadside collection.

Note: Imprint, "*LONDON,* Printed by *George Larkin,* at the *Coach* and *Horses* without *Bishopsgate.* 1687." For Larkin, see Plomer (1668–1725), p. 183. The broadside was licensed by Richard Pocock on 22 March 1687.

Dr. Wild's Ghost   104–108

Copy text: Harleian 7319 (*A*).

Collation: POAS, 2, 1703 (*B*). MSS.: B.M., Add. 29497 (*C*); Firth c. 16 (*D*); Advocate 19. 1. 12 (*E*); Folger 473.1 (*F*); Osborn, Box 89 #3 (*G*).

Note: Three distinct lines of transmission appear among the various witnesses to the text. The copy text represents the best of one line with *C, D, E* following it in that order of reliability. The single printed text, *B*, represents a separate and inferior line, as do MSS. *G* and *F*, the latter following and less reliable than *G*.

1. *How*] What *G, F*.   2. *Bilks*] Balks *B, G, F*.   4. *The Observator's pains of many*] The Observator's pains of twenty *All but B:* All Crackfart's labor'd scribbles twenty *B*.   7. *Halberstadt*] Hammerton *B*.   7–11. *Omit G, F*. 10. *tweedling music*] charming wheedling *B:* wheedling music *C*.   17. *sparks, implements*] blades, instruments *B:* sparks, employments *E*.   17–27. *Omit G, F*.   19. *Fled*] Fell *B*.   22–27. *Omit C*.   23. By worrying sectaries a pretty trade *D*.   25. *But . . . repentant*] And . . . repenting *B:* But . . . repenting *D*.   40–1. *Omit F*.   42. Sadly they toll their bells and wring their hands *B*.   43–53. *Omit B*.   50–1. *Omit C*.   *Following 55:*

> These Jesuits are cruel cunning elves,
> We would have none to spoil you but ourselves *B*.

59. The grid-iron grumbles at the frying pan *B*.   62–3. *Omit C, G, F*. 64–9. *But why this . . . On each occasion Papists*]

> But oh, ye champions, bring forth now and shew
> The foreskins of the Philistines you slew
> When in your power, Popery *B*.

72–7. *Omit B (see above, following 55)*.   78. *Well, rev'rend sirs*] But fear not Tribe of Smirk *B*.   82–3. *Omit B*.

On the Earl of Castlemaine's Embassy to Rome in King   112–113
James II's Reign, 1687

Copy text: John Wright's *Account,* 1688 (*A*).

Collation: POAS, 1697 (*B*).

Note: The title is from *B*. The title in *A* reads: "Upon the foregoing Account of his Excellency the Earl of Castlemaine's Embassy Extraordinary to Rome, Anno. 1687."

37. *Those seem'd to live*] And those e'en seem'd *B*.

The Entry of the Pope's Nuncio   114–115

Copy text: POAS, 1698 (*A*).

Collation: B.M., Add. 29497 (*B*), Douce 357 (*C*); Firth c. 16 (*D*); Dyce 43 (*E*); Vienna Nat. Lib. 14090 (*F*).

8–9. *Omit F*.   9. *tools*] fools *D, E*.   13. *he labors All:* they labor *A*.

The Hind and the Panther Transversed   118–145

Copy text: First edition, "London: Printed for W. Davis, MDCLXXXVII" (*A*), as reproduced by H. Bunker Wright and Monroe K. Spears in their edition of Prior's *Literary Works,* Oxford, 1959.

Note: A pirated edition appeared the same year in Dublin without designation of printer or place of publication. The poem was first printed among the State Poems in *POAS,* 1697 (Case, 211. I. c). For further bibliographical details see Wright-Spears.

In the final verse-citation, p. 144:
separate] separated *A. the other*] the t'other *A. fingers*] finger *A.*

On the Author of the Hind and Panther and On the Same 145–146

Copy text: Folger 473. 1 (*A*).

Collation: Ellis Correspondence, 1, 318–9 (*B*), a copy sent "To Mr. William Smith, at the Custom House in Dublin," 21 July 1687.

Note: Not cited in MacDonald.

14. *he B: Omit A.*

Dryden's Ghost   146–150

Copy text: Folger 473.1

Note: Not cited in MacDonald.

The Converts   153–158

Copy text: Firth b. 21 (broadside) (*A*).

Collation: Popery, 1, 1689 (*B*); *Muses Farewell,* 1689 (*C*); *POAS,* 1697 (*D*); *POAS,* 1705 (*E*). MSS.: B.M. Add. 29497 (*F*); Firth c. 16 (*G*).

Note: Normally, the text of *E* follows *D* from which it was pirated. The text of *G* introduces many minor variants not sufficiently interesting to warrant inclusion here.

25. *mistresses*] mistress *B*.   27. *'tis*] it's *D, E*.   73. *fathers*] father *B*.   75.
returned] returning *B, G*.   98. *example is they're*] excuse is they are *G*.
100. *the*] their *B, E*.   105. *Renounc'd his faith for piteous*] Who turn'd for
inconsid'rate *G*.

The Man of Honor   159–163

Copy text: Yale Quarto (*A*).

Collation: Popery, 1, 1689 (*B*); *Muses Farewell,* 1689 (*C*); *POAS,* 1697, continuation (*D*); *POAS,* 1705 (*E*); Montagu's *Works,* 1715 (*F*). MSS.: B.M., Add. 29497
(*G*); Douce 357 (*H*); Sloane 2332 (*I*); Doncaster e. 24 (*J*); Firth c. 16 (*K*); Folger
473.1 (*L*); Osborn, Box 89 #3 (*M*); Osborn, single sheet (*N*).

Note: Agreeing substantively, the printed texts represent a different line of
transmission from the MSS., six of which contain the additional couplet following 95. Witnesses *I* and *J* do not contain the couplet, but the latter stops after
87, and the former is in most respects an inferior example of the true MS. line.
MSS. *H, I, L,* and *M* are generally quite unreliable. Where they stand alone
against the other MSS., they are normally in error. In such cases I have felt
it unnecessary to cite their readings. Among printed texts, *E* follows *D*, from
which it is pirated. No place or printer in *A*.

Subtitle: by the] by reading of the *J. corr. to* by the *J*.

Ascription: Written by the Honorable Mr. Montagu *D, E*.

6. *Omit H*.   7. *base and*] rich or *K*: false and *L*.   8. *and with*] and a *I,
J, K, L, M, N*.   10. *storms*] frowns *L*.   11. *church*] court *L. in their cells*]
and their spells *L, M*.   12. *basis*] bases *K*.   13. *mighty*] weighty *L, M*.
14. *Omit H*.   15. *Honors*] Honor *K, L, M, N*.   18. *minds*] mind *H*: hand
M.   25. *last*] least *L, M*.   26. *must*] can *H, J, L, N*.   31. *our*] her *corr.
to* our *K*.   35. *and*] or *J*: or *corr. to* are *K*.   35–42. *Omit L*.   38. *a
heart*] yᵉ heart *G, K*.   45–46. *Omit M*.   46. *Have*] And *corr. to* Have *K*.
60. *once*] all *All MSS*.   63. *is*] as *K*.   67. *gathering*] *Omit H*.   72. *decline*] declin'd *K*.   73. *resign*] resign'd *K*.   75. *was the*] led like *All but
K. to the*] the *G, H, I, J, L, M, N*: to *K*.   78–9. *Omit M*.   79. *in vain*]
were vain *I*: 'em vain *J*: were *corr. to* 'em vain *K*.   87. *giv'n*] given *A*.   91.
ev'n] even *A*.   94. *colors*] figures *H, J, K, N*.   94–5. *Omit M. Following 95:*

Teach music as in graceful Molière's reign
Speak in a smoother tongue and softer strain
G, J, K, L, N.

98. *thought*] thoughts *G, H, I, M*.   101. *mis'ry*] misery *A*.   106. *dispose*]
expose *L, M*.   114. *Men*] such *J*.   114–29. *Omit M*.   116. *metal*] metals
J.   121. *Coins*] Coin *C, D, E, F*.   125. *searching*] glaring *J, K, L, N*:
glazing *H*.   130. *Prone*] But one prone *corr. to* Prone *K*.

The Men of Honor Made Men Worthy 163–168

Copy text: Firth c. 16 (*A*).

Collation: Harleian 7317 (*B*); Folger x. d. 198 (*C*).

Note: Lines 1–14 and 147–55, cancelled in *A*, are printed here within square brackets. Proper names are given in full by *B*.

Epigraph: versum] versus *A*.   *1–4. What shall . . . nauseous rhymes*]

> My honest Muse by indignation fir'd,
> And maxims of true loyalty inspir'd,
> With generous anger vents herself in rhymes
> Against the shameful vices of the times.   *C.*

5. knaves and fools] fools and knaves *B*.   *10. men, men*] men who *B*.
8–12. Ungrateful villains . . . me, unknown]

> Ingratitude aspires to honor's name;
> Like the dumb Roman, I was silent long,
> Whose father's danger first unti'd his tongue;
> But so much to an injur'd monarchy's due
> And to my country's future good I owe   *C.*

13. so] how *B*.   *20. he is*] thee art *B*.   *24. silent*] sullen *B*. *scandal*] dullness *B*.   *27. thy*] his *B*.   *28. could*] can *B*.   *36. sit*] set *B*.   *40–86. Omit B*.   *45. free*] safe *C*.   *47. your*] thy *C*.   *49. thee*] you *C*.   *69. plain*] main *C*.   *72. vitals*] victuals *C*.   *77. fain*] *Omit C*.   *84. streaming*] springing *C*.   *87. whose*] that *B*.   *88. So*] Who *B*.   *89. The*] Though *B*. *90. fool and knave*] knave and fool *B*.   *92. his*] the *B*.   *97. yet*] that *B*. *98. will damn*] he damns *B*.   *100. is slipp'd*] slipp'd once *B*.   *103. another*] another's *B*.   *105. this C:* his *A,B*.   *107. o'th'plot*] i'th'plot *B*.   *110. crucify*] sacrifice *B*. *his*] a *C*.   *117. nought*] nothing *B*.   *119. The height of ignorance*] His heights, ignorance, and *B*.   *122–23. Omit C*.   *127. fortune*] fortunes *B*.   *132. now*] *Omit C. turn'st the*] turns thy *B*.   *140. dwindle*] dwindled *B*.   *141. Popish*] Pope's *B*.   *144. out*] full *B*.   *146. glorious*] gracious *B*.   *147. stigmatized*] stigmatizing *B*.   *154. in*] of *C*.   *155. Your forfeit*] Your fine *C*.

Hounslow Heath 170–175

Copy text: Popery, 3, 1689 (*A*).

Collation: POAS, 1697 (*B*); POAS, 1705 (*C*). MSS.: B.M., Add. 29497 (*D*); Advocate 19. 1. 12 (*E*).

Note: As usual *C* is a piracy of *B*.

Epigraph: Omitted E. rare] brave *B, C.*

22. *to*] with *D*.   33. He scorns to stand in equal rank *D*.   41. *can*] does *E.*
55. His having not one promise broke *D*.   60. *Were he to*] If he might *E.*
82. *Sulla*] Sylla *A*.   88. *Heroes of*] Thus heroes *D*.   90. *instruments*]
instrument *All*.   94. *the*] their *D*.   97. *arrant*] hot-brained *D*.   105.
scene] seige *D*.   118. *that's*] 'tis *E*.   121. *thought*] grown *D*.   125. *way*]
ways *D, E.*   135. *his*] the *E.*   142–3. *Deep secrets . . . in theology*] Deep
mysteries in theology / And secrets in philosophy *D*.   147–8. *For which . . .
till hanged*] *Follows line 144 in E; D reads:* For which he has been reprehended/
But hain't his due till quite suspended.

To the Haters of Popery, &c.   178–180

Copy text: Popery, 1, 1689 *(A).*

Collation: Muses Farewell, 1689 *(B); POAS, 3,* 1704 *(C); POAS,* 1705 *(D).* MS.:
Rawl. Poet. 173 *(E).*

Note: As usual *D* follows *C*, from which it is pirated; *B* derives from the copy
text; *C* constitutes a variant version with separate—unknown—antecedents.
10. *that . . . first*] the . . . that *C, D.*   12. *consists of*] is rul'd by *C, D.*
17. *mercies*] mercy *C, D.*   21. *They're but your*] They are but *C, D.*
22. *for*] seek *C, D.*   23. On them, you see, they raving fix their paws *C, D.*
25. Knowing that they to death subject them all *C, D.*   27. And yield your
lives rather than yield the test *C, D.*   30. *count*] pay *B, E.*   34. *admire*]
submit to *C, D.*   35. *thou*] you *C, D.*   36. *that durst*] who dare *C, D.*
37. *your C, D:* their *A, B, E.*   39. *Omit C, D, E.*

Advice to the Test-Holders   180–185

Copy text: Popery, 3, 1689 *(A).*

Collation: B.M. Add. 29497 *(B)*; Burney 390 *(C)*; Harleian 7317 *(D)*; Stowe
305 *(E)*; Firth c. 16 *(F)*; Folger 473.1 *(G).*

Note: The texts fall into two major groups: *A, C, D* and *B, E, F, G.* Because
neither group is without numerous substantive errors, the second group has been
used where necessary to emend the readings of the first.

7–8. *Omit B, E, F, G.*   9. *He that by's liberty has*] He by his liberty hath *C*:
Has not the King by freedom *B, E, F, G.*   10. *in*] with *C, E.*   13. *pious*]
only *B, E, F:* secret *G.*   14. *priest he o'er the temple*] father o'er the pate he

B, E, F, G.   15. *'Twas well that beating*] 'Twas well that basting D, E, G:
And 'twas that basting B, F.   16. *i'th'* B, F: but C: Omit A, D, E, G.
18. *learned doctors arraign*] learned doctors harrangue D: . . . argue C: Jane
and Patrick argue B, E, F, G.   21. *Although*] In which B, F. *a stout*] a good
B, E, G: so good F.   22. And baffl'd us, yet [but F] in requittal we B, F.
23. *his lordship*] the statesman B, E, F, G.   27. *Like the two*] And like true
B, F. *and reign*] reign both B, F.   30–31. *Omit* A, D.   33. *We have on
a sure lock as well as they*] We have in . . . C: We have him on as sure a lock
as they B, F.   34. *Moray*] Murray E.   35. *circuit*] circle D, E.   44. *Whilst
not his soul we aim'd at but his money*] It was his soul we valued not his money
E: though 'twas . . . G: While [When B] 'twas his soul we sought he fearing's
money F.   45. *To toss the*] For tossing C: Cried toss B, F.   48. *Newport
late*] Maynard erst E.   50. *greater*] harder B, C, E, F, G.   54. *Omit* E.
56. *from court to*] leave [quit F] court turn B, F.   60. That e'er to boggle in a
case of conscience B, F.   62. *you your*] you of C: on your D.   *the wit*]
more wit C.   63. *side*] turn B, F: tide G.   72. It will save your money
and employments too E.   74. *shy*] sly E, F.   76–77. *Omit* B, E, F, G.
80–82. *Omit* B, E, F.   80. *Durhamite* C, G: quack A, D.   82. *endeavors*]
persuasions G.   85. *to see the land*] why will you be B, E, F.   87. *directions*]
evasions B, C, E, F, G.   88. *turnings*] turns B, C, F, G.

A Faithful Catalogue, &c.   191–214

Copy text: Phillipps 8301 (*A*).

Collation: Poems on Several Occasions (Dorset, 1686), 1714, and 2nd ed., 1720
(*B*). MSS.: Firth c. 15 (1686) (*C*); Firth c. 16 (*D*); Harleian 7319 (1687) (*E*);
Dyce 43 (*F*); Advocate 19. 1. 12 (*G*); Portland PwV 46 (1687) (*H*); Vienna Nat.
Lib. 14090 (1686/7) (*I*); Taylor 2 (1686) (*J*); Ohio State (*K*); Harvard Eng. 585
(*L*); Osborn, Box 89 #3 (*M*).

Note: Written on a single folio half-sheet, *A* exhibits at least two distinct hands.
The first is responsible for the text; the second has corrected the text in several
places, added lines twice, and provided calculations for copyists. These calculations include the note "six sheets," both at the beginning and end of the
poem. The note would seem to indicate the amount of paper required to tran-
scribe the poem in folio MS. Tick marks divide the text into 24 sections, equal
to the number of pages available to the copyist working with the prescribed
six sheets. From this it seems clear that *A* is a scriptorium master copy, or
exemplar, from which further transcripts were made. (The development of the
scriptorium has been traced by William Cameron, "A Late Seventeenth-Century
Scriptorium," *Renaissance and Modern Studies*, 7 (1963), pp. 25–52; see esp. pp.
45–6.) The text, written in the first hand, often errs. Though some of these
errors have been corrected by the second hand, many remain. These I have
emended with readings from witness *D*, a collateral MS. of high quality, bearing

a strikingly close relationship at times with the copy text. When in agreement
on a reading against the other witnesses, A and D provide a uniformly sure
guide for the editor. I have included a sampling of variants from other witnesses,
when the variants assist an understanding of the developments of the text.
For the most part, however, their readings are demonstrably inferior to those
contained in A and D.

6. *shall*] that *A (b.c.) D:* may *A (b.c.).*   14. *Pimp-statesmen*] Pimps, statesmen
D.   19. *vile All:* base *A.*   25. *Barbary*] Barbara *All but D.*   27. *that
All but A, H:* the *A:* thy *H.*   31–7. *Omit B.*   41. *confine All:* confirm *A.*
43. *which All:* that *A.*   47. *court'st All:* courts *A.*   54. *like*] as *A (b.c.).*
67. *Actaeon's fate*] his fate *A (b.c.).*   70. *adulterers D:* adulteress *A, D (b.c.).*
72. *his*] her *A (b.c.), D.*   80–4. *Added in A: Omitted in B, D.*   86–7. *Omit
I.*   88–92. *Omit B.*   92. *arse*] they *A (b.c.).*   96. *Southcot's E, L:*
Circuit's *A, B, C, D, F, H, J, K:* Cleveland *G:* Crevat's *M: see note.*
96–97. *Omit I.*   109. *for*] from *A (b.c.).*   110–15. *Omit B.*   122. *bust*]
burst *All.*   145–8. *Omit B.*   159. *Your All:* their *A, B, J.*   159–60. *Omit
I.*   168. *peril All:* perils *A.*   177. *just All:* own *A.*   179. *or All but A, L:*
and *A, L.*   180. *supports*] maintains *A (b.c.), D et al.*   183. *Amid All:*
Amidst *A.*   200. *like*] live *A (b.c.).*   211–14. *Omit B.*   217–20. *Omit B.*
218. *more All:* worse *A.*   223. *amour All but A, B, I:* amours *A, B, I.*
229. *That*] What *A (b.c.).*   230. *And*] That *A (b.c.).*   238. *save*] serve *I.*
meat D: meal *A:* bread *Others.*   250–54. *Omit B.*   257–60. *Omit all but
A, D.*   286. *Subdues All:* pursues *A.*   325. *He'll scarce be able e'er*] She's
sure he'll ne'er be able *A (b.c.), all others.*   326. *then*] you *D.*   339. *gloat
All but A, B:* dote *A, B.*   362. *swiving All but A, D: Omit A (with space left)
D.*   365. *Omit L, K, H.*   367. *o'th' All:* i'th' *A.*   374–5. *Omit C, E, F,
G, H, I, K.*   392–93. *Omit D. Following* 395:

> That batter'd fort which they with ease deceive,
> Pillag'd and sack'd, to the next foe they leave.
>   *C, E, F, G, H, I, J, K: see* 374–75.

434. *mortals' All:* mortal *A.*   443–44. *Omit L.*   446. *that All but A, H:*
the *A, H.*   470. *What All:* yet *A.*   470–1. *Omit I.*   482. *Caetera desunt*]
Omit D.

The Dissenters' Thanksgiving for the Late Declaration   219–220

Copy text: Popery, 3, 1689 (*A*).

Collation: POAS, 1697, continuation (*B*); *POAS,* 1705 (*C*). MSS.: Firth c. 16
(*D*); Osborn, Box 89 #3 (*E*).

Note: Witnesses *B* and *C* are misdated '1685'; *C* is a piracy of *B*.

Title: Anthem: to be Sung in the Lord Mayor's Chapel at the Reading of the
New Declaration (*E*).

2. *grace*] act *E*.   5. *misguided*] misguised *A*.   11. *Omit E*.   14. *are*] yet *D*: out *E*.   15. It may be put in occupation *E*.

The Clerical Cabal 220–222

Copy text: Dyce 43 (*A*).

Collation: Firth c. 16 (*B*); Harleian 7319 (*C*); Vienna Nat. Lib. 14090 (*D*).

Note: The text of *D* is extremely unreliable; normally I have felt it unnecessary to record its many variants.

12. *they're not quite*] they are not *B*.   23. *Tests were the*] Test was a *B*.
29. *loss*] laws *B*.   31. *That*] But *B*.   47. *salvo*] salve *B, D*.   48. *retract*] recant *B*.   55–7. *such respect . . . of displeasing*] *Omit D*.

The Sentiments 223–225

Copy text: Osborn, Box 89 #3 (*A*).

40. *hope*] hopes (*A*).

The Paradox, 225–229
Upon the Confinement of the Bishops and Their Bailing Out

Copy text: Popery, 3, 1689 (*A*).

Collation: Muses Farewell, 1689 (*B*). MS.: Firth c. 16 (*C*).

2. *their*] his *B, C*.   4. *bleeding*] bleating *C*.   6. *joy and pleasure*] unknown pleasures *B*: joys and pleasures *C*.   10. *tired*] tir'd out *C. below*] beneath *B*.
14. *prelates*] bishops *C*.   16. *o'th'faith and doctrine*] Of the true doctrine *B*.
19. *under sequestration*] are in tribulation *B*.   21. *that this is*] this is the *B*.   22. *means*] way *B*.   28. *wolves and bears*] ravenous wolves *B*.   33. *great*] old *C*.   33–6. *Omit B*.   41–4. *Omit B*.   45. I will believe Durham shall bail his grace *B*.   48. *make*] write *B*.   50. *shall*] would *B*.   51. *to be*] for their *C*.   53–60. *Omit B*.   66. *sue*] plead *B, C*.   68. *left*] lost *C*.
69–76. *Omit B*.   83. Out of respect to be sent back again *B*: With greater load to send 'em there again *C*.   84. *endeavor'd*] sworn are *B*: endeavor *C*.

A New Catch in Praise of the Reverend Bishops 229–230

Copy text: Popery, 1, 1689 (*A*).

Collation: Muses Farewell, 1689 (*B*); *POAS*, 1697 (*C*).

The Church of England's Glory   230–233

Copy text: Yale quarto.

Note: Licensed, "With allowance, July 3, 1688. C. N." Imprint, "London. Printed for R.W. 1688." The initials in the imprimatur probably should be "C. M.", designating Charles Middleton, one of James' secretaries of state. The printer may be R. Wells (Plomer, 1668–1725, p. 307).

The Story of the Pot and the Kettle   233–234

Copy text: Popery, 2, 1689 (*A*).

Collation: Muses Farewell, 1689 (*B*); *POAS,* 1697, continuation (*C*); *POAS,* 1705 (*D*). MSS.: Firth c. 16 (*E*); Rawl. Poet. 173 (*F*); Douce 357 (*G*); Sloane 2332 (*H*); Stowe 305 (*I*); Harvard Eng. 585 (*J*).

Note: The text of *D* is a piracy of *C; J* is an 18th-century copy.

Title: The Fable of the Two Pitchers in King James 2nd's reign *J. Story*] Fable *All. the Kettle*] Kettle *All but J. As it . . . King's hand*] As 'twas . . . *E:* Advice to the Whigs *F.*

2. *pot and a brass kettle*] . . . pitcher *I(b.c.)*: and a brazen pitcher *J.*   3. *heavy caldron*] ponderous pitcher *J. and distress'd*] in distress *J.*   4. *its*] his *All but H. the fierce*] fiercer *J.*   8. *expose*] oppose *J.*   9. *the*] the rude *J.* 11. There have been differences on both parts *J.*   12. *The*] Let *J. reconciles*] now unite *J.*   13. *Here*] Come *J. arm*] aid *I,J. this*] the *All.*   15. *made*] gave *J.*   16. *alliance does*] occasion doth *I(b.c.),J.*   17. *different*] differing *I,J. will*] can *J.*   18. *constitution is too rough*] constitution's much too hard *J.* 20. *to*] on *I,J.*   22. *from the shore, the*] from the shores, the *All but J,E:* force or shores or *I(b.c.),J:* from the angry *E.*   23. *I*] If *I(b.c.),J. and*] or *J.* 25. *To*] I'll *I(b.c.),J:* To *corr. to* I'll *E.*   26. *you Whigs, and*] ye Whigs and *All but I,J:* Dissenters act *I,J.*   28. *flatteries*] flatterings *J.*   30. *But*] And *J. this*] the *All. postscript:* incerto authore *J.*

The Council   240–241

Copy text: Muses Farewell, 1689 (*A*).

Collation: POAS, 1697, continuation (*B*); *POAS,* 1705 (*C*). MSS.: Douce 357 (*D*); B.M. Add. 29497 (*E*).

Note: The text of *C* is a piracy of *B*. For tune, see Chappell, 2, 446.

Title: The Thanksgiving *D:* Two Toms & Nat *E.*

2. *In council*] Together *D'*.   4. *And make a*] And form a *D:* In a daily *E.*
5. *thing in the air*] hopeful heir *E.*   9. *In her late, quaint*] All in her late *E.*
10. *to*] of *D.*   11. *Bequeath the*] Beg a *D:* Vow the *E.*   12. *With*] His *E.*
14–19. *With this . . . And is*]

> The Queen of Prayer,
> When it came there,
> Receiv'd the diamond bodkin;
> Then to conceive
> Our Queen had leave,
> And was
>
> ### *D:*
>
> So soon as e're
> The Queen of Prayer
> Had got her diamond bodkin,
> The Queen had leave
> For to conceive,
> And was
>
> ### *E*

21. *some*] most *E.*   22. *'tis come*] 't comes *B,C:* he comes *E.*

Upon the King's Voyage to Chatham to make Bulwarks against   242–243
the Dutch, and the Queen's Miscarriage thereupon

Copy text: POAS, 1, 1689 (A).

Collation: POAS, 1697, continuation (*B*); *POAS,* 1705. (*C*). MSS.: Dyce 43 (*D*);
Vienna Nat. Lib. 14090 (*E*).

Note: The text of *C* is a piracy of *B*.

Title: The Voyage to Chatham (1688) *MSS.*

4. *coming*] going *B,C*. *peep'd*] popp'd *MSS.*   7. *in*] back *MSS.*   8. *in our*]
on the *MSS.*   14. *stand in ships of*] stand of ships in *B,C:* in ships of *MSS.*
15. *the*] good *MSS.*   16. And I wish this great fright does not . . . *MSS.*
And] Omit *B,C.*   18. *did*] does *MSS.*   19. *on . . . pretext*] for . . . pretense *MSS.*   21. *a pretense he had*] an excuse had not *MSS.*   22. For his
fleet and his army, we are told, do increase *MSS.*   24. *Nay*] But *MSS.*   25.
Our . . . leave] That our . . . leaves *MSS.*   30. It would give us great comfort to say . . . *MSS.*   31. *the*] our *MSS.*   33. *never*] ne'er yet *B,C.*   34–6.
Omit *B,C.*   34. *we*] you *MSS.*   36. *did*] should *MSS.*

Britannia Rediviva   244–255

Copy text: Britannia Rediviva, London 2º, 1688 (*A*).

Collation: Edinburgh 4º, 1688 (*B*); London 4º, 1688 (c. 1691) (*C*).

Note: All texts bear the permission, as licenser, of Charles Middleton, second Earl of Middleton, secretary of state, dated 19 July 1688. Both *A* and *C* were "Printed for J. Tonson, at the Judges-Head in Chancery Lane, near Fleet Street." Following the text of the poem in *C* is an advertisement leaf which reads, in part: "The Works of John Dryden. Containing as follows, *Essay on Dramatic Poetry* . . . to be sold by Jacob Tonson . . . 1691." The Edinburgh text bears the following imprint: "Holyrood House, Reprinted by Mr. P. B. Enginier, Printer to the King's Most Excellent Majesty, for his Household Chapel and College, 1688." For fuller bibliographical information about these texts and for a brief account of the Holyrood House press, see Macdonald, pp. 46, 49–50.

An Excellent New Ballad   256–257

Copy text: Muses Farewell, 1689, supplement (*A*).

Collation: POAS, 3, 1704 (*B*). MSS.: Firth c. 16 (*C*); Harleian 7319 (*D*); Stowe 305 (*E*).

Note: Set out in two-line stanzas in *C* and *D*.

Title: Ballad] Song *B,C,D.*

Subtitle: Nations] Kingdoms *B,C,D.*

2. *Of*] Of a *B,C,D. has*] will have *B.*   8. *Here's*] There's *All.*   12. *sighing*] shitting *B,D,E:* snivelling *C.*   13. *we*] they *C,D.*   14. *It is*] 'Tis *E.*   17. *'Twere*] 'Twould be *B, C, D. determine*] distinguish *B.*   19. *for*] of *B,C,D.* 20. *for*] of *B:* for the *C,D.*

Tom Tiler, or the Nurse   257–259

Copy text: Wood 417 (*A*).

Collation: Popery, 1, 1689 (*B*); *Muses Farewell,* 1689 (*C*); *POAS, 3,* 1704 (*D*). MSS.: Firth c. 16 (*E*); B.M. Add. 29497 (*F*).

Note: As usual *C* and *B* agree substantively, the latter having been set originally from *A,* following it in error, though later in part corrected in press. Witness *C* generally follows the uncorrected state of *B* and adds its own errors.

8. *silver*] golden *E*.   15. *repair*] repeal *C*.   20. *to*] two *C*.   23. *That C,D:* That's *Others. Following 26:*

> That thou, in spite of all the priests
> Should'st long [draw *E*] for milk of heretic [from pagan *E*] breasts *All*.

29. *so*] too *E*.

The Audience   259–263

Copy text: New York Public Library broadside (*A*).

Collation: Popery, 1, 1689 (*B*); *Muses Farewell,* 1689 (*C*); *POAS,* 1697 (*D*); *POAS,* 1705 (*E*); *Minor Poets, 3,* 1749 (Stepney) (*F*). MSS.: Firth c. 16 (*G*); B.M. Add. 29497 (*H*).

Note: Witnesses *A, B,* and *C* bear the same relationship here as in *Tom Tyler* (see above). Witness *E* is a piracy from *D*.

10. *god*] gods *G*.   14. *Wise*] Loud *G. whisp'ring*] Blank left in *G*.   19. *audience*] answer *G*.   20. *prince*] king *G*.   25. *pilch C, D, E, G:* robe *A, B, H:* cross *G*.   28. To prostrate at your highness' bum *G. at C, D, E, G:* to *A, B, H*.   29. *yet*] and *G*.   42. *inward*] minor *G*.   52. *At*] With *G. pawn'd*] pull'd out *G*.   53. *And*] And at *G*.   56. *for*] in *G*.   68. *Holland*] Holland, Sir, *G*.   72. *your*] the *G*.   74. *affright*] him fright *G*.

A Poem on the Deponents   263–272
Concerning the Birth of the Prince of Wales

Copy text: Bodleian broadside collection, Vet. A3. C. 133 (*A*).

Collation: Popery, 2, 1689 (*B*); *POAS, 3,* 1704 (*C*); *POAS,* 1705 (*D*).

Note: I do not cite variant readings from *C* or *D*; *D* is a piracy of *C* which, in turn, derives directly from *B*. Normally, *B* gives only the initial letter of a proper name.

9. *summon'd*] summons *B*.   14. *come*] comes *B*.   18. *esquires*] squires *B*.   19. *locusts*] locust *A*.   24. *greatest*] Omit *B*.   29. *design . . . has*] designs . . . hath *B*.   38. *hasted*] hasten'd *B*.   41. *those*] these *B*.   62. *thought B:* thoughts *A*.   63. *the*] Queen's *B*.   69. *hast'ning B:* hasting *A*.   74. *guests B:* guess *A*.   75. *A*] and *B*.   82. *It's*] 'tis *B*.   101. *gone and*] Omit *B*.   104. *east*] both east *B*.   108 *coach Ed.:* cast *A, B*.   124. *Is spurious B:* Espurious *A*.   140. *his*] from his *B*.   142. *to town*] Omit *B*.   146. *follow B:* fellow *A. bear*] cast *B*.   148. *no*] we *B*.   153. *just B:* Omit *A*.   160. *England B:* England's *A*.   167. *horn*] horns *A*.   175. *T'allay*] To allay

the *B*.   179. *he is B:* he's *A*.   184. *so great concern*] indeed concern'd *B*.
202. *He doth believe 'twas*] Believes it was the *B*.   211. *It is B:* It's *A*.   221.
Nation's] Nation *B*.   223. *spurious*] espurious *A*.   226. *of*] o'th' *B*.   236.
to conclude] he concludes *B*.   237. *all*] ah *B*.

To the Prince of Orange: 275–277
A Packet of Advice, with the
Packet Boat Returned

Copy text: Popery, 2, 1689 (*A*).

Collation: Muses Farewell, 1689 (*B*); *POAS,* 1697, continuation (*C*); *POAS,* 1705
(*D*): MSS.: Douce 357 (*E*); Firth c. 16 (*F*); B.M. Add. 29497 (*G*); Dyce 43 (*H*);
Vienna Nat. Lib. 14090 (*I*).

Note: The printed texts, *B, C, D,* agree substantively with each other and offer
a version of the poem different from that of the copy text; variants from *B* are
cited as representative of this version of the text. MSS. *F, G, H,* and *I* contain
only the sections of "Advice," *E* only the responses. MS. *F* basically follows the
copy text. Witnesses *G, H,* and *I* follow each other in variant readings, with *H*
cited as representative of them. In his copy of *POAS* in the Bodleian, Thorn-
Drury notes a small folio broadside entitled, *The Age of Wonders: To the tune
of Chevy Chase* (1710), which begins "The year of wonders is arriv'd." It bears
no further resemblance to this poem. *Pepys Ballads, 4,* 193, is not, as Rollins
suggests, a sequel to the present poem. It attacks James in a reply to Henry
Care's scandalous newssheet *The Weekly Packet of Advice from Rome.*

1. *wonder*] wonders *H*.   3. *Crown*] Womb *B, H*.   4. *your*] the *B*.   5.
your jubilees] of jubilee *B*.   7. *lay by your hope*] give o'er your hopes *B*.
8. *Give up*] And yield *B*.   11. *Till*] Let *B*.   13. *You boast you've*] Ye talk
of *B*.   15. 'Twas joyful news when it came here *B:* Such news, you know is
welcome here *H*.   16–18. *Omit E*.   19. *Now*] Well *H*.   20. *some are*]
others *B*. *laid up*] laid by *H*.   21. *When . . . will*] Well . . . would *B*.
22. *as you would*] as if you'd *B*.   23. *But*] And *B*. *on the*] of the *E*.   25.
Besides, we've call'd our subjects home *B:* Besides, we have call'd home our
men *H*.   26–27. *Which in . . . let 'em come*]

Though here appears not one in ten:
Send all, or we'll send these again *H*.

27. *'tis said*] they say *B*.   31. *and seamen*] not officers *H*.   32–33. *Old England's . . . do the deed*]

Feather and scarf would do the deed,
And they that wear 'em scorn to bleed *H*.

34. *of arms*] and arm *B*.   37. Now, if you'd be victorious made *B:* If Europe's
terror . . . *H*.   38. *in*] on *B*.   41. *off to*] off *E*.   44. Do the same upon

the seas *B:* Pursue that frolic . . . *H.* 45. And then we'll meet you when you please *B.* *so when e'er*] so oft as *H.* 46. *Your taking*] The storming *B:* Your storming *E.* 51. *rest*] jest *H.* 52. *camps . . . sieges . . . shows*] camp . . . siege . . . sham shows *B.* 53. *Make B:* Makes *A.*

All Shams 277-279

Copy text: Muses Farewell, 1689 (*A*).

Collation: Dyce 43 (*B*); Vienna Nat. Lib. 14090 (*C*).

Note: For the tune, which Jonson employs in *Bartholomew Fair* and Gay in *The Beggar's Opera*, see Chappell, *1*, 123; *2*, 772.

2. *An*] Of an *MSS.* 3. *graver*] grave *MSS.* 10. *coxcomb*] *Omit A.* 13. *he can*] can he *B.* 16. *dreaded*] has dreaded *C.* 22. *it*] that *MSS.* 29. *off*] *Omit MSS.* 30. *Jamaica, Virginia*] Virginia, Jamaica *MSS.* 31. *Except*] But *MSS.* 33. *Nay, sail*] Or else *C.* 34. *Presbyter*] Prester *MSS.*

The Statesman's Almanac 279-284

Copy text: Harvard broadside (*A*).

Collation: Muses Farewell, 1689 (*B*); *POAS, 3,* 1704 (*C*); *POAS,* 1705 (*D*). MSS.: Firth c. 16 (*E*); B.M. Add. 27407 (*F*); Harleian 6914 (*G*), 7319 (*H*); Dyce 43 (*I*); Vienna Nat. Lib. 14090 (*J*).

Note: Witness *B* is set from *A,* a small folio broadside printed on both sides. The MSS. generally follow this text with little significant variation. The text of *C* and that of *D,* pirated from it, differ considerably, however, from *A.* For the tune, see Chappell *1*, 306–7, 309. Like that for *All Shams,* above, this tune was used by Gay in *The Beggar's Opera.*

Prologue] *Omit C.* 9. *And*] But *C.* 11. *There's never*] There is ne'er *C.* 16. *often been*] been often *C.* 18. *Have All:* Has *A.* 21. *excuses*] some excuses *C.* 25. *came*] comes *C.* 26. *harvest*] harvest's *C.* 33. *moon is*] moon's *C.* 34. *though it be strange*] sure it most strange is *C.* 35. *In all her change*] That in all her changes *C.* 39. *climates improve*] climes do improve *C.* Following 36. *The Almanac*] *Omit C.* 42. *offer*] offer for *C.* 46. *had not*] hadn't *C.* 47. *i'th'*] in the *C.* 51. *rouses*] knows *C.* 52. *trust*] trusts *C.* 54. *their breath infect the houses*] th'air infects the house *C.* 58. *i'th'*] in *C.* 68. *too hot*] hot *C.* 71. *much to*] to *C.* 72. *Being*] To be *C.* 74. *For*] For the *C.* 75. *Where . . . treasures*] When . . . treasure *C.* 76. *Of*] With *C.* 87. *But*] And *C.* 92. *for*] in *C.* 94. *For*] But *C.* 95. *What . . . does*] How . . . blows *C.* 96. *can hardly*] cannot *C.* 99.

chance, sirs] chancellor *C.*   105. *fortune*] their fortune *C.*   111. *people*]
the people *C.*   114. *thirteen of the*] up a baker's *C.*   119. *is half*] may be
C.   120. *faith I think not*] 'fore George it will never be *C.*

In Defiance to the Dutch   284–288

Copy text: Harvard broadside [1688] (*A*).

Collation: Harvard broadside [1672] (*B*); *Poetical Recreations,* 1688 (*C*).

Note: "Printed for W.S." (not listed by Plomer). Since, essentially, the copy
text must be considered a new poem, derived from the original version of 1672
(*B*), which *C* follows, but brought up to date to meet the circumstances of the
autumn of 1688, it has not seemed necessary to record variants from *B* and *C*.

11. *they: B, C:* the *A.*

The Advice   291–294

Copy text: Yale broadside (*A*).

Collation: Popery, 1, 1689 (*B*); *Muses Farewell,* 1689 (*C*); *POAS, 3,* 1704 (*D*);
Political Ballads &c., 1860 (*E*).

Note: The date of this poem must be after 8 Aug. 1688, when Henry Care died;
broadside copies in Firth b. 21 and *HMC, Le Fleming,* no. 3159, have been
wrongly dated in 1687 or early 1688.

15. *past, he did*] which he does *D.*   41. *at once*] Omit *D.*

Ballad   294–299
To the tune of "Couragio"

Copy text: Harvard broadside.

Collation: Popery, 1, 1689; *Muses Farewell,* 1689; *POAS, 3,* 1704.

Note: I am unable to locate the source of this tune.

The Plowman   299–303

Copy text: Osborn, Box 89 #3.

Song   303–305
To the tune of "Men in Fashion"

Copy text: Osborn, Box 89 #3.

Note: The tune, normally entitled "Would You be a Man of Fashion?," is in
180 Loyal Songs, 1685, p. 163. The MS. leaf is endorsed, "To the King."

The Orange   305–308

Copy text: Harvard broadside (*A*).

Collation: Popery, 1, 1689 (*B*). MSS.: B.M. Add. 29497 (*C*); Longleat, vol. 28
(*D*).

Note: For a description of the Prior papers in the library of the Marquis of
Bath (*D*), see Wright-Spears, *1,* xxix–xxx. Unless otherwise indicated, blanks are
filled in on the authority of *D*.

Title: Answer to an **Orange** *D*.

39. *of*] on *D*.   48. *Majestie's MS. insertion in Bodleian copy of broadside:*
Mistress's *B*: M——*Others*.   54. *Will . . . just*] Must . . . the *D*.   57.
Lobb, Penn] Penn, Lobb *B, D*.

A New Song   311–312
("Ho brother Teague, dost hear de decree")

Copy text: Luttrell broadside (*A*).

Collation: Harvard broadside (*B*); *Popery, 1,* 1689 (*C*); *Muses Farewell,* 1689
(*D*); *POAS, 3,* 1704 (*E*); *Political Ballads, 1* (*F*); *Bagford Ballads, 1* (*G*). MSS.:
B.M., Add. 29497 (*H*); Bodleian, Mus. Sch. c. 95 (*I*).

Note: For Luttrell's notes in *A*, see commentary. Witness *B* is the same as the
small folio broadside originally in the Thorn-Drury collection and as another
copy in Bodleian, Wood 417 (#168); this last bears a MS. note in Wood's hand
which dates this version "Decemb. 1688". None of the broadsides bears an imprint of place, date, or printer.

5. *Lero lero*] Lero laro *B throughout*.   7. *my shoul*] Shaint Tyburn *F*.   8.
cut de Englishman's] cut all de English *All*.   9. *Though*] Dough *F*. *my*] Omit
C.   10. *knows*] know *E*.   12. *Cart*] Carto *B*. *demselves*] dem *F*.   13. *And*]

For *F.*   15. *Who'll all*] Who'! all *A.*   17. *Oh*] Ara *F.*   19. *Now Tyrconnel is come*] But see de Tyrconnel is now *F.*   21. *to*] to de *F.*   22. *Shall*] Shall be *F.*

An Irish Prophecy   312–313

Copy text: Popery, 2, 1689 (A).

Collation: Muses Farewell, 1689 (B); POAS, 3, 1704 (C); Political Ballads, 1 (D); Bagford Ballads, 1 (E). MS.: B.M., Add. 29497 (F).

Note: A distinct poem, these lines sometimes occur as forming two additional stanzas to the previous poem (*A New Song*). Such is the case in *B, D,* and *F.*

2. *rul'd B, D:* ruin'd *A:* govern'd *F.*

The Second Part of Lilli burlero bullen a-la   313–314

Copy text: Popery, 2, 1689 (A).

Collation: Muses Farewell, 1689 (B); POAS, 3, 1704 (C); Bagford Ballads, 1 (D).

9–10. *Follows 24 in C.*

A New Song upon the Hogen Mogens   314–315

Copy text: Harvard broadside, #2 *(A).*

Collation: Harvard broadside, #1 *(B); Popery, 1, 1689 (C); POAS, 3, 1704 (D).*

Note: For a discussion of *A* and *B,* see commentary. Neither *A* nor *B* bears an imprint of place, date, or printer.

1. *D'ye*] Dost *B. news*] news that's *B.*   3. *That*] How *B.*   7. *dare*] once *B.*   8. *may*] will *B.*   11. *the*] their *B.*   12. *For*] For now *D. in pickle themselves shall*] now themselves shall in pickle *B.*   13. *they have*] they've *B.*   14. *thrive if't prove*] ere thrive in *B:* thrive if it prove *D.*   15. *Woe*] Then woe *D. them*] you *B:* 'em *D.*   16. *them*] you *B:* 'em *D.*   17. *Port-bay*] the Pom-pass *D.*   18. For, i'faggins, we the Orange will squeeze *D.*

A New Song   315–316
("*Our history reckons some kings of great fame*")

Copy text: Muses Farewell, 1689 (A).

Collation: B.M. Add. 29497 (*B*).

Note: After first stanza, *B* does not include the chorus lines. Blanks are filled in on authority of *B*.

1. *Our history reckons some kings*] History speaks of men *B*.   3. *before this who*] ever more *B*.   4. *Of*] Omit *B*.   7–8. *Follows 12 in B*.   7. *He*] And *B*. *fools and*] ignorant *B*.   8. *them*] 'em *B*.   9. *Then for the Church*] The Church to preserve *B*.   10. *He took as much care*] And kept it as right *B*.   11. *To*] For to *B*.   13–16. *yet, for . . . he dare*]

> But at last we have prov'd the Prince to be true,
> Which makes Orange Tawny to look very blue;
> And the Queen with her huswifery looks very big,
> Though the Prince never cost her the price of a pig *B*.

17–18. *Omit B*.   19. *What though the Dutch*] And the Protestants now *B*. 20. *To swear*] They'll prove *B*. *is*] to be *B*.   21–24. *Omit B*.

Song   317–319
("*The pillars of Popery now are blown down*")

Copy text: Popery, 2, 1689 (*A*).

Collation: POAS, 3, 1704 (*B*).

Note: The blanks in *A* are filled in on the authority of *B*.

3. *frighted*] frighten'd *B*.   19. *wise*] vile *B*.   21. *the*] though *B*.

A New Song, &c.   323–326

Copy text: Popery, 1, 1689 (*A*).

Collation: Muses Farewell, 1689 (*B*); POAS, 3, 1704 (*C*); POAS, 1705 (*D*).

Note: The text of *D* is pirated from *B*.

3–4. *Line-division incorrect in A: may be, /Since*.   24. *Foment their*] Be making *C, D*.   51. *graves*] braves *C, D*.   53. *counsellor*] confessor *C, D*. 55. *at*] on *C, D*.

The Scamperers   327–330

Copy text: Yale quarto [i.e. folio half-sheet] (*A*).

Collation: Popery, 1, 1689 (*B*); Muses Farewell, 1689 (*C*); POAS, 3, 1704 (*D*). MS.: Osborn, Box 89 #3 (*E*).

Note: The copy text bears no place, date, or printer. The title is taken from *C;* all other versions of the poem are simply called "Packington's Pound," the name of the old tune to which these verses are set. For the tune, see above, *All Shams.* Names are normally left blank in *C.*

15. *turns*] turn'd *D.*   17. *But to hasten his fate*] But a plague of ill [damn'd *E*] fortune *C, E.*   20. *religion*] religious *D, E.*   28. *noted for*] practic'd in *E.* *that's*] that is *C, D, E.*   29. *the making*] make *B.*   34. *on*] at *D.*   35. *hope*] hopes *E.*   36. *bout*] rout *D.*   39. *It's . . . if*] 'Tis . . . that *D.* 41. *that*] Omit *D.*   43. *pert*] brisk *D.*   47. *But each in due place have his*] In one line without having their *E.*   48. *Yet since*] But that *E.*   50. *While*] Since *E.*   54. *'em*] them *C.*   55. *Wi. Williams D, E:* W.W. *A.*   59. *Both . . . Britains*] Nay . . . judges *E.*   62. *Then try if your*] Nor is't thought all their *E.*   63. *you*] 'em *E.*   64. *Edward*] Neddy *D.*   69. *dumb idol-dressers*] idol-addressors *E.*   70. *that . . . which*] the . . . that *D.*   71. *Papist*] Papists *D.*

The Progress   330-333

Copy text: POAS, 1698.

INDEX OF FIRST LINES

GENERAL INDEX